TAXES AND POLITICS

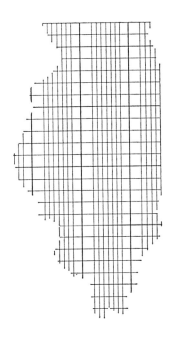

TAXES
AND
POLITICS

A Study
of Illinois Public
Finance

GLENN W. FISHER

UNIVERSITY OF ILLINOIS PRESS   URBANA · CHICAGO · LONDON   1969

PREFACE

Since the publication of *Financing Illinois Government* in 1960, I have spent six years on the staff of the Institute of Government and Public Affairs of the University of Illinois. This has provided many opportunities to observe the political processes which shape the financial policies of Illinois state and local governments. Close contact with colleagues in the Institute has provided new perspectives from which to view the whole financial process.

Because of these new perspectives, what started out to be a revision of the earlier work has become essentially a new book. New chapters deal with local government finance and with the politics of taxation. The chapter on expenditure has been expanded to present data on an agency basis since political decisions are made on that basis. The chapter on tax burden has been expanded in scope by drawing upon a doctoral thesis written by Arlyn J. Larson for numerical estimates of tax burden by income class. The final chapter reflects the author's changing perspectives more than any other. In it the politics of state finance are seen as part of the much larger process by which men deal with the innumerable conflicts and complexities of modern life. From this point of view it may be disappointing that the financial system of the state is not a model of equity and rationality, but it is not surprising.

As always, the author owes many debts. Some of the more specific of these are implicitly acknowledged in footnotes, but many other persons have provided information or insights. It is clearly impossible to identify all of them by name.

Three major contributors must be given specific acknowledgment. Richard Swenson updated most of the tables in *Financing Illinois Government* and prepared several new ones. His patient checking and cross-checking of sometimes conflicting data sources with computer outputs eliminated many errors. Ann H. Elder contributed far more than one expects from a graduate assistant. In addition to doing the usual unpleasant chores assigned to such persons, she gathered much of the data for Chapter 6, conducted some of the interviews, and wrote the first draft of the chapter. Also, she served as a "sounding board" for many ideas in the uncharted area between political science and economics. Professor Robert P. Fairbanks took charge of the manuscript after my departure on a sabbatical leave of absence, updated several chapters to take account of developments in the 1967 legislature, and served a valuable role as editor, critic, and advisor. Chapter 4 draws heavily upon findings of a study of municipal finance written by Professor Fairbanks and this author. (See *Illinois Municipal Finance: A Political and Economic Analysis* (Urbana and London: University of Illinois Press, 1968).)

The charts were drawn by Everett Conway. Jean Baker, Loretta McKeighen, and Lorena McClain typed and proofread the manuscript.

Francis Whitney read the entire manuscript and his expert knowledge of Illinois financial procedure saved me from several errors.

June, 1968   GLENN W. FISHER

CONTENTS

LIST OF TABLES

LIST OF CHARTS

1

INTRODUCTION

Statistics show that Illinois is one of the lowest tax states in the nation,[1] yet when Illinois grocery stores opened for business on July 1, 1967, they began collecting the highest sales tax upon food in the United States. The legislation which brought about this paradox was first introduced in the General Assembly as a Senate amendment to a House bill on June 29. It passed the Senate without hearing and the House of Representatives concurred at 12:35 A.M. on July 1.[2] As the first grocery stores opened that morning, the Governor's signature had not yet been affixed to the bill, but most merchants were aware that the bill would be signed and that the tax would be due on the entire day's sales.

Behind the figures that indicate Illinois' status as a low-tax state and the political drama that included stopped legislative clocks, angry charges of fiscal brinkmanship, and a crying lady senator, lies a complicated story of the interaction of political and economic factors which together determine the pattern of expenditure and the tax structure of a state.

Economically, taxes are compulsory extractions from the incomes of individuals and businesses. They reduce the funds available for spending in the private sector of the economy and thus reduce the output of privately produced goods and services. Taxes upon items

[1] Based on comparisons of total state and local tax collections and the personal income of Illinois residents. See Table 35.
[2] The legislative clock had been stopped at midnight; thus it was officially June 30.

1

of consumption may affect the relative consumption of the item taxed, and taxes upon businesses may affect decisions concerning business investment and the location of economic activity.

State expenditure results in the provision of economic services which substitute for, or supplement, goods and services produced in the private sector of the economy. Many of these are rendered directly to the ultimate consumer. They contribute to the economic well-being of the person receiving the services and are properly considered as part of his total consumption. Some state expenditure is in the form of cash payments, usually to the poor or disadvantaged, which are used to purchase privately produced goods and services. Other services are producers' services which are used by business firms or other governmental agencies in further production. These have an important impact upon the state's economy and contribute indirectly to the well-being of its residents.

Tax and expenditure decisions are political decisions. General policy decisions are made by the legislature within procedural rules established by the Constitution, case law, and custom. The courts interpret legislation and sometimes declare it void on the grounds that it is unconstitutional. Decisions made at the administrative level are political, too, in the sense that they represent an authoritative allocation of values in the face of conflicting pressures.

Economic analyses of public finance are typically concerned with the level and composition of governmental expenditure and with the effect of tax and expenditure policies upon private consumption and investment. Economists often inquire into the equity of the tax system and the efficiency with which governmental services are performed. Economists' inquiries into the decision-making process usually consist of attempts to construct models of rational decision-making which parallel the models used to explain the way decisions are made in a competitive private economy. Typically, these models assume the existence of individual "demands" which become politically effective because political survival of the decision-makers depends upon correctly judging the policy preferences of voters.

Much recent political research, on the other hand, suggests that the theory of an issue-oriented political process is overly simple. This research suggests that elections are often won on the basis of the candidate's image; that political "clout" rather than rationality or public demand determines the outcome of legislative debates; and that complex decisions are made by simple rules of thumb by persons who have neither the time nor the inclination to attempt to understand all the ramifications of the issue.

In the opinion of the author both approaches have something to contribute to an understanding of Illinois finance. There is little doubt that public demands for expenditure and opposition to particular kinds of taxation do influence political decisions. On the other hand, there are many instances in which public demand is based upon motives which an economist would call "irrational," and many important decisions are made casually, automatically, or by simple rules of thumb. Further, there is little reason to believe that the political power of the interest groups which play a part in financial decisions is proportional to the number of persons represented.

Unfortunately, there exists no integrated theory of the economics and politics of public finance which would serve as a framework for analyzing Illinois finance. Thus, two themes—the economic and the political—run throughout this book. The author hopes that it will be apparent that these themes touch each other at many points and become indistinguishably merged at a few.

THE ENVIRONMENTAL SETTING

Obviously, the financial affairs of state government affect and are affected by the environment in which the government operates. Among the most important environmental factors are density and distribution of population and the nature of the state's economy.

Population

The estimated population of the state of Illinois on July 1, 1966, was 10,722,000 persons. This amounted to 5.5 per cent of the population of the United States. Only three states are larger.[3]

Illinois' population has risen steadily since the admission of the state to the union, but in recent decades the rise has not been as rapid as that of the United States as a whole. From 1900 to 1966 Illinois' population rose from 4,822,000 to 10,722,000, but as a proportion of the nation's population, it fell from 6.4 to 5.5 per cent.

Geographically, there is a heavy concentration of population in the Chicago metropolitan area. In 1960, 61.7 per cent of the state's population lived in the six Chicago metropolitan area counties.[4]

[3] California, New York, and Pennsylvania.
[4] Cook, DuPage, Kane, Lake, McHenry, and Will.

Seven other standard metropolitan statistical areas[5] contained 16.4 per cent of the population while the remaining 21.9 per cent was in nonmetropolitan areas.

Not only is Illinois' population heavily concentrated in metropolitan areas, but the trend appears to be toward further concentration. While population has been increasing rapidly in urban places, rural counties, especially in the southern part of the state, have lost population. DuPage County, in the Chicago metropolitan area, more than doubled its population between 1950 and 1960. Kane and McHenry counties, also in the Chicago metropolitan area, had increases of more than 60 per cent in the same period. In contrast, Pope County, in the extreme southern part of the state, lost almost 30 per cent of its population. Chart I illustrates the county population changes which occurred between 1950 and 1960. It reveals that, except for counties in the East St. Louis area and Jackson County (Carbondale), virtually the entire southern one-third of the state is an area of declining population. Differences of this kind are of considerable importance for governmental finance. Areas of rapidly rising population are usually prosperous, but the need for new governmental facilities often exceeds the increase in tax collections. Areas of declining population, on the other hand, are often economically depressed areas which, in spite of decreased need for certain types of governmental services, may have an even more difficult time in financing those that are needed.

The recent rapid rate of population growth is the result of an increase in the birth rate and an increase in life expectancy. These factors have resulted not only in an increase in total population but also in a significant shift in the age composition of the population. Table 1 indicates the percentage of Illinois population in various age groups for the years 1940, 1950, and 1960.

The most important aspect of the changed age distribution is the growing importance of the nonworking ages. In 1940 persons under 15 and persons 65 or over made up only 28.8 per cent of the population, but by 1960 these groups made up 39.5 per cent. This shift has important public finance implications since persons in this age group create more demand for public services, particularly for welfare and educational services, but contribute little in the way of tax revenue.

[5] Champaign-Urbana (Champaign County), Decatur (Macon County), East St. Louis (Madison and St. Clair counties), Peoria (Peoria and Tazewell counties), Rock Island-Moline (Rock Island County), Rockford (Winnebago County), and Springfield (Sangamon County).

CHART I

COUNTY POPULATION CHANGES IN ILLINOIS, 1950–60

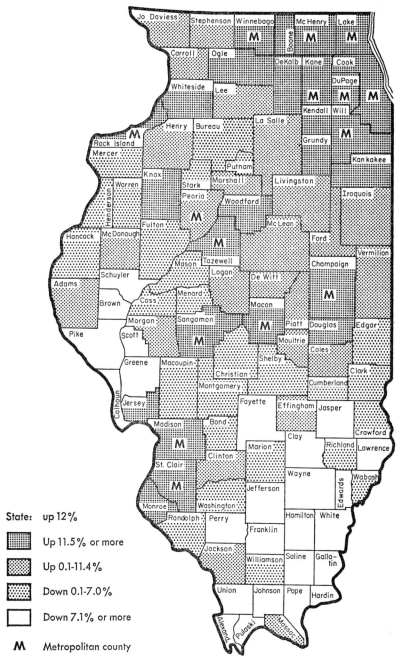

State: up 12%

Up 11.5% or more

Up 0.1-11.4%

Down 0.1-7.0%

Down 7.1% or more

M Metropolitan county

Source: U.S. Bureau of the Census.

TABLE 1

DISTRIBUTION OF POPULATION, BY AGE GROUP, 1940–60

Age	1940	1950	1960
	(per cent)		
Under 5	6.9	9.7	11.2
5 to 14	14.7	14.4	18.6
15 to 24	17.2	13.5	12.6
25 to 34	16.8	16.1	12.8
35 to 44	15.1	14.9	13.7
45 to 54	13.4	12.6	12.1
55 to 64	8.7	10.1	9.4
65 and over	7.2	8.7	9.7

Source: U.S. Bureau of the Census.

Personal Income

Total personal income in Illinois for the calendar year 1965 was $34.9 billion, a sum amounting to 6.6 per cent of the United States total of $532.1 billion. In only two states, New York and California, was total personal income higher than in Illinois.

Per capita personal income in calendar year 1965 was $3,280, well above the U.S. average of $2,746 and exceeded in only three states.[6]

A comparison with per capita personal income in the United States for the 1929–65 period is provided in Chart II. A ratio chart has been employed to make possible visual comparisons of relative change. Such a chart has the vertical scale so drawn that an equal distance anywhere on the scale measures equal percentage changes. For example, an increase from $500 to $1,000 raises the curve exactly the same as does an increase from $1,000 to $2,000. This chart shows that per capita personal income in Illinois fell more rapidly than in the nation as a whole in the early 1930's, but rose more rapidly in the latter half of the decade. During the war years Illinois per capita income rose less rapidly than did per capita income in the United States. Since 1949 the growth of per capita income in Illinois has closely paralleled that of the nation except that the rate in Illinois has been slightly lower.

Over the period as a whole, per capita income has not grown as fast in Illinois as in the nation. In the first three years of the period, Illinois per capita personal income averaged 131.5 per cent of the income of the nation, while for the last three years the average per-

[6] Connecticut, Delaware, and Nevada. U.S. Department of Commerce, *Survey of Current Business*, August, 1966, p. 13.

CHART II

PER CAPITA PERSONAL INCOME, ILLINOIS AND UNITED STATES, 1929–65

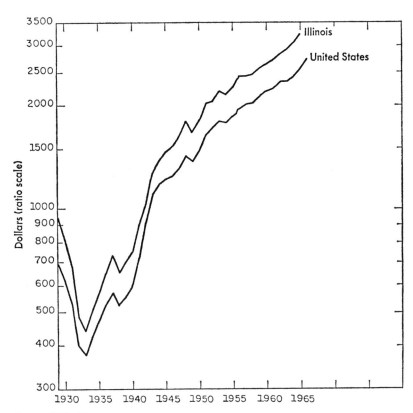

Source: Table A3.

centage was only 118.8. The failure of per capita income to grow as rapidly in Illinois as in the nation is characteristic of other high income states and appears to be in conformity with a national trend toward reductions in per capita differentials.

In 1965, 68.1 per cent of Illinois personal income was received in the form of wages and salaries. The relative importance of various types of income is indicated in Table 2. Wage and salary income is more important in Illinois than in the United States as a whole, while proprietors' income and transfer payments are somewhat less important.

Of key significance in describing a state's economy is the break-

TABLE 2

PERSONAL INCOME BY TYPE, ILLINOIS AND UNITED STATES, CALENDAR YEAR 1965

	Illinois	United States
	(per cent of total)	
Wages and Salaries	68.1	66.8
Other Labor Income	3.7	3.5
Proprietors' Income	10.0	10.5
Property Income	14.4	14.3
Transfer Payments	6.2	7.4
Total	102.4	102.5
Less: Personal Contributions for Social Insurance	2.4	2.5
	100.0	100.0

Source: U.S. Department of Commerce, *Survey of Current Business*, August, 1966.

down of personal income showing the amounts received by residents of the state from farming, government, and private nonfarm sources. Table 3 shows such a breakdown for Illinois and for the United States in selected years. Although Illinois is one of the most important farm states, farm income makes up a slightly smaller percentage of personal income in Illinois than in the nation. Personal

TABLE 3

BROAD INDUSTRIAL SOURCES OF PERSONAL INCOME,
SELECTED CALENDAR YEARS, 1929–65

	1929	1933	1940	1950	1955	1960	1965
	(per cent of total)						
ILLINOIS							
Farm	4.7	2.8	4.2	5.0	3.4	2.4	3.0
Federal Government	1.6	3.8	5.4	7.6	7.6	8.8	7.8
State and Local Government	4.3	9.5	6.9	4.8	5.1	6.4	6.9
Private Nonfarm	89.4	83.9	83.5	82.6	84.0	82.5	82.3
Total	100.0	100.0	100.0	100.0	100.0	100.0	100.0
UNITED STATES							
Farm	8.5	6.5	7.1	7.1	4.7	3.7	3.3
Federal Government	2.4	4.8	6.9	10.1	10.5	11.2	11.3
State and Local Government	4.7	9.9	7.3	6.0	6.3	7.4	8.3
Private Nonfarm	84.4	78.8	78.6	76.9	78.5	77.7	77.2
Total	100.0	100.0	100.0	100.0	100.0	100.0	100.0

Source: U.S. Department of Commerce, *Personal Income by States Since 1929* (Washington: U.S' Government Printing Office, 1956); U.S. Department of Commerce, *Survey of Current Business* August, 1961, and 1966.

income received from federal government and from state and local government makes up a substantially smaller percentage of the total in Illinois than in the United States, while private nonfarm income makes up a higher percentage.

Table 3 also reveals that in both Illinois and the United States there was a sharp decline in the importance of farm income and a rise in the percentage of income received from government between the years 1929 and 1965. These changes, especially those in farm income, have not always been slow and gradual but were sometimes abrupt and erratic. The percentage of income from farming fell sharply during the depression years, with the relative decline being greater in Illinois than in the country as a whole. This was followed by a sharp rise in the war years and a gradual decline to present levels. Income from government, as a percentage of total income, rose sharply between 1929 and 1933. Since that time, with the exception of war years for which no data are provided, government income, as a percentage of total income, has been fairly stable; but there have been marked changes in the relative importance of the federal government vis-à-vis state and local government. In 1929 income from state and local government was approximately twice as great as income from federal government in the United States and more than twice as important in Illinois. In the war and immediate postwar years these proportions were reversed with the federal government being the source of more than twice as much income as state and local governments. Since that time, however, the relative importance of state and local governments as a source of personal income has grown substantially.

The data in Table 3 provide the most detailed pictures of *total* income by source that is available because there is a lack of information concerning the industrial source of dividend and interest income. In attempting to describe the economy of a state, however, this lack of information is not as serious as it might seem, since the industrial source of income received for participation in current production[7] provides a better picture of economic activity within the state than would a similar breakdown of total income. Chart III illustrates the relative importance of the various sources of current production income in Illinois and the United States. Manufacturing and wholesale and retail trade are somewhat more important sources of personal income in Illinois than in the country as a whole. Farming, mining, services, and government are somewhat less im-

[7] Consists of wage and salary disbursements, other labor income, and proprietors' income.

CHART III

INDUSTRIAL SOURCES OF CIVILIAN INCOME RECEIVED BY PERSONS FOR PARTICIPATION IN CURRENT PRODUCTION, ILLINOIS AND UNITED STATES, CALENDAR YEAR 1965

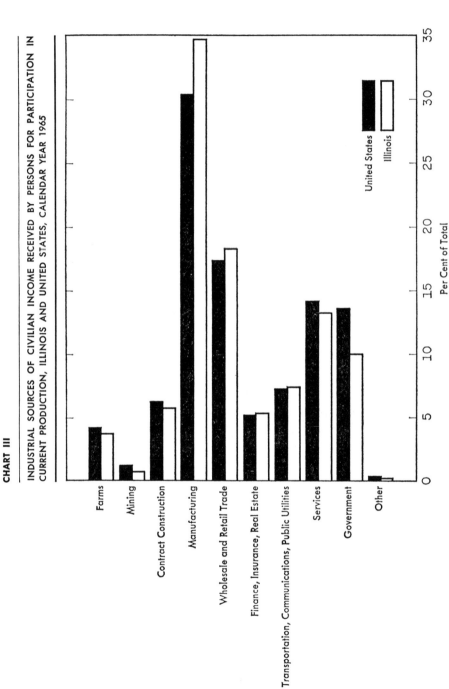

Source: U.S. Department of Commerce, *Survey of Current Business*, August, 1966.

portant, but, in general, the picture is one of fairly close conformity with the national pattern.

STATE AND LOCAL GOVERNMENT

American government is an intricate set of organizations varying greatly in size and function which are bound to each other in complex and varying ways. The federal government, of course, bulks far larger than any other unit in both geographic and financial terms. Under the federal system, however, the states retain many elements of sovereignty and are not merely subordinate units of the federal government. The many local governments are created by, and theoretically remain instruments of, the states. In terms of the practical political situation, however, local governments may be very much independent entities. Government in Illinois has long been characterized by emphasis upon the importance of local governmental units. This emphasis is reflected in the unusually large number of local governmental units and by the large percentage of state and local government funds which is expended by local governments.

Structure of State Government

Although it is common to speak of "the state" as if it were a single, unified entity, state government is actually a complex arrangement of officials, departments, legislative bodies, judicial bodies, boards, and commissions. Each of these has responsibilities and powers which overlap, limit, and reinforce those of the others. Chart IV, which is a simplified table of organization of the executive branch of Illinois state government, shows some of these relationships in a single branch of government. The top line shows the elected officials. The Governor, the most important elected official, appoints the heads of the code departments, but his appointments are subject to approval by the state Senate. Employees of the departments and of elected officials may be patronage employees subject to hiring and firing at will, or they may be covered by the civil service system. The powers, duties, and organization of departments are determined by the state legislature which also makes the biennial appropriations for operating the departments.

There are a large number of boards and commissions, not all of which are shown in the chart, composed of elected, appointed, or ex officio members. These have functions which range from very specialized regulatory activity to the operation of very large agencies such as the universities.

The legislative and judicial branches are far simpler in organization than is the executive branch but, even so, the situation is not simple. As of January 1, 1966, for example, there were 28 permanent and 26 temporary legislative commissions. Many of these legislative commissions have public as well as legislative members, and the membership of a few includes state officials on an ex officio basis. Some of these commissions were created to conduct research and recommend legislation in specific problem areas or to advise and watch over specific administrative agencies. The budgetary commission has the responsibility of reviewing departmental budget requests and making appropriate recommendations to the Governor and the legislature. Some commissions, such as the Legislative Reference Bureau and the Legislative Council, have a permanent staff to serve the legislative body.

The fiscal program of the state is determined by interacting activities of all three branches. Taxes are levied and appropriations made by the legislative branch which, in turn, must depend heavily upon the executive agencies for the information upon which decisions are based as well as for administration of programs once adopted. The judicial branch plays an unusually important role in Illinois fiscal matters because of the tradition of much tax litigation and the significant role which the question of constitutionality has played in shaping the tax system of Illinois.

Local Government Structure

Illinois has more local governments than any other state. The U.S. Bureau of the Census placed the number in existence in January, 1962, at 6,453.[8] All local units of government occupy a position subordinate to the state, but their powers and responsibilities vary greatly.

Counties, along with municipalities and townships, are units of general government which supply numerous and varied public services. Essentially, counties are local subdivisions of the state, created by the state as its agents to carry out administrative and judicial functions. The General Assembly has allotted a wide range of func-

[8] U.S. Bureau of the Census, *Census of Governments, 1962*, vol. I (Washington: U.S. Government Printing Office, 1963). For purposes of this census, a government was defined as an organized entity which, in addition to having governmental character, has sufficient discretion in the management of its own affairs to distinguish it as separate from the administrative structure of any other governmental unit.

CHART IV

SIMPLIFIED ORGANIZATIONAL CHART, EXECUTIVE BRANCH, ILLINOIS STATE GOVERNMENT

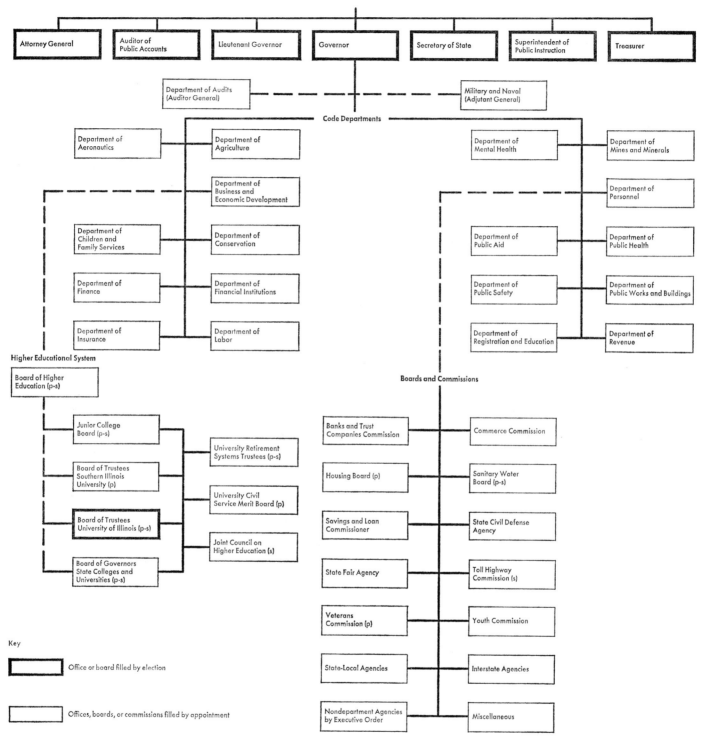

Attorney General | Auditor of Public Accounts | Lieutenant Governor | Governor | Secretary of State | Superintendent of Public Instruction | Treasurer

Department of Audits (Auditor General)

Military and Naval (Adjutant General)

Code Departments

Department of Aeronautics

Department of Agriculture

Department of Business and Economic Development

Department of Children and Family Services

Department of Conservation

Department of Finance

Department of Financial Institutions

Department of Insurance

Department of Labor

Department of Mental Health

Department of Mines and Minerals

Department of Personnel

Department of Public Aid

Department of Public Health

Department of Public Safety

Department of Public Works and Buildings

Department of Registration and Education

Department of Revenue

Higher Educational System

Board of Higher Education (p-s)

Junior College Board (p-s)

University Retirement Systems Trustees (p-s)

Board of Trustees Southern Illinois University (p)

University Civil Service Merit Board (p)

Board of Trustees University of Illinois (p-s)

Joint Council on Higher Education (s)

Board of Governors State Colleges and Universities (p-s)

Boards and Commissions

Banks and Trust Companies Commission

Commerce Commission

Housing Board (p)

Sanitary Water Board (p-s)

Savings and Loan Commissioner

State Civil Defense Agency

State Fair Agency

Toll Highway Commission (s)

Veterans Commission (p)

Youth Commission

State-Local Agencies

Interstate Agencies

Nondepartment Agencies by Executive Order

Miscellaneous

Key

☐ Office or board filled by election

☐ Offices, boards, or commissions filled by appointment

(p) Indicates commission, committee, or board; includes public members, generally nonsalaried.

(s) Indicates commission, committee, or board; includes state officials.

Where no composition of commission, committee, or board is indicated, members generally are salaried state employees.

Source: Adapted from a chart prepared by the Institute of Government and Public Affairs, University of Illinois, and distributed by Secretary of State Paul Powell, January, 1966.

tions to the county, some of the more important of which are the enforcement of state laws, the collection of property taxes, the administration of election machinery, and the recording of legal documents. The county also has an important role in constructing and maintaining roads.[9]

There are 102 counties in Illinois, and all areas within the state are served by organized county government. In size, counties vary from 166 to 1,173 square miles. Population varies from less than 5,000 to over 5,000,000. The major source of county revenue is the property tax, although large sums are also received as grants from the state and from charges and miscellaneous sources.

The township functions as a political and administrative subdivision of the county and state. The major functions of Illinois townships are the assessment of property for taxation, the maintenance of local roads, and general assistance. Eighty-five of the 102 counties in Illinois are organized into townships. There are a total of 1,433 townships in the state,[10] a number exceeded in only three states. The property tax is the major source of township revenue, but grants from the state and charges and miscellaneous revenue are also significant.

The 17 nontownship counties are divided into road districts which have the single function of providing local roads. Although the road districts may levy taxes with the approval of the county board and incur debt with the approval of the voters, the road district is not counted as a government in the Bureau of Census tabulation.

There are 1,251 municipalities in Illinois, more than in any other state. Illinois municipalities range in size from Chicago, the second largest city in the United States, to villages with only a handful of residents.

Municipalities, although units of general government, differ from counties and townships in that they are created at the request or by the consent of their inhabitants for the convenience of the locality rather than being created as an arm of the state.[11] Legally, municipalities occupy a somewhat higher ranking in the scale of corporate

[9] This list is by no means exhaustive. A more complete discussion of the legal status and functions of the county and other local government units is found in Neil F. Garvey, *The Government and Administration of Illinois* (New York: Thomas Y. Crowell Co., 1958), pp. 483–538; and Clyde F. Snider, Gilbert Y. Steiner, and Lois Langdon, *Local Taxing Units: The Illinois Experience* (Urbana: University of Illinois, Institute of Government and Public Affairs, 1954), pp. 1–68.

[10] Eleven geographic townships in Chicago are excluded because they do not perform governmental functions.

[11] Snider *et al., op. cit.,* p. 23.

existence than do townships or counties.[12] This does not mean, however, that municipalities are independent of the state. The courts have repeatedly held that all power exercised by a municipality is delegated to it by the state. In Illinois the state has not delegated power to municipalities in broad general terms by means of home rule charters. Instead, municipalities must look to the state statutes for specific and detailed delineation of their powers. Municipalities do, however, possess many powers for the performance of governmental functions within their boundaries. The statutes list more than one hundred specific powers vested in municipalities.[13] In terms of expenditures, the most important functions performed by Illinois municipalities are:

Roads and Streets
Police Protection
Sewerage and Sanitation
Fire Protection
General Control
Welfare
Hospitals

Although the property tax is the most important source of revenue for municipalities, other taxes such as the municipal sales tax and various license taxes, also produce large sums and are relatively more important to municipalities than to any other type of local government.

In January, 1962, there were 1,540 school districts in Illinois—a sharp reduction from the 12,138 which were in existence in 1942. The decline is largely due to various actions taken by the General Assembly to encourage or force school reorganization. The "dual system" of separate districts for elementary and secondary schools had been encouraged by tax and bonding limitations. Prior to 1945 no distinction was made between the taxing power of elementary school districts and of districts operating both high school and elementary grades. Even today, the constitutional debt limit is identical for every type of district. State aid in the form of flat per-pupil grants had contributed to the continuance of small independent and high school districts until postwar legislation provided for withholding of state aid from districts of less than a certain size. The General Assembly also speeded the consolidation of school districts by direct legislative fiat. Districts which had not maintained a school for two

[12] Garvey, *op. cit.*, pp. 517–19.
[13] Snider *et al.*, *op. cit.*, p. 23.

years were required to annex to an adjoining district, while many non-high school districts were forced to annex to adjoining districts.

By U.S. Bureau of the Census count, there are now 12 kinds of school districts in existence in Illinois.[14] Except for the Chicago School District, whose directors are appointed by the mayor, and special charter districts, whose boards may be elected or appointed, all are governed by elected boards.

Total school district expenditures are greater than the expenditures of any other type of local governmental unit in Illinois and are greater than those of the state itself if only direct general expenditures (excluding intergovernmental expenditure) are included. Revenue comes largely from the property tax and from state grants.

The sharp decline in the number of school districts contrasts with an opposite tendency in the case of special districts. In 1942 the U.S. Bureau of the Census counted 1,042 special districts. By January, 1962, the number had risen to 2,126 and exceeded the number in any other state. Some of the forces which lie behind this growth are described in the following quotation:

All too frequently the need for specific governmental services in an area will not be co-extensive with any general government unit; in an attempt to meet the demands, new units of an *ad hoc* character have been authorized by the legislature with boundaries fashioned to include the area needing the service. The circumscriptions of these units may include both urban and rural areas or they may cross-cut, divide, and disregard other existing borders in an attempt to define the benefited areas.

Although many districts have been organized to provide additional governmental services or to equalize the tax burden, others have been set up in order to permit borrowing or imposition of tax levies beyond constitutional or statutory limits already reached. The constitutional limitation on local indebtedness in Illinois is fixed at five per cent of the assessed valuation for each separate municipal corporation. Overlapping, and even coterminous districts with different corporate purposes, if authorized by the legislature, may each borrow up to the five per cent limit. In some counties of the state where the assessment ratio has been low, the constitutional limitation has frequently been unduly restrictive, and has resulted in the organization of new taxing units.[15]

The purposes of the various districts are indicated by the breakdown of special districts by type provided in Table 4. Most of the districts have the power to levy taxes. Some, such as the Chicago

---

[14] Chicago School District, common districts, community consolidated districts, community high school districts, community unit districts, consolidated districts, consolidated high school districts, high school districts (same boundaries as common districts), junior college school districts, non-high school districts, township high school districts and special charter districts.

[15] Snider *et al., op. cit.,* pp. 7–8.

TABLE 4

GOVERNMENTAL UNITS IN ILLINOIS, BY NUMBER AND TYPE, JANUARY, 1962

Type	Number
State	1
Counties	102
Townships	1,433
Municipalities	1,251
School Districts	1,540
Special Districts:	
Airport Authorities	24
Cemetery Maintenance Districts	19
Chicago Transit Authority	1
Drainage Districts	865
Fire Protection Districts	620
Hospital Districts	26
Housing Authorities	107
Metropolitan Fair and Exposition Authority	1
Mosquito Abatement Districts	18
Park Districts	179
Port Districts (special acts)	4
Public Library Districts	16
River Conservancy Districts	5
Sanitary Districts	81
Soil and Water Conservation Districts	99
Street Lighting Districts	13
Surface Water Protection Districts	4
Tuberculosis Sanitorium Districts	11
Water Supply Districts	33
Total	6,453

Source: U.S. Bureau of the Census, *Census of Governments, 1962*, I (Washington: U.S. Government Printing Office, 1963), 279–82.

Transit Authority and the housing authorities, are financed largely from charges for services. Others, such as the soil conservation districts, have power to levy compulsory charges against landowners for work performed.

In addition to the 6,453 state and local governmental units in Illinois, there are a number of agencies or areas which have some of the characteristics of governmental units but which are treated in Census statistics as subordinate agencies or areas of the state or local governmental units. Examples include forest preserve districts, land-clearance commissions, road districts, county health districts, and township health districts, all of which are subordinate to local units. Agencies or areas of the state government include the Illinois State Toll Highway Commission, the Chicago Medical Center Commission, mine inspection districts, registration districts (vital statistics), and the University of Illinois Foundation.

State-Local Fiscal Relations

The financial affairs of the state and local units of government in Illinois are interrelated in a number of ways.

Local units of government have been given a considerable amount of power over their own financial affairs. Most units have the power to levy taxes and to borrow money, and all have the power to make expenditures necessary in the performance of their authorized functions. However, the state has retained certain controls over the finances of the local units. For example, local units are subject to tax rate limits and to borrowing limits. Assessment and collection of the property tax are primarily local functions, but the state equalization program has important repercussions upon local fiscal affairs. This program, designed to equalize the general level of assessment in the various counties, is carried out by assigning multipliers to each county. Locally assessed values are adjusted in accord with the multiplier assigned and become the equalized values which are used in computing individual tax bills and in state aid distribution formulas. Since tax and debt limits are stated in terms of equalized assessed values, the level of the multiplier assigned greatly affects the tax and borrowing power of the local units which would, in most cases, be lower in the absence of application of the multiplier because of the low fractional level of original assessments.

A second kind of fiscal control exercised by the state is budgeting and accounting control. The statutes contain various scattered requirements with regard to the budgetary and accounting procedures to be followed by local units. In 1951 a law was enacted which, as amended, requires all municipalities except Chicago to have regular audits of their accounts and to file a copy with the Auditor of Public Accounts. A law providing for a standard method of accounting and requiring periodic audits of school district accounts became effective on July 31, 1959. By the end of the 1967 legislative session auditing requirements had been extended to all units of local government.

There are various statutes forbidding officers of a governmental unit from being a party to contracts entered into by the unit or requiring that certain purchases be made on the basis of competitive bidding. These provisions vary greatly in content as applied to the various kinds of governmental units and usually involve little, if any, administrative control by state agencies.[16]

One of the important developments in state and local finance in

---

[16] Garvey, *op. cit.*, pp. 574–75.

the last 30 years has been the growing importance of state grants as a means of financing local governmental units. Although local units in Illinois receive a smaller proportion of their revenue from this source than do local units in most states, the sums involved are substantial. Grants are largest in the fields of education and highways but are also substantial in the welfare and health fields.

These programs involve varying amounts of state control. Probably the closest supervision occurs in connection with highway aids. The state not only requires that the funds granted to the local unit be expended upon an approved project, but the projects are subject to state supervision and to approval at every stage. School districts, on the other hand, are given a wide range of discretion in utilizing state aids. The district must qualify by meeting minimum standards and must make certain reports to the state Superintendent's office, but has much the same freedom in expending state funds that it has in expending local tax revenue.[17]

The effect which state and local governmental units have upon units at the other level are by no means confined to formal programs of control or cooperation. For example, the provision of certain governmental services at one level may reduce the pressure for similar services at the other or, in certain circumstances, may make the demand for additional services more insistent. Similarly, the use or nonuse of a certain revenue source at one level may affect its use at the other.

NATURE AND LIMITATIONS OF THE ANALYSIS

The first problem involved in an attempt to study the economic and political aspects of Illinois state finance is to limit the scope of the study to manageable size. There are millions of facts about Illinois finance which might be included and hundreds of books and articles in political science and economics which might contribute to understanding Illinois state finance. The choice of a general approach to the subject, the choice of data to be presented, and the aspects of state finance which are given most attention in the analysis are influenced by the availability of data and the qualifications and interests of the author.

These factors have led, in this case, to an attempt to present a general synthesis which will provide the reader with a description of the expenditure programs and revenue sources of Illinois state government and, because of the close relationship between state

[17] *Ibid.*, pp. 575–76.

and local finance, with a description of some important aspects of local finance. This descriptive material provides the background for an analysis of the economic burdens imposed by the Illinois tax system and of the political forces which have created the existing system. The final chapter is a summary and appraisal of the political and economic aspects of Illinois finance.

Economically, the study is "micro" rather than "macro" or aggregative. It is assumed that the effects of the financial policies of the state of Illinois and its subdivisions upon the national economy are small enough to be neglected safely by the analyst and by state government decision-makers. On the other hand, the fact that the state is an open, rather than a closed, economy means that certain economic effects must be considered more closely than would be necessary in a study of national finance. Population, industry, and commerce are more mobile across state lines than across national boundaries. The quality of public services and the character of the tax system may affect both that movement and the character and rate of internal growth. The fact that this study deals with political as well as economic factors means that the political effects of economic mobility must also be considered.

Much information concerning expenditures and taxes is, of necessity, numerical. There are a number of problems involved in collecting and presenting such data. Although the financial data of most governmental units and agencies are a matter of public record, and although many units of government publish the minute details of their financial transactions, it is difficult to obtain data which provide an adequate, general description of the financial aspects of state and local government in Illinois. Basically, the problem arises from the fact that the data available are accounting data which have something other than general public information as their prime purpose. The purpose may be to control expenditures so that they do not exceed appropriations, to prevent defalcation, or to provide particular officials with information for internal decision-making purposes. Sometimes the form in which information is presented is based upon statutes or customs which had their origin in circumstances which no longer exist. At the state level, a number of detailed reports are published but none of these includes all the expenditures and receipts of the state government. The purposes for which the reports are issued vary. The State Treasurer's report is primarily designed to show cash receipts, cash expenditures, and cash balances in the various funds. The State Auditor's report, on the other hand, is designed to show appropriations to each fund and warrants issued against the appropriations. Unless the reader is familiar with the purpose of each fund and the intricacies of inter-fund transfers, these reports do not provide a very clear picture of the state's financial activity.

To compound the confusion further, the figures in the various state reports often cannot be reconciled with each other. There are a number of reasons for this. One is the difference in the timing of receipts and expenditures. For example, tax collections are recorded by the Department of Revenue when received, but the same funds are not recorded as receipts by the State Treasurer until cleared into the state treasury. The time lapse in this case is ordinarily short, but occasionally, as when the legality of a tax statute or tax assessment is being challenged in the courts, the delay may amount to several months. Expenditures may be recorded when the warrant is written, when the warrant is paid, or in the year for which the appropriation was made,[18] depending on the agency reporting and the purpose of the report.

Reports prepared by the Department of Finance probably come closer to providing an overall view of state finances than do any other state reports. However, even these reports have weaknesses. Data concerning certain operations which are independent of legislative financing are omitted completely, and there is a greater emphasis upon the funds from which expenditures are made than is desirable for the person who wants only a general view of state expenditure. As mentioned earlier, a person unfamiliar with the purpose and operation of the various funds will sometimes find it difficult to get a meaningful picture of state operations when information is arranged in this way.

At the local level, financial information is even more difficult to obtain. Certain items of information are collected by a state agency and are available on a statewide basis. For example, the state Department of Revenue collects information concerning property tax extensions in each county, and the State Auditor publishes information concerning local finance which is collected under the local auditing laws.

Because of the weaknesses of state and local sources of numerical data needed to provide an overall picture of state government expenditure and revenue, this study depends heavily upon statistics gathered by the Governments Division of the U.S. Bureau of the Census. Although these data are largely derived from state and local

---

[18] Obligations incurred against appropriations prior to June 30 of the second year of a biennium may be paid during the ensuing three months.

sources, their use has several advantages over the direct use of state and local reports when the purpose is to provide a comprehensive picture of the tax structure or expenditure patterns or to compare Illinois and other states.

Census data, of course, have their weaknesses. Since the data are derived from state sources, it is sometimes necessary for the Bureau of the Census to make rather arbitrary assignments of items to a particular classification. Occasionally, it is necessary for the Bureau to estimate particular items in order to obtain reasonable estimates of a financial total. Census data are often inferior to data provided in state or local reports for political analysis. For such an analysis it may be more important to know which agency receives funds and what controls have been placed upon their use than to know the function for which they are spent.

The analysis of economic aspects of Illinois finance is based primarily upon general revenue and general expenditure data, as reported by the Bureau of the Census. Insurance trust and liquor store[19] revenue and expenditure are the only items of revenue and expenditure which are excluded from this classification. Basic state data are available for fiscal years 1942–65.[20] Complete local government data classified on the same basis are available for 1942, 1957, and 1962. Less complete local government data are available for several other recent years. There have been some minor changes in classification, often involving only the combination or separation of a class, in the years involved. The author has sometimes combined Census classes to obtain comparability with other years or to shorten and simplify the presentation.

Census data are supplemented by information from official state and local sources when appropriate. Because of the problems mentioned above, it is often impossible to reconcile these figures with Census figures. For example, total expenditures for all state agencies shown in Appendix Table A6 differ considerably from Census expenditure figures for the same biennium shown in Table A8. This particular difference results largely from differences in coverage but there are also some differences in timing and definition involved.

When the processing of data for this volume began, 1965 fiscal year data were the most recent available. More recent data have been utilized at a few points, but, in general, 1965 data are the most recent utilized and the present tense is often used in referring to 1965.

[19] In states where applicable.
[20] Except for 1943, 1945, 1947, and 1949.

Reference to existing statutes, tax rates, and administrative arrangements describes the situation as it existed when the 1967 General Assembly recessed on June 30, 1967. Chapter 6 dealing with tax politics includes a review of developments in the 1967 legislative session.

Throughout this study, all financial data are on a fiscal year basis unless otherwise specified. The date attached to a fiscal year refers to the year in which the fiscal year ends. Thus, for the Illinois state government the fiscal year 1965 is the period from July 1, 1964, to June 30, 1965. Many Illinois local governments use the same fiscal year as the state but there are numerous exceptions.

A number of the larger and more detailed tables have been placed in an appendix. Many readers will find it unnecessary to refer to this material, but it will be useful to those who are interested in more detailed data.

Throughout the study, data are rounded when necessary to make them more manageable or to avoid the appearance of spurious accuracy. When such data were totaled, however, the total was computed before the individual items were rounded; thus, there may be a slight discrepancy between the detail and the total.

Unless otherwise noted, all per capita and percentage of personal income data used were computed using the population and income data shown in Tables A1, A2, A3, and A4. In computing per capita figures, the population at the beginning of the fiscal year was used.

2

EXPENDITURE TRENDS AND
PATTERNS, 1942–65*

In this chapter, Illinois state expenditure is viewed
from two different perspectives. In the first part of
the chapter, data are arranged by agency, and atten-
tion is focused upon the categories or classifications which are utilized by those who make political decisions about expenditure. This
involves an examination not only of expenditures by the various
agencies of government but of the funds from which appropriations
are made and the methods of classification utilized in the appropriation bills. Data classified in this fashion are useful for understanding
the decision-making process and for analyzing the political power
which a given appropriation represents. In the second part of the
chapter, expenditure data are viewed from an economic perspective.
Expenditures are classified by function and by economic character,
and the size of the government sector of the economy is related to
the size of the private sector.

POLITICAL PERSPECTIVES

The focal point of the decision-making process is the appropriation. Since no funds may be expended from the state treasury without a lawful appropriation,[1] the various agencies and departments
of state government must turn to the Illinois General Assembly once

* Unless otherwise noted, descriptive material in this chapter refers to the situation as it existed just before the opening of the 1967 General Assembly.
[1] *Constitution of the State of Illinois,* Article IV, Sec. 17.

every biennium for the funds needed to carry out and expand their programs. Every agency is in competition for available funds, and the legislators who must make the decisions are caught between conflicting demands for more spending and pressures to "hold the line" on taxes.[2] Many factors influence the outcome. Agencies with powerful constituencies or with powerful friends in the legislature have a clear advantage. The success of the department head and the budget officer in following the "rules" for spending money and submitting budget requests plays a role.[3] For some agencies and programs there are formulas or earmarked funds which affect appropriations. These are sometimes outside the legislature's control. Even when they are within legislative control, they are not frequently reexamined.

Agency Appropriations

The "appropriation book" for the seventy-fourth biennium contains 565 pages. In it are found the texts of 317 bills which appropriated over $4.5 billion. Appropriations were made to 129 different agencies, departments, and officers and ranged in size from $3,000 appropriated to the Spanish American War Veterans Commission to more than $1.1 billion appropriated to the Department of Public Works and Buildings.

Table 5 is based upon the report of the Department of Finance for the seventy-third biennium which began on July 1, 1963, and ended on June 30, 1965. It shows appropriations and expenditures of that biennium for major agencies. Smaller agencies are grouped together. Thus, expenditures of the General Assembly, 20 continuing legislative commissions, 17 interim commissions, and the General Assembly Retirement System are grouped under the heading "legislative agencies." Total appropriations to these agencies amounted to only .21 per cent of total appropriations. Funds appropriated to the judicial agencies are to pay operating costs of the Supreme Court and five appellate courts and to pay the salaries of officers of the circuit courts. The total appropriated for these purposes amounts to .6 per cent of total appropriations.

Elected state officials receive appropriations of funds to operate their offices, and, in addition, some receive funds which are to be distributed to other units of government or for debt retirement pur-

---

[2] The system which produces decisions to spend money has been analyzed in Thomas J. Anton, *The Politics of State Expenditure in Illinois* (Urbana: University of Illinois Press, 1966).

[3] Anton, *op. cit.*, pp. 49–53.

poses. For example, 98 per cent of the funds appropriated to the State Treasurer was for debt service and tax refunds, and 99.3 per cent of the appropriation to the Auditor of Public Accounts was for

TABLE 5

SEVENTY-THIRD BIENNIUM APPROPRIATIONS AND EXPENDITURES, BY AGENCY

Agency	Biennium Appro- priations	Expenditures		Amount Lapsed
		Fiscal 1964	Fiscal 1965	
	(in thousands)			
Legislative Agencies	$ 8,265	$ 2,459	$ 4,448	$ 1,358
Judicial Agencies	24,159	9,481	12,708	1,970
Elected Officials:				
Governor	604	292	302	11
Lieutenant Governor	112	53	58	1
Attorney General	3,656	1,692	1,953	11
Secretary of State	44,271	23,573	17,524	3,822
State Treasurer	84,241	40,088	39,899	4,288
Auditor of Public Accounts	460,392	222,417	236,842	1,133
Superintendent of Public Instruc- tion	98,527	52,569	59,039	7,011
Universities:				
University of Illinois	248,023	135,926	95,529	16,568
Southern Illinois University	104,737	54,750	32,254	17,733
Teachers College Board	93,893	49,052	39,025	5,816
Code Departments:				
Aeronautics	12,859	2,911	5,175	4,772
Agriculture	26,886	12,443	12,537	1,906
Children and Family Services	52,830	26,463	17,710	8,884
Conservation	21,446	10,564	7,707	3,176
Finance	297,454	117,789	95,125	85,140
Financial Institutions	5,171	2,239	2,404	529
Insurance	2,971	1,244	1,398	328
Labor	44,485	23,487	27,082	1,226
Mental Health	374,039	172,966	122,530	82,859
Mines and Minerals	1,489	704	746	38
Personnel	2,232	851	875	507
Public Aid	640,004	292,612	327,610	20,682
Public Health	48,129	26,053	15,053	13,534
Public Safety	77,883	37,379	34,407	6,096
Public Works	1,014,224	586,419	157,495	270,311
Registration and Education	9,755	4,389	4,883	483
Revenue	47,954	18,521	27,793	1,641
Boards, Commissions, and Noncode Departments:				
Department of Audits	686	519	153	14
Military and Naval Department	5,847	2,542	3,006	298
Youth Commission	22,544	9,993	10,881	1,688
Board of Economic Development	1,068	972	1,436	13
Civil Service Commission	186	79	80	27
Commerce Commission	4,934	1,820	2,082	1,032
Board of Higher Education	150	83	92	—
Illinois Building Authority	150	3,242	15,883	76
Scholarship Commission	5,177	2,153	3,010	13

TABLE 5 (Concluded)

Agency	Biennium Appro- priations	Expenditures Fiscal 1964	Fiscal 1965	Amount Lapsed
		(in thousands)		
School Building Commission	6,552	4,633	394	1,524
Illinois Veterans Commission	3,367	1,343	1,420	604
Board of Vocational Education	26,357	8,451	29,342	759
Retirement Systems:				
State Employees	14,728	7,817	6,788	123
Teachers	6,906	4,823	2,082	—
University	633	633	—	—
Other Boards and Commissions	11,204	5,199	5,865	916
Total	3,961,180	1,983,687	1,482,628	568,921
Total Includes:				
Expenditures of Federal Funds in Excess of Appropriation	—	—	2,568	—
Expenditures from Nonappro- priated Funds	—	26,809	44,678	—

Source: State of Illinois, Department of Finance, *Forty-Eighth Annual Report.*

aids and grants to be distributed to local governments in accordance with formulas established by state statutes.[4]

Code departments are headed by a director appointed by the Governor with the advice and consent of the Senate. They range in size from the Department of Public Works and Buildings, which received more than one-fourth of the total state appropriations in the seventy-third biennium, to the Department of Mines and Minerals, which received less than .04 per cent. The Department of Public Works, through its Division of Highways, has the responsibility of building and maintaining the state highway system and also supervises the use of state funds which are returned to local governments for the purpose of building streets and highways.

Other fiscally important code departments include the Department of Public Aid, which administers the federally aided public assistance program. This agency operated as a commission prior to 1963 when, in the midst of a furor over increasingly large expenditures and controversy over the extension of information concerning birth control to relief recipients, the agency was brought under gubernatorial control. The Department of Mental Health is responsible for the operation of an extensive system of mental hospitals

[4] Much of the appropriation to the Auditor was for grants to local schools from the Common School Fund. In the seventy-fourth biennium these funds were appropriated to the Superintendent of Public Instruction.

and clinics, and the Department of Public Safety operates the prison system and maintains the state police force.

Appropriations represent authority to spend rather than actual money, and lapse if not spent within the biennium for which appropriated. The statutes provide that all appropriated expenditures by code departments and other agencies not specifically exempted must be approved in advance by the Director of Finance. Appropriations for capital outlay provide that no obligation may be incurred without prior approval by the Governor, and the rate of expenditure of all agencies, except legislative and judicial agencies, is controlled by a system of quarterly allotments.

In view of the fact that agencies with small lapses are generally believed to fare better in the appropriations process, the rather large lapses shown in Table 5 may be somewhat surprising. Further analysis of the figures makes it possible to explain much of the lapsed appropriations. In the seventy-third biennium $374 million, or 65.8 per cent of total lapses, were of funds appropriated for capital outlay. Of this amount 68.9 per cent was lapsed by the Department of Public Works. Such large lapses occur in capital appropriations because many of the projects involved are large-scale projects which are not completed in one biennium. An agency must have an appropriation for a project before it can let a contract. If the project is not completed during the biennium, the legislature usually reappropriates the funds and a new contract for the completion of the project becomes effective.[5] In other cases, where earmarked funds are involved or where actual expenditure is controlled by a formula, appropriations may be intentionally generous since the formula or the availability of funds will limit expenditure regardless of the appropriation.

Table 6 illustrates these points. During the three-biennia period from July 1, 1959, to June 30, 1965, 17.17 per cent of all appropriations lapsed, but lapses of capital appropriations were 11.90 per cent of total appropriations of all character. Lapses of operating appropriations amounted to only 1.59 per cent of all appropriations during that period. Lapses in aids, grants, and debt service appropriations amounted to 3.68 per cent of appropriations of all character. Details of the 16 major departments shown reveal a considerable amount of variation from agency to agency.

Even after the appropriation and the quarterly allotment to the

[5] Lapses of this type, sometimes called temporary gross lapses, involve contracted obligations which the state is morally, if not legally, bound to carry out. True lapses involve no legal, moral, or ethical claims on the state.

TABLE 6

AGENCY LAPSES, BY CHARACTER, AS A PERCENTAGE OF TOTAL APPROPRIATION,
SELECTED AGENCIES, THREE-BIENNIA AVERAGE

Agency	Opera-ations	Capital	Aids and Grants	Debt Service	Total
Secretary of State	2.34%	7.81%			10.15%
State Treasurer	.18			21.09%	21.27
Auditor of Public Accounts	.06		.17%		.23
Superintendent of Public Instruction	4.07		4.31		8.39
Universities[a]	.48	16.61	—[b]		17.09
Department of Agriculture	7.16	1.51	1.11		9.77
Department of Children and Family Services	9.31	7.43	.08		16.82
Department of Finance	.33		28.01		28.34
Department of Labor	2.30				2.30
Department of Mental Health	4.48	27.68	.20		32.36
Department of Public Aid	.21		1.81		2.02
Department of Public Health	1.94	.36	19.04		21.34
Department of Public Safety	5.68	6.80			12.49
Department of Public Works	1.41	27.59	.16		29.16
Youth Commission	5.19	3.30			8.49
Board of Vocational Education	.71		2.84		3.55
Other Agencies	4.54	3.40	3.72	.21	11.87
All Agencies	1.59	11.90	3.23	.45	17.17

[a] Combined data for the University of Illinois, Southern Illinois University, and the Teachers College Board which operated four universities.
[b] Less than .005%.

Source: Computed from State of Illinois, Department of Finance, *Forty-Sixth Annual Report, Forty-Seventh Annual Report, Forty-Eighth Annual Report.*

agency is made, the agency does not have complete control over the funds since appropriations are itemized in considerable detail. First, appropriations to a given agency are classified by character. Table 7 shows the seventy-third biennium appropriations classified by character for 16 major agencies. In that biennium more than 41 per cent of all appropriations were for aids and grants and one-third of the total was for operating purposes, but there was great variation from agency to agency. For example, less than 0.7 per cent of the Auditor's appropriation was for operations as compared with more than 99.9 per cent of the Youth Commission's appropriation for the same purpose. In addition to classification by character, there are much more detailed classifications within the appropriation bill. For example, appropriations for ordinary and contingent (operating) expenses of the Auditor of Public Accounts are itemized both by organizational units and by major objects for each unit or

TABLE 7

AGENCY EXPENDITURES, BY CHARACTER, SEVENTY-THIRD BIENNIUM

Agency	Opera-tions	Capital	Aids and Grants	Debt Service[a]	Total
		(thousands)			
Secretary of State	$ 36,749	$ 4,348			$ 41,097
Treasurer	1,601		$ 35	$78,352	79,988
Auditor	3,049		456,210		459,259
Superintendent of Public Instruction	9,759		101,849		111,608
Universities and Colleges	289,868	112,109	4,561		406,538
Department of Agriculture	13,466	928	10,585		24,979
Department of Children and Family Services	28,675	12,016	3,482		44,173
Department of Finance	8,772		204,142		212,914
Department of Labor	43,365		7,204		50,569
Department of Mental Health	225,623	62,050	7,822		295,495
Department of Public Aid	64,441		555,781		620,222
Department of Public Health	22,317	44	18,746		41,107
Department of Public Safety	70,730	1,057			71,787
Department of Public Works	180,310	563,603			743,913
Youth Commission	20,865	9			20,874
Board of Vocational Education	7,958		29,836		37,794
All Other Agencies	126,634	24,019	25,009	28,341	204,003
Total	1,154,182	780,183	1,425,262	106,693	3,466,320

a Includes money for tax refunds.

Source: State of Illinois, Department of Finance, *Forty-Eighth Annual Report.*

division in the Auditor's office. The following divisions are specified:

Administration	County Audits
Accounting	Records Control
Investigative	Cemetery Care
Municipal Audits	Burial Trust

For each of these divisions there is, by statutory requirement,[6] standard "object and purpose" classifications reflecting major program responsibilities for each division. These standard classifications include such items as:

Personal Services	Permanent Improvements
Contractual Services	Land
Travel	Electronic Data Processing
Commodities	Contingencies
Equipment	Reserve

6 *Ill. Rev. Stat.*, ch. 127, sec. 149 (1965).

Fund Structure

To facilitate control of expenditures the state legislature has established a variety of funds.[7] Some are established by the legislature for the purpose of insuring that money from a specific source is used only for designated purposes.[8] For example, revenue from the sale of hunting and fishing licenses is earmarked for conservation purposes. A group of highway funds has been established to insure that certain highway user taxes are used only for highway purposes and to facilitate accounting for sums which are earmarked for highway use by local units of government. Other special funds are used to segregate monies held for building and debt service purposes, and there are a number of special funds established in connection with federally aided programs. Table 8 is based upon the fund classification used by the Department of Finance in its annual reports. A complete list of funds, including trust funds, is provided in Table A5 of the appendix.

A major portion of state tax revenues are deposited in the General Fund which supports all appropriations not specifically drawn against a special fund. The General Revenue Public Assistance Distributive funds are financed solely by transfers from the General Revenue Fund, and the Common School Fund is financed in part by transfers from the General Fund and in part by earmarking two-sevenths of the state sales tax for the fund.

The dominant highway fund is the Road Fund which receives federal aid monies directly from the U.S. Treasury and receives current collections of motor vehicle registrations and operators' license fees. Motor fuel tax collections are deposited in the Motor Fuel Tax Fund and then allocated to the Road Fund, the Grade Crossing and Protection Fund, and to the Motor Fuel Tax Distributive funds. Money from the latter funds is distributed to counties, municipalities, townships, and road districts upon the approval of the Department of Public Works.

Two funds, the Public Welfare Building Fund and the Universi-

---

[7] The word "fund" has a variety of technical meanings to accountants and financial experts. Within the context of this discussion it is sufficient if the word is understood to mean "an accounting device for the segregation of cash." The plural form of the word may also be used as a synonym for "cash" or "money." The context will indicate which meaning is intended.

[8] *Ill. Rev. Stat.*, ch. 127, sec. 137–176, contains general provisions dealing with state financial procedures and fund structures. Exceptions and modifications to these general provisions are sometimes contained in appropriation bills. The section entitled "The State's Fiscal System" in recent annual reports of the Department of Finance is an excellent brief description of fund structures and fiscal control mechanisms.

TABLE 8

APPROPRIATIONS AND EXPENDITURES, BY FUND, SEVENTY-THIRD BIENNIUM

Fund	Appropriations	Expenditures
	(thousands)	
General Revenue and Common School Funds:		
General Revenue	$1,079,640	$1,011,842
General Revenue Public Assistance:		
Distributive	475,342	465,363
Common School	451,878	451,556
Total	2,006,860	1,928,760
Highway Funds:		
Road	1,045,169	781,094
Grade Crossing Protection	2,411	786
Motor Fuel Tax	322,031	236,347
Road Bond Interest and Retirement	37	—
Emergency Relief Bond Interest and Retirement	—[a]	—
Total	1,369,648	1,018,227
Building Funds:		
Public Building	Not Approp.	19,051
Public Welfare Building	135,332	67,933
Universities Building	139,851	105,270
Total	275,183	192,255
Debt Service Funds:		
Public Welfare Building Bond Retirement and Interest	22,726	20,283
Universities Building Bond Retirement and Interest	27,902	26,595
Service Recognition Bond Interest and Retirement	29,111	28,810
Soldiers Compensation Bond Interest and Retirement	3	—[a]
Total	79,741	75,687
Educational Income Funds[b]	22,191	21,882
Other Special State Funds[b]	80,600	70,394
Special Federal Funds[b]	108,884	130,767
Funds Held Outside the Treasury[b]	Not Approp.	11,371
Revolving Funds[b]	18,072	16,971
Total Appropriations Expended	3,961,180	3,392,259
Expenditures in Excess of Appropriations		2,568
Expenditures from Nonappropriated Funds		71,487
Grand Total Expended		3,466,315

[a] Amount less than $500.
[b] See Appendix Table A5 for complete list of funds in this group.

Source: State of Illinois, Department of Finance, *Forty-Eighth Annual Report.*

ties Building Fund, received the proceeds from the sale of bonds authorized in a statewide referendum in 1960. Appropriations are made from these funds to construct buildings for the Department of Mental Health and Department of Children and Family Services and the state universities. Bond Interest and Retirement funds receive monies for the payment of the bond interest and principal. Such funds exist for each outstanding bond issue.

Educational income funds receive sums collected by the universities in payment of tuition, fees, and other revenue. These monies are then appropriated to the universities by the legislature.

There are 18 funds classified as "other special state funds." Included are such funds as the Agricultural Premium Fund which receives revenue from taxes on pari-mutuel betting and which is used to support appropriations of grants to local fairs and for certain expenses of the state fair. Another large special state fund is the Mental Health Fund which is financed entirely by charges for the care of mentally ill persons at state hospitals and is appropriated to the Department of Mental Health.

In the seventy-third biennium there were 51 special federal funds in which federal grants were held for specifically restricted purposes. The fact that total expenditures from these funds were greater than appropriations reflects the fact that not all expenditures by agencies of the state are supported by specific legislative appropriations. It is not uncommon for appropriation bills which authorize specific amounts of expenditure to include a clause authorizing the agency to spend additional sums that may become available from federal grants. Expenditures made under this type of authorization are referred to as "expenditures in excess of appropriation." In addition, there are a number of funds which are held outside the treasury from which expenditures are made without any specific appropriations. The Department of Finance refers to these as "nonappropriated" funds. Many of the nonappropriated funds are federal funds, but the category also includes the Psychiatric Research Fund, which is supported entirely by an allocation of revenue from charges for the care of patients in state mental hospitals and is expended by the Department of Mental Health. The Public Building Fund, also outside the state treasury, is supported by the sale of revenue bonds and is used to finance the construction of buildings which are "rented" to state agencies.

The statutes authorize the state universities to retain endowments, gifts, trust funds, federal aids, monies received in connection with research contracts, and receipts from the operation of dormitories, bookstores, farms, and other auxiliary enterprises. These monies are not only outside the treasury but are also outside the Department of Finance's reporting system and, thus, are not included in those tables in this chapter which are based upon Department of Finance data.

There are six revolving funds in the state treasury. The largest of these is the Working Capital Fund which receives the gross proceeds from the sale of items produced by industrial operations in state institutions. Appropriations for the operation of these industries are made from the fund. Another large revolving fund is the State Garage Revolving Fund which is used to maintain a fleet of motor vehicles for state use.

TABLE 9

EXPENDITURE FROM FEDERAL AND EARMARKED FUNDS, AS PERCENTAGE
OF TOTAL EXPENDITURE, SEVENTY-THIRD BIENNIUM

Agency	Earmarked State Funds[a]	Federal Funds
Secretary of State	69.2%	1.6%
State Treasurer	94.6	—[b]
Auditor of Public Accounts	.2	—[b]
Superintendent of Public Instruction	7.0	26.5
Universities[c]	33.8	0.0
Department of Agriculture	55.0	.2
Department of Children and Family Services	26.7	7.2
Department of Finance	96.3	.3
Department of Labor	0.0	95.6
Department of Mental Health	28.7	.8
Department of Public Aid	0.0	47.1
Department of Public Health	0.0	51.0
Department of Public Safety	39.5	0.0
Department of Public Works	43.6	54.4
Youth Commission	0.0	.1
Board of Vocational Education	.6	67.2

[a] See text for definition of earmarked funds.
[b] Less than .05 per cent.
[c] Data for universities includes only appropriated funds. Federal grants to universities are handled outside the state treasury and are not reported by the Department of Finance.

Source: Computed from State of Illinois, Department of Finance, *Forty-Eighth Annual Report.*

Table 9 indicates the importance of earmarked and federal funds for 16 major agencies. For purposes of this table, earmarked funds are defined as those which receive state revenues which, under existing laws, can be used only for a stated purpose. In general, this means that monies appropriated from funds other than the General Fund are classified as earmarked. Expenditures from the Common

School Fund are not included among earmarked expenditures since the earmarked revenue received by this fund is heavily supplemented by transfers from the General Fund. The term "earmarked," when used alone, is to be understood to mean *state* funds. Actually, all federal monies granted to the state are also earmarked.

Earmarked monies received by the Secretary of State come from the Road Fund, since a large part of the operating cost of his office arises from responsibilities for the licensing of vehicles and vehicle operators.

Appropriations to the State Treasurer from earmarked funds are from the various bond interest and retirement funds for the purpose of meeting debt service costs.

A large part of the earmarked and federal monies received by the Superintendent of Public Instruction are for distribution to local school districts as grants and aids. These include money from the state Driver's Education Fund, which is used for driver education programs in local schools, and monies from a number of federal programs in the field of education.

Earmarked monies expended by the universities come from income funds, which are supported largely by tuition and fees, and from the Universities Building Fund, which was established with borrowed monies.

The Department of Agriculture receives more than one-half of its appropriation from funds which are financed by the various taxes upon horse and harness racing. The Department of Children and Family Services does not ordinarily spend from earmarked state funds, but in the seventy-third biennium it received appropriations for building purposes from the Public Welfare Building Fund. This fund, like the Universities Building Fund, was established as a result of a 1960 referendum which approved the sale of $150 million of bonds.

That portion of motor fuel tax receipts which is returned to local units of government for street and highway purposes is appropriated to the Department of Finance, although release of the monies must be approved by the Division of Highways of the Department of Public Works and Buildings. Operating expenses of the Department of Finance are paid largely from the General Fund.

The Department of Labor receives almost all of its appropriation from federal grants. These grants include the 100 per cent grant for purposes of administering the unemployment compensation system and grants under such programs as the Manpower Development and Training Act.

The Department of Mental Health receives appropriations from the Mental Health and the Psychiatric Training and Research funds. Both are supported by charges for the care of patients. In the seventy-third biennium the department also received appropriations for capital purposes from the Mental Health Building Fund.

Approximately one-half of the expenditures of the Department of Public Aid and of the Department of Public Health come from federal grants, but neither department receives monies from earmarked state funds. The Board of Vocational Education made over two-thirds of its expenditures from federal funds.

Earmarked revenue for the Department of Public Safety was largely from the Road Fund and is used to operate the state police system.

The Department of Public Works which, among other things, builds and maintains the state highway system, makes almost all of its expenditures from the Road Fund which is financed by highway user taxes and federal aid.

Importance of Technical Factors

It may appear strange that a section entitled "Political Perspectives" has been devoted almost entirely to a description of technical factors such as the form of appropriation, fund structures, and lapse procedures. In fact, there is a close relationship between these matters and the process of political decision-making.

Anyone who thumbs through the appropriation book is apt to realize that the complexity of state government operations is such that the legislators who vote upon appropriation bills cannot possibly have a detailed knowledge of the many activities which are financed by state government. It is also clear that the appropriation process is an important one which affects the lives and fortunes of many persons and, thus, might be expected to become the basis of intense political conflict. In fact, such conflict sometimes occurs but the great majority of appropriations move through the legislative process with considerable dispatch and there is little apparent conflict.

This suggests that there are informational and decision-making mechanisms which have a remarkable capacity for simplifying complex decisions and for avoiding or ameliorating overt conflict. These mechanisms have been described in detail by Professor Anton[9] and need not be described again, but it is important to emphasize the

[9] Anton, *op. cit.*

close relationship between decision-making and the technical aspects of finance.

Thus, it is important that appropriations are made to specific agencies rather than for specific functions. Economic analysts often discuss public expenditure decisions in terms of needs and demands for particular kinds of services. Clearly, needs and demands do influence decisions, but appropriations are made to agencies and there is rarely a perfect correspondence between agency responsibilities and any commonly used functional classification. Since legislators and executive budget-makers focus their attention upon agency expenditures, expenditures for a particular function may be affected by the agency to which it is assigned or by the way it is split among the agencies.

Expenditure decisions are also influenced by the fund from which appropriations are made. The device of "earmarking" certain taxes for particular expenditures tends to routinize decisions. The legislature need only know the estimated receipts from the tax in order to make the appropriation. Occasionally, of course, pressure for a change becomes great and the fundamental earmarking decision is reconsidered, but, in general, earmarking tends to ameliorate conflict over appropriations. Sometimes formulas, such as the one used to determine the amount of equalization aid to be paid to local school districts, are utilized for the same purpose.

Similarly, conflict is avoided and decisions are simplified when appropriations are made from federally aided funds. Often the federal government prescribes important details of the program so that the principal decision to be made is whether or not to "buy" the program which is offered. Since federal grants usually call for matching funds, the cost in terms of state-collected tax dollars is lower and the decision is apt to be in the affirmative.

There are also interrelations between the technical aspects of state finance and the political power represented by appropriations. It is clear, first of all, that the authority to spend public funds does represent political power. An administrator who has the power to hire personnel, to decide which section of a highway to improve or which kind of equipment to buy has power which can be used politically. It is, however, power which is subject to many different kinds of restrictions. The detailed classification which is common in appropriation bills is an important legal restriction. Funds appropriated to the State Treasurer for debt service purposes represent relatively little political power as compared with funds appropriated to the Secretary of State for the employment of personnel. Funds appropriated to the Department of Public Health for the employment of personnel may represent less political power than an equal sum appropriated to the Secretary of State. The Department of Public Health is subject to the personnel code (civil service) and to restrictions upon the political use of federal aid funds. Few of the Secretary of State's employees are subject to the personnel code and he spends little federal money.

The legal restrictions upon the use of appropriated funds are imposed by the legislature in a deliberate effort to limit or control the use of funds by the Governor and agency heads. There are, in addition, many informal controls. For example, legislators often make it clear that too much activity or not enough activity of certain types is apt to have an unfavorable effect upon future appropriations. For example, during a 1964 dispute over an action of the Illinois Fair Employment Practices Commission, a prominent state senator was widely quoted as saying, "It will be interesting to see how they can continue to operate next year without any money." [10] In fact, the Commission received a larger appropriation than it had in the preceding biennium but the legislature did cut a substantial sum from the appropriation bill, added provisions prohibiting the Commission from expending any funds for legal services, and severely limited the conditions under which education and research programs could be conducted.[11]

Public opinion and precedent may also limit both legislators and administrators in their use of funds. Certain positions are customarily filled by patronage employees while others are filled by professionally qualified persons with little or no attention to party affiliation or political activity. Thus, the Secretary of State makes no secret of the fact that his employees are expected to spend election day "getting out the vote" and that campaign contributions are expected from all employees. In contrast, a similar policy on the part of a university president would bring an immediate chorus of censure from both the public and the legislature.

Trends in Agency Expenditure

One of the factors which simplifies decision-making and ameliorates conflict over the allocation of state funds is the fact that it is never necessary to allocate all expenditures *de novo*. There are powerful political factors which tend to prevent reduction in agency appropriations. It is ordinarily assumed that every agency will receive a sum sufficient to permit it to carry on at a level of operations

[10] *Chicago Daily News*, November 12, 1964.
[11] *Chicago Tribune*, June 28, 1965, and House Bill 1313, approved July 16, 1965.

at least equal to the present level. In fact, the device of presenting budget requests to the budgetary commission in the "basic-supplemental" format represents a tacit recognition that there is little likelihood that the basic budget needed to carry on at the existing level will be cut, but that legislative decision-makers will take a close look at any proposal to expand operations. At the same time, the fact that the budget is presented in this fashion tends to reinforce the tendency not to cut the current level of operations, and the budget problem becomes largely one of determining how much of an increase each agency will receive.

In the nine biennia beginning July 1, 1947, and ending June 30, 1965, the expenditures reported by the Department of Finance rose from $1.3 billion to almost $3.5 billion. However, expenditures in the first biennium included $311 million of nonrecurring expenditure for veterans' bonuses by the Service Recognition Board. If this nonrecurring expenditure is excluded from consideration, then there was a 251.3 per cent increase in expenditures in the 18 year period. There are, however, large differences in increases among agencies. When the data are adjusted for major reorganizations of departmental functions, such as the transfer of the operation of five institutions of higher education from the Department of Registration and Education, the percentage increases in the 18 year period range from a low of 30.7 per cent for the Department of Mines and Minerals to a more than 8,000 per cent (eighty-fold) increase for the Superintendent of Public Instruction. Similar data for 27 agencies are shown in Table 10. Charts V through VIII show the trend of expenditures of several agencies during the nine-biennia period. These charts, used along with Table 10, reveal much about the rate of growth and the absolute size of the agencies during the period. They also raise the question as to the reason for the great difference in the rate of growth. It has been hypothesized that large agencies and agencies with access to federal or earmarked state funds will be most successful in the battle for increased appropriations,[12] but attempts to test these hypotheses statistically produced little evidence to support them.[13]

ECONOMIC PERSPECTIVES

Political decisions to spend public money produce several economic consequences. One direct consequence is the production of

[12] See Anton, *op. cit.*, pp. 255–61.
[13] See Appendix B.

CHART V

EXPENDITURE TRENDS, ELECTED STATE OFFICIALS

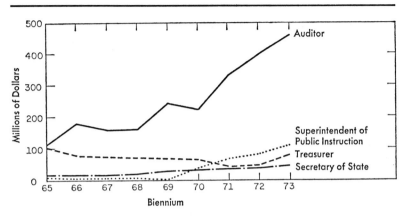

Source: State of Illinois, Department of Finance, *Annual Report,* various years.

CHART VI

EXPENDITURE TRENDS, STATE UNIVERSITIES

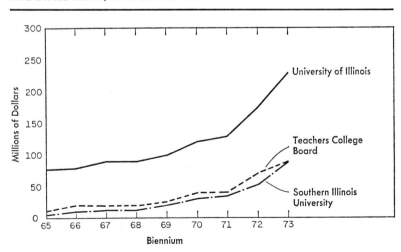

Source: State of Illinois, Department of Finance, *Annual Report,* various years.

CHART VII

EXPENDITURE TRENDS, FOUR LARGE DEPARTMENTS

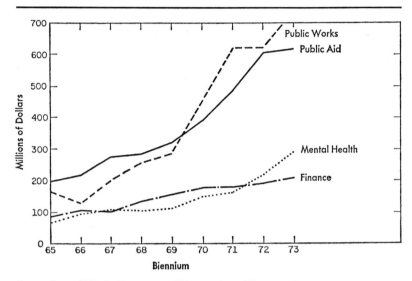

Source: State of Illinois, Department of Finance, *Annual Report,* various years.

CHART VIII

EXPENDITURE TRENDS, FIVE SMALLER DEPARTMENTS

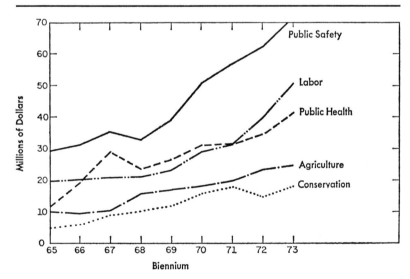

Source: State of Illinois, Department of Finance, *Annual Report,* various years.

TABLE 10

PERCENTAGE GROWTH IN AGENCY EXPENDITURES,
SIXTY-FIFTH TO SEVENTY-THIRD BIENNIUM

Legislative Agencies	171.6%
Judicial Agencies	447.1
Elected Officials:	
Governor, Lieutenant Governor, Attorney General	99.7
Secretary of State	235.0
State Treasurer	53.0
Auditor of Public Accounts	270.0
Superintendent of Public Instruction	8,279.0
Universities:	
University of Illinois	210.0
Southern Illinois University[a]	1,731.3
Teachers College Board[a]	537.5
Code Departments:	
Aeronautics	85.6
Agriculture	141.6
Children and Family Services[a]	336.4
Conservation	254.3
Finance	140.3
Insurance	65.4
Labor	153.3
Mental Health[a]	284.2
Mines and Minerals	30.7
Public Aid	210.8
Public Health	256.2
Public Safety[a]	146.4
Public Works	348.7
Registration and Education[a]	88.5
Revenue	84.5
Boards, Commissions, and Noncode Departments:	
Youth Commission[a]	287.6
Vocational Education	146.8
All Agencies	251.3

[a] Data from which computations were made were adjusted to allow for major reorganization of departmental functions.

Source: Computed from State of Illinois, Department of Finance, *Annual Report*, various years.

goods and services which have immediate want-satisfying power for those who benefit from them. Another economic consequence is the provision of income to government employees and business firms which supply goods and services to the state government.

In addition to these direct effects upon the economic system, there are indirect and feedback effects upon the economic and political system. Among the indirect effects upon the economic system are those resulting from the influence which government services exert upon the private sector of the economy. Many governmental services become an integral part of the productive process in the private sector and may properly be considered as "agents of production." Some of these are as immediate and tangible as the highway system over which component parts and finished goods are transported, and others are as distant and intangible as the educational and social services rendered to a child who will someday manage a private firm. Other indirect effects include those resulting from government competition with private firms and the stimulation of demand for the products of private firms. Often the same government operation does both. For example, a state park may contain a lodge which competes directly with similar private establishments yet stimulates the demand for other privately produced tourist services.

Feedback occurs when the actual and potential economic consequences of a political decision about expenditure influence the political decision-making process. For example, political decision-makers do not lightly reduce services to which voters have become accustomed or alter the spending pattern in such a way as to eliminate the livelihood of persons dependent upon government expenditure. Furthermore, arguments that a given policy will promote industrial development or encourage the location of industry in the state are among the most effective that a lobbyist can use.

For describing and analyzing economic aspects of public expenditure, data assembled by the U.S. Bureau of the Census are often more useful than are data published at the state level. Census data are more comprehensive than are Department of Finance data because they include expenditures not included in the Department of Finance data which have been utilized thus far in this chapter. Among these items are expenditures of the Toll Road Commission, expenditures from university funds which are not part of the state treasury, and expenditures from pension and insurance trust funds. Census classifications emphasize the purpose and nature of expenditure rather than the agency or the fund, and the nationally uniform system of classification facilitates interstate comparisons. For these reasons Census data are utilized in the remainder of the chapter.

The Census classifies as general expenditure all state expenditure except insurance trust and, in states where applicable, liquor store expenditure. Interest expenditure is classified as miscellaneous general expenditure, but sums paid out in repayment of debt are not considered to be expenditure. Total general expenditure for the fiscal year 1965 was $1.9 billion and insurance trust expenditure was $165 million. Debt repayment amounted to $34.5 million.

Chart IX is a graphic presentation of 1965 general expenditure by

CHART IX

ILLINOIS STATE GOVERNMENT GENERAL EXPENDITURE, BY FUNCTION, 1965

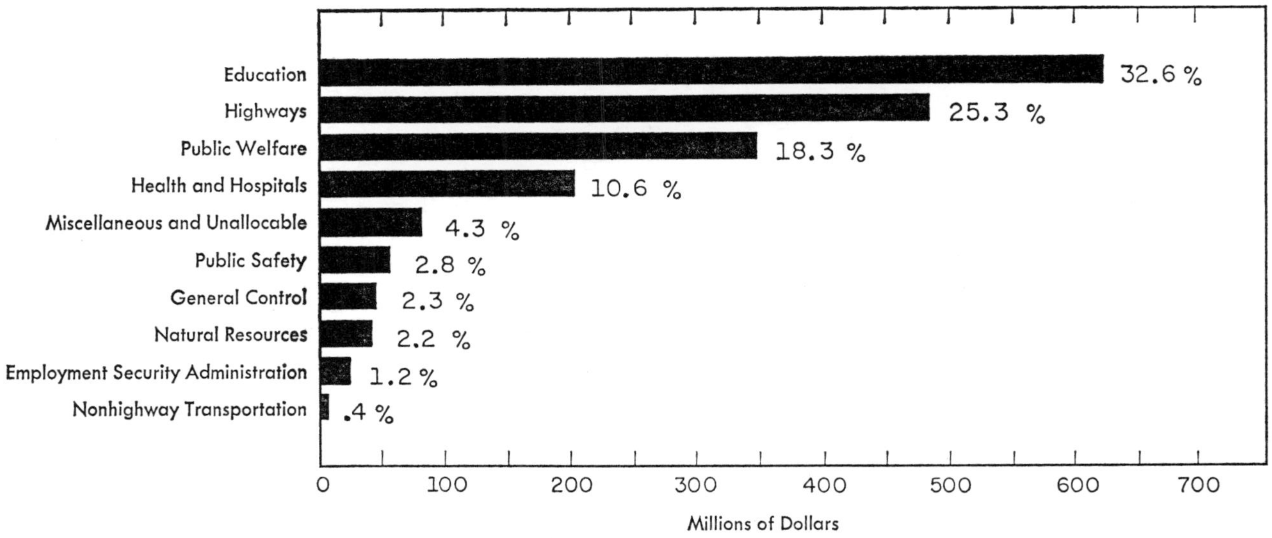

Source: Table A8.

major function. Appendix Table A7 provides a detailed breakdown of these data.

The most expensive single function in 1965 was education which accounted for almost one-third of state general expenditure. Of the $620 million expended for that function, 47.2 per cent was for higher education. Virtually all of this went for the operation and expansion of the University of Illinois, Southern Illinois University, and the four universities under the control of the Teachers College Board.[14] Comparison of these data with those of Table 5 reveals that only about 57 per cent of the total expenditure for higher education is from appropriated funds.[15]

Intergovernmental expenditure for education amounted to almost as much as did expenditures for higher education. Most of this expenditure was in the form of state grants to local school districts and came largely from state tax funds, although federal funds for this purpose have increased in importance in recent years.

A total of $482 million was expended for highways in fiscal 1965. Seventy-two per cent of this was for the construction and maintenance of state highways by the Division of Highways of the Department of Public Works and Buildings. Twenty-six per cent was in grants to counties, townships, and municipalities for the construction and maintenance of streets and highways under their jurisdiction.

Public welfare expenditure amounted to $347 million, making it the third most expensive function. Most of this sum was spent by the Public Aid Department, which administers the federally aided categorical assistance programs, but some expenditure by other state agencies is included as public welfare expenditure.

Well over one-half of the health and hospital expenditure was for the operation and construction of mental hospitals. The remainder of health and hospital expenditure was for a variety of public health services and for payments to hospitals maintained by private sources or other governmental units.

Public safety expenditures include expenditure for correctional purposes and for police protection.

[14] Since renamed the Board of Governors of State Colleges and Universities.
[15] Figures derived in this way must be considered approximations since there are other reasons for differences in Census and Department of Finance figures. One of these is that the Department of Finance reports expenditures as of the date of obligation while the Census reports as of the date of payment. This probably results in a relatively minor difference in higher education data but is a major difference in the case of highway expenditure, since obligations for highway construction are heavily concentrated in the first year of the biennium.

Expenditures classified as natural resources by the Bureau of the Census include expenditures for fish and game conservation and for forestry and park purposes, but the largest portion of these expenditures went for various agricultural programs.

Expenditures for administration of unemployment compensation, public employment services, and related services, called employment security administration by the Census Bureau, amounted to $23.3 million.

General control or "general government" expenditure amounted to $44.0 million. Of this, over half went for financial administration and the remainder to judicial, legislative, and executive agencies of the state.

Miscellaneous and unallocable expenditures amounted to $80.3 million of which $35.4 million consisted of interest payments. The remainder was made up of a variety of small expenditures which could not be classified elsewhere.

The Census Bureau's "character and object" classification is a five-fold one. Current operation expenditures consist of direct expenditure for compensation of officers and employees and for supplies, materials, and contractual services except for capital outlay amounts. Capital outlay includes expenditures for construction of buildings, roads, and other improvements and for purchase of equipment, land, and existing structures, as well as additions and major alterations to structures. Intergovernmental expenditures include amounts paid to other governments as fiscal aids in the form of shared revenues and grants-in-aid, as reimbursements for performance of general government activities, and for specific services in lieu of taxes. Assistance and subsidies consist of cash payments for public assistance, veterans' bonuses, and other payments to individuals or private organizations which are neither subject to repayment nor in return for goods or services. (It excludes cash benefits for insurance trust programs since expenditures in connection with such programs are not classified as general expenditure.) Chart X provides a graphic breakdown of 1965 expenditures on the basis of this classification.

Table 11 is a cross-classification of expenditure by function and by character and object. As would be expected, there is considerable variation in the character and object of expenditure for the different functions. For example, almost 60 per cent of highway expenditure is capital outlay and 26 per cent is intergovernmental expenditure. In contrast, more than 50 per cent of public welfare expenditure is for assistance and subsidies and only 1 per cent is capital outlay.

CHART X

ILLINOIS STATE GOVERNMENT GENERAL EXPENDITURE, BY CHARACTER AND OBJECT, 1965

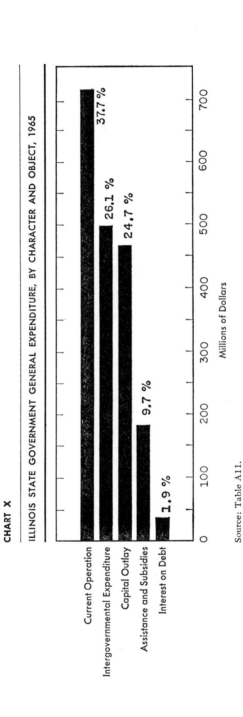

Source: Table A11.

TABLE 11

ILLINOIS STATE GENERAL EXPENDITURE, BY FUNCTION AND BY CHARACTER AND OBJECT, 1965

Function	Current Operation	Capital Outlay	Intergovernmental Expenditure	Assistance & Subsidies	Interest	Total
			(thousands)			
Education	$217,377	$102,851	$291,741	$ 7,872		$ 619,841
Highways	66,021	287,823	127,751			481,595
Public Welfare	99,120	3,508	68,355	176,375		347,358
Hospitals	126,735	45,939	2,258			174,932
Health	23,255	1,147	1,721			26,123
Police	13,832	2,123				15,955
Correction	30,351	6,490				36,841
Natural Resources	34,352	7,440	533			42,325
General Control	20,500	209				20,709
Financial Administration	22,765	557				23,322
Employment Security Administration	23,183	144				23,327
Housing and Urban Renewal	956	5				961
Airports	27	3,873	1,116			5,016
Water Transports and Terminals	2,045	77	274			2,396
Protective Regulations and Inspection, n.e.c.	20,389	334				20,723
General Public Buildings	3,600	5,033				8,633
Veterans Services	1,352			56		1,408
Libraries	1,894					1,894
Interest on General Debt					35,408	35,408
Miscellaneous and Unallocable	8,450	1,471	2,293			12,214
Total	716,204	469,024	496,042	184,303	35,408	1,900,981

Source: U.S. Bureau of the Census, *Compendium of State Government Finances in 1965* (Washington: U.S. Government Printing Office, 1966), and unpublished census worksheets.

Debt Service Payments

As noted above, interest payments are included as expenditures in Census data but debt retirement payments are excluded from expenditure figures. Similarly, receipts from borrowing are excluded from revenue. This treatment of debt transactions is appropriate when attention is focused upon the long-run aspects of the state's financial problem, but it should be recognized that the problem which legislators face every two years may be greatly affected by the necessity of meeting debt service costs. Conversely, borrowing by the state and its agencies may permit spending without an immediately corresponding increase in taxes or other revenue.

Long term state debt outstanding at the end of the fiscal year 1965 was as follows:[16]

	Amount (in thousands)
State Institutions of Higher Education	$ 397,739
Toll Highways	436,853
Veterans' Bonuses	87,623
Other and Unallocable	164,700
Total Long Term Debt	$1,086,915

Out of the total long term indebtedness of the state, only $397 million is backed by the full faith and credit of the state. Bonds issued by the state institutions of higher education are revenue bonds backed by the pledge of income from dormitories and other student facilities.[17] The toll highway bonds are revenue bonds secured by income from the operation of the toll highway system.

During fiscal year 1965 Illinois issued $45.5 million in long term debt and retired $34.5 million, resulting in a net increase in indebtedness of $11 million.

Employment Patterns

Another view of the size and character of the state governmental sector of the state's economy can be obtained by examining public employment data. These data give a less comprehensive picture than do expenditure data because of wide differences in expenditure per employee for the various functions. For example, more than twice as many persons are employed by the state of Illinois in the field of

[16] U.S. Bureau of the Census, *Compendium of State Government Finances in 1965* (Washington: U.S. Government Printing Office, 1966), pp. 40–41.
[17] Apparently, Bureau of the Census data for state institutions of higher education include the general obligation bonds issued for uinversity buildings following the 1960 Universities and Public Welfare Bond referendum.

higher education as are employed in the area of highways, although highway expenditures are much higher than higher education expenditures. The explanation, of course, is that much highway expenditure involves contract construction and intergovernmental payments, while much expenditure in the field of higher education is for services rendered directly by state employees. For some purposes, however, employment data are more useful than expenditure data. They are, for example, a better measure of "direct" production of governmental services.[18]

In October, 1965, there were 93,937 state employees. Of these, 73,269 were full-time employees and the remainder were employed on a part-time basis.[19]

When the number of part-time workers is discounted by applying full-time earning rates, it is found that "full-time equivalent" employment was 78,190. Table 12 reveals that more state employees were employed in higher education than in any other field and that state hospitals were the second largest source of state employment.

Comparisons with Other States

Comparisons of per capita general expenditure of the state of Illinois with per capita general expenditure of all states combined indicates that expenditures in Illinois are considerably below the average. Per capita state general expenditure in Illinois in 1965 was $180.39 while the corresponding figure for all states was $210.66. In Table 13 Illinois state general expenditure, by function, is compared with that of the United States as a whole. These data reveal that Illinois spends less than the national average for every function except health and hospitals, and public welfare. These data are of limited usefulness as a basis for comparing the level of governmental services provided to residents of Illinois with that provided to residents of other states because of the wide differences in the way

---

[18] The relationship between the governmental and private sectors of the economy is a complex one, and the degree to which political decisions replace market decisions varies greatly. When the government hires men to produce a service which is provided free, political decisions are dominant. When subsidies and assistance payments are made (transfer payments in the national income accounts), the government changes the distribution of income but otherwise does not interfere with the market mechanism. Between these extremes, political decisions may determine the form which output is to take (e.g., a highway of certain specifications from point A to point B), but the goods may be produced by the private firm making the lowest bid and using construction methods determined largely by cost considerations.

[19] U.S. Bureau of the Census, *Public Employment in 1965* (Washington: U.S. Government Printing Office, 1966), p. 13.

TABLE 12

FULL-TIME EQUIVALENT, ILLINOIS STATE EMPLOYEES,
BY FUNCTION, OCTOBER, 1965

Function	Full-time Equiva-lent Employees
Higher Education	22,039
Other Education	1,575
Highways	9,715
Public Welfare	3,697
Hospitals	19,358
Health	965
Police	1,763
Natural Resources	3,327
Correction	3,799
Employment Security Administration	2,798
Financial Administration	2,702
General Control	977
Other and Unallocable	5,476
Total	78,190

Source: U.S. Bureau of the Census, *Public Employment in 1965* (Washington: U.S. Government Printing Office, 1966).

responsibility for the various governmental functions is distributed among the levels of government. Data showing combined expenditure of state and local government in Illinois are provided in Chapter 4.

TABLE 13

PER CAPITA STATE GENERAL EXPENDITURE,
BY FUNCTION, ILLINOIS AND UNITED STATES, 1965

Function	Per Capita	
	Illinois	U.S.
Public Safety	$ 5.01	$ 5.25
Public Welfare	32.96	28.40
Education	58.82	75.94
Highways	45.70	51.44
Health and Hospitals	19.08	15.37
Natural Resources	4.02	6.53
Employment Security Administration	2.21	2.39
General Control	4.18	5.01
Miscellaneous and Unallocable	8.41	20.33
Total	180.39	210.66

Source: Tables A1, A8, A9.

TABLE 14

PER CAPITA STATE GENERAL EXPENDITURE, BY CHARACTER
AND OBJECT, ILLINOIS AND UNITED STATES, 1965

	Per Capita	
Character and Object	Illinois	U.S.
Current Operation	$ 68.28	$ 72.67
Capital Outlay	44.72	47.94
Assistance and Subsidies	17.57	11.69
Interest on Debt	3.38	4.29
Intergovernmental Expenditure	47.29	74.06
Total General Expenditure	181.24	210.66

Source: Table A12.

Table 14 reveals that Illinois expends more per capita in the form of assistance and subsidies than does the average state, but that in all other object and subject classifications Illinois spends less. In view of the fact that local governments are given somewhat greater functional responsibilities in Illinois, it is particularly noteworthy that the state expenditure for intergovernmental grants is so much smaller than the national average.

Comparison of full-time equivalent employment in Illinois and

TABLE 15

FULL-TIME EQUIVALENT STATE EMPLOYMENT PER 10,000 POPULATION,
ILLINOIS AND UNITED STATES, OCTOBER, 1965

Function	Illinois	United States
Higher Education	20.7	23.7
Other Education	1.5	2.5
Highways	9.1	14.6
Public Welfare	3.5	3.2
Hospitals	18.2	18.5
Health	.9	1.7
Police	1.7	2.1
Natural Resources	3.1	5.8
Correction	3.6	3.6
Employment Security Administration	2.6	3.3
Financial Administration	2.5	4.1
General Control	.9	1.4
Other and Unallocable	5.1	5.1
Total	73.5	89.7[a]

[a] Excludes state liquor store employment.

Source: Table A1; U.S. Bureau of the Census, *Public Employment in 1965* (Washington: U.S. Government Printing Office, 1966).

the United States (Table 15) reveals that employment per 10,000 population is substantially lower in Illinois than the national average. Only public welfare employment per 10,000 population is higher in Illinois than in the United States.

It is difficult to say exactly what the above data on state public expenditure and employment mean in terms of the quantity and quality of government services provided to the residents of the state. Lower expenditure and lower employment in Illinois result, in part, from the fact that local government performs more services in Illinois than in many states. There are also variations in governmental efficiency and geographic variations in the cost of providing governmental services which are very difficult to measure.

Trends in Total Expenditure

State and local government expenditure in the United States has risen sharply in the postwar period. For the United States as a whole, the rise in state expenditure from 1942 to 1965 was 786 per cent. All of this rise occurred in the postwar period. There was a slight decline during World War II.

In Illinois state general expenditure rose from $225 million in 1942 to $1.9 billion in 1965, a rise of 746 per cent. The relative rise of state general expenditure in Illinois and in the nation as a whole is illustrated in Chart XI. Except for 1948, when a sharp rise in ex-

CHART XI

INDEX OF STATE GENERAL EXPENDITURE, ILLINOIS AND UNITED STATES, 1942–65

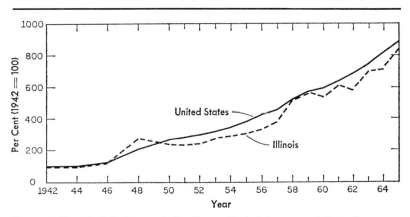

Source: Table A8; U.S. Bureau of the Census, *Revised Summary of State Government Finances, 1942–1950* (Washington: U.S. Government Printing Office, 1952); U.S. Bureau of the Census, *Compendium of State Government Finances,* 1951–65 (Washington: U.S. Government Printing Office, 1952–66).

penditure resulted from the payment of a veterans' bonus, the index of general expenditure for Illinois has been below that for the nation. In 1957 and 1958, however, the Illinois index rose more sharply than the index for the United States. Expenditure for the construction of toll roads were big factors in these sharp rises.

Many factors have contributed to the rising trend of state and local government expenditure in the United States. There is no standard method of classifying these factors, and a certain amount of overlapping is inevitable, but several of the most important can be identified.

One important factor is the high degree of prosperity which has existed in the postwar period. Prosperity inevitably brings about an increased demand for some types of governmental services. For example, production of more (and more powerful) automobiles in the private sector of the economy results in increased demand for highways. Higher and more secure family income increases the percentage of young people enrolled in public institutions of secondary and higher education. Prosperity has also been a factor in broadening the horizons of both public officials and citizens in a way which has created new demand for public services. There has been a demand for better schools and better teaching methods, for roads of new design, and for better recreational and cultural facilities.

A second factor is the inflation which has occurred in this period. Governmental expenditure has had to expand in order to avoid an actual decrease in the quantity and quality of services provided.

A third factor is the large backlog of needed public works which accumulated during the depression and war years.

The large increase in population which has occurred is a fourth factor which has created pressure for the expansion of state and local governmental services in the United States, particularly for increased expenditures on public schools.

A fifth factor is the change in political philosophy which has taken place. The traditional American distrust of government has been softened and, to some extent, replaced by a tendency to turn to government for the solution of difficult problems.

Sixth, most state governments entered the postwar period with surplus revenues and found that yields of existing taxes rose rapidly. Thus, there was a period of several years in which many states could initiate or enlarge programs without imposing new taxes or increasing the rates of existing taxes. However, local units of government were not so fortunate. Heavily dependent upon the property tax, most local units found that "automatic" increases in tax revenue were far from adequate. Sharp increases in assessments and tax rates were necessary and resulted in pressure for increased state aid, which became an additional drain on state revenue.

The remainder of this chapter describes general expenditure trends in Illinois and analyzes some of the causes of these trends. Obviously, some of the factors discussed above do not lend themselves to exact numerical analysis. However, a great deal can be learned by examining trends and by comparing expenditure trends with other relevant data.

The years under consideration have been ones of rapidly rising prices. The consumer price index for the United States rose by 101.9 per cent, while the implicit price deflator for goods and services purchased by state and local governments rose by 236.4 per cent.[20] The much more rapid rise in the price of goods and services purchased by state and local governments is the result of several factors, but probably the most important of these is the relatively large proportion of governmental expenditure which goes for personal services. Productivity (output per man) in agriculture and manufacturing has risen rapidly during the period under consideration, and the price of manufactured and agricultural goods has risen less rapidly than the price of labor. As a result, the price of the package of goods and services purchased by the average consumer has risen much less rapidly than the price of the package of goods and services purchased by governments.

Neither the consumer price index nor the implicit price deflator is designed specifically for deflating Illinois state expenditure, but, used together to deflate appropriate components of state expenditure, they can be used to obtain a reasonable estimate of "constant dollar" expenditure.[21]

This estimate indicates that total general expenditure, in dollars

[20] The consumer price index, computed by the U.S. Department of Labor, measures the cost of a "market basket" of goods and services. Quantities and qualities of goods in the "market basket" are based upon studies of actual expenditure by city wage earners and clerical workers in certain years. The implicit price deflator for goods and services purchased by state and local governments is computed by the U.S. Department of Commerce in connection with the national product accounts. Weighting is in proportion to expenditures incurred each year rather than being calculated from a constant or infrequently changed base year.

[21] A number of difficulties, both conceptual and statistical, are involved in an attempt to deflate state governmental expenditures. Although there is no serious conceptual problem involved in constructing an index of the cost of goods and services purchased, the Department of Commerce reports that data on the composition of purchases by state and local units of government are inadequate. For some types of governmental payments such as assistance, subsidies,

of 1958 purchasing power, rose by 206.3 per cent in the period from 1942 to 1965. This compares with a 746 per cent increase in expenditures measured in current dollars.

Estimated Illinois population has risen from 8,054,000 at the end of fiscal year 1942 to 10,641,000 at the end of fiscal year 1965—an increase of 21.1 per cent. It is likely that increased population results in a greater than proportionate increase in demand for governmental services because the increase is apt to be in age groups which require more than an average amount of public services and because increases in population often cause an immediate increase in capital outlay by government. However, this possibility is ignored here and it is assumed that the effect of population change can be isolated by expressing expenditure on a per capita basis.

The relationship between per capita estimated real general expenditure and per capita general expenditure in current dollars is illustrated in Chart XII. Estimated real general expenditure, per capita, has risen by 131.8 per cent in the 24-year period. Comparison of this figure and the 746 per cent rise in expenditure unadjusted for price rise or population increase indicates that a large part of the increase in state general expenditure in Illinois is a result of population and price change and does not represent an expansion of real government services per resident. It should not be concluded, however, that the increase in government expenditure is negligible. An expansion of 131.8 per cent in a 24-year period represents a substantial rate of growth, and further analysis is needed to identify the factors which explain this growth.

and interest, there is a problem of determining just what is being measured.

In making the estimates of real expenditures shown in Chart XII and Table A16, the implicit price deflator was used to deflate current operation and capital outlay expenditure on the assumption that the composition of goods and services purchased bears a close resemblance to those purchased by all state and local governments. It also must be assumed that prices paid are the same. This last assumption is undoubtedly reasonably accurate with respect to goods purchased and even for construction projects. There could, however, be a considerable variation in the wages paid to state employees in any given year. The implicit deflator was also used to deflate intergovernmental expenditures on the assumption that, in making such grants or expenditures, the state is providing the receiving government with the means to purchase goods and services. The consumer price index was used to deflate assistance and subsidy payments on the assumption that the state is attempting to provide the recipients with the means to purchase consumer goods. Interest payments were deflated in the same way, although there is a difficult conceptual problem involved in the question of what index should be used to deflate interest payments. Fortunately, interest payments are small enough that it makes relatively little difference which index is used.

CHART XII

INDEX OF PER CAPITA ILLINOIS STATE GENERAL EXPENDITURE, 1942–65

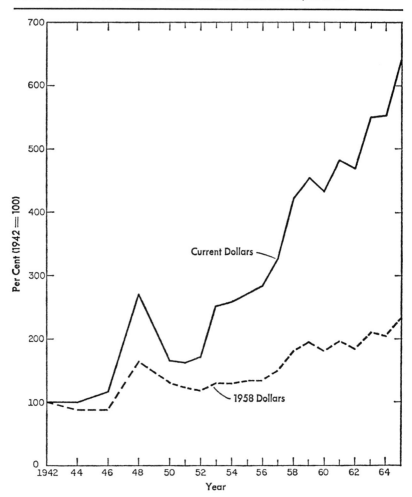

Source: Tables A9, A16.

The Impact of Economic Growth

One of the factors explaining the increase in real per capita expenditure is economic growth. The real output of the private sector of the Illinois economy rose substantially in the 1942–65 period. Had the state government sector done no more than keep pace with the growth in the private sector, there would have been a substantial increase in governmental expenditure.

Probably the most satisfactory method of indicating the relative importance of the state governmental sector is to express state general expenditure in relation to state personal income.[22] This relationship is illustrated in Chart XIII which shows that state general expenditure

CHART XIII

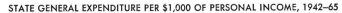

STATE GENERAL EXPENDITURE PER $1,000 OF PERSONAL INCOME, 1942–65

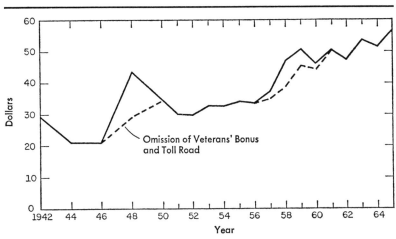

Source: Table A10.

per $1,000 of personal income has doubled in the 24-year period. As would be expected, there was a decline in the ratio of state expenditure to personal income in the war years of rapidly rising income and declining or slowly rising state expenditure. The relative stability of the ratio in the 1951–56 period was followed by a substantial rise, caused partly by large expenditures for toll road construction in fiscal years 1957–58.

It should be emphasized that the data illustrated in Chart XIII do

[22] This procedure is not without its faults. Not all personal income is available for use in consuming privately produced goods and services or for use by the state, since federal and local personal taxes must be paid from personal income. On the other hand, state general expenditure is financed in part by revenue obtained from sources other than the personal income of its residents. Many state taxes on business are ultimately paid by customers and stockholders in other states and by the federal government (state taxes are deductible in computing federal income tax and corporation tax). This means that state expenditures financed by certain types of taxes can be enlarged more than personal income (less direct taxes) is decreased. Nevertheless, the use of personal income has an important advantage. It is the most comprehensive measure of state economic activity which is available on a consistent basis for many years and which is widely accepted by statisticians and economists.

not necessarily mean that the consumption of governmental services relative to consumption of privately produced goods has doubled. The more rapid rise in the price of goods and services purchased by government undoubtedly means that it would be necessary to devote an increasingly large portion of total income to governmental purposes merely to maintain the same relative levels of consumption in the public and private sectors.[23]

Trends in Educational Expenditure

The dramatic increase in state expenditure for education in the postwar period is a prime example of the many interactions between the private and public sectors of the economy. Many of the technological developments which have made possible the rapid growth in the productivity in the private sector of the economy are possible only because of the success which the educational system has had in developing and transmitting technical knowledge. At the same time, growing technical specialization requires large numbers of highly educated workers and thus creates demand for more education at the same time that rising incomes make it possible for more people to undergo a longer period of educational training. During the period covered by our data, public attention was sharply focused upon the importance of education by Russia's early lead in the space race.

The response to these developments in Illinois has been a fourfold increase in the proportion of personal income expended for education by the state. During this period there has been a roughly equal division of expenditure between intergovernmental aid to local schools and expenditure for higher education by the state.[24] Chart XIV graphically portrays this growth.

[23] The lack of a measure of governmental output, as distinct from input, is troublesome at this point. It is known that the increase in output of the private sector of the economy has come both from an increase in inputs and from more efficient utilization of these inputs (productivity), but we have little data concerning governmental productivity. In general, productivity in processes such as manufacturing, which lend themselves to standardization and other mass production techniques, has increased more rapidly than has productivity in service type industries. Since governmental services performed directly by governmental employees (as distinct from activities like road construction which are performed by private firms on a contract basis) are predominantly of the service type, it seems likely that governmental productivity has increased more slowly than has productivity in the private sector of the economy. If so, the proportion of inputs going to government must increase in order to hold the ratio of governmental outputs and private sector outputs constant.

[24] As noted above, a substantial proportion of state higher education expenditure comes from sources other than state taxation.

CHART XIV

ILLINOIS STATE EDUCATION EXPENDITURE PER $1,000 OF PERSONAL INCOME, 1942–65

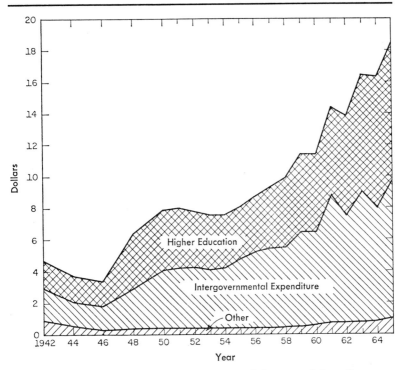

Source: Table A4; U.S. Bureau of the Census, *Revised Summary of State Government Finances, 1942–50* (Washington: U.S. Government Printing Office, 1953); and *Compendium of State Government Finances, 1951–65* (Washington: U.S. Government Printing Office, 1952–66).

Common Schools Public school education is traditionally a local function, but there is a long history of state financial assistance to local units. In fact, the first state appropriation for public school education in Illinois was made in 1825.[25]

Since 1927 the basis for state payments to local school districts has been a combination of flat grants and equalization. A flat grant is made for each student in average daily attendance. Equalization aid is computed by deducting the per-pupil yield of a property tax levy at the "qualifying rate" and the amount of the flat grant from the "equalization level." This means (1) that the district must levy a minimum tax to show that it is attempting to support its schools and

[25] Eugene S. Lawler, Jacob O. Bach, and Edward Griffin, "The Common Schools," *Report of the Commission on Revenue* (Springfield, 1963), p. 179.

(2) that the state must determine the cost to the district of maintaining the minimum program. The basic cost of the foundation program which the state will support is presently $400 per pupil in both elementary and high schools. The minimum tax rates which must be levied by school districts (the qualifying rates) are now .84 per cent of equalized assessed valuation for elementary and high school districts and 1.00 per cent for unit districts.[26]

There are also other sources of state aid for school districts in Illinois. These are aids which support such programs as the program for the gifted, driver's education, educational television, and vocational education. The state also contributes to the downstate Teachers Retirement Fund and the Chicago Teacher Retirement Fund. There are other minor appropriations which pay tuition for orphans and for residents of state-owned housing. In recent years there has been a substantial increase in the number of federal aid programs. Funds from these are often channeled through the office of the State Superintendent of Public Instruction.

There appear to be three major reasons for the rapid rise in state expenditure for elementary and secondary education in the period since World War II.

1. The number of children has increased. In 1942 there were 1,-518,000 persons aged 5 to 17 inclusive in Illinois. In 1965 there were 2,664,000 in the same age group.[27] The average daily attendance in public schools in the state has increased at an almost identical rate.[28]

2. Total expenditure per child enrolled has risen very rapidly. In the period from 1949–50 to 1959–60, current expense per pupil in average daily attendance rose from $258.46 to $437.74, a rate of increase which is clearly much faster than the increase in personal income in the state.[29] This undoubtedly results, in part, from the unavoidable increases in costs but also represents a deliberate effort to improve the quality of education offered to the children of the state.

3. The state now assumes a higher proportion of the total educational costs. In the 1941–43 biennium state appropriations were only 12.8 per cent of total school operating costs. In recent biennia state appropriations have stabilized at about 24.0 per cent. This has been accomplished by periodic changes in flat grants and in the equalization formula and by institution of new programs, several of which are federally aided.

[26] *Ill. Rev. Stat.*, ch. 122, sec. 18-8 (1967).
[27] See Table A2.
[28] Cf. Table A2 and Lawler *et al.*, *op. cit.*, p. 180.
[29] *Ibid.*, p. 191.

Higher Education   In 1942 the state of Illinois operated six institutions of higher education. Five of these were teachers' colleges under the control of the Department of Registration and Education and the sixth was the University of Illinois, which is governed by an elected board of trustees. Since that time Southern Illinois University has been given a separate board of governors and has opened a branch campus in the St. Louis area. The other four teachers' colleges have been granted university status and placed under the control of governing boards now known as the Board of Governors of State Colleges and Universities and the Board of Regents. Beginning in 1965 the Board of Governors also assumed control of the two teachers' colleges formerly under control of the Chicago Board of Education. The University of Illinois has opened a large branch campus in Chicago and continues to operate the professional schools at the Medical Center in Chicago. A system of state-coordinated junior colleges is rapidly being created.

The pressures which brought about the rapid expansion of higher education expenditures include a large number of persons of college age, a higher enrollment rate, and the failure of private institutions of higher education to expand fast enough to maintain their proportionate share of enrollment. The first two factors combined between 1950 and 1963 to produce an increase of 68.6 per cent in the number of degree-credit students enrolled in Illinois institutions of higher education. However, enrollment in public institutions expanded by 159.9 per cent while enrollment in nonpublic institutions expanded only 20.6 per cent.[30]

Another factor which tends to increase expenditure for higher education is the larger number of students enrolled in graduate and professional schools. Studies by the Illinois Board of Higher Education indicate that the operating costs involved in educating an advanced graduate student may be 3.5 times greater than for lower division students.[31]

Highway Expenditure

State expenditure for highway purposes is closely related to the availability of specific revenues. Motor fuel tax receipts and vehicle license fees are largely earmarked for highway construction and maintenance,[32] and large amounts of federal funds for highway

[30] Illinois Board of Higher Education, *Report of Master Plan Committee A: College Enrollments* (Springfield, 1963), p. 38.

[31] Illinois Board of Higher Education, *A Master Plan—Phase II* (Springfield, 1966), p. 64.

[32] A portion of these receipts is utilized to support judicial and administrative agencies which carry out functions related to motor vehicle ownership and use.

purposes are received. Toll roads are constructed from funds obtained from the sale of revenue bonds.

Since 1942 there have been three major changes in the revenue system with a major impact upon highway expenditures. The first of these was the series of highway tax increases enacted during the administration of Governor Stevenson. These increases were precipitated by the evident deterioration of highways which had occurred in the war and early postwar years and included two one-cent increases in motor fuel taxes and a substantial increase in truck registration fees.

The second major development was the creation by the 1953 legislature of the Illinois Tollway Commission with authority to issue revenue bonds and to construct and maintain a system of toll highways in the state. In October, 1955, the Commission sold $415 million of revenue bonds. This revenue bond sale, the largest ever to occur in the United States, was to finance the first 193 miles of a 568-mile tollway system. Actually, only the first portion was ever built. Scandals in the program, rising interest rates, and the initial failure of revenue from completed portions of the toll system to reach expected levels were all factors which contributed to the cessation of toll road building in the state, but the most important single factor was the approval of the Interstate Highway Program by Congress in 1956. This program of 90 per cent federal financing of high quality, limited access highways made the need for tollways less urgent and caused fear that competition from these free roads would reduce the earning capacity of toll highways below that needed to meet bond service costs.

The effects of all three postwar developments can be seen in Chart XV. The tax increases of the early 1950's affected both intergovernmental expenditure and direct spending for state highways since local government allocations are a fixed percentage of motor fuel tax collections. Most of the toll road expenditures occurred during a four-year construction period and then declined to a relatively small maintenance expenditure. Regular state highway expenditure rose rapidly in the first two years of the interstate program and then leveled off as interstate highway spending was stabilized.

Public Welfare Expenditure

Public welfare expenditure is one of the few expenditure categories which has not risen substantially as a percentage of income since 1942. There have, however, been important period-to-period fluctuations and major changes in the nature of program expenditures. In

1942 about one-half of all public welfare expenditures by the state of Illinois consisted of cash payments to recipients of Old Age Assistance. This program, established on a federal-state matching basis by the Social Security Act of 1935, has declined in importance as more and more aged persons become eligible for Social Security

CHART XV

ILLINOIS STATE HIGHWAY EXPENDITURE PER $1,000 OF PERSONAL INCOME, 1942-65

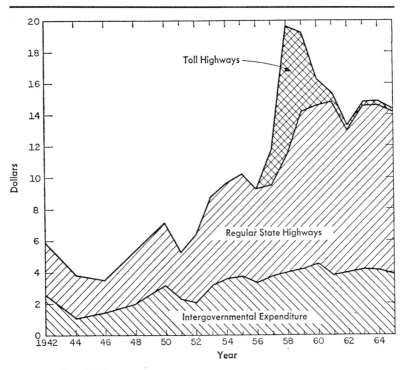

Source: See Chart XIV.

benefits. At the same time, the importance of medical vendor payments in behalf of Old Age Assistance recipients has risen greatly. Unfortunately, vendor payments data are not available for the entire time period shown in Chart XVI, but data compiled in 1963 indicate that vendor payments under the Old Age Assistance program were approaching the magnitude of cash payments.[33]

In contrast to expenditure for Old Age Assistance, expenditure for

[33] Glenn W. Fisher, "Public Assistance Expenditure," *Report of the Commission on Revenue* (Springfield, 1963), p. 125.

another federally aided welfare program, Aid to Dependent Children (now called Aid to Families with Dependent Children) has risen rapidly. This program was originally conceived as a program which would reduce the number of children placed in institutions by providing cash payments to the mother or other surviving relative who

CHART XVI

ILLINOIS STATE EXPENDITURE FOR PUBLIC WELFARE PER $1,000 OF PERSONAL INCOME, 1942–65

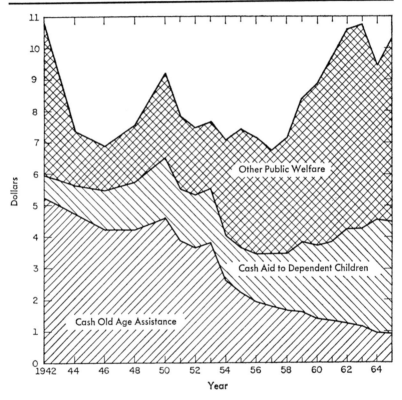

Source: See Chart XIV.

would maintain a home for the child. However, changing social and economic conditions have transformed the program into one whose beneficiaries are primarily families with illegitimate or deserted children and whose recipients are concentrated in Chicago and other metropolitan centers in the state. An analysis of this program published in 1963 indicates that expenditures for ADC rise sharply in recession years but that the rise is not fully counteracted by declines in years of economic recovery.[34]

Other federally aided welfare programs include the Aid to the Blind program, Aid to the Disabled, and Aid to the Medically Indigent Aged (Kerr-Mills) program. Expenditure for these programs are included in "other" in Chart XVI.

The "other public welfare" category also includes the nonfederally aided General Assistance Program. Recipients of general assistance are needy persons not eligible for any of the federally aided categorical programs. Initial administrative responsibility for these programs is in the hands of townships, but those townships which levy and expend the proceeds of a one-mill property tax are eligible to apply for 100 per cent state grants for all expenditures above that amount. In some recent years expenditures on this program have been greater than expenditure on Old Age Assistance (including vendor payments) and have been almost as high as expenditure on Aid to Dependent Children. Since there is no federal matching for general assistance, expenditure from state sources for general assistance is greater than expenditures for either ADC or OAA.

Other expenditures classified as welfare include the operation of welfare institutions such as the Illinois Soldiers and Sailors Children's School and the Visually Handicapped Institute and expenditure of the Child Welfare Division of the Department of Children and Family Services.

During the early years of the Kerner administration a state fiscal crisis focused attention upon rapidly rising welfare expenditure. This occurred as a result of the economic effects of the 1959 recession and was aggravated by policy changes implemented by the new and inexperienced state administration. Returning prosperity, legislative action, and changes in administrative personnel and policy combined to reverse this rise in spite of the fact that the scope of the federally aided program has been expanded by federal action.[35]

Expenditure Elasticity

Expenditure for most state functions is growing more rapidly than is the personal income of Illinois residents, but there is considerable variation in the rate of growth. Charts XIV, XV, and XVI are diagrammatic representations of the relationship between growth of

[34] *Ibid.*, pp. 103–21.
[35] Gilbert Y. Steiner, *Social Insecurity: The Politics of Welfare* (Chicago: Rand McNally and Co., 1966), pp. 205–37, and Fisher, "Public Assistance Expenditure," pp. 96–157.

expenditure for particular functions and income. A somewhat more concise and, for some purposes, more useful method of showing this relationship involves the use of coefficients of income elasticity. These are numbers which express the relationship between the growth of expenditure and personal income. For example, a coefficient of 1 indicates that expenditures for the function in question grow at the same rate as does personal income. A coefficient of 1.5 indicates that each 1 per cent increase in personal income is accompanied by a 1.5 per cent increase in expenditure.

TABLE 16

STATE EXPENDITURE ELASTICITY, BY FUNCTION, 1950–65

Function	Coefficient of Elasticity	Coefficient of Correlation
	(b)	(r)
Public Safety	1.10	.90
Public Welfare	1.40	.93
Education, Total	2.27	.97
Higher Education	2.27	.95
Intergovernmental	2.24	.98
Highways, except Toll Roads	2.30	.96
Intergovernmental	1.69	.93
Health and Hospitals	1.41	.92
Natural Resources	1.47	.95
Employment Security Administration	1.35	.91
General Control	1.40	.97
Miscellaneous and Other	1.64	.93
All Functions	1.86	.98

The elasticity coefficients shown in Table 16 are for the period 1950–65 and were computed by fitting an equation of the form log $Y = a + b \log x$, where Y is expenditure and X is personal income. This equation is an "estimating" equation which could be utilized to estimate expenditure when personal income is known. The "b" term is the coefficient of elasticity. The coefficients of correlation shown in Table 16 indicate how well the equation fits actual data in the period 1950–65. A correlation of 1.0 would indicate a perfect fit while a coefficient of zero would indicate that there is no relationship between income and expenditure.

Since the coefficients of elasticity given in Table 16 are based upon 1950–65 data, they can be accepted as reasonable estimates of the future relationship between personal income and expenditure only if economic and political conditions approximate those in this 16-year period. For example, they tell little or nothing about the relationship which might exist during a period of economic depression or during a major war and make no allowance for the possibility of a major political upheaval which might result in a radical change in the growth and quality of services provided by state government.

The relatively high coefficients of correlation suggest that there is a systematic relationship between the personal income of Illinois residents and state expenditure. The fact that all coefficients of elasticity are greater than one shows that state expenditure has risen more rapidly than personal income. The variation in the magnitude of the elasticity coefficients shows that there is considerable variation in the growth rate of expenditures for the various functions. It is clear from these figures that the most rapid growth has occurred in highway and educational expenditure. Welfare, health, and "general" government expenditure have risen at a far more modest pace.

3

STATE GENERAL REVENUE

The general revenue of state government comes from three main sources. The most important of these is taxation, which, in fiscal year 1965, provided about 66 per cent of all the general revenue of the state of Illinois. Intergovernmental revenue, which includes amounts received from other governments as fiscal aid and funds received as reimbursement for services performed, made up 26 per cent of Illinois general revenue. The third major source, charges and miscellaneous revenue, is defined by the U.S. Bureau of the Census as including all general revenue except taxes and intergovernmental revenue. It includes sums received by the state from the sale of goods and services, interest, rentals, donations, and similar items. Revenue from these sources in 1965 was about 8 per cent of total general revenue.

From a political perspective, the revenue system is the result of a complex decision-making process that determines who shall pay for the goods and services produced by the government. The focal point of this process is the state legislature, but judicial and administrative decisions play an important role.

Constitutional limitations upon legislative action in the revenue field are so pervasive in Illinois that it is difficult to explain the overall revenue system or to describe the structure of many individual taxes without reference to the state constitution and the court cases which have interpreted it. Other limitations upon the legislature, such as those imposed by the U.S. Constitution and by economic conditions, are often interrelated with state constitutional limitations. For example, states are open economies with governments whose taxing and borrowing powers are economically and constitutionally limited. State services may make the state more attractive as a place of residence or as a business location, but they must be paid for by means which are apt to reduce its attractiveness. This poses a dilemma for decision-makers and provides a ready-made argument for interest groups advocating a particular expenditure or revenue policy. The spectre of lagging economic development is raised by proponents of both increased spending and of lower taxes. Economic statistics are ammunition in many of the political wars that shape the revenue structure of the state.

Day-to-day administration of tax statutes requires that thousands of administrative decisions be made. These decisions define the tax base and administrative procedure and, thus, have a significant impact upon the distribution of the tax burden and the yield of the revenue system.

GENERAL REVENUE: STRUCTURE AND TRENDS

The structure of the Illinois state revenue system is graphically illustrated in Chart XVII. A much more detailed breakdown is provided in Appendix Table A17. Table 17 compares the yield of major state revenue sources in Illinois and in the United States as a whole.

Perhaps the most striking features of the Illinois revenue structure are the heavy dependence upon the general sales tax and the absence of income taxes. Table 17 shows that the average state receives 16.4 per cent of its revenue from general sales taxation, 8.9 per cent from the individual income tax, and 4.7 per cent from corporation income taxes—a total from these sources of 30.0 per cent. In contrast, Illinois receives 33.7 per cent from general sales taxation and nothing from income taxation. The other important difference is that Illinois receives only 7.9 per cent of its revenue from charges and miscellaneous sources as compared with 11.0 per cent received from this source by the average state.[1]

Chart XVIII reveals that the relative importance of the general sales tax as a source of state revenue has fluctuated within rather narrow limits. In 1942 it provided 30.6 per cent of general revenue. In 1948 it reached a peak of 35.1 per cent and in 1959 a low of 29.1 per cent.

---

[1] The apparent difference in receipts from utility taxation is, in part, a statistical discrepancy, since several states tax utility receipts under the general sales tax statute. In Illinois the utility tax is imposed by separate statutes, and receipts are reported separately from the general sales tax receipts.

CHART XVII

ILLINOIS STATE GENERAL REVENUE, BY SOURCE, 1965

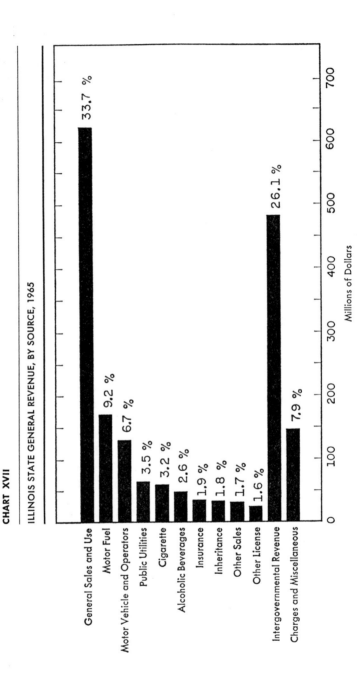

Source: Tables A18, A20.

The motor fuel tax provided 15.5 per cent of general revenue in 1942, but the percentage dropped sharply during the war years and remained in the 10 to 11 per cent range until the increase in tax rates occurred in fiscal years 1952 and 1953. In 1954, the first fiscal year in which these rates were in effect for the full year, motor fuel taxes provided 16.8 per cent of general revenue. Since that time there has

TABLE 17

STATE REVENUE STRUCTURE, ILLINOIS AND UNITED STATES, 1965

| | Per Capita | | Per Cent of Total | |
Source	Illinois	United States	Illinois	United States
Taxes[a]				
Sales and Gross Receipts:				
General Sales and Gross Receipts (37)	$ 59.11	$ 35.07	33.7%	16.4%
Motor Fuel (50)	16.13	22.47	9.2	10.5
Alcoholic Beverages (50)	4.55	4.79	2.6	2.2
Tobacco Products (48)	5.61	6.71	3.2	3.1
Insurance (50)	3.32	3.89	1.9	1.8
Public Utilities (39)	6.06	2.60	3.5	1.2
Other	3.02	3.16	1.7	1.5
License Taxes:				
Motor Vehicle and Operators (50)	11.69	9.77	6.7	4.6
Other	2.88	7.05	1.6	3.3
Individual Income Taxes[b] (36)	—	19.11	—	8.9
Corporation Net Income Taxes[b] (38)	—	10.08	—	4.7
Property Taxes (45)	.15	4.00	.1	1.9
Inheritance Taxes (49)	3.13	3.82	1.8	1.8
Other Taxes	—	4.00	—	1.9
Total Taxes	115.65	136.52	66.0	63.8
Intergovernmental Revenue	45.74	53.93	26.1	25.2
Charges and Miscellaneous	13.91	23.43	7.9	11.0
Total General Revenue	175.30	213.88	100.0	100.0

[a] Numbers in parentheses indicate number of states using tax.
[b] Individual income tax data include corporation net income tax collections for New Mexico.

Source: Tables A19, A20, A21, A22.

been a steady decline in relative importance and only 9.2 per cent of general revenue came from that source in 1965.

Revenue from taxes on alcoholic beverages and cigarettes has also exhibited a tendency to decline in relative importance, although the trend has been interrupted by occasional increases in tax rates. This is most marked in the case of alcoholic beverage taxes whose contribution to general revenue has declined from 8.4 per cent in 1942 to

CHART XVIII

MAJOR REVENUE SOURCES AS PERCENTAGE OF TOTAL, 1942–65

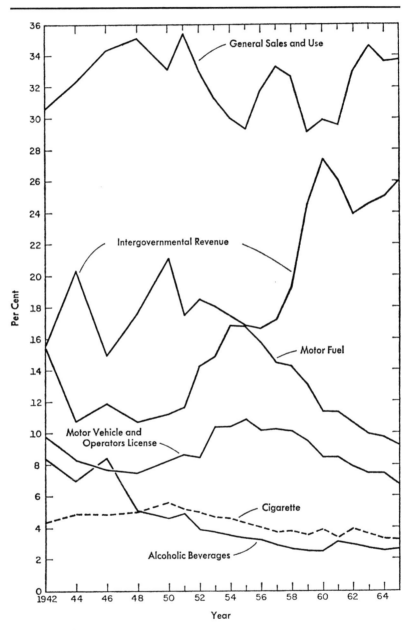

Source: Table A20.

2.6 per cent in 1965 in spite of a 50 per cent increase in rates which were effective in fiscal 1960.

Motor vehicle license taxes increased sharply in importance as the result of rate increases in the early 1950's but have declined steadily since. The percentage of revenue received from intergovernmental sources (chiefly federal grants) has risen from 15.6 per cent in 1942 to 26.1 per cent in 1965, but the upward course has been somewhat irregular.

THE GENERAL SALES TAX

Taxes upon the sale of goods or services may take several forms. Selective sales or excise taxes are levied upon the sale of specific commodities such as cigarettes, alcoholic beverages, or motor fuel. The base may be the sales price or it may be a physical quantity such as number of items or gallons sold.

General sales taxes are levied upon the sale of a broad class of goods or services and may be either single stage or multiple stage. Single stage taxes are levied at only one level in the distribution process, such as the sale by the manufacturer, wholesaler, or retailer. Multiple stage taxes are levied at two or more of these stages.

Since the 1930's American states have made wide use of general retail sales taxes. Usually these apply only to the sales of tangible personal property, but several states depart from a pure form of the tax and tax the sale of certain services. Some exempt the sale of some commodities such as food and medicine.

Major problems with state sales taxes may result from the fact that states cannot tax interstate commerce and from the fact that residents who live near a state line may feel that it is profitable to shop in neighboring non-sales tax states. This problem was partially solved in 1937 when the U.S. Supreme Court upheld a compensating use tax imposed by the state of Washington upon the use or storage of goods upon which no sales tax had been paid.[2] In upholding this form of taxation, the court stressed the fact that the tax was designed to insure equal taxation since it did not apply to items upon which the sales tax had been paid somewhere else.

The history of the Illinois retail sales tax provides unsurpassed examples of the interaction of economic, constitutional, administrative, and political factors. The virtual breakdown of the property tax in the economic depression of the early 1930's led the legislature to pass a graduated state income tax. This tax was ruled unconstitu-

[2] *Henneford v. Silas Mason Co.*, 300 U.S. 577 (1937).

tional by the state Supreme Court in a sweeping opinion which declared that the state's power to tax is limited to property taxes on a valuation basis, occupation taxes, and privilege and franchise taxes.[3] In March, 1933, the legislature attempted to tax retail sales by imposing a retailers' occupation tax to be measured by gross sales. This measure was declared unconstitutional on the grounds that it violated uniformity by exempting the sale of motor fuel and farm products from the measure of the tax and because proceeds of the tax were unconstitutionally appropriated back to counties.[4] A new measure, without these features, was promptly passed and became effective July 1, 1933. Since the tax was legally upon the retailer rather than upon the sale, the retailer had no legal right to collect the occupation tax, as a tax, from the purchaser, but it was customary for retailers to collect an amount equal to the tax in addition to the quoted price.[5]

Partly because of widespread doubts about the constitutionality of a general use tax, none was in force in Illinois before 1955. However, in 1951 the legislature enacted a cigarette use tax. After this tax was upheld by the courts,[6] it became the pattern for the general use tax which became effective on August 1, 1955. On November 26, 1956, the Illinois Supreme Court declared the general use tax to be unconstitutional but later, on rehearing, reversed itself and sustained the tax.[7]

Unlike the retailers' occupation tax, the use tax is levied upon the purchaser. In some cases it is collected by the seller and in others is paid directly to the Department of Revenue. In order to satisfy the uniformity provision of the constitution, it applies to all purchases in Illinois as well as to out-of-state purchases of property to be used in Illinois. An offsetting provision allows the retailer to keep the use tax to the extent that he is liable for the occupation tax on the same transaction. Thus, the actual effect is to tax the out-of-state purchase of property for use in Illinois to the same extent as if the purchase were made within the state. Legally, the use tax legislation resulted in a basic alteration in the relationship of the retailer and the customer.[8] Since the enactment of the use tax, the retailer has a legal obligation to collect the tax from the customer and to quote the tax

---

[3] *Bachrach* v. *Nelson*, 349 Ill. 579 (1932).

[4] *Winter* v. *Barrett*, 352 Ill. 441 (1933).

[5] Paul E. Malone, "The Sales Tax," *Report of the Revenue Laws Commission of the State of Illinois* (Springfield, 1949), p. 268.

[6] *Johnson* v. *Halpin*, 413 Ill. 257 (1952).

[7] *Turner* v. *Wright*, 11 Ill. 2d 161 (1957).

[8] This point is developed in detail in John F. Due, "The Unique Illinois Use Tax," *National Tax Journal* (September, 1959), pp. 260–64.

separately from the price of the item. The state now prescribes a
bracket schedule which retailers are required to post. Under the old
law, the state carefully refrained from prescribing a bracket
schedule.

In 1947 the General Assembly authorized municipalities to levy
a retailers' occupation tax at a rate not to exceed 0.5 per cent upon
approval of the voters in a municipal referendum.[9] In the years 1947–
55, only six referenda were held, and all were defeated.[10] The 1955
legislature eliminated the referendum requirement, after which this
form of taxation spread rapidly. By June 30, 1958, sales taxes were
imposed by more than 1,000 municipalities. In 1959 counties were
given authority to impose a similar tax in unincorporated areas of the
county. Both the municipal and county taxes are collected by the state
Department of Revenue, and the proceeds, less a collection fee, are
remitted to the local governments. The collection fee, originally fixed
at 6 per cent, was reduced to 4 per cent by the 1959 legislature. Although local sales tax revenues are held temporarily in a special trust
fund of the state treasury, they are not considered to be part of state
revenue. In this study, following Bureau of the Census practice, the
receipts from the collection fee are included as part of state sales
tax collections.

The rate of the *state* sales tax has varied from time to time, as follows:

July 1, 1933–June 30, 1935	2.0	per cent
July 1, 1935–June 30, 1941	3.0	per cent
July 1, 1941–June 30, 1955	2.0	per cent[11]
July 1, 1955–June 30, 1959	2.5	per cent
July 1, 1959–June 30, 1961	3.0	per cent[12]
July 1, 1961–June 30, 1967	3.5	per cent[12]
July 1, 1967–present	4.25	per cent[12]

Since adjournment of the 1967 legislature, most sales within the state
are taxed at a total rate of 5.0 per cent since the local sales tax of
0.75 per cent is usually imposed.

[9] Clyde F. Snider, "Potential New Sources of Municipal Revenue," *Report of
the Revenue Laws Commission of the State of Illinois* (Springfield, 1949), pp.
362–64.
[10] Jack F. Isakoff, Gilbert Y. Steiner, and June G. Cabe, *Illinois Municipal Revenue*, 2nd ed. revised (Urbana: University of Illinois, Institute of Government
and Public Affairs, 1958), p. 51.
[11] During the 1941–55 period, the rate was technically 2 per cent of 98 per cent
of gross receipts. Since the Illinois tax was legally imposed upon the retailer,
any additional sum added because of the tax was considered as part of gross
receipts and therefore taxable. The actual rate upon the true sales price was
therefore 1.9992 per cent, computed as follows:
$$1.02 \times .98 \times .02 = 1.9992$$
Since July 1, 1955, the definition of gross receipts used in administering the tax
excludes the use tax collected by the retailer.
[12] Less a 2 per cent collection fee retained by retailers.

The Sales Tax Base

Both the economic and political impact and the yield of a sales tax depend to a large extent upon the composition of the tax base. Many states have exempted the sale of certain items, such as food and medicine, from the sales tax base. Although the uniformity provision of the Illinois constitution is generally believed to prevent "exemptions," there have been hundreds of cases involving the definition of the tax base, and court rulings have freed from taxation the sale of many items which would be taxable in other states. Attempts by the legislature to reverse these decisions have often been unsuccessful, but there is evidence that the trend to an ever narrower tax base has been reversed since 1961.[13]

The retailers' occupation tax is imposed upon persons engaged in "the business of selling tangible personal property at retail," [14] and the base of the tax is the amount of the "sale at retail." [15] Many of the problems of determining taxability of a given transaction have turned upon the definition of "the business of selling tangible personal property at retail" and "sale at retail." [16]

Determining whether a firm is engaged in the business of selling tangible personal property at retail often involves determining whether the firm is selling tangible personal property or providing a service. Many transactions involve both the transfer of tangible personal property and the rendering of a service by the seller. In some cases the court has held that the two elements can be separated. Thus, it was held that a funeral director who sells tangible personal property such as caskets and provides embalming and other services was engaged in severable occupations. He was ruled taxable in the first and exempt in the second.[17]

Generally, however, the courts have held that transactions which involve both the sale of taxable property and the rendering of a service are wholly taxable or wholly exempt.[18] If the sale represents the substance of the transaction and the rendering of service is inci-

[13] Legally there are now four different taxes: the retailers' occupation tax, the use tax, the service occupation tax, and the service use tax. The leasing occupation tax and the leasing use tax were repealed by the 1967 legislature. Unless the context indicates otherwise, the term sales tax or general sales tax is used in this chapter to refer to all six, or as many as were in effect at the time in question.

[14] *Ill. Rev. Stat.*, ch. 120, sec. 441 (1967).

[15] *Ibid.*

[16] Willard Ice, "The Retailers' Occupation Tax Act and Related Laws," *The University of Illinois Law Forum* (1961), pp. 619–28.

[17] *Ahern* v. *Nudelman*, 374 Ill. 237 (1940).

[18] Ice, *op. cit.*, p. 624.

dental, the entire transaction is taxable; otherwise the entire transaction is exempt.

This approach led to the exemption of a great many sales which would have been taxable in most sales tax states. The following examples illustrate the situation as it existed in 1960:

1. Sales of newspapers, magazines, books, sheet music, phonograph records, and similar items were excluded from the tax base on the grounds that the purchaser buys the services of the writer, composer, or musician. Similar reasoning was applied to the sales of graphic art products, photographs, tags, bookkeeping forms, sales tickets, order blanks, and similar items which are imprinted or made to special order in such a way as to have value only to the purchaser.

2. Sales of machinery and tools made to special order and having value only to the purchaser were excluded from the tax base on the grounds that the purchaser was paying primarily for the services of the designer or draftsman rather than for tangible personal property.

3. The sale of custom-tailored clothing was considered to be the sale of a service rather than of tangible property.

4. Sales of portieres, drapes, curtains, venetian blinds, window shades, screen and storm doors and windows, floor coverings, tents, awnings, signs, and similar items made to order and having no value other than salvage value to anyone but the purchaser, were not part of the tax base. Sale of such items was considered to be the sale of services.

5. Sales of monuments and gravemarkers were not considered to be sales of tangible personal property when such services as engraving or inscribing were rendered.

6. No sale of tangible personal property was considered to occur when property such as medicine, glasses, or dentures was furnished by physicians, optometrists, and dentists in connection with professional services.

In 1961 the following wording was added to the Retailers' Occupation Tax Act:

A person who holds himself out as being engaged (or who habitually engages) in selling tangible personal property at retail is a person engaged in the business of selling tangible personal property at retail hereunder with respect to such sales (and not primarily in a service occupation) notwithstanding the fact that such person designs and produces such tangible personal property on special order for the purchaser and in such a way as to render the property of value only to such purchaser, if such tangible personal property so produced on special order serves substantially the same function as stock or standard items of tangible personal property that are sold at retail.[19]

[19] *Ill. Rev. Stat.*, ch. 120, sec. 440 (1967).

This addition to the statutes had the effect of partially eliminating the exemption for producers of special order merchandise. For example:

1. Sales of books, phonograph records, and sheet music became taxable. Sales of newspapers and magazines were not subject to taxation on the grounds that the information contained therein has only fleeting value.[20] Sales of graphic art products and *personalized* tangible property such as pencils, matchbooks, and bookkeeping forms were made taxable when the items serve substantially the same function as stock or standard items and have value to the purchaser. Personalized items such as business cards have no commercial value to anyone other than the purchaser and no liability for retailers' occupation tax is incurred.

2. Many sales of machinery and tools made to special order continued to be exempt on the grounds that the seller is employed primarily for his skill in designing the product and that the property has value only for the specific purpose for which it was produced and only to the purchaser. However, such sales were ruled taxable in case of a simultaneous order for 50 or more identical items or where the sale is a repeat order for an item previously designed by the seller for the purchaser.

3. Custom-made clothing, portieres, drapes, curtains, venetian blinds, window shades, screen and storm doors, and similar items become taxable if they serve substantially the same purpose as a stock item.

4. Sales of monuments and gravemarkers become taxable, even if produced on special order, since they serve the same purpose as stock or standard items, but inscribing and other services rendered in connection with the sale were not considered part of the taxable transaction.

5. The rule regarding the taxability of items such as medicines, glasses, or dentures furnished by physicians, dentists, or optometrists remained unchanged. Such items continued to be nontaxable when furnished as part of a professional service.

Before the proceeds of a transaction may be included in the base to determine a retailer's tax liability, it is also necessary that the transaction be a "sale at retail." This term is defined in the statutes to mean "any transfer of ownership of, or title to, tangible personal property to a purchaser, for use or consumption and not for resale in any form as tangible personal property, for a valuable consideration. Transactions whereby the possession of the property is transferred

[20] S. B. 568, *Ill. Laws* (1961).

but the seller retains title as security for payment of the selling price shall be deemed a sale." [21]

In early cases the Supreme Court defined "use" to mean a long continued possession and employment of a thing for the purpose for which it is adapted, as distinguished from a possession and employment that is merely temporary or occasional. Consumption was defined to mean destruction by use.[22]

Application of these definitions meant that sales to contractors and servicemen of tangible items which were for later transfer to their customers as part of services rendered were not taxable, since the serviceman or contractor was not using or consuming the product. In view of the very broad concept of services adopted by the court this meant that a great many final sales of tangible personal property went untaxed.

In 1941 the General Assembly tried to change this result by adopting the following definition of "use or consumption."

Use or consumption in addition to its usual and popular meaning shall be construed to include the employment of tangible personal property by persons engaged in service occupations (including construction contracting and other service occupations of like character), trades or professions, in the rendering of services, where as a necessary incident to the rendering of such services, transfer of all or a part of the tangible personal property employed in connection with the rendering of said services is made from the person engaged in the service occupation (including construction contracting and other service occupations of like character), trade or profession, to his customer or client.[23]

In 1944 the Supreme Court held this amendment unconstitutional as being beyond the scope of the title of the act and as being in conflict with the definition of "sale at retail" in the act.[24] This case was later overruled by the court, but, in the meantime, the General Assembly had repealed the 1941 amendment, and the court voided an attempt by the Department of Revenue to include sales to servicemen and contractors in the tax base in the absence of specific statutory authorization.[25]

As the situation stood in 1960, the definition of "business of selling tangible personal property at retail" was very narrow. Sales of such items as custom-made suits, wall-to-wall carpeting, and many kinds of machinery and equipment were considered as the rendering of services and not within the statutory definition. At the same time,

[21] *Ill. Rev. Stat.*, ch. 120, sec. 440 (1967).
[22] *Reuzan v. Nudelman*, 370 Ill. 180 (1938).
[23] *Ill. Rev. Stat.*, ch. 120, sec. 440 (1941).
[24] *Stolze Lumber Co. v. Stratton*, 386 Ill. 334 (1944).
[25] Ice, *op. cit.*, pp. 621–22.

the sale of many items to those engaged in performing these services was not considered to be a "sale at retail." Thus, the sale of cloth to the tailor, carpeting to the installer, and steel to the machinery manufacturer often went untaxed because it was not for use and consumption as defined by the courts. The "last sale" concept utilized in defining retail sales in many states was not applied in these cases.

Several developments which had the effect of narrowing this gap occurred in 1961. One of these was the amendment which broadened the definition of "business of selling tangible property at retail" to include made-to-order items which serve the same purpose as stock items. In the same year the state Supreme Court upheld the Department of Revenue in an attempt to tax sales of building material to real estate developers and speculative builders.[26] The court said that use is any act which takes personal property off the retail market. As a result, both contractors and speculative builders became subject to the retailers' occupation tax upon materials purchased.

The 1961 legislature also passed the Service Occupation Tax Act and the Service Use Tax Act. This legislation places a tax upon service occupations based upon the cost of tangible personal property purchased and retransferred as an incident to sales of services.[27]

The 1961 legislature also passed bills designed to tax rental receipts in much the same way as receipts from sales. In 1962 the state Supreme Court held these amendments to the Retailers' Occupation Tax Act unconstitutional on the ground that they caused the act to contain a subject not expressed in the title which refers to selling and not to leasing.[28] The 1965 General Assembly reimposed the tax as a separate leasing tax. The act and the related leasing use tax and municipal leasing tax acts have been sustained by the state Supreme Court,[29] but in 1967 the Department of Revenue asked for and obtained repeal of these acts.

One of the most unusual consequences of the fact that Illinois legally taxes the "occupation of retailing," rather than the transaction, relates to sales made to the federal government. It is well established that the U.S. Constitution prohibits state taxation of the federal government and its instrumentalities, but when the tax is legally upon

[26] G. S. Lyon & Sons Lumber and Manufacturing Company v. Department of Revenue, 23 Ill. 2d 180 (1961).
[27] Purchases of materials by contractors are also taxable under these acts, but the Department of Revenue chose to utilize the G. S. Lyon decision and apply the retailers' occupation tax. This action was upheld in Materials Service Corporation v. Isaacs, 25 Ill. 2d 137 (1962).
[28] International Business Machines Corporation v. Department of Revenue, 25 Ill. 2d 503 (1962).
[29] International Business Machines Corporation v. Korshak, 34 Ill. 2d 595 (1966).

the seller, as in Illinois, there seems to be no general bar to including sales to the federal government in the tax base. Thus, in 1948 the Department of Revenue changed its rules to require that sales to the federal government be included in the tax base. In 1953 the Illinois General Assembly amended the Retailers' Occupation Tax Act to exempt sales to the state of Illinois, to local governments, and to charitable, religious, or educational organizations and institutions. On February 24, 1961, a federal court held that it is unconstitutional discrimination for Illinois to collect taxes on the proceeds from sales to the federal government when sales to the state and its local governments are exempt.[30] The state appealed this decision to the U.S. Supreme Court. In May, 1961, however, the Illinois Supreme Court held that the 1953 amendment was invalid because sales to the federal government were not included within the exemption.[31]

On July 31 the Governor approved legislation removing the exemption of sales to the state of Illinois and its local units.[32] As a result, sales to both the federal government and to Illinois state and local governments were included in the tax base after August 1, 1961. The constitutionality of this procedure was upheld by the U.S. Supreme Court in October, 1963.[33]

This rapid series of developments had focused attention upon the fact that Illinois was one of a very few states to include sales to the federal government in its tax base At the same time, much interest was being expressed in obtaining a larger share of federal contracts in Illinois, and there was much concern about the lag in government-sponsored research and development activities in Illinois. This, plus widespread complaints by local and state officials, led the 1963 legislature to reverse the action of the previous legislature and exempt sales to all governmental bodies or agencies from the tax. The bill carried an emergency clause and was approved by the Governor on March 21, 1963.[34]

Sales Tax Administration

The yield of a tax depends not only upon the rate and the legal definition of the base but also upon the quality of administration. This, in turn, depends upon policy as articulated by the top admin-

---

[30] *United States* v. *Department of Revenue*, 191 F. Supp. 723 (1961).
[31] *Holland Coal Co.* v. *Isaacs*, 22 Ill. 2d 477 (1961).
[32] *Ill. Laws*, 1961, pp. 2312–14.
[33] *United States of America and Olin Mathieson Chemical Corporation* v. *Fasseas*, 371 U.S. 21 (1963).
[34] *Ill. Laws*, 1963, pp. 735–36.

istrative officials and the quantity and quality of personnel available for enforcement.

It is not possible to trace or appraise all of the developments which have occurred in the field of sales tax administration in Illinois, but it is clear that 1961 began a period of activity and change as attention was focused upon improved administration and broadening of the base as a means of escaping the intense financial problem facing the new administration of Governor Otto Kerner.

In March, 1961, a state representative, formerly employed by the Department of Revenue, reported to a legislative committee that sales and use tax evaders were costing the state $150 million every two years.[35] It was also reported that the new Director of Revenue, Theodore Isaacs, was planning to reduce the number of investigators in the department and to replace them with nonpatronage auditors.

In 1962 the Department of Revenue followed up the Supreme Court's favorable ruling on the taxation of building materials by organizing a drive to collect taxes from about 4,000 dealers in building materials. A task force of almost 100 auditors, about half of whom were borrowed from private firms, was organized. The Director also formed a special advisory council with the express purpose of "brain picking" ideas that would improve the effectiveness of the existing tax system.[36]

Suits were brought against officers of corporations which had gone out of business without paying taxes due the state, and a major drive was launched against the nonpayment of taxes by automobile dealers. An office of the Department of Revenue was opened in New York to permit more effective auditing of firms who maintained their records in eastern offices.

These administrative measures were accompanied by a good deal of legislation designed to make collection more effective. For example, the Department of Revenue was given power to require that bonds guaranteeing payment of sales taxes be filed by certain firms, payment of the occupation or use tax upon automobiles was made a condition of licensing, and provisions were enacted which provided for the withdrawal of liquor licenses from firms with sales tax delinquencies.

Legislation permitting the Attorney General to obtain summary judgments against delinquent taxpayers was ruled unconstitutional by the Supreme Court. Under this procedure, judgment would have

[35] Statement by Rep. James P. Loukas as reported in the *Champaign-Urbana Courier,* March 22, 1961.
[36] *Chicago Sun-Times,* July 11, 1962.

been automatic 35 days after the department made final assessments, but the taxpayer would have had the right to petition for rehearing any time within two years.

Another plan worked out early in Isaacs' administration resulted in mutual tax collection agreements with neighboring states. Under these agreements, merchants who make sales for delivery in a state which is party to the agreement must collect the *use* tax imposed by the purchaser's home state. The initial agreements with Iowa and Missouri became effective in February, 1962. Agreements with Indiana and Kentucky were reached in 1964.

Efforts to require out-of-state mail order houses to collect the use tax upon merchandise shipped into the state suffered a setback in 1967, when the U.S. Supreme Court ruled against the Department of Revenue.[37] Although it has long been established that firms with a place of business in a state may be required to collect use taxes upon sales made directly from an out-of-state mail order branch, the court ruled that National Bellas Hess, which had no office or agent within Illinois, could not be required to collect the tax. Thus, although the purchaser remains liable for the tax, enforcement becomes very difficult and firms within the state are placed at a competitive disadvantage.

Yield of the Sales Tax

Mathematically, the yield of a sales tax is obtained by multiplying the tax rate by the tax base. The tax base is the result of legislative, judicial, and administrative definition and its size varies with variations in economic conditions. Although it is very difficult to separate the effects which these factors play in the changing yield, it is possible to draw some general conclusions from available data.

There seems to be little doubt that the yield of a tax upon the sale at retail of tangible items of personal consumption does not rise as fast as personal income. This is true because consumption of services becomes a more important element in total consumption as income rises.[38]

Existing sales tax bases actually include some items sold for nonconsumption purposes, may include some services, and often do not include all retail sales of tangible consumption goods. However,

[37] *National Bellas Hess* v. *Illinois Department of Revenue*, U.S. Supreme Court, May 8, 1967.
[38] In 1953 services made up 34.8 per cent of personal consumption expenditure in the United States. In 1966 the percentage was 40.7 per cent. U.S. Department of Commerce, *Survey of Current Business*, February, 1967, p. 6.

empirical studies of the past behavior of sales tax yields conclude that the yield of the tax will, in the absence of rate or base changes, rise somewhat more slowly than personal income. In other words, the elasticity of the sales tax is less than unity. In projecting tax yields into the future, however, it is not uncommon to use an elasticity of one on the grounds that some broadening of the base will occur.[39]

TABLE 18

ILLINOIS STATE SALES TAX COLLECTIONS, 1942–65

Year	Total Collections	Per Capita Collections	Collections per 1% of Rate per $1,000 of Personal Income
	(thousands)		
1942	$ 85,589	$10.71	$5.52
1944	89,932	11.58	4.39
1946	107,378	14.11	4.54
1947	142,514	17.46	5.46
1948	159,528	19.12	5.47
1949	172,817	20.21	5.78
1950	166,951	19.26	5.47
1951	187,556	21.43	5.57
1952	191,934	21.93	5.29
1953	205,475	23.06	5.35
1954	208,557	23.17	5.25
1955	205,532	22.44	5.00
1956[a]	267,326	28.70	4.84
1957[a]	282,767	29.82	4.80
1958[a]	287,060	29.76	4.74
1959	308,273	30.99	4.92
1960	374,949	37.55	4.76
1961	383,957	38.09	4.72
1962	466,430	46.11	4.72
1963	545,076	53.13	5.26
1964	558,584	53.87	5.12
1965	622,857	59.11	5.31

[a] Data for these years are corrected for inadvertent omission of municipal sales tax administration fee and, thus, differ from those shown in appendix tables.

Source: Tables A1, A4, A18, A19; U.S. Bureau of the Census, *Compendium of State Government Finances*, 1947, 1949 (Washington: U.S. Government Printing Office, 1948, 1950).

For the period 1950–65 the income elasticity of the Illinois sales tax was .924. This figure is in line with computations of sales tax

[39] Robert Harris, *Income and Sales Taxes: The 1970 Outlook* (Chicago: Council of State Governments, 1966), pp. 28–29.

CHART XIX

SALES TAX REVENUE IN RELATION TO PERSONAL INCOME, 1950–65

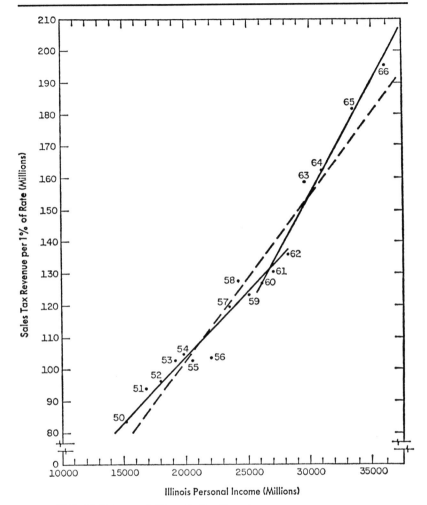

Illinois Personal Income (Millions)

Source: Table 18. Data corrected for collection discount.

elasticity in other states,[40] but a closer look at Illinois data reveals that there was a marked change in relationships beginning with the 1963 fiscal year. Table 18 reveals that the yield per 1 per cent of rate had a tendency to decline prior to that year. The magnitude of the reversal is shown more dramatically by Chart XIX. The broken

[40] Harris, *loc. cit.*

line is fitted, by the least squares method, to data for 1950–66. The solid lines are fitted to 1950–59 and 1960–66 data, respectively. The greater slope of the 1960–66 line shows the impact that measures taken in the 1961–63 period had upon the sales tax yield. Extension of the 1950–59 regression line reveals that the 1966 tax yield would have been $170 million per 1 per cent of rate as compared with the actual yield of $195 million. Multiplying these figures by the rate in effect in 1965 [41] reveals that sales tax collections in fiscal year 1966 were $85 million higher than could have been expected had 1950–59 relationships between income and tax yield continued. Unfortunately, it is not possible to separate the results of the broadening of the base from any that may be attributable to improved administration.

Comparison with Other States

Because of the wide variation in sales tax statutes in the various states, it is difficult to detail the differences in sales tax bases. Most of the 37 sales tax states levy single stage retail sales taxes, and several also make levies at the wholesale or manufacturing stage. All levy upon some kinds of services such as restaurant meals, admissions, transit lodgings, or utility services. Certain types of sales of tangible goods are excluded from the tax base. Sales of materials that become a constituent part of a final product which will be sold at retail are generally excluded. A few states exempt machinery and other items used directly in production. The fuel used in manufacturing processes is exempt in more than half the states. Sales of feed, seed, and fertilizer are exempt in almost all states and agricultural products sold by producers are not usually taxable. Alcoholic beverages and tobacco products are subject to both selective and general sales taxes in most sales tax states, but motor fuel is usually exempt from general sales taxation. [42]

Several states have extended exemptions to certain necessities in order to reduce the burden on low income groups. Food and medicine are exempt in a number of states and a few states exempt clothing. [43]

Table 19 shows the yield per 1 per cent of rate per $1,000 of per-

---

[41] The rates utilized in these calculations are corrected for the discount for collection expenses which has been allowed the retailer in recent years.
[42] Advisory Commission on Intergovernmental Relations, *Tax Overlapping in the United States, 1964* (Washington: U.S. Government Printing Office, 1964), p. 105.
[43] *Ibid.*

TABLE 19

COMPARATIVE YIELDS OF STATE RETAIL SALES TAXES

State	Revenue, 1965 Fiscal Year	Rate as of Sept., 1964	Yield Per 1% of Tax Per $1,000 Personal Income	Food Exempt
	(thousands)	(per cent)		
Hawaii	$ 77,296	3.5	$11.24	—
West Virginia	112,174	3.0ᵃ	10.57	—
Washington	324,884	4.0	9.79	—
Indiana	257,811	2.0	9.79	—
New Mexico	63,068	3.0	9.47	Lᵇ
Mississippi	108,818	3.5	8.80	L
Louisiana	119,316	2.0	8.49	L
Nevada	22,995	2.0	8.17	—
Wyoming	13,548	2.0	8.12	—
Arizona	88,260	3.0	8.10	—
Georgia	207,564	3.0	7.69	—
Utah	51,276	3.0	7.55	—
Arkansas	76,230	3.0	7.46	L
North Dakota	23,494	2.25	7.25	—
Tennessee	160,553	3.0	7.24	L
South Carolina	92,758	3.0	6.92	L
Iowa	92,741	2.0	6.79	—
South Dakota	18,230	2.0	6.60	—
Florida	260,647	3.0	6.43	Yes
Oklahoma	69,198	2.0	6.43	L
Missouri	215,910	3.0	6.32	—
Michigan	593,961	4.0	6.28	—
Kansas	90,709	2.5	6.25	—
Kentucky	116,868	3.0	6.24	—
Colorado	63,494	2.0	6.15	—
Alabama	155,053	4.0	6.10	L
North Carolina	168,468	3.0	5.82	L
California	943,780	3.0	5.44	Yes
Maine	46,499	4.0	5.41	Yes
ILLINOIS	622,857	3.5	5.34	—
Texas	221,988	2.0	4.64	Yes
Rhode Island	36,972	3.5	4.36	Yes
Ohio	324,120	3.0	3.88	Yes
Connecticut	122,927	3.5	3.78	Yes
Maryland	113,993	3.0	3.73	Yes
Pennsylvania	549,434	5.0	3.60	Yes
Wisconsin	83,406	3.0	2.60	Yes

ᵃ 2% plus 1¢ per $1.00 for sales in excess of $1.00.
ᵇ L indicates limited exemption.

Source: Column 1: U.S. Bureau of the Census, *Compendium of State Government Finances, 1965* (Washington: U.S. Government Printing Office, 1966). Columns 2 and 4: Tax Foundation, Inc., *Facts and Figures on Government Finance*, 13th ed. (Englewood Cliffs, N.J.: Prentice-Hall, 1965), p. 188. Column 3: Computed using 1964–65 average personal income data. No correction for collection fees retained by retailers or inclusion of receipts from nonretail components of tax.

sonal income in 37 sales tax states. The yield of the retail portion of the tax is somewhat overstated for the first six states listed since the taxes levied in these states contain substantial nonretail elements. Hawaii taxes manufacturers and wholesalers at a .5 per cent rate in addition to the 3.5 per cent retail sales tax. Mississippi taxes wholesale sales at one-eighth of 1 per cent. Washington and West Virginia have taxes of broad coverage on the receipts of a wide range of business firms, and the receipts shown for Indiana include receipts from a .5 per cent gross receipts tax which is paid by firms when the amount is greater than would be paid under the 2 per cent net income tax.

Despite the fact that the Illinois Supreme Court's interpretations seem to preclude exemptions, the Illinois tax is a narrow one. Illinois ranks 30th among the 37 states in yield per 1 per cent of rate per $1,000 of personal income. All of the states which rank below Illinois exempt food from taxation.[44]

It is not clear whether the relatively poor yield from the Illinois sales taxes is due to poor administration or to narrow legislative and judicial definition of the base, but it is clear that recent efforts to improve administration and broaden the base have not succeeded in making the tax as productive a source of revenue as it is in many states.

TAXATION OF PUBLIC UTILITY SERVICES

Shortly after the enactment of the Illinois retailers' occupation tax in 1933, the Department of Finance ruled that persons engaged in the business of providing electricity, gas, and water to persons for use or consumption were subject to the tax. However, the Supreme Court held that such businesses were not within the scope of the act.[45] An attempt by the 1935 legislature to subject the gross receipts of public utilities to taxation was thwarted by the Court, but a 1937 act imposing a tax "upon persons employed in the business of transmitting telegraph or telephone messages or of distributing, supply-

[44] Since many state sales tax bases include public utility sales in the base, the yield of the utility tax should properly be included when making comparisons of this kind. Including the yield of this tax would raise the Illinois collection figure shown in Table 19 to $5.98. Similar adjustments would be needed in several other states.

[45] Montgomery S. Winning, "The Revenue System of Illinois," 120 *Ill. Anno. St.*, pp. 57–58.

ing, furnishing or selling gas or electricity to persons for use or consumption and not for resale" was sustained. The administrative provisions of this act were taken almost verbatim from the retailers' occupation tax then in effect.[46] The utilities tax was re-enacted in 1945 as three separate acts (messages, gas, and electricity).

Although the rate of the public utility service tax has not always been the same as that of the sales tax, the two taxes can, for many purposes, be considered together. Both are consumption taxes. Rates and administrative procedures are similar. In many states public utility services are taxed under general sales tax statutes and collections from this source are reported as sales tax revenue.

The tax rate was 3 per cent until August 1, 1965, when the rate increased to 4 per cent of gross receipts. The additional 1 per cent was effective through August 31, 1966. Thereafter, the "excess rate" was the rate which would have yielded $19 million in the previous year but could not exceed 1 per cent. The rate was to be computed annually by the Department of Revenue.[47] The 1967 legislature deleted the "excess rate" provision and increased the flat rate to 5 per cent of gross receipts (*Ill. Laws*, Smith-Hurd, ed., 1967, Act 642).

Also included as public utility sales tax revenue by the Bureau of the Census are receipts from the Illinois Central Railroad tax. This tax is unusual—perhaps unique—among state taxes in the United States. It results from an 1851 act providing for the construction of the Illinois Central Railroad and granting certain lands to the railroad company. This act provided for a gross receipts tax and exempted the charter lines of the railroad from other forms of taxation. The courts have held that this constitutes a contract between the state and the railroad company which cannot be changed without the consent of both parties.[48] The result is that the Illinois Central continues to pay a gross receipts tax of 7 per cent of its charter line revenues and is exempt from all other state and local taxes on these lines.

Revenue from the two forms of public utility taxation totaled almost $64 million or $6.06 per capita in 1965. Of this amount $60 million came from the tax on utility services and the remainder from the Illinois Central tax. In 1965 these taxes provided 3.5 per cent of state general revenue as compared with 4.6 per cent in 1942.

[46] *Ibid.*, p. 58.
[47] *Ill. Rev. Stat.*, ch. 120, sec. 469, par. 2 (1967).
[48] *Neustadt* v. *Illinois Central Railroad Co.*, 31 Ill. 484 (1863); *Illinois Central Railroad Company* v. *Emmerson*, 299 Ill. 328 (1921).

The Motor Fuel Tax

The largest revenue producer among the Illinois selective sales taxes is the tax on motor fuel. The tax was first imposed in 1929 as a tax upon the privilege of operating motor vehicles upon the state's public highways. Later the scope of the tax was expanded to include operation of motor vehicles on public waters. The original three cent per gallon rate was increased to four cents in 1951 and to five cents on January 1, 1953.

The tax is collected from motor fuel distributors who file monthly returns with the Department of Revenue. The distributors are allowed an amount up to 2 per cent of collections as reimbursement for the cost of collecting and remitting the tax. Sales made to the fed-

TABLE 20

ILLINOIS MOTOR FUEL TAX COLLECTIONS, 1942–65

		Collections Per One Cent of Tax			
Year	Total Collections	Total	Per Capita	Per $1,000 of Personal Income	Per Registered Vehicle[a]
	(thousands)	(thousands)			
1942	$ 43,418	$14,473	$1.81	$1.87	$7.31
1944	29,835	9,945	1.28	.97	5.73
1946	37,305	12,435	1.63	1.05	6.66
1947	45,159	15,053	1.84	1.15	7.36
1948	48,821	16,274	1.95	1.12	7.32
1949	51,280	17,093	2.00	1.13	7.08
1950	56,339	18,780	2.17	1.23	7.09
1951	61,602	20,534	2.35	1.22	7.36
1952	82,435	20,609	2.35	1.13	7.25
1953	97,217	21,604	2.42	1.12	7.30
1954	116,288	23,258	2.58	1.17	7.53
1955	117,306	23,461	2.56	1.14	7.18
1956	128,152	25,630	2.75	1.16	7.52
1957	129,441	25,888	2.73	1.10	7.37
1958	138,424	27,685	2.87	1.14	7.76
1959	138,158	27,632	2.78	1.10	7.51
1960	141,865	28,373	2.84	1.08	7.51
1961	146,302	29,260	2.90	1.08	7.58
1962	149,942	29,988	2.96	1.06	7.54
1963	155,786	31,157	3.04	1.05	7.59
1964	161,087	32,217	3.11	1.03	7.57
1965	170,002	34,000	3.23	1.01	7.66

[a] Passenger cars, trucks, and buses only; motorcycles and trailers excluded.

Source: Tables A1, A4, A18; Illinois Division of Highways.

eral government and sales made to operators of local bus systems are not taxable. Taxes paid upon fuel used off the public highways or public waters and upon fuel lost or destroyed are refunded upon application.

Money received from this tax is deposited in the Motor Fuel Tax Fund. After the payment of refunds and administrative costs, $100,-000 monthly is transferred to the Grade Crossing Protection Fund and $84,000 monthly is transferred to the State Boating Act Fund. Thirty-five per cent of the balance is transferred to the Road Fund and the remainder is allocated to local governments for street and highway purposes.

Column 4 of Table 20 reveals that the yield of the motor fuel tax, corrected for rate change, has risen more slowly than personal income during most of the postwar period. As a result of the relatively low elasticity of the tax and the infrequent rate increases, the proportion of total state revenue provided by the motor fuel tax declined from 15.5 per cent in 1942 to 9.2 per cent in 1965.

In 1965 Governor Kerner proposed a three cent increase in the tax on motor fuel. However, only one-third of the increase was to be used for highway purposes. This proposal to divert motor fuel tax money to nonhighway purposes encountered strong opposition from highway lobbyists, and the entire proposal became entangled in the controversy over reapportionment. The session ended with no increase in the motor fuel tax and with each political party blaming the other for the lack of highway funds. The 1967 legislature passed a one cent increase and provided that one-half of the increase would go entirely for state highway purposes. The other half is to be divided between state and local governments in the customary way.

Motor Fuel Taxes in Other States

State gasoline tax rates in the 48 contiguous states range from five to eight cents per gallon as follows:[49]

Rate per gallon	Number of States
$.05	5*
.055	0
.06	15
.065	4
.07	21
.075	3

Alaska levies an eight cent tax and rates in Hawaii range from

[49] Tax Foundation Inc., *Facts and Figures on Government Finance*, 14th ed. (New York, 1967), p. 190. Data as of September 1, 1966; asterisk denotes rate category into which Illinois fell on that date.

8.5 to 11 cents depending upon the county. Eleven states impose higher rates on diesel fuel, and one state does not tax diesel fuel but imposes higher license fees on vehicles using diesel. The other states, including Illinois, impose the same rate on diesel and other special fuels as upon gasoline.

TAXATION OF ALCOHOLIC BEVERAGE SALES

Like tobacco, liquor has long been a favorite target of special excise taxation at both the state and federal levels. The high rates imposed upon liquor are often rationalized on the grounds that they reduce consumption and provide funds to pay the heavy social costs of the liquor industry. The remarkable revenue-raising ability of this form of taxation also does much to explain its popularity. Few other industries could flourish under a combined federal and state tax load which is several times the cost of production. Increases in the tax rate usually result in only a slight decline in sales.[50]

Alcoholic Beverage Tax Rates and Yields

Taxes on alcoholic beverage sales are commonly graduated according to alcoholic content and type of beverage and are levied on a gallonage, rather than an ad valorem, basis. In Illinois the rate schedule is as follows:[51]

Alcohol and spirits	$1.52
Beer	.06
Wine—14% or less	.23
Wine—over 14%	.60

Since 1942 there have been only two increases in the tax on alcoholic beverages. In 1957 the rate on alcohol and spirits was increased by two cents a gallon and in 1959 all rates were increased by approximately 50 per cent.

Gallonage taxes produced $47.9 million or $4.55 per capita in 1965. In that year 63.8 per cent of total receipts came from taxes on distilled spirits, 26.8 from beer, 1.8 from wines of less than 14 per cent alcoholic content, and the remaining 7.7 per cent from wines of more than 14 per cent.[52]

[50] The low elasticity of demand for alcoholic beverages greatly reduces the sumptuary effects of taxation. A tax which succeeds in greatly reducing consumption would yield little revenue. It should also be noted that to the extent that purchases over state lines are possible, the elasticity of demand for alcoholic beverages purchased within a given state may be considerably higher than the elasticity of total demand.

[51] Lower rates apply to wine made from grapes grown in Illinois.

[52] Breakdown based on Department of Revenue data.

Since 1942 collections from taxes on the sale of alcoholic beverages have increased far less than have collections from other major revenue sources in Illinois. Although the period from 1942 to 1965 was a period of great economic and population growth, liquor gallonage tax collections have only doubled—even with a 50 per cent increase in tax rates.

When per capita collections are converted to a constant rate basis, it appears that there has been little change in taxable consumption of alcoholic beverages during the period. However, conversion of the data in the last column of Table 21 to a constant rate basis would

TABLE 21

ILLINOIS ALCOHOLIC BEVERAGE TAX COLLECTIONS, 1942–65

Year	Total Collections	Per Capita Collections	Collections Per Capita 18 and Over
	(thousands)		
1942	$23,574	$2.95	
1944	19,505	2.51	
1946	26,197	3.44	
1947	23,683	2.90	
1948	23,122	2.77	$3.79
1949	22,193	2.59	3.54
1950	22,966	2.65	3.64
1951	25,915	2.96	4.08
1952	22,098	2.52	3.54
1953	24,340	2.73	3.87
1954	24,461	2.72	3.90
1955	23,362	2.55	3.68
1956	26,262	2.82	4.10
1957	25,653	2.71	3.98
1958	25,137	2.61	3.88
1959	26,558	2.67	
1960	31,623	3.17	4.76
1961	40,612	4.03	6.11
1962	41,419	4.09	6.25
1963	42,376	4.13	6.35
1964	41,691	4.02	6.22
1965	47,952	4.55	7.08

Source: Tables A1, A2, A18, A19.

show that there has been a modest rise in collections per person within the age group most likely to consume alcoholic beverages.

Taxes on the Sale of Alcoholic Beverages in Other States

It is difficult to compare alcoholic beverage tax rates in the various states because of the wide variety of tax and control measures used. In the 17 states which operate state liquor stores, profits from these stores supplement or replace taxes as a source of revenue. In license states there is a wide variation in the way rates are graduated. In some states brandy, vermouth, sparkling wines, or other specified beverages are taxed at different rates from general liquors or wines, and some also provide different rates for malt beverages depending upon the alcoholic content. The following tabulations, based upon data collected by the Tax Foundation,[53] do not allow for all of these variations but are sufficiently complete to indicate the general range of rates employed by the states in which sale of alcoholic beverages is through licensed liquor stores.

In the 32 license states which tax on a gallonage basis,[54] rates are distributed as follows:

Rate (per gallon)	Number of States
$1.00–1.49	6
1.50–1.99	10*
2.00–2.49	6
2.50–2.99	8
3.00–3.49	0
3.50–3.99	1
4.00–4.49	1

The asterisk indicates the group in which Illinois falls. These rates are in addition to the federal tax of $10.50 per proof gallon.

Rates on wines containing 14 per cent alcohol or less vary from one cent to $1.15 per gallon and are distributed as follows:

Rate (per gallon)	Number of States
$ .01– .24	16*
.25– .49	8
.50– .74	3
.75– .99	2
1.00–1.24	3

On wines containing 14 to 21 per cent alcohol, rates vary from two cents to $2.00 per gallon and are distributed as follows:

[53] Tax Foundation Inc., *op. cit.*, p. 192.
[54] Hawaii and several monopoly states tax on an ad valorem basis.

Rate (per gallon)	Number of States
$ .01– .24	9
.25– .49	8
.50– .74	8*
.75– .99	3
1.00–1.24	1
1.25–1.49	0
1.50 and over	2

One of the 32 license states is not included on this table because there is more than one rate applicable to wine of this class.

Since state liquor stores do not monopolize the sale of beer in the nonlicense states, it is possible to tabulate beer tax rates for 49 states. The following tabulation shows rates for draught beer. In some cases the rate for a gallon of bottle beer differs.

Rate (per gallon)	Number of States
$.01–.049	11
.05–.099	15*
.10–.149	6
.15–.199	3
.20–.249	3
.25–.299	4
.30 and over	7

THE CIGARETTE TAX

The cigarette tax was first adopted in Illinois in 1942. The original rate was two cents per pack and the proceeds were earmarked for the Emergency Relief Fund. In 1946 an additional one cent per pack tax was adopted, with the proceeds of the additional levy going to service the debt created to pay a bonus to Illinois veterans of World War II. In 1958 the voters rejected a proposal to increase the levy by one cent to finance a bonus for veterans of the Korean War. The 1959 legislature, however, voted a temporary one cent per pack increase to finance a bonus for combat veterans only. This additional tax was in effect from July 31, 1959, to June, 1960, and from May 1, 1961, to July 8, 1961, the date the additional levy became permanent. The rate remained at four cents per pack until August 1, 1965, when the rate became seven cents per pack. The 1967 legislature increased the rate to nine cents per pack.

The tax is collected by the Department of Revenue from cigarette distributors who are required to affix a stamp or meter impression to each package. Prior to 1963 the distributor received a 5 per cent discount as reimbursement for the cost of affixing the stamp or meter impression. The 1963 legislature imposed a sliding discount scale which provided a smaller discount for large volume distributors. The additional revenue which the state expected to receive was reduced when the distributor that handles more than one-third of all cigarette sales was split into two corporations. One of these does the stamping for both.[55] Since 1951 a cigarette use tax has been in effect as a means of reducing avoidance of the tax by out of state purchases. House Bill 1288 of the 1963 legislature amended the Cigarette Tax Act to place the legal incidence on retailers, rather than distributors, and required that distributors state the tax as separate items when billing retailers.

In 1965 cigarette tax revenue in Illinois totaled $59 million, almost five times as much as in 1942. In 1966 this jumped to over $98 million as a result of the three cent per pack increase in the rate. Table 22 reveals that there has been a substantial rise in per capita collections even when corrected for rate changes.

TABLE 22

ILLINOIS CIGARETTE TAX COLLECTIONS, 1942–65

Year	Total Collections	Collections Per One Cent of Tax	
		Total	Per Capita
	(thousands)	(thousands)	
1942	$12,448	$ 6,224	$ .78
1944	13,712	6,856	.88
1946	15,367	7,683	1.01
1947	20,913	8,365	1.02
1948	27,343	9,114	1.09
1949	28,661	9,554	1.12
1950	28,328	9,443	1.09
1951	27,828	9,276	1.06
1952	28,919	9,640	1.10
1953	30,867	10,289	1.15
1954	31,777	10,592	1.18
1955	30,261	10,087	1.10
1956	32,904	10,968	1.18
1957	33,437	11,146	1.18
1958	36,727	12,242	1.27
1959	37,477	12,492	1.26
1960	49,320	12,592	1.26
1961	43,064	13,599	1.35
1962	54,869	13,717	1.36
1963	56,002	14,000	1.36
1964	55,449	13,862	1.34
1965	59,128	14,782	1.40

Source: Tables A1, A18, A19.

[55] *Chicago Sun-Times,* September 10, 1963.

Tobacco Taxes in Other States

Forty-seven states impose cigarette taxes on a per-cigarette or per-pack basis. Fifteen of these also tax other tobacco products. Two states impose ad valorem taxes upon all tobacco products, including cigarettes.

The rates on the most common size of cigarettes in the 47 states range from 2.5 cents per pack of 20 and are distributed as follows:[56]

Rate (per pack)	Number of States
$.025	2
.03	1
.04	3
.05	3
.06	3
.065	1
.07	7*
.08	19
.09	1
.10	4
.11	3

INSURANCE PREMIUM TAXES

All 50 states impose taxes upon the gross premium of insurance companies. This form of taxation has developed primarily because the taxation of the insurance business in any other way presents a number of special problems. Tangible property typically makes up a small portion of an insurance company's assets. Thus, in most states insurance companies pay little property tax.[57] Because net income is a questionable concept for mutual companies and is difficult to determine for stock companies, especially for life insurance companies whose contracts extend for long periods of time, it is difficult to tax the income of insurance companies.

State taxation of insurance companies has also been complicated by constitutional considerations. The U.S. Supreme Court at one time

[56] Tax Foundation, Inc., *op. cit.*, p. 196. Rates shown were in effect September, 1966. The asterisk indicates into which group Illinois falls.

[57] It has been pointed out that insurance companies would find it difficult to evade the property tax on intangibles by failing to report intangibles owned as private owners of securities generally do. See William J. Shultz and C. Lowell Harriss, *American Public Finance* (Englewood Cliffs, N.J.: Prentice-Hall, Inc., 1965), p. 294.

According to Illinois law, all intangibles having taxable situs in the state are subject to property taxation, and the gross *receipts* of agents of foreign fire insurance companies are to be reported and taxed as personal property. In practice the amounts assessed under these provisions are very small.

held that insurance is not commerce,[58] thus removing the insurance business from the protection of the interstate commerce clause and permitting states to discriminate against foreign (outstate) companies. This discrimination has been greatly reduced in recent years through reciprocal and retaliatory provisions in insurance tax laws, although some states, including Illinois, continue to exempt domestic companies from the tax. A 1943 decision of the U.S. Supreme Court holding insurance to be commerce may have been a factor in reducing discrimination, although this case did not deal with taxation.[59]

Insurance Premium Taxation in Illinois

An annual tax of 2 per cent is levied on the gross premiums of foreign and alien insurance companies except fraternal benefit societies authorized to do business in Illinois. Taxable premiums are the gross amount of premiums received on direct business, including annuity considerations, on risks within Illinois after deducting (1) the amount of returned premiums on policies covering Illinois risks and (2) the amount returned to policyholders on Illinois risks as dividends paid in cash or used to reduce premiums. The amounts of the fire department tax against fire premiums which may be levied by municipalities or fire protection districts is deducted from the tax due the state. The premium tax is in lieu of all license fees or privilege or occupation taxes levied by any local unit of government. A complementary tax, known as the surplus line agent tax, applies to business written by agents or brokers in companies not authorized to do business in Illinois.

An additional tax, not to exceed 0.5 per cent, is levied by the Department of Insurance upon the premiums of all foreign and domestic fire insurance companies for the purpose of maintaining the state fire marshal's office.

In 1965 the tax on premiums of foreign companies yielded over $33 million and the surplus line agent tax produced $374,000. The fire marshal tax produced $762,000. The total of almost $35 million produced by these taxes compares with less than $8 million in 1942. On a per capita basis, revenues from this source have increased from $.97 in 1942 to $3.32 in 1965.

Insurance Premium Taxes in Other States

It is difficult to make exact comparisons of taxes on insurance in the several states because of the variety of taxes imposed and because

---

[58] *New York Life Insurance Co. v. Deer Lodge County,* 231 U.S. 508 (1913).
[59] *United States v. Southeastern Underwriters Association,* 322 U.S. 533 (1944).

of the complex of retaliatory laws in effect. One recent analysis suggests that most states tax insurance companies more heavily than does Illinois.[60] This study reveals that premium taxes and fees as a percentage of gross premiums in 1960 ranged from a high of 3.30 per cent to a low of 1.27 per cent. Illinois ranked 43rd with an effective rate of 1.47 per cent. Among the six states with lower ratios, two impose an income tax on domestic companies in addition to the premium taxes included in the comparison.

The relative rankings of the individual states depend upon the rates levied, the definition of the premium base, and credits or offsets allowed. Since 2 per cent is the most common rate, it is not possible to explain the relatively low yield of the Illinois tax on the basis of its low rate. Probably the most important single factor is that Illinois is one of 10 states which exempt all domestic insurers from the premium tax. Five of these 10 states levy an income tax on domestic insurers, leaving Illinois as one of five states which impose neither an income tax nor a gross premium tax on domestic companies. This has encouraged tax avoidance in Illinois, as it is possible to place business in an in-state company and then arrange for 100 per cent reinsurance in a foreign company, thus avoiding the premium tax which would be due if the insurance were placed directly in the foreign company.[61] In 1961 about 30 per cent of all premiums written in Illinois were in domestic insurers and thus not subject to tax.

OTHER SALES AND GROSS RECEIPTS

In Illinois the principal source of revenue classified as "other sales and gross receipts taxes" is the tax on pari-mutuel betting. Smaller sums come from the tax on admissions to races and athletic exhibitions.

In 1941 Illinois imposed a 2 per cent tax on money wagered at horse races. In 1946 an additional tax of 4 per cent plus one-half the breaks[62] was imposed to service the debt created to pay a bonus to veterans of World War II. In the same year legislation reduced by 1 per cent the take of the track. The 1947 legislature reduced the total tax by 1 per cent and restored the take of the track to its

---

[60] Robert I. Mehr, "Taxation of Insurance Companies," *Report of the Commission on Revenue* (Springfield, 1963), pp. 760–94.

[61] *Ibid.*, p. 788.

[62] Breaks are the sums resulting from the fact that winning tickets are not figured to the nearest cent. In Illinois winning tickets are paid in full ten cent amounts. Thus, if a ticket is computed to pay $3.58, the holder actually receives only $3.50.

original level. The results of these changes were that the 6 per cent rate was in effect from the beginning of the 1947 racing season until July 12 and then dropped to 5 per cent, where it remained until it was again raised to 6 per cent in 1951. The rate continued to be 6 per cent plus one-half of the breaks until 1965 when a system of graduated rates was introduced. Rates now range from 5 per cent to 8.5 per cent, depending upon the annual mutuel handle at the track.[63]

A tax of 2 per cent of the pari-mutuel handle on harness races was imposed in 1946. In 1949 the rate was increased to 5 per cent. The 1951 legislature added a .5 per cent levy to be paid into the Illinois Fund for Illinois Sired Colts. In 1965 a graduated rate schedule similar to that used in running races was substituted for the 5.5 per cent flat rate previously in effect. The 5.5 per cent rate now applies to the first $30 million of annual handle at a track. This rises by increments to 8.5 per cent on handle above $60 million.

The tax on admission to running and harness races is 20 cents per ticket. For boxing and wrestling exhibitions the tax is 10 per cent of gross receipts.

MOTOR VEHICLE AND OPERATORS' LICENSES

Motor vehicle and motor vehicle operators' licenses produced almost $130 million in 1965. These receipts were distributed as follows:[64]

Motor Vehicles:	
Registrations	$120,064,000
Common and Contract Carriers	681,000
Certificate of Title and Other	2,412,000
Motor Vehicle Operator:	
Drivers	5,436,000
Chauffeurs	1,010,000

In 1942 receipts from these sources were only $27 million, but this was a larger proportion of total state revenue than was the $130 million of receipts in 1965.[65]

---

[63] At tracks within 100 miles of Chicago the 5 per cent rate applies to the first $5 million of mutuel handle. The rate rises by increments of one-half or 1 per cent to a rate of 8.5 per cent which applies to amounts above $60 million. Elsewhere in the state the first $10 million is subject to the 5 per cent rate and rates rise to 8.5 per cent on amounts exceeding $60 million.
[64] Appendix Table A17.
[65] Appendix Table A20.

Motor Vehicle Registration Fees

Passenger car registration fees range from $8.00 to $24.00 per car depending upon the actual horsepower. Trucks and buses are taxed according to weight and number of wheels, with the fees ranging from $5.00 to $1,210.00. Operators of trucks and buses may elect to pay a mileage-weight tax in lieu of the annual license fee. The minimum mileage-weight tax ranges from $21.00 to $568.00, with an additional fee being charged for each mile driven in excess of the amount permitted by the minimum fee. Small fees are also levied for such services as the issuance of duplicate plates and registration of vehicles owned by state and local governments.

Except for the addition of $.50 per vehicle to cover the cost of reflectorized plates in 1965 and slight increases in 1967, the schedule of registration fees for passenger cars has not been changed since 1919, but the average fee has risen as the horsepower of passenger automobiles has increased. For trucks and buses the schedule was increased rather markedly by the 1951 legislature. This became effective January 1, 1952. A further increase was to go into effect on January 1, 1954, but the 1953 General Assembly amended the schedule again to eliminate the proposed 1954 increases, holding fees at the 1952 level. The 1953 General Assembly also increased the rates for mileage-weight tax (which is an elective substitute for the fees) and specified a required minimum payment of the elective mileage-weight tax. The regular fee on a vehicle in the 12,000–14,000 pound weight class, for example, was raised from $50 to $86 (including the flat $5 basic fee); the fee on a vehicle in the 50,000–59,000 pound weight class was raised from $350 to $894 (including the $5 basic fee). The mileage-weight tax on the 12,000–14,000 pound vehicle was raised from five to 14 mills per mile, with a minimum fee of $40.50 (including the $5 basic fee); for the 50,000–59,000 pound vehicle, it was raised from 28 to 89 mills, with a minimum fee of $444.50 (including the basic $5 fee). Litigation held up collections from the new schedule in 1952, but the collection statistics show a marked rise from 1952 to 1953. Averages for various classes of vehicles are shown in Table 23.

Since 1957 Illinois has entered into agreements with 18 states under which large trucking concerns are allowed to register part of their fleet in other states. Proration is based on mileage traveled in each state, but trucks with out-of-state license plates are not permitted to do intra-state hauling.

Because of the wide variation in formulas used to calculate registration fees, it is difficult to make direct comparisons between Illinois rates and rates in other states. Only three states other than Illinois base the registration fee for automobiles exclusively on horsepower.

TABLE 23

AVERAGE LICENSE FEES, CALENDAR YEARS 1942–65

Year	Passenger Cars	Trucks and Buses	Trailers
1942	$ 9.47	$ 31.27	$ 8.10
1943	9.50	32.12	8.56
1944	9.54	32.44	8.43
1945	9.44	32.96	8.20
1946	9.35	35.20	7.86
1947	9.47	37.74	8.16
1948	9.47	38.48	8.34
1949	9.59	39.93	8.84
1950	9.77	41.94	9.05
1951	10.09	44.13	9.25
1952	10.35	64.99	12.01
1953	10.47	84.90	13.38
1954	10.81	83.43	12.26
1955	11.31	84.98	11.14
1956	12.04	88.93	10.48
1957	12.63	92.20	10.08
1958	13.17	95.81	9.63
1959	13.48	98.45	9.24
1960	13.78	99.41	8.98
1961	13.97	98.06	8.84
1962	14.07	98.81	8.70
1963	14.24	99.77	8.58
1964	14.54	101.68	8.70
1965	14.85	102.46	8.76

Source: Illinois Department of Public Works, Division of Highways.

Many states tax passenger cars on a weight basis, some combine weight with other factors to determine the fee, and some levy a flat fee on passenger cars. Other formulas involve horsepower, age, or value of the car.[66] Trucks are taxed on the basis of various combinations of capacity, gross weight, net weight, value, number of wheels, number of axles, and type of tires.

[66] Robert W. Harbeson, "Highway-User Charges," *Report of the Commission on Revenue* (Springfield, 1963), p. 582.

The tabulation below indicates the average license fee paid by passenger cars in various states:[67]

Average Fee	Number of States
Under $ 4.00	1
$ 4.00– 6.99	7
7.00– 9.99	10
10.00– 12.99	8
13.00– 15.99	10*
16.00– 18.99	3
19.00– 21.99	2
22.00– 24.99	4
25.00– 27.99	4
28.00 or over	1

Comparisons among truck license fees are even more difficult to make because the average fee paid depends not only upon the rate levied, but upon the proportion of heavy trucks included. It is clear, however, that the increase in truck license fees in the early 1950's placed Illinois fees among the highest in the United States.

Administration of motor vehicle and operators' license fees is in the hands of the Secretary of State. In mid-1966 investigators from this office and the Cook County Sheriff's police set up road blocks and stopped hundreds of trucks in an investigation of a racket in which, according to newspaper accounts, trucking companies had been cheating the state out of millions of dollars in license fees.[68] Later, the newspapers reported allegations of bribery and corruption in truck licensing extending high in public office and printed evidence that truckers were permitted to avoid Illinois taxes and license fees by registering fleets in small Indiana villages with low property tax rates.[69]

Early in 1967 sharp criticism was levied against the Illinois Motor Vehicle Laws Commission which ended a study of the scandal with calls for new legislation and regulation but which failed to "get to basic causes." The executive director of the Better Government Association said there were reports of huge cash donations to Commission members, and several of them were reported to have acknowledged to reporters of the *Chicago Tribune* that they had accepted cash from truckers.[70]

[67] Wilbur Smith and Associates, *Illinois Highway Needs and Fiscal Study, Summary Report* (Springfield, 1966), p. 11.
[68] *Chicago Tribune*, June 18, 1966.
[69] *Chicago Sun-Times*, November 26, 1966.
[70] *Chicago Tribune*, January 9, 1967.

OTHER LICENSE TAXES

In 1965 Illinois received $24 million from a wide variety of other license taxes or fees. The most important of these was the corporate franchise tax, which is based upon the estimated share of stated capital and paid-in surplus employed in Illinois. The annual rate was one-twentieth of 1 per cent. A supplemental rate was added by the 1967 legislature of one-twentieth of 1 per cent, bringing the combined annual supplemental rate to 0.1 per cent and imposing a minimum combined tax of $100 and a maximum of $1,000,000.

As a result of a court decision involving prior law and a ruling of the Attorney General that the minimum tax, as applied to foreign corporations, is unconstitutional, the Secretary of State does not assess it against foreign corporations. A $10 minimum imposed in another section of the statutes is collected.

Domestic corporations also pay an initial license fee at the time the corporation files its first report of issuance of shares and when additional shares are issued or whenever there is an increase in stated capital or paid-in surplus. Foreign corporations pay an initial fee when they file application for authority to operate in Illinois and when the amount of stated capital or paid-in surplus represented in the state is changed. There are also a variety of small filing fees charged for services performed by the Corporation Division of the Secretary of State's office.

In 1965 receipts from the various general corporation license and franchise taxes amounted to $8 million.[71]

Other license tax collections in 1965 were:

License	Amount (thousands)
Alcoholic Beverages	$1,144
Amusements	823
Hunting and Fishing	3,364
Water Craft	125
Occupation and Business, n.e.c.:	
Oil Inspection	1,258
Grain Inspection	1,051
Insurance Agents and Brokers	1,001
Insurance Companies	1,559
Bank and Building and Loan Examination	1,025
Beauty Culture	586
Real Estate	416
Other	3,490

[71] For a detailed description and analysis of corporation taxation in Illinois see Ruth A. Birdzell, "General Corporation Taxes," *Report of the Commission on Revenue* (Springfield, 1963), pp. 602–45.

Receipts from taxes and fees included in the "other license" category have risen from less than $7 million in 1942 to almost $24 million in 1965. On a per capita basis receipts from these sources have risen from $.83 per capita to $2.88 per capita, but there has been a substantial decline in the percentage of revenue obtained from these sources. Collections per capita from these sources are much smaller in Illinois than in the United States as a whole. In 1965 per capita collections is the United States were $7.05 as compared with $2.88 in Illinois.

STATE PROPERTY TAXES

The state has not levied a general property tax since 1932, but it does receive the revenue from the taxes on operating personal property of private railroad car companies. The sums shown in Appendix Table A18 as state property tax collections for the years 1942–65 also include small amounts representing the collection of general property taxes levied by the state in prior years.

INHERITANCE TAXATION

Three types of wealth transfer taxes are in use in the United States. The inheritance tax is imposed upon the privilege of succession to property and is levied on the share of the estate left to a particular beneficiary. Exemptions and rates depend upon the relationship of the heir to the decedent. The basic death tax imposed by most states takes this form. The estate tax is imposed upon the privilege of transferring property at death and is levied upon the net value of the estate without regard to the number of heirs or their relationship to the decedent. For the federal government and a few states, the estate tax is the basic form of death taxation. In addition, many states use a supplemental estate tax as a means of insuring that the full federal credit is absorbed. The gift tax is imposed upon gifts between living persons as a means of checking avoidance of inheritance and estate taxes.[72]

Illinois has imposed an inheritance tax since 1895. The present rate schedule is as follows:

[73] Gifts made in contemplation of death are almost always taxed under the estate or inheritance tax. The tax on *inter vivos* gifts applies to those gifts which cannot be proved to be in contemplation of death.

Beneficiary	Exemption	Bracket	Rate
Lineal ancestors or descendant	$20,000	– 50,000	2 per cent
of decedent, wife or husband		$ 50,000–150,000	4 per cent
of decedent, wife or husband		150,000–250,000	6 per cent
of decedent's child		250,000–500,000	10 per cent
		500,000–	14 per cent
Brother or sister	10,000	Same as above	
Uncle, aunt, niece, nephew,	500	– 20,000	6 per cent
and lineal descendants		20,000– 70,000	8 per cent
thereof		70,000–170,000	12 per cent
		170,000–	16 per cent
Other	100	– 20,000	10 per cent
		20,000– 50,000	12 per cent
		50,000–100,000	16 per cent
		100,000–150,000	20 per cent
		150,000–250,000	24 per cent
		250,000–	30 per cent

In addition, a supplemental estate tax is imposed in order to take full advantage of the 80 per cent federal credit.[73] In this report, receipts from this tax are included as part of the yield of the inheritance tax. Illinois levies no gift tax.

In 1967 the inheritance tax law was amended. First, the full value of property would be included in the determination of the value of an inheritance for tax purposes unless the survivor had contributed to the purchase price of the property. As the law stood prior to amendment, only one-half of the value of the property held in joint tenancy was included in value determination. Second, the $20,000 exemption in the old law was raised to $30,000 for a wife and $25,000 for a husband. Finally, life insurance proceeds to a designated beneficiary had not been included in determination of the value of an inheritance under the old law. Revisions in the law provided that life insurance proceeds would be included in determining value with a $20,000 exemption for husbands and wives and a $5,000 exemption for minor children. Reaction to these changes in the inheritance tax law were such that these new provisions were repealed when the legislature met in extended session in October, 1967.

Responsibility for enforcement of the inheritance tax is diffused. Tax returns are filed with the county clerk and a copy is sent to the Attorney General. After his office reviews the return he agrees to

[73] The federal estate tax is actually two separate taxes, the *basic* estate tax and the *additional* estate tax. A credit of up to 80 per cent of the basic tax is allowed for state estate or inheritance taxes paid. Prior to 1949 it sometimes happened that the Illinois inheritance tax was not great enough to absorb the full federal credit. Upon recommendation of the Revenue Laws Commission, the 1949 legislature enacted the supplemental estate tax to ensure that the state imposes all the tax which can be imposed without increasing the overall burden on the estate.

the entry of an order determining the tax. A hearing is held before the circuit judge, who, in an administrative capacity, approves the assessment and issues an order determining the tax. The estate then pays the tax to the county treasurer who forwards the money to the State Treasurer. Ultimately a receipt, issued by the county treasurer and signed by the State Treasurer, is filed with the probate court as proof that the tax has been paid. The county receives 4 per cent of the tax for administering the hearing and collecting the tax.[74]

Receipts from the inheritance tax rose from $8 million in 1942 to $33 million in 1965. On a per capita basis, collections rose from $.98 to $3.13. Because of the great amount of administrative discretion involved in valuing the estate for tax purposes and the importance which a small number of large estates have in collections for a given year, inheritance tax receipts may fluctuate considerably from year to year. Table 24 illustrates the rapid changes in yield that can occur even though there has been no change in rates. The large increase in collections in 1961 is particularly striking.

Death Taxation in Other States

All states except Nevada impose some form of death tax. Twelve states also impose a gift tax. Because of the wide variation in the form of the tax, in the way heirs are classified, and in the rate brackets used, it is difficult to present a simple, meaningful tabulation of rates and exemptions. Comparisons of death tax rates have sometimes been made by computing the tax which would be paid on a hypothetical estate in each state. This procedure is not entirely satisfactory since it is difficult to make allowances for the rather wide differences in the definitions used in determining the value of the taxable estate.[75]

Because of these difficulties, no attempt has been made to provide a detailed comparison of Illinois inheritance tax rates and those of other states. An examination of rates in those states levying the inheritance form of death taxation does suggest that the 2 to 14 per cent rates on inheritance by a spouse, child, or parent in Illinois are relatively high. Of the 37 states, 13 levy a 2 per cent tax on the first

[74] A staff report to the 1963 Commission on Revenue recommended that administration of the tax be transferred to the Department of Revenue. See Robert N. Corley, "Inheritance Tax," *Report of the Commission on Revenue* (Springfield, 1963), p. 565.
[75] Tabulations of rates and exemptions may be found in the following sources: Advisory Commission on Intergovernmental Relations, *Tax Overlapping in the United States, Selected Tables Updated: A Supplement to Report M-23* (Washington: U.S. Government Printing Office, 1966), pp. 41–45; Tax Foundation Inc., *op. cit.*, pp. 198–99.

bracket, and one levies a 3 per cent rate. In the other 23 states the first bracket rates are lower than 2 per cent. In only three states does the top bracket rate for this class of heirs exceed the Illinois rate of 14 per cent. On the other hand, the Illinois rates on inheritances by brothers or sisters are lower than in many other states, especially in the lower brackets.

TABLE 24

ILLINOIS INHERITANCE TAX COLLECTIONS, 1942–65

Year	Total Collections	Collections Per Capita	Collections Per $1,000 of Personal Income
	(thousands)		
1942	$ 7,816	$ .98	$1.01
1944	5,481	.71	.53
1946	7,459	.98	.63
1947	7,926	.97	.61
1948	8,954	1.07	.61
1949	8,295	.97	.55
1950	7,090	.82	.46
1951	8,618	.98	.51
1952	11,439	1.31	.63
1953	12,437	1.40	.65
1954	12,191	1.35	.61
1955	15,065	1.64	.73
1956	19,976	2.14	.90
1957	19,245	2.03	.82
1958	20,372	2.11	.84
1959	21,123	2.12	.84
1960	22,027	2.21	.84
1961	33,455	3.32	1.23
1962	31,682	3.13	1.12
1963	31,981	3.12	1.08
1964	35,783	3.45	1.15
1965	33,031	3.13	.99

Source: Tables A1, A4, A18, A19.

The exemptions allowed to children, parents, brothers, and sisters in Illinois are among the highest, but a number of states allow larger exemptions to a spouse.

The importance of death and gift tax revenue varies greatly from state to state. In the three fiscal years 1964, 1965, and 1966 these taxes provided only .39 per cent of the total state tax revenue in Alaska but provided 9.01 per cent in New Jersey. In Illinois the inheritance tax made up 3.08 per cent of total state tax revenue. The following tabulation indicates the extent of this variation in the 49 states which levy death or gift taxes:

Death and Gift Taxes as Percentage of Total State Tax Revenue	Number of States
.2– .9	12
1.0–1.9	15
2.0–2.9	10
3.0–4.9	8*
5.0 and over	4

The variation, of course, results both from differences in rates and differences in the amount of wealth transferred. Most of the states in which this form of taxation is more important than in Illinois are eastern states, and all, with the exception of Maine, are wealthy states.

INTERGOVERNMENTAL REVENUE

Intergovernmental revenue is made up of amounts received from other governments as fiscal aids or as reimbursement for performance of general services for the paying government. It excludes any amounts received from other governments for sale of property, commodities, and utility services.

Illinois state government received $474 million from the federal government in 1965, most of which was in the form of grants-in-aid.

A breakdown of receipts from the federal government in 1965 (Appendix Table A17) reveals that $225 million of this total was received for highway purposes. These grants are in the form of matching grants as determined by allocation formulas under the various federal programs. Interstate highway construction grants are on a 90–10 matching basis, but grants for other eligible classes of highways are on a 50–50 basis.

Public welfare grants totaled $145 million in 1965. Most of these funds were received as matching grants in connection with categorical aid programs such as Old Age Assistance, Aid to Families with Dependent Children, and Aid to the Blind.[76] Federal payments are conditioned upon state compliance with certain specified conditions and are calculated so that the federal government's percentage contribution falls as the average payment declines. For example, the federal government pays five-sixths of the first $18 average monthly

[76] For a detailed analysis of these programs in Illinois see Glenn W. Fisher, "Public Assistance Expenditure," *Report of the Commission on Revenue* (Springfield, 1963), pp. 96–157.

payment to AFDC recipients plus 50 per cent of the next $14. Federal grants for payments to recipients of public assistance, unlike most federal grants, are open-ended. Thus, there is no ceiling on the number of recipients to whom the federal government will make payments. Prior to 1962 the federal government matched administrative costs on a 50–50 basis, but since that time the federal government pays 75 per cent of certain costs incurred to reduce dependency and permit recipients to become self-supporting.

Grants for education, totaling almost $65 million in 1965, were made up of payments for a variety of programs including school milk and school lunch programs, vocational education, and manpower development and training. A substantial proportion of the total consists of payments made directly to institutions of higher education in connection with federal research programs.

Federal grants for health and hospital purposes amounted to almost $7 million. Grants are for a variety of specific programs in the field of mental health, public health, and hospital construction.

Federal grants for employment security administration represent the full administrative cost of the unemployment compensation system and the employment service. The unemployment compensation system was established as a result of a provision in the Social Security act imposing a federal payroll tax, 90 per cent of which is remitted if the employer is paying into an approved state unemployment compensation system. In addition, the federal government pays the state the full cost of administering the system. These payments to Illinois amounted to $22 million in 1965.

Receipts from local governments totaled $8 million and were composed largely of receipts connected with highway construction or maintenance.

CURRENT CHARGES AND MISCELLANEOUS GENERAL REVENUE

Current charges are amounts received for the performance of specific services benefiting the person charged and from the sale of commodities and services. Current charges are distinguished from license taxes, which relate to privileges granted by the government or to regulatory measures for the protection of the public. Illinois received $114 million from current charges in 1965. Of this sum, almost $38 million were receipts from the commercial activities of state institutions of higher education such as residence halls, dining facilities, athletic contests, and bookstores operated by the institutions. Institutions of higher education also collected $20 million in other charges, largely tuition and fees.

More than $32 million were collected from state-operated toll facilities and another $4 million were collected from other highway-related charges.

Fifteen and one-half million dollars were collected in connection with state hospitals—primarily as reimbursement for care and maintenance of patients in state hospitals.

Although institutions of higher education, toll highways, and state hospitals are the major sources of current charge revenue, many departments and agencies collect small sums in return for a variety of services. Some of these are classified in Appendix Table A17.

Interest earnings are a substantial source of revenue to the Illinois state government, amounting to more than $25 million in 1965. Other miscellaneous revenue includes fines and donations. Donations are largely in the form of gifts and endowment funds to institutions of higher education.

COLLECTION AND DISPOSITION OF STATE REVENUE

Most of the revenue data presented in this chapter has been classified according to Bureau of the Census classifications. These classifications emphasize the economic character of the revenue and treat the state as a single entity. Actually, state revenues are collected by several different agencies and not all are expended through the state treasury. Within the treasury, revenues may be placed in the state general fund or in a number of special funds.

Statutory provisions dealing with the major taxes are grouped in Chapter 120 of the statutes, but many provisions dealing with taxation are found elsewhere in the statutes. For example, the provisions authorizing two forms of sales taxation (pari-mutuel and admission) and several license taxes upon promoters and participants in horse racing are found in the chapter of the statutes which deals with animals.[77] Provision for various kinds of business license and privilege taxes are found in the section of the statutes dealing with the authorization and regulation of that particular business or organizational form.

Table 25 is a reconciliation of the Census classification and the legal and administrative classification of major Illinois taxes. The classifications in the left stub of the table are Census classifications listed in the same order as in Appendix Table A17. Statutory citations are to the 1967 edition of *Illinois Revised Statutes*. Other columns indicate the rate, agency charged with administering the tax, and the fund into which the proceeds are paid.

[77] *Ill. Rev. Stat.*, ch. 8 (1967).

TABLE 25

MAJOR ILLINOIS TAXES, ADMINISTRATIVE AGENCY AND FUND, JANUARY 1, 1968

Tax	Statutory Citation (Ill. Rev. Stat., 1967)	Rate	Administrative Agency	Fund
Sales and Gross Receipts:				
Retailers' Occupation	ch. 120, sec. 440–53	4.25%	Dept. of Revenue	⅚ General Revenue, ⅔ Common School
Use	ch. 120, sec. 439.1–439.22	4.25%	Dept. of Revenue	
Service Occupation	ch. 120, sec. 439.101–439.121	4.25%	Dept. of Revenue	
Service Use	ch. 120, sec. 439.31–439.51	4.25%	Dept. of Revenue	
Motor Fuel	ch. 120, sec. 417–434	6¢ per gallon	Dept. of Revenue	Motor Fuel Tax Fund
Alcoholic Beverage (gallonage)	ch. 43, sec. 158	Alcohol and Spirits $1.52 / Beer .06 / Wine (14% or less) .23[a] / Wine (over 14%) .60[a]	Dept. of Revenue	General Revenue
Cigarette	ch. 120, sec. 453.1–453.30	4.5 mills per cigarette (9¢ per pack)	Dept. of Revenue	4.0 mills General Revenue, .5 mill Service Recognition or Fair & Exposition Authority Reconstruction
Cigarette Use	ch. 120, sec. 453.31–453.67	4.5 mills per cigarette	Dept. of Revenue	General Revenue
Insurance:				
Foreign	ch. 73, sec. 1021–1025	2%	Dept. of Insurance	General Revenue
Surplus Line	ch. 73, sec. 1057	3%	Dept. of Insurance	General Revenue
Fire Insurance	ch. 127½, sec. 16	Up to .5%	Dept. of Insurance	Fire Prevention
Public Utilities:				
Public Utilities (electricity)	ch. 120, sec. 468–481a	4%[b]	Dept. of Revenue	General Revenue
Gas	ch. 120, sec. 467.16–467.30	5%[b]	Dept. of Revenue	General Revenue

Messages	ch. 120, sec. 467.1–467.15	5%[b]	Dept. of Revenue	General Revenue
Ill. Central R.R.	ch. 120, sec. 373–374	7%	Dept. of Revenue	General Revenue
Pari-Mutuel: Running Races	ch. 8, sec. 37e–37f	5%–8.5%	Racing Board	Service Recognition, Agricultural Premium, Fair and Exposition, and General Revenue
Harness Races	ch. 8, sec. 37s19	5.5%–8.5%	Racing Board	Fund for Illinois Colts, Agricultural Premium, and General Revenue
Amusements: Racing Admissions	ch. 8, sec. 37e–37f	20¢ per ticket	Racing Board	General Revenue
Harness Racing Admissions	ch. 8, sec. 37s8	20¢ per ticket	Racing Board	Agricultural Premium
Boxing and Wrestling	ch. 10⅓, sec. 25	10% of receipts	Athletic Commission	General Revenue
Hotel Operators' Occupation	ch. 120, sec. 481b.31–481b.39	3%	Dept. of Revenue	General Revenue
License: Motor Vehicle	ch. 95½, sec. 3-801.1–3-801.10	See text	Secretary of State	Road
Operators'	ch. 95½, sec. 6-124	$5.00[c] (3 years)	Secretary of State	Drivers Education, Road
Chauffeurs'	ch. 95½, sec. 6-124	$5.00[c] (1 yr.)	Secretary of State	Road
Corporation Franchise	ch. 32, sec. 157.129–157.140	⅒% of stated capital value and paid-in surplus	Secretary of State	General Revenue
Corporation Filing Fees	ch. 32, sec. 157.127–157.130	Varies	Secretary of State	General Revenue
Alcoholic Beverage	ch. 43, sec. 115, 117, 118	$10.00–$2,500.00	Liquor Control Comm.	General Revenue
Amusements: Running Races	ch. 8, sec. 37c-2, 37d, 37f	Varies	Racing Board	General Revenue
Harness Races	ch. 8, sec. 37s8, 37s24	Varies	Racing Board	Agricultural Premium
Boxing and Wrestling (promotors, officials, and participants)	ch. 10⅓, sec. 114, 126, 127	$5.00–$50.00[d] per year	Athletic Commission	General Revenue

TABLE 25 (Concluded)

MAJOR ILLINOIS TAXES, ADMINISTRATIVE AGENCY AND FUND, JANUARY 1, 1968

Tax	Statutory Citation (Ill. Rev. Stat., 1967)	Rate	Administrative Agency	Fund
Occupations and Business, n.e.c.	—ᵉ	Varies	Varies	General Revenue
Hunting and Fishing:				
Hunting	ch. 61, sec. 172.02, 187, 189	Varies	Dept. of Conservation	Game and Fish
Fishing	ch. 56, sec. 228	Varies	Dept. of Conservation	Game and Fish
Property:				
Private Car Lines	ch. 120, sec. 372.1–372.12a	Statewide average rate	Dept. of Revenue	General Revenue
Inheritance	ch. 120, sec. 375–403c	See text	Attorney General, State Treasurer, Circuit judges	General Revenue

ᵃ Lower rates apply to wine made from Illinois grapes.
ᵇ The cigarette tax is a tax on the sale of cigarettes. The cigarette use tax is a tax on the use of cigarettes. Thus, the total tax on cigarettes is 8.5 mills.
ᶜ Chauffeurs' renewal license is $3.00.
ᵈ Includes referee, trainer, etc.
ᵉ There are a large number of business license fees. Statutory provisions are usually found in section providing for licensing or regulation of the occupation. Collections are usually paid into the General Revenue Fund.

Source: Ill. Rev. Stat., 1967.

MAJOR ILLINOIS NONTAX REVENUE, BY FUND OR INSTITUTION

Source	Fund	Statutory Citation (Ill. Rev. Stat., 1967)
Intergovernmental Revenue:		
Federal	Generally paid into special funds in the state treasury. Some funds are paid directly to state institutions. In cases where no designation of purpose is made by the federal government, the Governor shall make the designation.	ch. 127, sec. 1766
Charges and Miscellaneous:		
State Institutions of Higher Education:		
Tuition, laboratory, and library fees and excess income from auxiliary enterprises	Teachers College Board Income Fund	ch. 127, sec. 142a
	Southern Illinois University Income Fund	ch. 127, sec. 142a1
	University of Illinois Income Fund	ch. 127, sec. 142d
Endowment funds, gifts, trusts, federal aid, research contracts, and revenue from auxiliary operations necessary for their support, and revenue necessary to discharge obligations	Treasury of the institution	ch. 127, sec. 142a, 142a1, 142a2, 142d, 142g
Varying amounts from the receipts of each institution	Working Cash Fund of the institution	ch. 127, sec. 142a, 142a1, and 142e
SIU receipts of sale of revenue bonds under the SIU Revenue Bond Act	Southern Illinois University Treasury	ch. 127, sec. 142a3
University of Illinois: $1 million receipts	Stores and Service Fund	ch. 127, sec. 142f
Toll Highway Charges	Illinois State Toll Highway Fund	ch. 121, sec. 314a45
Health & Hospital Charges:		
State Hospitals	¾ to Mental Health Fund, ¼ to Psychiatric Training & Research Fund (not to exceed $1,000,000 per fiscal year; the total not to exceed $2,000,000. Excess goes to Mental Health Fund).	ch. 91½, sec. 12-22
Interest	General Revenue unless otherwise specified, e.g., interest accruing to principal of county school funds are to be distributed to townships.	ch. 122, sec. 19-1
Donations	As designated by donor.	
Fines and Fees	To General Revenue Fund unless otherwise specified, e.g., Road Fund and State Boating Act Fund fees and fines related to motor vehicles and boats, respectively.	ch. 95½, sec. 320-1, ch. 95½, sec. 235

Source: *Ill. Rev. Stat.*, 1967.

Table 26 provides similar information concerning nontax revenues. Intergovernmental revenues are usually received for specific purposes and often federal statutes and regulations have an effect upon accounting procedures as well as upon the program. Appendix Table A5 indicates the variety of funds which have been set up in the state treasury in connection with federal grants. Some federal money also goes directly to state institutions of higher education—usually in connection with research grants or contracts.

Most charges and miscellaneous revenues are earmarked for the department or agency which earns the revenue. Sometimes the revenue is paid into a special fund in the state treasury and appropriated back to the department or agency by the legislature. In other cases the money is retained and expended by the state agency on the basis of general statutory authorization.

4

STATE FINANCE AND
LOCAL GOVERNMENTS

Local governments are created by the state which also
determines the types of revenue which may be raised
by local governments and the purposes for which it
may be expended. State law spells out the financial procedures which
local governments must follow in levying and expending taxes and
in expending state and federal grants. Local taxes tap the same income stream as do state taxes and a substantial portion of local government revenue is received as grants from the state. Many services
provided by local government are complementary to or competitive
with those provided by the state.

Decisions made at one level influence and are influenced by decisions at the other. For example, increases in state school aids may
make it easier for local officials to avoid raising local taxes while
changes in school safety standards exert pressure in the opposite
direction. Legislators often make a choice between expanding state
programs and permitting or requiring expansion at the local level.
This choice, in turn, may be influenced by the adequacy with which
local programs have been supported in the past.

LOCAL EXPENDITURE

One of the most important facts about the relationship between
state and local finance is that local governments spend more money
than does the state. Local expenditure in 1965 was $2.5 billion as
compared with state expenditure of $1.9 billion, but almost $500

million of state expenditures were in the form of grants to local government. If these intergovernmental payments are excluded and only direct expenditures are considered, local government expenditures amounted to 63.9 per cent of total state and local expenditures.

Expenditure by Function and Type of Government

Another important fact about the relationship between state and local government expenditure is that some functions are performed almost entirely by local governments while other functions are shared by state and local governments. It is clear from Table 27 that func-

TABLE 27

STATE AND LOCAL GOVERNMENT DIRECT EXPENDITURE, BY LEVEL
OF GOVERNMENT AND FUNCTION, 1964–65

Function	Illinois		Local as Percentage of Total	
	State	Local	Illinois	U.S.
	(millions)			
Education	$ 328.1	$1,143.6	77.7%	78.4%
Local Schools	3.6	1,121.0	99.7	99.2
Institutions of Higher Education	292.6	22.6	7.2	10.3
Other	31.9	—	—	—
Highways	353.8	254.9	41.9	32.8
Public Welfare	279.0	98.0	30.0	52.5
Health and Hospitals	197.1	119.5	37.7	49.6
Police Protection	16.0	146.9	90.2	86.4
Fire Protection	—	68.0	100.0	100.0
Sewerage	—	97.2	100.0	100.0
Other Sanitation	—	45.4	100.0	100.0
Local Parks and Recreation	—	72.1	100.0	100.0
Financial Administration	23.3	28.7	55.1	52.3
General Control	20.7	65.3	75.9	77.2
Interest on General Debt	35.4	100.9	74.0	67.0
All Other General Expenditure	151.5	246.9	62.0	58.7
All Direct General Expenditure	1,404.9	2,487.6	63.9	64.9

Source: U.S. Bureau of the Census, *Governmental Finances in 1964–65* (Washington: U.S. Government Printing Office, 1967), pp. 34–35.

tions such as elementary and secondary education, police protection, fire protection, sewerage, and other sanitation are largely local functions.[1] In contrast, only one function, higher education, comes close to being purely a "state level" function.

[1] The 100 per cent figures for fire protection, sewerage, other sanitation, and local parks and recreation result from the way the U.S. Bureau of the Census defines the functions, and somewhat overstate the case, but, except in the case of parks and recreation, use of any reasonable alternative definition would result in relatively small changes.

The final two columns of Table 27 permit comparison of the distribution of expenditure between state and local governments in Illinois with that in the United States as a whole. They reveal that the distribution of total expenditure is very similar, but there is considerable difference for some individual functions. Local governments in Illinois make a higher proportion of highway expenditure and a lower proportion of public welfare and health and hospital expenditure than in the nation as a whole.

Within the local government sector, expenditures are made by many types of governmental units. Table 28 shows the distribution

TABLE 28

DISTRIBUTION OF ILLINOIS LOCAL EXPENDITURE, BY FUNCTION AND
TYPE OF GOVERNMENT, 1962

Function	Counties	Munici- palities	Town- ships	School Districts	Special Districts
		(per cent of total)			
Education	.1	—	—	99.9	—
Highways	32.0	56.7	11.3	—	—
Public Welfare	78.9	.8	20.3	—	—
Health and Hospitals	52.3	28.9	—	—	18.8
Police Protection	6.6	93.4	—	—	—
Fire Protection	—	92.4	—	—	7.6
Sewerage	—	38.0	—	—	62.0
Other Sanitation	.1	99.9	—	—	—
Local Parks and Recreation	10.5	16.4	—	—	73.1
Financial Administration	48.6	41.8	9.7	—	—
General Control	49.6	39.5	10.9	—	—
Interest on General Debt	9.7	32.5	.8	39.6	17.4
All Other General Expenditure	8.2	47.9	1.5	—	42.4
All Direct General Expenditure	11.6	31.4	2.3	39.7	15.0

Source: U.S. Bureau of the Census, *Government in Illinois, 1962* (Washington: U.S. Government Printing Office, 1964), p. 26.

among various types of local government in 1962.[2] Financially, the most important local government in Illinois is the school district. These districts, which are charged with the single function of maintaining elementary and secondary schools, make 99.9 per cent of

[2] Detailed local financial statistics are available only for the years for which a complete Census of Governments has been taken. 1962 is the last year available as this is written.

local education expenditure and almost 40 per cent of local expenditure for all purposes. Municipal governments, which make expenditure for every governmental function listed except education, are the second most expensive type of government. Municipalities have an especially important role in providing such services as police and fire protection and in maintaining streets and highways. Special districts are important providers of several types of governmental service. Sanitary districts make 62 per cent of the local expenditure for sewerage. Park or forest preserve districts make more than 73 per cent of local park and recreation expenditure. Public health districts are important in providing health and hospitals. Other special districts provide services ranging from the building and operating of airports to mosquito abatement.

Counties provide a great many general governmental services such as recording of documents and also serve as agencies of the state in many law enforcement activities. They play an important role in property tax administration. The bulk of county expenditures for public welfare, health, and hospitals was made by Cook County, which has been given more responsibility for administering public aid and related programs than downstate counties.

Townships are of little importance financially, although they do expend funds for road purposes, for general assistance, and for the salaries of township assessors.

Geographic Variation in Local Expenditure

One of the rationalizations for leaving expenditure decisions for local determination is that it permits expenditure programs to be tailored in response to variations in local conditions. Since few states vary as much in economic and demographic conditions as does Illinois, it would not be surprising to find that expenditure patterns differ greatly from one part of the state to another. In order to determine what variation does exist, 42 selected counties were divided into representative groups according to geographic and economic characteristics. Three of the five groups comprise counties which are predominately urban, one group is made up of counties in southern Illinois, and the final group is made up of prosperous agricultural counties in central and northern Illinois.[3]

Cook County (considered a "group") contains roughly one-half of

---

[3] The groups are the same as those used in an earlier study except that McHenry has been added to the list of suburban counties surrounding Cook County. See Glenn W. Fisher, "Illinois Local Finance, Geographic Variations," *Illinois Government*, No. 13 (April, 1962), entire issue.

the population of the state. It is an area of moderately increasing population, very high population density, and is almost entirely urbanized. Per capita income is higher than in any other group of counties and is about 50 per cent higher than the national average.

The five Chicago area suburban counties include areas of very rapid population growth and all are high income counties. All seven of the downstate urban counties have more than 70 per cent of their population living in urban places. Five of them have the major portion of their population in a single, isolated urban area.

The southern group consists of 16 counties in the extreme southern part of the state. It is an area of low income and declining population.

The 12 agricultural counties are characterized by heavy dependence upon agriculture as a source of income. Income is high as compared with other rural counties in the nation. They might be characterized as stable, prosperous, agricultural areas.

Table 29 shows the 1962 local government expenditure, by function, of these groups of counties. It reveals that Cook County gov-

TABLE 29

PER CAPITA LOCAL GENERAL EXPENDITURE, BY FUNCTION AND
COUNTY GROUP, 1962

Function	Cook	Chicago Suburban	Downstate Urban	Southern	Agri-cultural
Education	$ 90.48	$116.10	$102.55	$ 81.30	$117.87
Highways	27.64	16.67	18.56	17.95	27.08
Public Welfare	11.75	3.12	8.09	13.97	5.02
Health and Hospitals	11.63	6.29	5.77	10.84	5.97
Police Protection	20.36	7.27	6.38	4.12	5.27
Fire Protection	8.02	3.92	5.17	1.99	4.42
Sewerage	12.45	6.46	4.92	2.73	1.44
Other Sanitation	7.99	1.62	2.06	.36	.27
Parks and Recreation	12.18	3.70	5.90	1.57	2.84
Financial Administration	2.86	2.59	2.26	2.04	2.61
General Control	6.31	5.68	5.26	5.25	7.75
Interest on General Debt	12.86	7.54	8.04	4.64	4.65
All Other General Expenditure	39.79	12.38	18.13	13.26	8.89
Total General Expenditure	264.34	193.33	193.08	160.02	194.08

Source: U.S. Bureau of the Census, *Census of Governments, 1962*, VII, no. 13 (Washington: U.S. Government Printing Office, 1964), 43–52. Population estimates by Bureau of Business and Economic Research, University of Illinois.

ernments expended $264.34 per capita as compared with $160.02 in
the southern counties. The other groups have almost identical expenditures of about $193.00 per capita.

Variations in expenditures for particular functions are greater than
total variations and reveal a great deal about local government and
the demands upon it in different parts of the state. Cook County
governments spend heavily upon such "urban-type" services as parks,
sewerage, sanitation, fire protection, police protection, health and
hospitals, and public welfare. Cook also spends more for highways
than any other group.

Governments in the suburban counties spend heavily upon education. Police expenditure is far below that of Cook County but is
above that in other groups. Less is spent on some "urban-type" services such as fire protection, other sanitation, and parks than is spent
by downstate urban counties.

Agricultural counties are distinguished by heavy expenditures on
education and highways. In contrast, governments in the southern
counties spend heavily upon public welfare, health, and hospitals.
This is a reflection not of urban characteristics, but of the depressed
economic conditions in the area.

TABLE 30

LOCAL GOVERNMENT GENERAL EXPENDITURE, BY FUNCTION AND
COUNTY GROUP, AS PERCENTAGE OF PERSONAL INCOME, 1962

Function	Cook	Chicago Suburban	Downstate Urban	Southern	Agri-cultural
Education	$2.92	$4.01	$4.42	$ 5.37	$5.71
Highways	.89	.58	.80	1.18	1.31
Public Welfare	.38	.11	.35	.92	.24
Health and Hospitals	.38	.22	.25	.72	.29
Police Protection	.66	.25	.27	.27	.26
Fire Protection	.26	.14	.22	.13	.21
Sewerage	.40	.22	.21	.18	.07
Other Sanitation	.26	.06	.09	.02	.01
Parks and Recreation	.39	.13	.25	.10	.14
Financial Administra-tion	.09	.09	.10	.13	.13
General Control	.20	.20	.23	.35	.38
Interest on General Debt	.42	.26	.35	.31	.23
All Other	1.29	.43	.78	.88	.43
Total	8.54	6.68	8.32	10.56	9.41

Source: U.S. Bureau of the Census, *Census of Governments, 1962*, VII, no. 13 (Washington: U.S.
Government Printing Office, 1964), 43–52. Personal income estimates by Bureau of Business and
Economic Research, University of Illinois.

Table 30 shows expenditure of local governments in the county groups as a proportion of personal income. It reveals that governmental expenditure is a higher proportion of personal income in the southern counties than in any other group. Agricultural counties rank next highest and suburban counties spend the smallest portion of personal income for governmental services.

THE PROPERTY TAX

Table 31 reveals that the property tax plays a very important role in local finance. It provides 56.5 per cent of local government revenue and 72.5 per cent of the revenue which local governments receive from their own sources.[4]

TABLE 31

ILLINOIS STATE AND LOCAL GENERAL REVENUE, BY SOURCE, 1964–65

Source	State	Local	Local as Percentage of Total
	(millions)		
Taxes:			
Property	$ 1.5	$1,427.4	99.9%
Other	1,217.2	189.0	13.4
Charges and Miscellaneous	146.6	351.3	70.6
Total from Own Sources	1,365.3	1,967.7	59.0
Intergovernmental Revenue:			
From Federal Government	473.9	39.0	7.6
Other	8.2	521.3	—a
Total General Revenue	1,847.3	2,528.0	65.7

a Not computed because of duplication caused by local-local and local-state payments.

Source: U.S. Bureau of the Census, *Governmental Finances in 1964–65* (Washington: U.S. Government Printing Office, 1967), p. 31.

These figures do not express the full importance of the property tax in Illinois government finance. In the early history of the state, both state and local governments were financed almost entirely by property taxation. Since the early 1930's the state has turned to other sources of revenue and has provided increasing amounts of nonproperty tax revenue to local governments, yet the financial procedures of local government are still closely tied to property taxation. Tax and debt limits are expressed as percentages of assessed values. Local budgeting procedures, borrowing procedures, and even the choice

[4] "Own source" revenue excludes intergovernmental payments.

of a fiscal year are closely related to property taxation. Every proposal to make a major change in the state revenue system or to reorganize local governments has property tax implications, and the major program of state aid to local units involves a formula which has both assessed value and a tax rate among its terms.

The role of the property tax can best be understood in historical context. To understand how the idea of a uniform, universal, general property tax influenced tax policy-makers and to understand the pressures and administrative difficulties which have forced repeated departures from the ideal during the 150 years of Illinois statehood would be to understand much about Illinois tax politics and much about the present distribution of the tax burden in Illinois. The pages that follow sketch some of the main features of these developments.

Early History of the General Property Tax

Property taxes in the United States are generally referred to as *general* property taxes. The distinctive feature of a general property tax is that *all* property is valued uniformly and taxed at uniform rates. In practice, of course, there are many exceptions and qualifications, but the concept has played an important role in the history of the tax.[5] In Illinois this concept has had a crucial impact upon state and local taxation.[6]

The idea of taxing property can be traced back to the semi-feudal doctrine that all land belongs to the sovereign and that the actual users of the land can be required to pay a "quitrent" in order to be freed of the sovereign's claims.[7] In England the quitrent and other feudal charges evolved into the present system of "rates" which are based upon rental value of real property.

In colonial America property taxes were usually imposed only upon selected types of property which were taxed according to more or less arbitrary schedules of value with different rates applied to different types of property. The adoption of the federal constitution deprived states of custom duties and forced them to depend more heavily upon property taxation. As public expenditure rose, the need for more revenue resulted in a broadening of the tax base, but there were few constitutional requirements for uniform taxation in effect when the first Illinois Constitution was adopted. This document,

[5] Jens Peter Jensen, *Property Taxation in the United States* (Chicago: University of Chicago Press, 1931), p. 1.
[6] The Illinois Supreme Court clearly regards the Illinois Constitution as requiring uniform, universal taxation of property even though the wording is not as specific as it is in many states. See *Bachrach* v. *Nelson*, 349 Ill. 579 (1932).
[7] Jensen, *op. cit.*, pp. 19–20.

adopted in 1818, provides that: "The mode of levying a tax shall be by valuation so that every person shall pay a tax in proportion to the value of the property he or she has in his or her possession." This provision had little impact upon tax practice for at least 20 years. The tax law of 1819 merely modified the previous system of classification. Three types of property—land, bank stock, and Negro slaves —were singled out as the principal base of taxation, but a tax for county purposes could also be levied upon town lots, carriages, distilleries, stock-in-trade, and other personal property. Each taxpayer was to declare the land he owned and the class to which it belonged. The first class was valued at $4.00 per acre, the second at $3.00 per acre, and the third at $2.00 per acre. The tax rate for 1819 was fixed at five mills per dollar. Cities came into existence by special act of the legislature, and each municipal tax was authorized by special act which specified the purposes for which it could be spent and the property subject to valuation. Taxation for municipal purposes usually exempted the property from county taxation.[8]

This system of classification, with some modification, continued in effect until 1839. Apparently the question of squaring the practice with the constitutional provision was not raised. Probably few were aware of the implications of the constitutional requirement.[9]

The 1839 tax law moved the system into much closer conformity to the Constitution. It specified that both land and personal property should be assessed according to value and made the total value of taxable property the base for all state and local taxes.

In 1841 the legislature took a step away from taxation by value when a law was passed providing that no land was to be valued at less than $3.00 per acre. This provision was repealed in 1849.[10]

In 1843 wording was added which specifically stated that all real and personal property except certain enumerated exceptions was taxable.[11]

The Constitution of 1848 prescribed a property tax in the following language:

[8] *Ibid.*, pp. 46–47.
[9] *Ibid.*, p. 46.
[10] The reasons for the minimum valuation requirement are not entirely clear, but it is likely that the principal motive was to prevent extreme undervaluation of property. Assessors were also required to swear "particularly" that they would "in no instance value any land at three dollars an acre, that he, in his conscience, believes to be worth more." R. M. Haig, *A History of the General Property Tax in Illinois*, University of Illinois Studies in Social Science (Urbana: University of Illinois, 1914), p. 83.
[11] Nontaxable property included cemeteries, church property, property of literary societies, and governmental agencies.

The General Assembly shall provide for levying a tax by valuation, so that every person and corporation shall pay a tax in proportion to the value of his or her property; such value to be ascertained by some person or persons elected or appointed in such manner as the General Assembly shall direct and not otherwise; but the General Assembly shall have power to tax peddlers, auctioneers, brokers, hawkers, merchants, commission merchants, showmen, jugglers, inn-keepers, grocery keepers, toll bridges and ferries, and persons using and exercising franchises and privileges, in such manner as they shall from time to time direct.[12]

This clause marks no great departure from the theory of taxation then in effect except that the idea of uniform taxation by value was in conflict with the requirement for minimum valuation of land. This statutory provision was repealed the following year.

In 1853 the legislature adopted a new revenue code which was to remain in effect for 15 years without a single amendment of consequence. Furthermore, this act established the system of taxation which, in its essential elements, is in effect in Illinois today. The first section of the act specified the property to be taxed in these words:

That all property, whether real or personal, in this state; all moneys, credits, investments in bonds, stock, joint-stock companies, or otherwise, of persons residing in this state, or used or controlled by persons residing within this state; and the property of all banks, or banking companies, now existing or hereafter created, and of all bankers and brokers, except such property as is hereinafter expressly exempted, shall be subject to taxation; and such property, moneys, credits, investments in bonds, stocks, joint-stock companies or otherwise, or the value thereof, shall be entered on the list of taxable property, for that purpose, in the manner prescribed in this act.[13]

Real estate was defined to include buildings and improvements. Personal property was to include "every tangible thing being the subject of ownership, whether animate or inanimate, other than money and not forming part or parcel of real property." Money included bank deposits and cash on hand. "Credits" were defined as ". . . every claim or demand for money, labor, or other valuable thing, due or to become due, or every annuity or sum of money receivable at stated periods, and all money invested in property of any kind which is secured by deed, mortgage, or otherwise, which the person holding such deed or mortgage, or evidence of claim, is bound by any lease, contract or agreement, to reconvey, release, or assign, upon the payment of any specific sum or sums." [14]

Pensions were specifically excluded from this definition and provision was made for the deduction of all bona fide debts. No person

[12] *Constitution of 1848,* Article IX, Sec. 2.
[13] *Illinois Laws, 1853* as quoted in Haig, *op. cit.,* p. 100.
[14] *Ibid.*

was required to list any portion of credits that he believed to be uncollectible.

Shares of stock in companies which were required to pay taxes on property or capital stock within the state were not to be listed by the owners. Foreign (outstate) insurance companies were taxed at regular property tax rates upon gross receipts in the state. Merchants were assessed on the average value of their stock during the preceding year and manufacturers were assessed on the average value of materials. There were the usual exemptions for property used for educational, charitable, and governmental purposes.

The Theory of General Property Taxation

In order to put the historical development of the Illinois property tax in perspective, it is useful to turn from the historical chronology and examine the theory of general property taxation which greatly influenced thought on tax matters in the middle and later parts of the nineteenth century.

It may well be that movement from the system of arbitrary classification and taxation of specific items of property toward a general property tax levied upon all property by valuation, had its origins as much in the need for additional revenue as in theories of tax equality. There is no doubt, however, that the theory did develop and that it played an important role in later development of the Illinois tax system. This theory is based upon the idea that the value of property is a good measure of an individual's ability to support government or, alternatively, of his obligation to support government. During the formative period of American state tax systems, many scholars and men of affairs not only accepted the idea that the general property tax was a good tax, but believed that virtually all state and local tax revenue should be obtained from it.

Unfortunately, there are difficulties with such a theory. The most basic difficulty is that income, not wealth, is the proper basis for measuring the ability to pay taxes. For an individual or a nation, income is the annual product, the consumable increment which can be spent or consumed without reducing the stock of capital.[15] Taxes are the price of government and the services which it renders and can be more logically related to income than to wealth.

[15] In this brief statement it is not possible to define all terms with precision or to make a full statement of all the issues involved. It will be recognized, however, that the word "income" is used in a generic sense of "product" and not the technical definitions found in national income accounts or in tax laws. The word "wealth" is used to include both produced and natural means of production—land and capital to an economist. To use an old analogy, wealth is the tree and income is the fruit.

Apparently, early proponents of the general property tax believed that there was a constant relationship between wealth and income. If this were so, it would make little difference which is used as the tax base. The property tax would, in effect, be a flat rate income tax but the levy would be against property rather than income. Given the nature of the nineteenth century economy and the state of tax administration, this was clearly preferable to an attempt to tax income directly.

It is also probable that the relationship between income and wealth comes close to being constant in an agricultural economy such as the one which existed in the first years of Illinois statehood. An individual's income or product was probably closely related to the amount of land, livestock, and machinery he owned.[16] The relationship is less close in a specialized, industrialized economy. The product of tangible capital becomes more and more dependent upon the way it is organized into an integrated, productive system. Thus, the "going concern" value of a corporation may be far more or far less than the value of tangible capital owned. Many individuals acquire skills which are neither property nor wealth but which are the source of much earning power.

A second problem involves the definition of property. The legal concept of property as a "bundle of rights" is often very different from the economic concept of wealth. The quantity of property in a modern economy greatly exceeds the quantity of economic wealth since property includes not only the capital items such as machinery, but many intangible claims such as stocks, bonds, mortgages, and all manner of future or reversionary interests. A uniform tax upon all property, as the word is legally defined, would fall very unequally upon wealth, economically defined. Presumably the theory of the uniform general property tax contemplates a uniform tax upon wealth; provision must be made to eliminate the tax upon many intangible property rights. Not all intangible property rights can be freed from taxation since some intangible property, such as going concern value, represents wealth above the value of tangible wealth. Although the problem of taxing only economic wealth is not too difficult conceptually, administrative difficulties are greatly increased by "state line" problems. Intangible property rights relating to a

---

[16] From a temporal distance of well over 100 years it may be easy to overstate the closeness of the relationship. The list of occupations singled out for special taxation in the constitution of 1848 indicates that the writers felt that many persons would not pay their fair share of taxes under the property tax alone.

given piece of tangible wealth are often held by a large number of persons living outside the state in which the wealth is located, and many intangible property rights may constitutionally be taxed simultaneously in several states.

A final problem involves determining the valuation of the property. In the absence of an actual sale, value cannot be determined—it must be estimated. The property tax and the inheritance tax are the only major state or local taxes which have a subjectively determined base.

Later Developments in Property Taxation

Since 1853, Illinois has grown from a thinly populated agricultural state to one of the great industrial areas of the world. Chicago is the second largest city in the United States; large industrial plants are found in many of the smaller cities and, occasionally, amid the corn-fields of rural areas.

During this period there have been many changes in the laws governing property taxes, but none have changed the fundamental nature of the system. The constitution of 1870—still in effect—reaffirmed a commitment to the uniform general property tax as the major source of state and local revenue. The list of occupations which could be taxed in such maner as the General Assembly should direct was increased by the addition of liquor dealers, insurance, telegraph, and express interests, business vendors of patents, and corporations owning or using franchises or privileges. The exemption clause was made somewhat more specific.

Basically, the period was one of rapidly changing political and economic conditions and slowly changing constitutional and statutory law. The result was a number of adaptations, many of them extra-legal, which have resulted in a property tax system which differs greatly from that which the constitution writers of 1848 and 1870 envisaged. It is impossible to describe all of these adaptations but some of the most important ones are discussed here.

Taxation of Capital Stock The framers of the revenue law of 1872 recognized that part of the wealth of a business corporation is in the form of intangible value which cannot be reached by local assessors. In an attempt to solve this problem they established a system whereby the state board of equalization would assess the corporate excess (and other intangible property) of corporations chartered in the state.

The basic theory of the tax is simple. It is assumed that the total value of a corporation is the market value of its securities. If the locally assessed value of all tangible property is subtracted from this, the result is the value of all intangible assets including such items as good will or going concern value.

Unfortunately, statutory and administrative weaknesses plus inherent administrative difficulties prevented the capital stock tax from contributing to uniformity. Today it ranks as a principal exhibit in any attempt to prove that the Illinois property tax is neither uniform nor universal.

As early as 1875 the legislature weakened the law by providing that companies organized for manufacturing purposes, for the printing and publishing of newspapers, or for the improvement and breeding of stock were to be assessed by the local assessors rather than by the state board of equalization. Assessment of coal mining companies was delegated to local assessors in 1893. Professor Haig reports that these acts were generally construed as complete exemptions, even though the statutes provided for local assessment.[17] In 1905 the legislature went further and specifically exempted manufacturing and mercantile companies from the tax. This action was blocked by the state Supreme Court and assessment of these corporations was returned to the local assessors.

The law requires corporations to submit information concerning the amount of capital stock, its market value, the amount of funded debt, and the assessed value of local property, but neither the state's enforcement agencies nor local assessors have ever been given adequate power to verify this information from the corporation books or to require the submission of supporting information. As a result, reports were defective and dishonest from the beginning. Haig reports that in the first year of operation of the law many managers were under the impression that funded debt would be subtracted from the value of stock to determine the value of the corporation. As a result, this item was greatly inflated in many reports. Later, it was realized that debt is added to the value of the stock to determine the value of the corporation, and the debt item was reported at much lower amounts in later reports. Largely for this reason the net assessed value of capital stock declined from almost $21 million in 1873 to $11.7 million in 1874 and to $4.8 million in 1875.[18]

In 1899 and 1900 the Teachers' Federation of Chicago began an investigation of property tax administration as a result of an announcement by the Board of Education that revenue was not great

---

[17] Haig, op. cit., p. 201.
[18] Ibid., p. 205.

enough to permit a planned new salary scale to be put into operation. In Haig's words:

Looking about for a means of relief, the Teachers' Federation investigated revenue conditions and soon uncovered grave abuses in the assessment of property. The assessment of corporate excess by the state board of equalization was chosen as the most promising point of attack. Here a large increase of revenue could be hoped for without antagonizing the general public by an increase in the tax rates. The methods of the board were notoriously lax and the federation found little trouble in finding specific evidence of gross errors in assessment. Twenty-three public service corporations were chosen for attack in a test case. It was claimed by the teachers that the real value of the securities of these companies was $268,108,312. They were taxed on the merest fraction of this amount by the local assessors and yet most of them were assessed nothing at all on their corporate excess by the state board.[19]

Eventually the case reached the U.S. courts and the board of equalization was forced to raise assessments from less than $5 million to more than $21 million. Although there have been changes in the details of the law since that time, the main features are unchanged. The important features can be summarized as follows:[20]

1. The tax applies to all corporations organized under the laws of the state. In 1875 the Illinois Supreme Court said there was no doubt about the legislature's power to tax foreign corporations but that additional legislation would be required if such application was desired. Intangible personal property of foreign corporations which is legally located in the state and used in business transacted in the state is taxable.

2. Companies "organized for manufacturing and mercantile purposes, for the mining and sale of coal, for printing and publishing of newspapers, for breeding and improving livestock, and banks and savings and loan associations" are assessed by the local assessor. All other corporations are assessed by the Department of Revenue.

3. The value of the capital stock is listed for taxation in the district in which the principal office or place of business is located.

4. The Department of Revenue has power to adopt rules, not inconsistent with law, for ascertaining fair value.

5. When a person refuses to make out a personal property schedule, the assessor has the power to list property according to his best knowledge and judgment and to add a 50 per cent penalty to the valuation.

[19] *Ibid.*, pp. 206–7.
[20] Ruth A. Birdzell, "General Corporation Taxes," *Report of the Commission on Revenue* (Springfield, 1963), pp. 610–11.

Many local assessors lack the ability, motivation, and authority to administer the law so that it contributes to uniform taxation. A recent survey of local administration of the capital stock tax revealed that in 70 counties nothing or virtually nothing was being done toward local assessment.[21] Local assessors who were interviewed indicated that there were no corporations having capital stock, or that they didn't want to antagonize firms which were turning in "pretty good" values for personal property. One assessor believed that a corporation could never be worth more than its paid-in surplus, others simply did not know how to assess the tax.

In 32 counties local officials reported that they made an active effort to assess capital stock. Twenty-five of them used the same formula as the Department of Revenue, but in most counties the locally assessed capital stock assessments make up a very small portion of total property assessments.

The Department of Revenue is in a somewhat better position to make accurate assessments than are most local assessors, but the fact that the capital stock tax does not apply to foreign corporations prevents both the Department and local assessors from making adequate assessments. Ruth Birdzell explains the situation: "It sometimes happens that when the capital stock assessment begins to come near to a fair figure or even merely exceeds what the company is willing to pay, the corporation simply incorporates in another state, dissolves the Illinois corporation, and thereby avoids the tax altogether. Where such an outcome appears likely, the Department has to decide how far it can proceed toward the fair value of the corporate excess without prompting the firm to become a foreign corporation so that the entire value of its corporate excess is lost." [22]

When it is noted that the annual cost of maintaining an average size corporation in Delaware is often less than $150 per year and that such a corporation has all the privileges within the state that an Illinois corporation does, it is easy to see that powerful constraints are placed upon effective administration of the tax.

The one major exception to this conclusion involves public utility corporations, which must, by law, be incorporated in Illinois. As a result, public utility assessments make up a large share of the total capital stock assessments in the state. Ironically, public utilities probably have a far lower ratio of intangible to tangible property than do most other corporations.

[21] *Ibid.*, p. 617.
[22] *Ibid.*, p. 613.

Another oddity of capital stock taxation is that corporations have had a considerable amount of freedom in choosing the location of their principal office or place of business and thus the place at which the capital stock assessment will be taxed. The result is that several of the large public utilities have established "principal offices" in small rural counties with low tax rates. One telephone company has its general office in Bloomington, where the 1960 tax rate was about $3.00 per hundred, but maintains its principal office in Monticello where the rate was $.79. An electric power company with general offices in Decatur also has its principal offices in Monticello. The result is that Piatt County, in which Monticello is located, received 22 per cent of the assessed valuation made by the Department of Revenue. Adams County, Kane County, and Kankakee County also have large capital stock assessments as the result of a large utility having its principal office within the county.[23]

Assessment of Other Intangibles   The idea of taxing corporate excess is consistent with the theory of a uniform, universal, general property tax, even though in practice it has failed to contribute to uniformity. The attempt to tax other types of intangibles has also failed in practice and, in some cases, is defective in theory.

Intangibles which are legally taxable in Illinois include money, bank deposits, shares of stock, bonds, franchises, patents, copyrights, good will, capitalized earning power, notes, accounts receivable, accrued interest, annuities, royalties, and other credits. There is no statutory exemption for the intangibles of domestic corporations, but the value of these intangibles would automatically be included in the capital stock assessment if correctly computed. Debts may be deducted from "net credits" such as notes, mortgages, and accounts receivable.

Shares of stock in corporations that have had property assessed or taxed under the capital stock tax (domestic corporations) or that have had *any* property assessed or taxed within the state are exempt. This means that a corporation can protect its stockholders against the possibility of their shares being assessed by reporting any piece of tangible or intangible property, no matter how small. Interestingly, the exemption is not lost even if the tax resulting from the assessment is not paid by the corporation. The shares of several thousand foreign corporations are exempt under this provision. Other intangible property is exempt because of statutory and constitutional provisions regarding charitable, religious, and governmental organizations.

[23] *Ibid.,* p. 615.

Clearly, the provisions regarding the taxation of intangibles are not in conformity with the theory of general property taxation. Many of the intangibles which are legally subject to taxation are claims against tangible property which has been taxed in Illinois or in other states. Other intangibles might logically be taxed but present very difficult administrative problems. For example, it would be almost impossible to assess currency, and attempts to assess bank accounts result in large sums being moved to out-of-state banks just before assessment day. Assessment of many intangibles at full value would, at existing tax rates, confiscate the value of the property.[24]

Both the theoretical and administrative weaknesses of an attempt to tax intangibles have been discussed elsewhere.[25] It is sufficient to say here that both tax administrators and the general public regard taxation of intangibles as unfair and impossible and that very little intangible property is assessed for taxation. Although it has been estimated that the amount of intangible property which is legally subject to taxation is at least equal to the amount of tangible property, intangibles make up only 2.7 per cent of total assessed valuation and over one-half of that is made up of state-assessed capital stock.[26]

Assessment of Tangible Property The theory of the general property tax requires that all property be uniformly assessed at its true or market value. Illinois statutes state: "(1) Each tract or lot of real property shall be valued at its fair cash value, estimated at the price it would bring at a fair, voluntary sale." [27]

The provisions dealing with various kinds of personal property vary slightly in wording but all make reference to fair cash value, current price, or some similar concept.

Assessed value is determined by a local assessor. In township coun-

---

[24] Economists sometimes argue that it is impossible to confiscate the value of property by ad valorem taxation. The argument is that the value of an intangible is determined by its after-tax earning power. The imposition of an ad valorem tax would reduce its value and thus would require a lower assessment. Eventually, equilibrium would be reached at a figure more than zero. This argument is not applicable in an open economy where taxes vary from state to state. For example, if an intangible yielding 4 per cent of its face value is taxed at a 4 per cent rate in Illinois, the value does not fall appreciably in a national market. The owner would have a strong incentive to sell the security to someone not taxable by Illinois and invest the proceeds where the tax could be passed on or avoided.

[25] H. K. Allen, "General Property Tax," *Report of the Commission on Revenue* (Springfield, 1963), pp. 454–91.

[26] Illinois Department of Revenue, Property Tax Division, *Illinois Property Tax Statistics*, 1964, p. 119.

[27] *Ill. Rev. Stat.*, ch. 120, sec. 501 (1965).

ties there are elected assessors in every township. In about half of these there is also an appointed supervisor of assessors who aids and advises the township assessors. In the 17 commission counties the county treasurer is also the assessor unless the county board appoints an assessor. St. Clair County has an elected board of assessors and Cook County has an elected assessor.

In every county there are boards of review charged with correcting assessor errors and hearing taxpayer appeals. In counties with township assessors there are boards of equalization which have power to make changes in the assessments of a township in order to insure that each township is assessed at the same level. The state Department of Revenue has the power to make county-wide changes in order to equalize the level of assessment among counties.

Examination of statistical evidence concerning the quality of assessment indicates that, in practice, assessments are far from uniform. Table 32 provides evidence of the poor quality of assessment of single-family, nonfarm houses in 19 of the larger counties and in the

TABLE 32

INDICATORS OF THE LEVEL AND UNIFORMITY OF ASSESSMENT
OF NONFARM HOUSES, SELECTED COUNTIES, 1961

County	Median Assessment Ratio	Coefficient of Dispersion from Median
Champaign	47.3%	21.8%
Cook	37.2	26.1
Chicago	34.3	32.4
DuPage	53.3	16.9
Kane	47.5	19.2
Knox	51.7	28.0
Lake	51.8	16.2
LaSalle	48.5	15.1
McHenry	54.1	30.1
McLean	50.2	13.7
Macon	44.6	32.3
Madison	49.6	22.4
Peoria	45.6	31.6
Rock Island	44.8	24.1
St. Clair	53.4	33.5
Sangamon	45.7	24.5
Tazewell	57.6	28.8
Whiteside	46.5	36.3
Will	38.6	26.7
Winnebago	52.4	21.6

Source: U.S. Bureau of the Census, *Census of Governments, 1962*, II (Washington: U.S. Government Printing Office, 1963), 142–43.

city of Chicago. These measures of uniformity were computed by the U.S. Bureau of the Census from data obtained by comparing sales prices in bona fide, arms-length sales with the assessed values of the same properties. Column 1 of the table shows the median ratio of assessed tax value to sales price. If the statutory directive to assess all property at its full value were followed, these ratios would all be 100 per cent. Actually, they vary from 34.3 per cent in the city of Chicago to 57.6 per cent in Tazewell County.

The second column shows the coefficient of dispersion from the median ratio for each county. This coefficient is the percentage by which the assessments in the sample differ, on the average, from the median assessment ratio.[28] In other words, if a county has a median assessment ratio of 50 per cent, a coefficient of dispersion of 20 per cent means that individual assessments differ from the median by an average of 10 percentage points (20 per cent of 50).

In recent years it has been common to accept a coefficient of dispersion of 20 per cent or less as a "good" assessment. Examination of Table 32 reveals that only four counties achieved this goal in 1961. To further put these data in perspective, however, it is important to note two additional facts. The first point is that the "acceptable" 20 per cent coefficient of dispersion represents a degree of variation that would be considered intolerable in the administration of most other taxes. Who would say that sales or income tax administration was "good" if the average taxpayer payment varied from the amount legally due by an average of 20 per cent? The second point is that "single-family, nonfarm houses" is probably the easiest class of tangible property to assess correctly. It has not been possible to collect sales-assessment ratio data for many kinds of property because sales are so infrequent. Undoubtedly, if it were possible to measure the quality of assessment of these kinds of property, it would be revealed to be far worse than is the assessment of single-family houses.

Very little data regarding the quality of assessment of tangible personal property exists, but it is well known that such assessment is often haphazard and falls most heavily upon easily visible property. Commonly, household goods and personal effects are valued by rough rule-of-thumb methods. In many counties of the state, automobile registration lists are checked and automobiles are assessed at some fraction of "bluebook" prices. In rural areas, farm machinery

---

[28] Computed by measuring the difference between the median assessment ratio and each of the individual ratios, adding these differences (disregarding plus or minus signs), dividing this sum by the number of items, dividing this result by the median assessment ratio, and multiplying by 100.

and livestock are often assessed according to a schedule which is roughly related to current market prices. Industrial machinery and inventories make up a substantial portion of tangible personal property assessment,[29] but rarely are these assessments based upon scientific appraisal methods. Rarely, for example, do assessors determine inventory valuation by examining the taxpayers' books or utilize the services of a valuation engineer familiar with the kinds of machinery being assessed.

De Facto Classification in Cook County The examples already cited have made it clear that the uniformity clause has not produced uniform or universal property taxation. Only in Cook County, however, has the departure taken the form of an admitted policy of classification.

When J. L. Jacobs was appointed Cook County Assessor in 1931, he reorganized the system of classification which was in effect. Since that time various classes of intangibles have been assessed at different percentages of true value, and ordinary household goods and personal effects have been considered to have no market value and thus are not assessed. Personal automobiles are ordinarily not assessed in Chicago but they may be in other parts of Cook County.

Real estate classification has been achieved by adjusting the values and formulas in the *Assessors' Manual* rather than by public announcement of the specific percentage ratio used for particular classes of property. It is possible, however, to calculate the percentages at which the various classes are assessed, on the average, by using the results of sales ratio studies conducted by the Department of Revenue. Table 33 shows the median assessment ratios for 16 classes of property in Chicago and Cook County.[30] This table clearly shows that single-family homes and small apartments are given favorable treatment as compared with large industrial businesses and commercial properties. Large apartment buildings seem to occupy an intermediate position.

Downstate there is no system of classification comparable to that in Cook County, but it is not uncommon for specific properties or groups of property to receive special treatment. It is difficult to generalize since the details vary from place to place, but it appears that

[29] In 1964 machinery and equipment (including farm machinery) made up 43.2 per cent of the assessed value of tangible personal property. Merchandise, goods on hand, and goods in process made up 18.8 per cent. Illinois Department of Revenue, Property Tax Division, *loc. cit.*
[30] Most of the 16 classes shown are combinations of two or more of the classes used in the *Assessors' Manual.*

in the downstate area special concessions are much more likely to be given to business and industrial property—just the reverse of the situation in Cook County.

TABLE 33

ASSESSMENT RATIOS, BY TYPE OF REAL PROPERTY,
CHICAGO AND COOK COUNTY, 1962

| | Median Assessment | |
Type of Property	Chicago	Cook County Total
Cottages and bungalows	24%	26%
Split-levels, 1 and 2 story modern residences, modern row houses	28	28
Old style residences	22	22
Old style, 2 story 2-flat and 4-flat	19	19
Modern apartments, not over 6-flat	28	28
One story stores, super-markets, shopping centers	38	36
Old style stores, loft and apartment buildings	28	28
Modern stores, offices, and apartment buildings	45	44
One story, nonfireproof public garages	38	38
Gasoline stations	38	34
Vacant—no buildings	21	20
Private garages, shacks, and garlows	21	21
Nonfireproof hotels and apartments (over 6-flat), motels	46	45
Factories, warehouses, quonset buildings, other industrial	56	49
Department stores, large offices, mercantile and loft buildings, and public garages	58	57
Hotels, theaters, clubs, lodges, hospitals, large apartment buildings (fireproof)	—	—
Bank buildings (not over 4 stories), real estate offices, and other types not otherwise classified	—	41

Source: Illinois Department of Revenue, Property Tax Division, *Property Tax Statistics, 1964.*

Railroad Assessment The problem of assessing railroads illustrates several of the most difficult aspects of taxing complex industrial properties. Because of the shift to other means of transportation, railroads own many facilities which would probably not be built today. Some of these facilities would be worth more if railroads were permitted to discontinue services and sell them for other purposes; others have little value for any purpose. Some branch lines appear to contribute little to the company's profit but may contribute indirectly by feeding traffic into more profitable main lines. As a result of these factors, appraisal methods based upon a cost approach may yield results far different than do methods based upon an income approach. The sales approach can be used only to the extent that the total market value of the corporation's securities can be consideerd to represent a sale price.

The problem would be even more difficult if the local assessor were required to assess that small portion of a railroad lying within his district. Consequently, Illinois has long followed the general practice of assessing railroads at the state level and apportioning the value to the local unit on the basis of mileage. Thus, railroads are appraised at the state level by an expert appraiser who specializes in assessing railroad property, but are taxed locally along with property assessed by a local assessor. In view of the pressure to keep assessments low which is felt by a local assessor, it is alleged that the situation almost guarantees that railroads will be assessed at a higher percentage of value than will local property.

In the 1950's Illinois railroads began a long court battle to obtain relief from such discrimination.[31] In three cases the railroad attack centered upon the methods used by the Department of Revenue. All these cases were lost by the railroads, but out of them came the tactic which was to enable them to win in the 1960's. This was to prove constructive fraud by showing that railroad property was subject to discriminatory assessments as compared with locally assessed property.

This tactic had its first success in *People* ex rel. *Hillison* v. *C. B. & Q. Railroad*.[32] The state Supreme Court upheld the lower court's finding that the road was assessed by the Department at 100 per cent of full, fair cash value while locally assessed property was at no more than 55 per cent of full value and that such a differential constitutes constructive fraud. In making this finding, the court accepted sales-assessment ratio studies conducted by the state and by the U.S. Bureau of the Census as evidence of the level of local assessment.

In another case, decided the same day, an attempt to prove that the railroad's property was also assessed at less than the statutory 100 per cent was turned down by the courts after the railroad called expert witnesses from the Department of Revenue to testify that they were assessing at the statutory 100 per cent of full value.[33]

Several other cases confirmed the use of the doctrine of construc-

---

[31] For a more complete description of these cases see Leo Cohen, "Recent Railroad Tax Litigation and the Valuation of Railroads," *Proceedings of the National Tax Association, 1965*, pp. 183–87.

[32] 22 Ill. 2d 88 (1961).

[33] *People* ex rel. *Kohorst* v. *G. M. & O.*, consolidated with *People* ex rel. *Kohorst* v. *Chicago & N. W.*, 22 Ill. 2d 104 (1961).

tive fraud and the validity of sales-assessment ratio studies, and the 1963 legislature, in effect, affirmed the court's holding by adding the following language to the statutes: "The Department shall determine the equalized assessed value of the property of every railroad company, other than non-carrier real estate, by applying to its determination of the fair cash value of such property of every railroad company an equalization factor, which factor shall be the statewide average ratio of the equalized assessed value of locally assessed property to the full, fair cash value of such locally assessed property." [34]

Other issues were unsuccessfully raised against the railroad's position in later cases. The circuit court of Cook County denied the railroad's claim for a refund when the State's Attorney made the argument that railroad property was not, in fact, assessed at 100 per cent of value. Evidence included comparisons of assessed values with the prices of small pieces of railroad property sold during the period 1947–61. The state Supreme Court rejected this claim on the ground that several of the transactions were between related corporations. There is reason to believe that Cook County authorities gave serious consideration to arguing this case on the grounds that railroad properties are not overassessed in relation to other *industrial* properties in Cook County. Such an argument might well have changed the outcome of the case, but having such evidence on the court record might have invited litigation by owners of industrial property which could upset the entire Cook County classification scheme.

Relation of the State to Local Units

Since 1932 the property tax has been entirely a local tax. However, every detail of property taxation continues to be affected by the great volume of statutory and case law, much of which goes far back into the history of the tax. Many of these provisions are so detailed that local government officials and local citizens find it difficult to understand the process. The following examples illustrate the situation.

Tax Calendar   The administrative cycle of the property tax takes almost two years to complete.[35] The county clerk begins the process by preparing the real property assessment books during November and December. These books are supplied to the assessing officials

---

[34] *Ill. Rev. Stat.*, ch. 120, sec. 561 (1965).
[35] For an illustrated explanation of the entire cycle see Thomas Page, "Administrative Cycle of the Illinois Property Tax," *Illinois Government*, No. 8 (1960), entire issue.

who are to value real property as of January 1 of quadrennial years. Between January 1 and June 1 in these years, real estate is assessed and the values are entered on the books. Between April 1 and June 1 of every year, personal property is assessed. The board of review convenes in June and the revised books are returned to the county clerk on dates that vary from September 7 to December 31, depending upon the population of the county.

During this same period of time, the various local units are levying, in dollar amounts, the taxes needed for the year. The exact date on which the levy must be made varies, but it is noteworthy that many units of government make the levy for a fiscal year which has already begun.

The Department of Revenue certifies the value of state-assessed property within each taxing unit and also the multiplier (equalization factor) to be applied to the local assessed values. The county clerk then has the information necessary to compute the tax rate which applies to each piece of property and to compute the tax bills. These are mailed, usually in April. The first installment of real estate taxes becomes delinquent on May 1 in Cook County and on June 1 downstate. The second installment of real estate taxes becomes delinquent on September 1. In October the process of obtaining tax judgments, which eventually leads to the sale of delinquent property, begins.

From the viewpoint of the local government unit this entire cycle is far too long. Many units of government complete their fiscal year before any taxes levied for that year are collected. They must finance the year's operations by selling tax anticipation warrants or by maintaining a working cash revolving fund. Accounting is complicated and it is almost impossible for the average citizen to understand which year's budget is supported by a particular tax payment. Public confusion is further compounded by the fact that the tax bill, which arrives a few months after the assessor's visit, is based on the previous year's assessment.

Appropriation and Levy Ordinances State law spells out certain procedures which must be followed if tax levies are to be valid. Although there is considerable variation in the requirements for the various local governments,[36] there is usually a requirement that the tax levy be preceded by the passage of a tax levy ordinance or a budget. In many cases these ordinances must be itemized in great detail. Generally the line-item format is required. This method of presentation puts the emphasis upon a detailed statement of what

[36] Ann H. Elder, "Effects of Budgeting by Local Governments in Illinois," *Illinois Government*, No. 19 (1967), entire issue.

items will be purchased, rather than upon the services which will be provided or the efficiency of performance. Failure to follow statutes or case law with regard to details of levy procedure and the format of ordinance can become the basis for a tax protest.[37]

Administrative Assistance to Local Governments Although state law is the basis of detailed procedures which must be followed, the state provides a minimum amount of supervision and assistance to local governments in property tax matters. The Property Tax Division of the Department of Revenue does prepare an assessor's manual and also conducts one-day assessors' meetings in various parts of the state before each assessing season. This Division has never been given the personnel or the authority to provide continuing, detailed help to local assessors or to make binding regulations and rulings on property tax and other local fiscal matters. Even statistical services have been minimal. In 1963 the Department did resume publication of a mimeographed volume, *Illinois Property Tax Statistics,* which gives information on tax rates and assessed valuations of local government units in the state. This volume also contains a county-by-county breakdown of the tax base. Unfortunately, the categories utilized reflect the agricultural past rather than the industrial present. The personal property breakdown, for example, provides data on the assessed value of swine (.08 per cent of the total assessed value of real and personal property), but lumps together all industrial and agricultural machinery (5.58 per cent of the total assessed value). The statistics on the assessed value of real estate are even less useful. The principal classifications—unimproved lands and lots, improved lands and lots, and improvements—tell almost nothing about the nature of the property.

The resulting lack of information about the nature of the Illinois property tax base has not only handicapped local government planning, but, as is explained in Chapter 6, it has had an important impact upon state tax decisions.

Tax Limitation and Equalization In contrast to the passive, but important, role which the state plays in many areas of local finance is the very active role which the state plays in property tax limitation and equalization.

The state statutes authorize each type of local government to levy taxes for a great number of special purposes or "funds." [38]

---

[37] Glenn W. Fisher and Robert P. Fairbanks, "The Politics of Property Taxation," *Administrative Science Quarterly,* 12, no. 1 (June, 1967), 48–71.

[38] Sometimes the statutes direct the establishment of a fund into which the tax

Municipalities, for example, are authorized to levy for more than 40 funds. In almost every case the state also prescribes the maximum rate which may be levied for a particular purpose or fund.[39] Dissatisfaction arose in the early 1940's because wide differences in the level of assessment from district to district meant that tax limits restricted some governmental units much more severely than others. Also, the failure of assessing officials to raise assessed values as fast as the market value of property rose meant that many local districts had difficulty meeting the rising cost of government.

In 1945 the General Assembly passed legislation, known as the Butler Bills, directing the Department of Revenue to equalize assessments at full value. Since it was believed that this would double the assessed valuation of the state, legislation was also passed which halved all statutory rate limits. However, in a few counties assessments averaged more than 50 per cent of true value, and in many they were well below 50 per cent. The results of these provisions would have been to decrease the permitted levies in those counties in which assessments were more than 50 per cent and to increase the permitted levies in those in which assessments averaged less than 50 per cent of true value. To protect both taxpayers and governmental units from abrupt changes, the legislature devised a transitional formula for determining rate limits for a five year period. Confusion immediately arose concerning the interpretation of this formula. The interpretation of the Illinois Supreme Court was not acceptable to the 1947 General Assembly, which revised the formula and extended the transition period for two additional years.

Although designated as a transition formula, the 1947 formula did not contain any "transit" provisions, and it had the effect of freezing many of the nonuniformities which the Butler Bills had been designed to correct in the first place. At the expiration of the "transition" period the legislature was still unwilling to allow the statutory rates to go into effect, and legislation was passed which had the general effect of freezing limits then in effect.

The entire tax limit program has been the subject of great confusion and uncertainty. There have been many amendments and

is paid and out of which expenditures for a given purpose are made. In other cases the statutes merely state that a tax levy for a particular purpose is permitted. In these cases it is common for accountants to establish a separate fund to insure that the monies collected are used properly.

[39] Major exceptions include bond service funds and employee retirement funds which do not have rate limits but whose levy is fixed in the bond agreement or by state statutes. Limits for major Cook County governments are in dollar amounts (pegged levies). There is no limit on the Chicago corporate fund.

much litigation.[40] School districts have been freed of most of the "formula" provisions but municipalities, townships, and counties are still subject to them. A study of municipal tax rate limits in 1964 and 1965 revealed that many officials concerned with municipal finance are uncertain as to what rate limits apply.[41] The equalization program has promoted equalization among counties and undoubtedly has kept the level of assessment higher than it would otherwise be. However, the data in Table 32 shows that county average assessment levels are far from uniform and far from 100 per cent.[42]

State-local relationships in the equalization program differ from those in many areas of state-local fiscal relations in that there is continuous administrative action on the part of a state agency. By raising or lowering the "multiplier" assigned to a county, the state Department of Revenue can change the amount of revenue which local governments can legally raise from property taxation and also affect the amount of aid payable under the equalization formula.

The Tax Rate Limit Commission   The 1965 legislature established the Commission to Study Full-Value Assessments and Tax Rate Limitations. This commission was composed of six persons experienced and knowledgeable in the field of local finance. It was chaired by Senator W. Russell Arrington, President Pro Tem of the Senate, and much technical assistance was provided by Mr. Maurice Scott, Executive Secretary of the Taxpayers' Federation of Illinois, who was also a member of the commission. This commission heard many witnesses and presented a comprehensive series of recommendations intended to improve property tax administration and to reduce inequities in the tax limitation program. These recommendations called for a great expansion in state assistance to local property tax administrators, for improved assessment appeals procedures, for mandatory county supervisors of assessment, and for consolidation of smaller townships. It was recommended that tax rate limits of many major funds be set at a point near the median of existing rates but that a "grandfather clause" be utilized to permit existing higher limits to remain in effect. Such action raises the tax rate limit on funds presently below that figure and relieves administrators of the problem of determining and defending the rate limit set by formulas or ref-

[40] For a detailed description see Glenn W. Fisher and Robert P. Fairbanks, *Illinois Municipal Finance* (Urbana: University of Illinois Press, 1968), Ch. 4.
[41] *Ibid.*
[42] For an examination of some of the political and technical factors involved in assessment administration, see Fisher and Fairbanks, "Politics of Property Taxation," pp. 48–71.

erenda some time in the past. Funds having a higher limit are un-affected.

Most of the recommendations providing for expanding state as-sistance and those dealing with tax rate limits were enacted and signed by the Governor well before the end of the session. Those dealing with township consolidation and requiring the appointment of supervisors of assessment were defeated as a result of opposition from local officials.

NONPROPERTY TAX REVENUES

Local government revenues from sources other than property taxes are of three types: nonproperty taxes, intergovernmental grants, and charges and miscellaneous revenue.

Nonproperty Taxes

About 95 per cent of the nonproperty taxes levied by Illinois local government are received by municipalities. Most of the remainder are received by county governments.

The principal source of the nonproperty tax revenue of munici-palities is the sales tax supplement described briefly in Chapter 2. Almost all municipalities in the state impose this tax at the maximum rate.[43] It is collected by the state and the proceeds are returned to the municipal government. A study of the finances of the 41 largest municipalities revealed that revenue from this source in 1962 ranged from a low of $3.73 per capita in Calumet City to a high of $11.38 in Kankakee.[44] In the average city in this group, general sales tax revenue amounted to about one-third as much as did property tax revenue. In a few smaller cities with large shopping centers, the general sales tax provided a much larger proportion of total tax revenue.

Municipalities are also empowered to license motor vehicles owned by residents. This tax, popularly known as the wheel tax, is levied by a majority of larger municipalities and by many smaller ones. In Chicago fees upon not-for-hire passenger vehicles are limited to $15.00 and $30.00, depending on horsepower. In other municipalities the limits are $10.00 and $20.00.

Wheel tax receipts must be utilized for paving and repairing or maintaining streets and other public roadways except that munici-

[43] The maximum was raised from .5 per cent to .75 per cent by the 1967 legis-lature. As this is written, it appears that most cities will impose the new maxi-mum rate.
[44] Fisher and Fairbanks, *Illinois Municipal Finance*, pp. 139–40.

palities of more than 3,000 population may use up to 35 per cent of the gross receipts for the salaries of traffic policemen, and municipalities of more than 40,000 population may use the funds for constructing and operating vehicle testing stations. Wheel taxes are administered locally and evidence of payment is a numbered decal affixed to the windshield of the vehicle.

Another source of municipal government revenue is business occupation taxes. Liquor licenses are by far the most lucrative of these, but licenses granted to other businesses provide considerable revenue to many municipalities.

Taxes upon public utilities are growing in importance as a source of municipal revenue. These taxes take two forms. Franchise fees are sometimes paid to the municipality by privately owned utilities in exchange for the right to use public streets and alleys. These are usually established in long term agreements—called franchises—between the city and the utility company. Franchise fees are collected by relatively few Illinois cities but have been a substantial source of revenue for a few cities with favorable agreements.

A more important form of utility taxation is the tax upon sales of utility services. Since 1955 municipalities have been permitted to levy a tax at rates up to 5 per cent of gross receipts upon messages originating in the city or upon the consumption or use of gas, electricity, and water within the city limits. Chicago levied the tax immediately, but other cities were slow to follow. In 1964 only 48 municipalities, many of them small, levied the tax. Since that time the tax has spread more rapidly and a number of municipalities, including several of the larger Chicago suburbs, have adopted the tax.

Intergovernmental Revenue

Local governments are receiving increasingly large grants directly from the federal government, but by far the largest part of intergovernmental grants received by local governments are from the state.[45] Table 31 revealed that intergovernmental revenue from the federal government amounted to $39.0 million in fiscal 1965 and that revenue from other sources amounted to $521.3 million. Table 34 provides a more detailed breakdown of the $496 million which the Illinois state government paid to local government.[46]

[45] Some federal grants are routed through state government, but most state grants in Illinois are paid from state tax funds.
[46] The difference between the $521.3 million of Table 31 and the $496 million in Table 34 is accounted for by local-local payments and possible discrepancies resulting from the fact that the fiscal years of some local governments represented in Table 31 are not identical with the state's 1965 fiscal year.

TABLE 34

STATE GRANTS TO LOCAL GOVERNMENT, BY TYPE OF RECEIVING GOVERNMENT
AND FUNCTION, 1965

	Amount	Percentage of Total
	(thousands)	
By Type of Government:		
Counties	$ 79,660	16.1%
Municipalities	63,353	12.8
School Districts	289,720	58.4
Townships	16,589	3.3
Special Districts	3,518	.7
Other and Unallocated	43,202	8.7
Total	496,042	100.0
By Function:		
Education	291,741	58.8
Highways	127,751	25.8
Public Welfare	68,355	13.8
All Other	8,195	1.7
Total	496,042	100.0

Source: U.S. Bureau of the Census, *Compendium of State Government Finances in 1965* (Washington: U.S. Government Printing Office, 1966), p. 38.

Educational Grants   Well over half of the state's grants to local government are for educational purposes. The bulk of the money involved is paid from the Common School Fund.

Payments from the Common School Fund can be divided into two classes. The first class of payments has priority over all other claims and is sometimes designated as "prior claims." It consists of:

1. Contributions to the Chicago teachers' retirement fund.

2. Contributions to downstate teachers' retirement.

3. Salaries of county superintendents and their assistants.

4. Supervisory expense fund ($1,000 per county per year).

5. Orphans' tuition

6. Grants to districts in lieu of taxes on state-owned property (including state-owned student housing).

7. Military encampment claims (supplemental to federal payments to school districts adversely affected by military installations).

The School Problems Commission estimated these claims for the 1965–67 biennium to be $122 million, of which more than 80 per cent were for the retirement funds.[47]

[47] School Problems Commission No. 8, *Illinois School Problems* (Springfield, 1965), p. 69.

The "distributive" portion of common school payments consists of flat grants, equalization grants, and summer school grants. Flat grants are paid at the rate of $47.00 per pupil in average daily attendance in elementary school districts and in districts maintaining grades 1 through 12. High school districts are paid at a rate of $54.05 per pupil. Equalization grants are computed under a formula which is intended to insure that every district which makes a reasonable effort will be provided the funds needed to make certain "equalization level" expenditure possible. The formula for an elementary or non-high school district can be expressed as follows:

$$G = E - (QA + \$47.00)$$
where   G = Equalization grant per child
        E = Equalization level per child
        Q = Qualifying tax rate
        A = Assessed value per child

The 1967 legislature set the qualifying rate at .84 per cent for elementary school districts and 1.00 per cent for school districts maintaining grades 1 through 12. High school districts have a .84 per cent qualifying rate and have a 1.15 weight added to their total attendance figures. The equalization level was set at $400 per child.

Computation of the equalization grant for a district maintaining grades 1 through 12 with an average assessed value of $25,000 per child would be as follows:

$$G = \$400.00 - (.01 \times \$25,000 + \$47.00) = \$103.00$$

The School Problems Commission has the responsibility of providing the legislature with an estimate of the amount that will be needed in the Common School Fund each biennium. The statutes provide that "prior claim" items are to be paid in full from the amounts appropriated into the Common School Fund. "Distributive claims" are to be scaled down if the fund balance is not sufficient to pay claims in full. In recent biennia, however, the legislature has made supplemental appropriations, when necessary, to permit payment in full.

In the postwar period there have been frequent changes in the equalization level and the qualifying rate. The net effect of these changes has been to raise state grants from 13 per cent of the cost of school operation in the 1943–45 biennium to 24 per cent in the 1963–65 biennium.[48] The increase has not been continuous, however.

[48] School Problems Commission No. 9, *Illinois School Problems* (Springfield, 1967), p. 58.

State grants were 24.9 per cent of cost in the 1959–61 biennium and dropped to 24.0 in the following two biennia.

It is important to note the close connection between the equalization formula and intercounty property tax equalization. In the absence of state property taxation, the principal reason for intercounty property tax equalization is to achieve a fair distribution of school funds. Taxpayers in a county with a low assessment ratio would gain at the expense of those in a county with a higher ratio since the yield of the qualifying rate would be lower and the equalization grant higher than it would otherwise be. This would provide a great incentive for local assessing authorities to assess at a small fraction of real value and would lead to competitive undervaluation among assessing officials.

The state legislature can change the distribution of school costs between state and local governments by changing the amount of flat grants or by changing the equalization formula. The Department of Revenue can achieve the same result by changing the general level at which property assessments are equalized.

Other educational grants received by school districts include others administered by the Superintendent of Public Instruction. These include pupil transportation and special programs for the gifted, adult education, and driver education. The Superintendent also administers programs under the Federal Civil Defense Act, National Defense Education Act, and the school lunch and school milk programs which involve the grant of federal funds to local units.

Highway Grants After the payment of refunds, administrative costs, and fixed sums into the Grade Crossing and Protection Fund and the Boating Act Fund, the proceeds of the motor fuel tax are distributed as follows:

State Road Fund	35%
Municipalities	32%
Counties other than Cook	12%
Cook County	11%
Townships and road districts	10%

The statutes specify the purposes for which these funds may be utilized by the local governments and require that the Division of Highways approve plans and specifications before bids can be advertised and contracts let. The statutory authorizations are quite generous in that expenditure can be for a wide variety of purposes related to the construction and maintenance of streets and highways or for the repayment of bonds issued for an approved project. Al-

most every session of the legislature adds to the list of permitted
expenditures. There has, however, been much dissatisfaction with
the cost and delay resulting from the paperwork required by the
Division of Highways.[49]

Funds remain in the state treasury until released to pay for a specific approved project. Since many local governments prefer to construct one major project every few years rather than to spend its
allotment every year, many units of local government accumulate
sizable balances. The action of the 1961 legislature in borrowing
from motor fuel tax funds for state purposes created concern among
local governments that this would create a precedent which might
lead to larger transfers and perhaps eventual failure to repay. It
also focused attention upon the fact that local governments receive
no interest on "their funds" from the time of allotment to expenditure.

Motor fuel tax funds make up a substantial part of the revenue
expended for street and highway purposes by local units of government in Illinois. For 1962 the U.S. Bureau of the Census reported
that Illinois local governments spent $247 million for street and
highway purposes.[50] In the same year the state made highway grants
to local government which totaled almost $112 million.[51] This indi-
cates that over 45 per cent of local street and highway expenditure
in that year was made from state motor fuel grants.

Public Welfare   The principal welfare grants to local units are
in connection with the general assistance program. Unlike the categorical public assistance grants[52] which are administered by the state
and receive federal aid, the general assistance program is locally administered and, under certain conditions, receives state aid.

In township counties this program is administered by the township supervisor, in commission counties the county board designates
a supervisor, and in Cook County responsibility rests with the Department of Public Aid. If the local unit levies a tax of one mill for
general assistance purposes, it may, upon application, receive a state
grant for all costs in excess of the amount raised by the levy. Funds
for these grants are appropriated to the Department of Public Aid,

---

[49] For a more detailed discussion of this controversy as it relates to municipal
governments see Fisher and Fairbanks, *Illinois Municipal Finance*, pp. 44–46.
[50] U.S. Bureau of the Census, *Census of Governments, 1962*, VII, no. 13 (Washington: U.S. Government Printing Office, 1964), 26.
[51] U.S. Bureau of the Census, *Compendium of State Government Finances in
1962* (Washington: U.S. Government Printing Office, 1963), p. 25.
[52] Old Age Assistance, Aid to Families with Dependent Children, Blind Assistance, Disability Assistance, and Assistance to the Medically Indigent Aged.

which assumes general supervision over administration of the program in units which receive state aid.

Other grants to local governments for welfare purposes include grants for the care of neglected children, administered by the Department of Children and Family Services, and grants of federal funds for manpower training and vocational education, administered by the Board of Vocational Education.

Charges and Miscellaneous General Revenue

No detailed breakdown of this classification is available, but it includes a wide variety of miscellaneous receipts. A substantial portion of the revenue involved comes from charges made for services rendered. These include items as diverse as parking fees, textbook rentals, golf course admissions, and recording fees.

Another important source of miscellaneous revenue is special assessments. These are usually levied by municipalities against property owners to pay for improvements which are of special benefit to the property. Drainage districts receive most of their revenue from assessments against benefiting property owners. The classification also includes a wide variety of miscellaneous items such as gifts, fines, forfeiture, and sale of property.

STATE AND LOCAL DECISIONS

Legally, local governments are creatures of the state. The state creates, or authorizes the creation of, local units of government and determines the powers and responsibilities thereof. Yet, the power of the state over local government is not complete. The essence of local government is that many decisions are made at the local level. There are practical administrative reasons for decentralizing many decisions, and there is the hard political reality that local government is cherished by many who respond to local officials' well-organized efforts to protect their power and position. The result is that many battles over financial matters are fought at both state and local levels. For example, proponents of increased spending for education or for city streets may find that they can be effective at the local level, or they may find that success requires legislative action to increase tax rate limits or state grants to local government. The quest for these may well bring them into conflict with business or taxpayers' groups as well as with advocates of spending for other purposes and may range over issues of state and local tax structure that seem far afield from the original objective.

The existing local tax and expenditure structure is the result of many such battles, fought over a long period of time during which economic and social conditions were changing rapidly. Throughout these battles, the property tax has remained the major source of local revenue for several reasons:

1. Habituation. A tax system changes slowly because people seldom complain about a tax to which they have become accustomed. The property tax is an old one. In many cases property has been purchased with full knowledge of the property tax levy and at values adjusted to the tax. Yearly changes in the tax levy on a given piece of property are ordinarily small, since the tax rates are computed to several decimal places to meet a given levy. This contrasts with other taxes whose rate changes are often in full percentage points.

2. Adaptability to local administration. Few taxes are as well adapted to local administration as the real estate tax. The items to be taxed are visible and ordinarily cannot be moved to avoid the tax. There is rarely any dispute as to which units of government have jurisdiction to tax. Administration, except for the assessment of specialized property, does not require highly trained experts. Perhaps most important, the tax is levied against the property—not against an individual. Unless the taxpayer takes overt action to stop it, the tax automatically becomes a lien against the property which cannot be sold until the lien is cleared.

3. Diffusion of responsibility. Related to the second point is the fact that responsibility for levy and collection of the tax is diffused so that the administrator does not suffer the intense personal pressure that would be brought to bear upon a person who had clear responsibility for taxing his friends and neighbors. Levy of the tax is the responsibility of the governing board of several different local units. Assessment is by one official, equalization is by a state agency, the county clerk computes the tax, and the county or township collector collects it. If a sale of property for taxes is required, the sheriff is responsible. Often when the tax is levied at the legal limit, the taxpayer believes that the rate is set by the state. It may well be that this diffusion of responsibility and the resulting uncertainty as to who is to blame for tax increases makes it possible to raise more from the tax than would otherwise be the case.

It is noteworthy that several of the reasons for the continuing importance of the property tax would not apply to a true general property tax but that they all apply to the modification which has evolved in Illinois. Assessment practice has modified the tax to prevent rapid changes in assessment, even when values change rapidly. Intangible property and certain kinds of tangible property which are hard to find and are susceptible to moving to avoid taxation are rarely assessed or are assessed at a small fraction of true value. Even real estate taxation has been modified to some extent since taxation can affect the value of a given type of property in the long run. Thus, in Chicago the classification system reflects the fact that the Loop is a virtually irreplaceable location for certain business activities while the suburbs are excellent substitutes as a location for single-family houses.

Dissatisfaction with the modified general property tax comes from several sources. Farm groups generally believe that the property tax hits them unusually hard because of the high ratio of capital to income used in farming and the visible, easily assessable nature of farm property. Education groups believe that the great district-to-district differences in the assessed value of property per school child means that many children will not have an adequate education. Academic critics and reformers generally point to the inequity of the tax as evidenced by its departures from both the principle of uniformity and of commonly accepted tax principles such as benefit or ability-to-pay.

The most commonly suggested changes are to improve the administration of the tax, to increase state grants to relieve the property tax, or to provide local units with additional tax powers. All these, of course, require state action and all meet resistance. Whatever course is followed, it is clear that state and local finances are inextricably intertwined. Chapter 5 deals with one economic aspect—the tax burden—of state and local taxation, and Chapter 6 reveals some of the interconnections between local taxation and state tax politics.

5

STATE AND LOCAL TAX BURDENS: ILLINOIS AND OTHER STATES

The term "tax burden," although widely used, is rather indefinite and sometimes misleading in its implications.

Whether or not it is proper to regard a tax as a burden depends entirely upon the context in which the term is used.

In the aggregate, taxes are the price which is paid for government and the services which government performs. When one considers what life would be like without courts of law and police protection, without public highways and public schools, without public health services and all the other services performed by government, it is difficult to consider taxes as a burden. There may well be differences of opinion as to how much should be spent for specific services and complaints about government "inefficiency," but, from the aggregative standpoint, it makes little sense to equate tax levies and tax burdens. It is more realistic to avoid the term "burden" and consider the distribution of economic resources between public sector and private sector goods that results from decisions to tax and spend at the governmental level.

From the viewpoint of an individual within the society, however, the situation is very different. Most governmental services are free to all or have eligibility requirements which are not related to taxes paid by the recipient of the service. The connection between paying and consuming which characterizes the private sector of the economy is missing. As a result, it is perfectly logical for an individual to consider taxes as a burden and to use all legitimate means to shape the tax structure and his private affairs in a way which will minimize the share which he will pay. The situation is complicated by the fact that the ultimate economic burden or incidence of the tax may not rest upon the person who initially pays it. Taxes upon business firms or business transactions may affect prices and outputs in such a way that the tax is shifted, in whole or in part, to someone other than the person or firm upon whom the tax was initially imposed. In addition, taxation may influence economic behavior in a way which does not result in identifiable tax shifting but which does produce collateral economic effects such as a reduction in output or a shift in the location of economic activity. Further complications are added by the fact that a person attempting to minimize his own tax burden cannot always ignore the effects which his action will have upon the level of government services. Successful attempts to reduce tax burdens may reduce service levels if the taxpayer concerned pays a relatively large portion of the tax or if major changes in tax structure are involved.

This chapter considers the level of taxation and tax burden in Illinois from several viewpoints. The first section is concerned with the level of state and local taxation and expenditure. The next three sections deal with the impact and incidence of Illinois taxes upon some major economic groups. The fifth section reviews other economic effects of taxation, and the final section briefly considers the relationship between economic and political impacts of taxation.

THE OVERALL LEVEL OF TAXATION AND EXPENDITURE

There are no objective standards of need for governmental expenditure. Although many professional groups have worked out standards or codes of adequate performance in their fields, these are usually stated in physical terms and include such items as a maximum number of pupils per teacher or maximum travel time from a fire station to the most distant property. These standards can be converted to dollar cost, but they still remain nothing more than expert judgments as to what would be desirable. Expenditure decisions often involve choosing among many desirable alternatives.

Comparisons among states do not indicate what ought to be spent but are useful indicators of the preference for public expenditure as expressed through the political process in the various states.

Table 35 shows state and local taxes on a per capita basis and as a percentage of income in each of the 50 states. It reveals that Illinois taxes in 1965 amounted to $268.86 per person. The range in other states was from a low of $161.22 in Arkansas to $376.34 in

TABLE 35

STATE AND LOCAL TAXES, PER CAPITA AND AS PERCENTAGE OF INCOME, 1965

Per Capita		As Percentage of Income	
1. Arkansas	$161.22	1. Alaska	7.7%
2. South Carolina	162.11	2. Virginia	8.1
3. Alabama	169.35	3. Ohio	8.3
4. Mississippi	171.67	4. ILLINOIS	8.5
5. Kentucky	175.95	5. New Jersey	8.6
6. Tennessee	180.39	6. Missouri	8.7
7. North Carolina	190.59	7. Nebraska	8.8
8. West Virginia	190.73	8. Connecticut	8.9
9. Virginia	192.01	9. New Hampshire	8.9
10. Georgia	193.55	10. Kentucky	8.9
11. Texas	210.26	11. Arkansas	9.0
12. Oklahoma	217.88	12. Maryland	9.0
13. Nebraska	220.67	13. South Carolina	9.1
14. Missouri	223.92	14. Alabama	9.1
15. New Hampshire	224.28	15. Texas	9.2
16. Louisiana	225.04	16. Pennsylvania	9.2
17. Ohio	227.40	17. Georgia	9.2
18. Maine	234.18	18. Tennessee	9.2
19. Florida	239.36	19. Delaware	9.4
20. South Dakota	241.37	20. Indiana	9.5
21. Pennsylvania	245.69	21. North Carolina	9.5
22. Idaho	246.66	22. Rhode Island	9.6
23. New Mexico	246.99	23. West Virginia	9.8
24. North Dakota	249.08	24. Oklahoma	9.9
25. Alaska	252.80	25. Michigan	10.0
26. Utah	259.10	26. Florida	10.0
27. Indiana	259.47	27. Nevada	10.2
28. Rhode Island	264.82	28. Massachusetts	10.2
29. Montana	266.38	29. Oregon	10.4
30. Maryland	267.14	30. Washington	10.5
31. ILLINOIS	268.86	31. Kansas	10.6
32. New Jersey	273.10	32. Maine	10.7
33. Kansas	274.23	33. Hawaii	10.7
34. Iowa	275.84	34. Idaho	10.8
35. Arizona	276.58	35. Iowa	10.9
36. Vermont	278.54	36. Utah	11.1
37. Wyoming	279.29	37. Mississippi	11.1
38. Oregon	283.57	38. Louisiana	11.1
39. Michigan	292.02	39. Colorado	11.2
40. Connecticut	296.26	40. Wyoming	11.3
41. Washington	296.33	41. Montana	11.3
42. Colorado	296.90	42. New Mexico	11.6
43. Hawaii	299.15	43. California	11.6
44. Minnesota	301.82	44. North Dakota	11.6
45. Massachusetts	304.31	45. New York	11.7
46. Delaware	307.46	46. Minnesota	11.8
47. Wisconsin	312.17	47. Arizona	11.8
48. Nevada	337.95	48. Wisconsin	11.8
49. California	371.92	49. South Dakota	11.9
50. New York	376.34	50. Vermont	12.4
Mean	250.25		10.3

Source: U.S. Bureau of the Census, *Governmental Finances in 1964–65* (Washington: U.S. Government Printing Office, 1967); U.S. Department of Commerce, *Survey of Current Business*, August, 1966. Population data as of July 1, 1964, used to compute per capita values. Personal incomes for calendar years 1964 and 1965 were averaged to compute taxes as percentage of income.

New York. The states with the lowest per capita taxes are low-income southern states. States with high per capita taxes include such wealthy states as Nevada, California, and New York, but also include such states as Wisconsin and Minnesota, which rank nearer the center of the income scale. Illinois ranks 31st in per capita collections.

The right side of the table shows taxes as a percentage of personal income. Illinois taxes amounted to 8.5 per cent of personal income. Only three states had lower taxes in relation to income. At the other end, there is also much diversity. The high tax states include such widely different states as South Dakota, Wisconsin, Arizona, and New York.

In recent years there have been a number of multiple correlation analyses of the relationship between the level of state and local expenditure and various economic, demographic, and social factors.[1] Multiple correlation analysis has an important advantage over simple correlation or the ranking method used in Table 35. It permits several variables to be considered at the same time and often brings out the importance of a variable which is overshadowed or overlooked if simpler methods are used. Even multiple correlation has its limitations, however. It does not prove a cause-effect relationship and tells nothing directly about the mechanism by which the relationships arise.

Because there is no generally accepted theory of the determination of the level of public expenditure, these studies have been of an exploratory nature. There has been a good deal of variation in the variables used and some disagreement upon procedure. This makes it difficult to sum up the findings of the several studies, but it is possible to draw some general conclusions.

1. There is a relationship between economic and demographic conditions in the state and the level of expenditure of state and local governments. These factors "explain" more than half of the statistical variation in most cases.[2] This indicates that analysis which

[1] Seymour Sacks and Robert Harris, "The Determinants of State and Local Government Expenditures and Intergovernmental Flows of Funds," *National Tax Journal* (March, 1964), pp. 75–85; Glenn W. Fisher, "Interstate Variation in State and Local Government Expenditure," *National Tax Journal* (March, 1964), pp. 57–74; Ernest Kurnow, "Determinants of State and Local Expenditure Reexamined," *National Tax Journal* (September, 1963), pp. 252–55; Elliott R. Morss, "Some Thoughts on the Determinants of State and Local Expenditure," *National Tax Journal* (March, 1966), pp. 95–103; Thomas Dye, *Politics, Economics and the Public* (Chicago: Rand McNally & Co., 1966), 314 pp.

[2] Again it should be noted that the correlation analysis itself does not prove the existence or direction of causation. It is assumed on the basis of other knowl-

focuses entirely upon political organization and political process would not be able to explain all the differences in the variation without taking into account factors which are external to the political system.

2. The most powerful explanatory factors are those relating to income, wealth, or tax capacity of the areas in question.

3. There are clearly differences in the need for different governmental services. Some of these differences, such as population density and degree of urbanization, are indirectly measured by statistics. A few can be measured directly.

4. Differences in the political system and in preference for governmental services vis-à-vis privately provided services play a role, but, to date, there has been little progress in measuring these in a way that permits incorporation of the measure into statistical analysis.

TABLE 36

COEFFICIENTS OF CORRELATION AND STANDARDIZED REGRESSION COEFFICIENTS, PER CAPITA FINANCIAL ITEMS, 50 STATES, 1965

		Standardized Regression Coefficient		
Item	Coefficient of Multiple Correlation	Per Capita Income	Population Density	Urbanization
Total Taxes	.83	.76	−.24	.23
Revenue from Federal Government	.57	.66	−.24	−.59
Charges and Miscellaneous Revenue	.63	.70	−.53	−.25[a]
Total Expenditure	.73	.95	−.37	−.32
Education Expenditure	.73	.78	−.60	.01[a]
Local School Expenditure	.79	.87	−.50	.03[a]
Highway Expenditure	.68	.80	−.23	−.75
Welfare Expenditure	.29	−.22[a]	−.07[a]	.42

[a] Indicates that the regression coefficient divided by the standard error is less than 1.5, and is assumed not to be statistically significant.

Table 36 shows the results of a multiple correlation analysis of 1965 per capita financial items. The first column is the coefficient of multiple correlation, (R). This coefficient is an index which indicates the degree of association between the dependent variable

edge of the social system that the independent variables influence the dependent (financial) variables rather than the other way around. The word "explain" must be understood in that context.

(taxes or expenditure per capita) and the independent variables. The square of this coefficient can be interpreted as the percentage of variation which has been statistically explained. Thus $(.83)^2$ or 69 per cent of the variation in per capita state and local tax collections in the 50 states is explained by differences in per capita income, population density (population per square mile), and urbanization (percentage of population living in urban places).

The size (disregarding sign) of the standardized regression co-efficients indicates the relative importance of the three independent variables in explaining variation in the dependent variables. The sign attached indicates whether the relationship is direct or inverse. Thus, per capita income is the most important factor explaining per capita tax collections and the relationship is direct. That is, states with high per capita income tend to have high per capita tax collections. Population density and urbanization are far less important than per capita income but are almost equal to each other in importance. Population density is inversely related; that is, thickly populated states have lower per capita taxes than do thinly populated ones, when differences in per capita income and urbanization are also taken into account.

The three independent variables are less highly correlated with per capita revenue from the federal government. The coefficient of correlation, (R), is only .57 ($R^2 = .29$). Of greatest interest here is the strong inverse effect of urbanization and revenue. In view of the great amount of publicity which federal aid to cities has received, it is interesting that per capita federal aid is negatively associated with the degree of urbanization. The explanation for this probably lies in the highway aid program which makes up a substantial part of federal aid to state and local governments. Distribution of the mileage of the interstate highway system is such that per capita federal aid is often higher in states with fewer large cities. The effect of this distribution is also evident in the regression coefficients for highway expenditure. Urbanization is inversely associated with highway expenditure and is almost as important an explanatory variable as is per capita income.

Except in the case of welfare expenditure, the three independent variables explain a substantial part of interstate variation. Per capita income is the most important explanatory variable in every case except welfare. Population density is inversely correlated in every case. This undoubtedly reflects the fact that certain governmental services are provided more economically when the population is grouped more closely together. This fact is overlooked when simpler methods of analysis are used, since densely populated states are also high income states and the income effect is much stronger than the density effect. A simple correlation or grouping of states would show that the densely populated states have the highest level of tax collections and expenditure per capita.

Urbanization is inversely associated with total expenditure and highway expenditure. It is directly associated with expenditure for several urban-type functions such as police, fire protection, and sanitation, for which data are not given.

The unexplained portion of the variation can probably be attributed to other factors which create differences in need and differences in public preference, and to the nature of the political system. Success in finding statistical data which measures, or serves as a proxy measure for, these variables has been rather limited; but it is sometimes possible to develop measures of need for specific services. For example, the need for expenditure on elementary and secondary schools is related to the number of children of school age and the proportion of these who attend public, as opposed to private, schools. These data are available and can be utilized to obtain the approximate percentage of the population which attends public schools. When this new variable is added to the analysis of local school expenditure, the coefficient of correlation increases from .79 to .87 and the resulting standardized regression coefficients are:

> 1.07 Per capita income
> −.28 Population density
> .00 Urbanization
> .49 Percentage of population attending public school

Unfortunately, this success cannot be repeated with expenditure for all functions since measures of need are not always so easily obtainable.

Table 35 revealed that Illinois taxes are low in relation to the level of income. Another method of comparing Illinois expenditure with that of other states is to use the regression equations generated in connection with the correlation analysis to predict per capita revenues or expenditures from per capita income, population density, and degree of urbanization in the state and to compare this figure with the actual one. The difference represents the influence of factors not utilized in the regression analysis. Table 37 shows that actual tax collections and expenditures in Illinois are well below the predicted values.

In other words, Illinois tax collections and expenditures per capita are substantially below that of other states when allowance is made

TABLE 37

PREDICTED AND ACTUAL PER CAPITA FINANCIAL ITEMS, THREE-VARIABLE
REGRESSION ANALYSIS, 1965, ILLINOIS STATE AND LOCAL GOVERNMENT

Item	Predicted[a]	Actual	Deviation
Total Taxes	$319.22	$268.86	−$ 50.36
Revenue from Federal Government	89.29	48.63	− 44.66
Charges and Miscellaneous Revenue	78.71	47.22	− 31.49
Total Expenditure	505.31	369.13	− 136.18
Educational Expenditure	191.50	139.57	− 51.93
Local School Expenditure	145.64	106.65	− 38.99
Highway Expenditure	92.69	57.73	− 34.96

[a] Predicted values computed from regression equations generated in correlation analysis. See text and Table 36.

for differences in per capita income, population density, and degree of urbanization. An analysis of expenditure for local schools including a fourth variable, estimated percentage of population enrolled in public schools, produces a predicted expenditure of $138.13 per capita as compared with the actual expenditure of $106.65.

Some of the reasons for the low relative level of taxation and expenditure in Illinois undoubtedly involve the political system and the attitude of Illinois people toward government and governmental services. These are difficult to measure, but the analysis of Illinois tax politics in Chapter 6 does contribute something by way of explanation.

TAX STRUCTURE AND TAX BURDEN

When attention shifts from aggregate levels of taxation and expenditure, the question ceases to be one of how much service the taxpayers are collectively buying and becomes a question of who is burdened by the tax. Clearly, different tax structures result in different distributions of the tax burden upon individuals and groups. The heavy dependence upon sales and property taxes in Illinois and the virtual absence of general business or corporation taxes mean that the tax burdens in Illinois differ from those in states which place heavier taxes upon businesses and upon incomes.

In general, heavy dependence upon sales taxation means that a substantial percentage of taxes are paid by purchasers of tangible personal property such as food, clothing, furniture, appliances, cigarettes, gasoline, and liquor. It also means that the retailer or distributor of these products bears a part of the cost of collecting the tax and takes the brunt of taxpayer complaints about increases in the tax rate.

Another kind of "burden" results from the fact that taxpayers may change their behavior as a result of the tax. A sales tax on tangible property has the effect of making such property more expensive in comparison with nontaxed services and may encourage residents of Illinois to spend more on services and less on tangible goods. This may benefit sellers of services at the expense of merchants who sell tangible items.

Heavy dependence upon the property tax means that much of the Illinois tax burden is related to the consumption of housing. In fact, if it were possible to compute the present value of all future property tax payments upon a newly built house, it would undoubtedly be discovered that the property tax is equivalent to a sales tax at a rate several times higher than the existing rate. Clearly this tax places a high burden upon those who choose to spend heavily upon housing and thus discourages such expenditure. This has adverse effects upon the home construction industry and related industries and has important effects upon the residential and other land use patterns in the state.

It is incorrect to assume, of course, that all residential property is taxed at the same percentage of value. Not only are there differences in tax rates in different governmental jurisdictions, but inaccuracies in assessment mean that similar properties in the same jurisdiction pay very different tax bills.

A portion of the property tax is levied upon business or agricultural property. Because of variations in the amount of tangible property used to produce a given amount of net or gross income in various industries, because of de facto classification in Cook County, because of the practice of tax negotiation, and because of the great difficulties which assessors have in assessing complex business property, it is very difficult to make meaningful generalizations about the impact of property taxes upon Illinois firms or Illinois industries. It seems clear, however, that the agricultural industry pays an unusually heavy property tax burden. One estimate is that farm property taxes in 1960 amounted to 13.3 per cent of all property taxes, although net farm income amounted to only 2.4 per cent of total personal income, and farm population amounted to only 5.6 per cent of the population.[3] This seems to result from the fact that farming has become a highly capital-intensive industry and that farm property is highly

[3] R. G. F. Spitze and W. H. Heneberry, "Burden of Property Taxes on Illinois Agriculture," *Report of the Commission on Revenue* (Springfield, 1963), p. 494.

visible and relatively easy to value. Farm property is unlikely to escape the eye of the assessor or be subject to the gross undervaluation that sometimes results from attempts to assess complex industrial property.

The entire problem of tax burden is complicated by the fact that taxes on business and agriculture may be passed on to someone other than the original payer. This usually comes about through shifts in the supply curve which affect the prices and outputs in the taxed industries. These changes, in turn, may affect the level of particular kinds of employment and lead to changes in industrial and residential location. Professor Musgrave has described the effects of public finance upon the economy in these words:

> When taxes are imposed, the statute places the legal liability upon particular consumers or firms. When public expenditures are made, they go to purchase specific resources from specific markets or involve gifts to particular people. There is a clearly defined point of impact at which the public-revenue or -expenditure flow is inserted, but the eventual distribution of costs or benefits may differ greatly from the way in which the initial liabilities or outlays are placed. The final results depend not only on how budget payments are inserted into the system but also on how the economy adjusts thereto. Only if we can predict these adjustments can we determine what policies are needed to accomplish given objectives.[4]

Musgrave points out that the most satisfactory way of studying the burden of a tax would be to hold expenditure constant, substitute one tax for another, and then make a "global" comparison of the economy before and after the change. If such a comparison were possible, it would permit an analyst to say how the position of every individual had changed as a result of the tax and would render the question "who pays" obsolete. Unfortunately, such a comparison is not possible in an economy which is characterized by constant change. The traditional "partial" analysis which attempts to trace the money burden of the tax from impact to incidence and to separately analyze some of the important secondary effects is more useful for the purposes of this chapter.

In tax burden analysis, tax *impact* refers to the initial money burden of the tax. *Shifting* refers to the process by which the original payer shifts the burden to someone else. Usually, this occurs through a change in prices of items bought or sold by the person or firm upon which the tax has its impact. *Incidence* refers to the ultimate resting of the tax upon some person who cannot shift it further. Economic

[4] Richard A. Musgrave, *The Theory of Public Finance* (New York: McGraw-Hill Book Co., 1959), pp. 105–6.

effects refer to economic consequences which are collateral to the incidence of the tax or are too remote to be considered as part of the money burden. Changes in the level of employment or shifts in industrial location are among the possible effects of taxation.

Clearly it is not easy to trace the process of shifting or to determine the final incidence of a tax, but there is broad agreement among economists as to important general principles of shifting and incidence. Using these principles and available statistical data, it is possible to make rough estimates of the incidence of a tax upon various income groups. It is generally agreed, for example, that taxes which have their impact upon individuals rather than upon business firms cannot be shifted.[5] Taxes upon business firms may be shifted forward to customers in the form of higher prices, backward to suppliers in the form of lower prices, or may be absorbed by the firm, reducing the earnings accruing to the benefit of the stockholders. The extent to which this is likely to occur depends upon the kind of tax and the nature of the business. Thus, the first step in analyzing tax incidence is to estimate the portion of each kind of tax which has its impact upon various economic groups.

THE IMPACT OF ILLINOIS TAXES

The classification of taxes and economic groups used in impact analysis should be chosen to facilitate shifting analysis. Ideally, this classification would be such that the entire amount of each entry in a tax impact table would be shifted in an identical fashion. Limits of theoretical knowledge and statistical data make it impossible to construct such a table, but Arlyn J. Larson has estimated the impact of major Illinois taxes upon four large economic groups:[6] private, agricultural, commercial, and industrial. The private group consists of taxpayers in an individual sense. It is a class of taxpayers who are subject to direct tax levies, or who bear the burden of a tax, such as a sales tax, which is legally the obligation of a business firm but which is usually shifted to customers.

---

[5] Taxes upon individuals may well have effects, such as changing the number of hours the taxpayer desires to work, but these are changes difficult to measure. In fact, in many instances the individual has little control over the number of hours he works, rather accepting employment for some standard number of hours, e.g., 40 per week.

[6] Arlyn J. Larson, *The Burden of State and Local Taxes on Income Classes in Illinois,* unpublished doctoral dissertation (Urbana: University of Illinois, 1964), p. 15.

The agricultural group was allocated those taxes which are the result of being in the business of agriculture. The industrial group was defined to consist of firms in manufacturing, mining, transportation, and public utility services, and the commercial group was composed of all other types of business.

Tables 38 and 39 show the impact of 1960 state and local taxes as estimated by Professor Larson. It should be noted that these data are estimates. For example, the estimated impact of the property tax is based upon extensions, rather than collections, and in several cases the distribution of taxes among the economic groups was according to a percentage distribution of some related economic series rather than by actual tax collections. It is also important to note that the classification of taxes differs somewhat from that used elsewhere in this volume, and that a few minor taxes are not included.

Larson assumes that the impact of general and selective sales taxes is upon the purchaser of the goods—even though the retailer or distributor actually mails the check to the state. Because of the regulated nature of the public utility industry, it is assumed that utility taxes are passed on to customers, even if the tax is not separately billed. Even the portion of the corporate franchise tax paid by utilities is assigned to customers.

According to these estimates, almost 60 per cent of Illinois state and local taxes fall upon private taxpayers and thus are not subject to further shifting. A much larger portion of general and selective sales taxes falls into this category. It is estimated that almost 83 per cent of the general sales tax impacts upon private groups, and 100 per cent of several of the selective categories are so assigned.[7]

In contrast, only 17.4 per cent of the personal property tax and 10.9 per cent of the corporate franchise tax fall upon private groups.

Personal property taxation falls heavily upon the industrial group, and motor vehicle registration taxes fall more heavily upon commercial and industrial groups than do taxes in general.

Real and personal property taxes fall far more heavily upon agriculture than does any other kind of taxation. In fact, 87.7 per cent of the taxes which have their estimated impact upon agriculture are property taxes.

[7] Assignment of 100 per cent of such selective excises as liquor, cigarette, and pari-mutuel taxes to private groups somewhat overstates the case. In view of the large amounts of business entertaining which involve use of the products and services covered by these taxes, it would seem that some portion of these should have been assigned to commercial and industrial groups.

TABLE 38

ESTIMATED IMPACT OF STATE AND LOCAL TAXES,
BY TAX AND ECONOMIC GROUP, 1960

Tax	Private	Agricultural	Commercial	Industrial	Total
			(thousands)		
Real Property	$ 592,462	$122,808	$156,499	$178,699	$1,050,469
Personal Property	43,650	21,619	52,329	132,768	250,366
State and Local Sales	362,051	10,655	27,998	37,139	437,843
Motor Vehicle Registration	46,784	5,222	20,853	27,398	100,257
Motor Fuel Taxes	93,993	3,781	24,694	22,691	145,159
Motor Vehicle Operators	4,597	—	—	—	4,597
Liquor	32,831	—	—	—	32,831
Cigarette	49,320	—	—	—	49,320
Insurance	16,783	325	4,686	6,178	27,972
Public Utility	42,415	165	15,726	19,366	77,672
Corporation Franchise	604	4	2,191	2,766	5,565
Pari-Mutuel	16,863	—	—	—	16,863
Amusement (State)	1,055	—	—	—	1,055
Amusement (Local)	1,254	—	—	—	1,254
Inheritance	22,027	—	—	—	22,027
Miscellaneous	—	—	—	4,836	4,836
Total	1,326,690	164,579	304,976	431,841	2,228,086

Source: Arlyn J. Larson, *The Burden of State and Local Taxes on Income Classes in Illinois*, unpublished doctoral dissertation (Urbana: University of Illinois, 1964), pp. 21–52.

TABLE 39

ESTIMATED IMPACT OF STATE AND LOCAL TAXES, BY TAX AND
ECONOMIC GROUP, 1960, PERCENTAGE DISTRIBUTION

Tax	Private	Agricultural	Commercial	Industrial	Total
Real Property	56.4%	11.7%	14.9%	17.0%	100.0%
Personal Property	17.4	8.6	20.9	53.0	100.0
State and Local Sales	82.7	2.4	6.4	8.5	100.0
Motor Vehicle Registration	46.7	5.2	20.8	27.3	100.0
Motor Fuel Taxes	64.8	2.6	17.0	15.6	100.0
Motor Vehicle Operators	100.0	—	—	—	100.0
Liquor	100.0	—	—	—	100.0
Cigarette	100.0	—	—	—	100.0
Insurance	60.0	1.2	16.8	22.1	100.0
Public Utility	54.6	.2	20.2	24.9	100.0
Corporation Franchise	10.9	.1	39.4	49.7	100.0
Pari-Mutuel	100.0	—	—	—	100.0
Amusement (State)	100.0	—	—	—	100.0
Amusement (Local)	100.0	—	—	—	100.0
Inheritance	100.0	—	—	—	100.0
Miscellaneous	—	—	—	100.0	100.0
Total	59.5	7.4	13.7	19.4	100.0

Source: Table 38.

THE INCIDENCE OF ILLINOIS TAXES

Estimating the impact of taxes is only the first step in determining the ultimate economic burden of the tax.

Taxes which have their impact upon the private groups may be "exported" to other states in reduced federal income tax liabilities. Federal income tax law provides that taxpayers who itemize their deductions may subtract most state and local taxes in arriving at taxable income. This means that the federal government, in effect, pays a portion of state and local taxes for such taxpayers. The portion ranges from 65 per cent for taxpayers in the highest federal tax bracket down to zero for taxpayers who take the standard deduction or who owe no federal income tax.

Business and agricultural taxpayers also export part of the taxes which impact upon them via the federal income tax route since they have the same privilege of deducting state and local taxes in computing taxable income for federal purposes. In addition, these taxpayers are often able to shift the taxes which they pay in the form of higher prices for products sold.

Analysis of the process of tax shifting is a complicated problem in economic analysis which requires many assumptions about the nature of competition for the product and other conditions in the economic system.

Generally, economists treat taxes as an addition to business costs which shifts the supply curve and raises the price of the product. This means that at least part of the tax has been shifted to purchasers in higher prices and that total sales of the product have been reduced.

There are many variations of this process, depending upon the nature of the tax and conditions of the industry. For example, if the tax is imposed upon only a few producers in the industry, the market price may be unaffected and the taxed producers may find it necessary to absorb the tax. This is a common situation when state and local taxes are imposed on firms which sell in a national market. However, if the taxed producers enjoy the advantages of a protected local market or are the beneficiaries of a strong brand preference for their product, they still may be able to shift the tax.

Other variations in the shifting situation result from the nature of the tax. For example, it is generally assumed that taxes upon land fall upon the landowner, through capitalization, rather than upon the tenant, because the supply of land is fixed and does not decrease as a result of the tax. Even here, however, there may be exceptions due to particular customs and institutional arrangements.

It is never possible to determine with certainty what proportion
of the tax is shifted. Larson's estimates are based upon a general
knowledge of shifting theory and available economic statistics. He
concludes that 6.3 per cent of the taxes which impact upon agriculture are shifted, as are 65.8 per cent of those upon commercial groups
and 100 per cent of those on industrial groups.[8]

The conclusion that all taxes upon industrial groups are shifted is
based upon two crucial assumptions. These are (1) that industrial
products are sold in a national market and (2) that the taxes upon
these concerns are lower in Illinois than in most other states. Under
these conditions the price would be set high enough to cover taxes
in an average or high tax state,[9] and would be more than sufficient
to cover the Illinois taxes on producers located in the state.[10]

Some of the taxes which are shifted are shifted to out-of-state
residents and some are borne by Illinois residents. The following
tabulation summarizes Larson's estimates with regard to the shifting
of taxes upon the economic groups:

	Total Tax Impact	Shifted in State (thousands)	Shifted out of State
Agricultural	$164,579	$ 8,910	$ 1,753
Commercial	304,976	190,940	9,623
Industrial	431,841	329,328	102,513

The much higher proportion of industrial taxes shifted out of state
reflects the fact that a much higher proportion of the output of such
concerns is sold outside the state. These data do not include any
allowance for taxes "exported" via reductions in federal income taxes
as a result of deducting state and local taxes.

Chart XX reveals the final results of Professor Larson's analysis
of tax burdens. It shows the estimated burden of various taxes as a
percentage of family income at different levels. These are based on
estimated final incidence of taxes upon industrial, commercial, and

[8] Larson, *op. cit.*, p. 99.
[9] The results would be similar whether the market is competitive or characterized by administered prices.
[10] This example illustrates some of the complexities of shifting analysis. If the
situation is as Larson assumes, Illinois producers may enjoy an "economic surplus" or excess profit from the fact that the national market prices are set high
enough to cover higher state and local taxes than are paid by Illinois firms.
However, any increase in Illinois taxes would result in a reduction of this profit
(economic surplus). Thus it is not correct to say that an *additional* tax would
be shifted.

CHART XX

STATE AND LOCAL TAXES AS A PERCENTAGE OF MONEY INCOME,
BY INCOME CLASSES, 1960

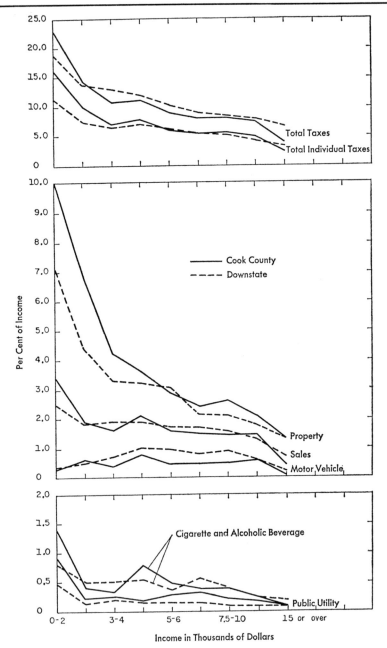

Source: Arlyn J. Larson, "Estimated Burden of State and Local Taxes in Illinois," *Illinois
Government*, No. 22 (1964).

agricultural groups. It is assumed that taxes on private groups were not shifted. Allowance is made for tax exporting and for federal tax offsets.

These data reveal that all Illinois taxes shown are regressive; that is, they take a higher portion of the money income of low income families than of higher income families. There is considerable difference in the degree of regressivity. Clearly the property tax contributes heavily to the regressivity of the total tax system. Its burden on all income classes is greater than any other tax and it is substantially regressive throughout the entire income range. The general sales tax is sharply regressive only at the extreme ends of the income range. Between the $2,000–2,999 and $10,000–14,999 income classes it is only mildly regressive.[11]

The two lower lines in the top panel of Chart XX show the burdens of individual taxes imposed upon various private income groups, and the upper lines include the burden of taxes upon agricultural, industrial, and commercial business. Detailed examination of the data upon which this chart was based reveals that business and agricultural taxes add to the regressivity of the tax system, although they are less regressive than property taxes levied upon individuals and, in extreme income ranges, less regressive than the sales tax.

The total state and local tax burden amounted to 7.69 per cent of money income in Cook County and 9.40 per cent downstate. The tax system seems to be considerably more regressive in Cook County where the burden ranged from 22.97 per cent on incomes under $2,000 to 3.99 per cent on incomes over $15,000. Downstate the range was from 18.80 to 6.69 per cent.

There were many estimates and assumptions involved in deriving these estimates, and minor differences from tax to tax or from income group to income group could well be the result of statistical error or faulty assumptions. But there is little doubt about the conclusion that the Illinois tax system is very regressive. In view of the heavy reliance which Illinois puts upon sales and property taxation, this conclusion is not surprising. Perhaps the most surprising finding of Larson's study is that the property tax is much more regressive than the sales tax throughout the middle income ranges.

---

[11] It should be noted that annual money income may not be a good measure of ability to pay taxes at the extreme low end of the income scale. Some portion of the persons in this income class are families who have substantial assets, but low money income. These may be elderly persons living off capital, students, or other persons who are temporarily unemployed.

SOME ECONOMIC EFFECTS OF ILLINOIS TAXES

Traditional analysis of tax incidence is concerned with "who ultimately pays" the tax. There are, however, many possible economic effects of state and local taxation which are not encompassed within the scope of such an analysis. For example, if a tax affects hours of work or the rate of capital formation, there may be economic results which cannot be measured by analysis directed toward determining the money burdens of the tax.

At the state level, few possible tax effects are potentially as important as are those involving industrial location and economic growth within a state or locality. Clearly, businessmen seeking plant locations and individuals seeking a place of residence should be interested in low taxes and high quality in those government services which are most important to them. However, many other factors enter into the decisions. The critical question is the relative importance of taxation upon economic development.

There is no doubt that taxation could be the deciding factor in a decision involving the location or expansion of a plant, office, or residence. If all other things are equal, it is clear that most persons would choose the location with the low tax.

It can also be asserted with some confidence that the smaller the geographic area covered by a governmental unit, the greater will be the role which tax considerations will play in economic decisions. This results from two factors. The first of these is that the smaller the governmental units involved, the greater the possibility of non-tax factors being equal. Alternative locations a few blocks apart are likely to be very similar with regard to transportation facilities, nearness to market, and labor supply. Living conditions for executives, climate, and topography are unlikely to vary greatly. A second and related consideration is that there is apt to be more spillover of government benefits when small units are involved. The search for a low tax area where one can enjoy the benefits of higher expenditures in surrounding areas is far more likely to be successful if the units of government are small. The ultimate success of such a search is exemplified by the tax enclave—a municipality or school district which contains a large industrial plant but few people. The plant is subject to a low level of taxation but workers and executives are able to enjoy a high level of services provided by surrounding governments. Another successful outcome of such a search is to live in a small, low tax suburb where one is able to use the streets and recreational and other facilities of other governmental units.

Studies of the effect of taxation upon business location are of three main types. One approach is to make statistical comparisons of economic growth rates and the level of taxation in various states or localities. Some of these have been relatively crude comparisons between per capita taxes and overall growth rates in various states, while others have been more sophisticated econometric studies in which growth rates of specific industries are compared with taxes upon those industries at the same time that allowance is made for other factors which are believed to affect growth. Studies of this type have generally failed to discover a significant correlation between taxes and economic growth. Although this is not conclusive proof that there is no connection between taxation and economic growth, it is clear that taxes are not producing economic stagnation as opponents of higher taxes often claim.[12]

A second approach to the study of taxes and location is the interview approach. These studies have involved asking businessmen who have a role in making location decisions what factors are considered. Generally, when interviewers simply ask respondents which factors are important, taxation has rated very low on the list. When taxes are specifically mentioned by the interviewer, they tend to be rated somewhat higher in importance.

A third approach is to study the importance of state and local taxes in total costs of a firm. Generally, these studies show that state and local taxes are a small part of costs. Ordinarily, taxes are a small fraction of such costs as labor or raw material. Sometimes they are much below transportation or advertising costs. On the other hand, there is a great deal of difference from firm to firm and tax costs may be substantial when compared to net profits.

Professor John Due summarizes the conclusions of a number of studies utilizing all three approaches in these words:

1. On the basis of all available studies, it is obvious that relatively high business tax levels do not have the disastrous effects often claimed for them. While the statistical analysis and study of location factors are by no means conclusive, they suggest very strongly that tax effects cannot be of major importance.

2. However, without doubt, in some instances the tax element plays the deciding role in determining the optimum location, since other factors balance. This is most likely to be the case in the selection of the precise site in a metropolitan area (property taxes being the ones of chief concern), or when a suitable area for site location straddles a state border.

[12] John F. Due, "Studies of State-Local Tax Influences on Location of Industry," *National Tax Journal* (June, 1961), p. 164. Due's paper is a summary of a large number of studies of the subject which were published in the 1950's. There have been relatively few such studies in the 1960's, and this article is still an excellent summary of available knowledge about this subject.

But state and local taxes represent such a small percentage of total costs that the cases in which they are controlling cannot be very significant.

3. The tax climate factor, as one element in the general business reputation or climate of the state, without doubt influences some location decision making, by causing firms to exclude certain states or urban areas from consideration. Again, these cases are probably not a significant portion of the total.[13]

Most of the studies of the economic effects of state and local taxation have been concerned with effects upon the location and growth of industrial businesses. In recent years, however, rising sales tax rates have focused attention upon the possible adverse effects of sales taxation upon commercial concerns. This concern arises from the incentive to purchase outside the state which may be created by sales taxation.

There are three major ways in which Illinois residents may avoid sales taxation. One of these is to purchase items from unregistered mail-order concerns. The major mail-order houses have places of business in Illinois and are required to collect the tax from all sales in Illinois, even upon sales made from an out-of-state branch; however, the National Bellas Hess case[14] prevents the Department of Revenue from requiring concerns with no office or agent in the state to collect the tax. The purchaser remains liable for the use tax but, in most cases, collection is almost impossible.

The second method permits the purchaser to enjoy the advantages of personal shopping but to arrange the transaction so that it becomes interstate commerce. For example, a purchase from a St. Louis store which is delivered to an Illinois address is an interstate transaction and cannot be subjected to a *sales* tax. The recent agreements between Illinois and several adjoining states appear to have greatly reduced this opportunity for tax avoidance. In the example, the St. Louis store would be required to collect the Illinois *use* tax.

A third method of avoiding the Illinois tax is for an Illinois resident to purchase and take delivery of an item in a state having no sales tax or a lower rate. Although he must pay the tax, if any, in the state of purchase, he will save money since no adjoining state has a sales tax as high as Illinois. With the exception of purchases of automobiles, which must be registered, and certain very large, visible purchases by businesses, the purchaser runs little risk of being required to pay the Illinois use tax.

The last two methods of avoidance are most feasible for persons

[13] *Ibid.,* p. 171.
[14] *National Bellas Hess* v. *Illinois Department of Revenue,* 385 U.S. 809 (1967).

who live near a state line and are often referred to as "border problems." Studies show that the sales tax has a measurable impact upon the pattern of retail trade in border areas. One Illinois study shows that in 1958 retail sales were 1.51 per cent of personal income in interior counties, but only 1.39 per cent in border counties.[15] There was considerable variation from county to county, apparently depending upon the rate of tax in the adjoining state and the shopping facilities available there. Studies in other states using somewhat different methods show results which are generally similar.[16]

POLITICAL EFFECTS

Just as different taxes vary in incidence and other economic effects, so they vary in political effect. Under certain circumstances a change or proposed change in the tax system will create many political repercussions. Under other circumstances, there will be few repercussions.

Unfortunately, there is no developed theory of the political effects of taxation, but it is possible to identify some of the more important factors and to sketch some of the interrelations between the economic and political aspects of taxation.

Basically, political effects result from taxpayers' attempts to minimize the economic burdens of the tax upon themselves by influencing the decision-makers. Taxes vary in political impact because of variations in perceptions of the burdens imposed and the political effectiveness of taxpayer efforts to minimize these burdens. A taxpayer is most concerned about a tax if he believes its incidence is upon him. Taxes which have adverse economic effects are cause for concern, but such taxes are generally preferable to a tax of equal magnitude having its incidence upon the individual in question. Thus, a merchant would oppose a sales tax upon the items which he sells, but may prefer it to a tax which he believes he will bear himself.

Perceptions of both burdens and political effectiveness are closely related to taxpayer organization. Although political decision-makers are influenced by "public opinion" as expressed in private letters and conversations, organizations are far more effective in influencing decisions. This is true not only because organizations carry more po-

[15] James Heins, "Sales and Use Taxes," *Report of the Commission on Revenue* (Springfield, 1963), pp. 691–94.
[16] Harry E. McAllister, "The Border Tax Problem in Washington," *National Tax Journal* (December, 1961), pp. 362–74; William Hamovitch, "Sales Taxation: An Analysis of the Effects of Rate Increases in Two Contrasting Cases," *National Tax Journal* (December, 1966), pp. 411–20.

litical "clout," but because organizations have access to legislators and to experts who understand the technical aspects of taxation. Many organizations interested in influencing taxation not only make the services of these experts available to legislators and other decision-makers, but pass their opinions back to their members and to the general public. Thus, organizations both influence taxpayer perceptions of tax burdens and aid in making these perceptions politically effective. It follows that incidence analysis is of greatest value in understanding the political impact of taxation when the burden is related to politically effective groups.

It may well be that Larson's impact analysis is of greater value in understanding the political impact of taxation than is the incidence analysis. Taxpayers may be very aware of taxes which impact upon them, but businessmen may be skeptical of economists' assurances that they will be able to shift the tax. This is understandable when it is realized that the tax becomes an immediate addition to cost but that shifting, if it occurs, may come about through long term price adjustments which may not have an obvious relation to the tax. Furthermore, three of the four economic groups utilized in the impact analysis correspond reasonably well to politically organized groups. Agriculture is well represented in the Illinois political process by one general organization, the Illinois Agricultural Association, which has been very active in the tax field. Business and commercial groups are represented by a number of organizations—some general and some specialized. Occasionally, the interests and policies of these business organizations conflict, but on many major tax issues they perceive much common interest and often make joint presentations of their position.

Private taxpayers are poorly organized for making their influence felt in the field of taxation, but they do have one powerful weapon —many votes. For this reason organized interests make a considerable effort to influence public attitudes and to stimulate expressions of public opinion. Newspapers, except possibly when their own taxes are involved, expend considerable effort in providing objective information concerning tax matters.

6

THE POLITICS OF TAXATION
IN ILLINOIS

The decisions which have shaped the Illinois tax structure and the resulting distribution of tax burdens have been made over a long period of time. Each has been made under a unique set of circumstances. Not only do the decision-makers and the demands made upon them change from time to time, but economic conditions, constitutional law, and public attitudes undergo almost constant change. Every decision which is made changes the existing tax system and insures that the next decision will be made under different circumstances.

In spite of the changes, Illinois tax politics in the postwar years have been characterized by certain recurring themes, and the broad character of the tax structure has remained the same. Rates have been increased, collections have multiplied, and there have been changes in the definition of the base of several taxes, but Illinois remains a low tax state with a narrow tax structure based primarily upon sales and property taxes. In a real sense, the defenders of the status quo have been victorious, even though pressures for change appear to be increasing.

This chapter identifies some of the groups which have been active in attempting to influence policy, describes the process of decision-making, and analyzes some of the factors which have been influential in determining the outcome.

THE PARTICIPANTS

The constitution, as interpreted by the state Supreme Court, provides the basic "rules of the game" within which tax policy decisions are made. It places limits upon the kinds of taxes that may be imposed and spells out the procedures which must be followed to enact tax legislation. It places responsibility for appropriation and tax legislation in the hands of the Governor and the legislature and establishes the courts which interpret legislation and rule upon the constitutionality of legislative and administrative acts.

The Governor has the responsibility for presenting a biennial fiscal program to the legislature. Measures passed by the legislature become law only with his approval, and he has power to veto particular items in appropriation bills without vetoing the entire bill. Much of the tax revenue is collected by code departments which are under his control, and he has power to prevent or delay certain expenditures for which appropriations have been made.

As holder of the purse strings, the legislature is crucial in the formation of tax policy. The approval of both houses of the General Assembly is necessary to enact new tax legislation. Obtaining approval is made more difficult by the fact that the House and Senate are seldom both of the same party as the Governor. Even when they are, cumulative voting in House districts virtually insures a close split between Republicans and Democrats in that body. This heightens the importance of swing groups or blocs which can hold any essential piece of legislation hostage and gives the House a somewhat unpredictable character.

Although the ultimate responsibility for tax decisions rests with the legislature and the Governor, the list of participants in the decision-making process must be extended to include a large number of organized interest groups which attempt to influence policy. These groups can be classified into four categories: taxpayer groups,[1] pro-expenditure groups, civic groups, and local government organizations.

Among the taxpayers' groups is a powerful bloc composed of business organizations such as the State Chamber of Commerce, the Illinois Manufacturers' Association, the Chicago Association of Commerce and Industry, and the Illinois Association of Retail Merchants. These groups are not entirely homogeneous in their membership, since all include both large and small businesses and some of them represent interests ranging from small retail stores to large industrial concerns. In general, however, all stand for maintaining the status

---

[1] The term, as used here, is not confined to groups organized solely to influence tax policy, but includes business, agricultural, and labor organizations which represent the interests of their members as taxpayers as well as in other capacities.

quo and the retention of a "favorable business climate" in tax matters.[2] The Illinois Association of Retail Merchants has objected to further increases in the general sales tax but has not made a major effort to reduce it from present levels or to propose an alternative form of taxation.

Other organizations which might be classified in the taxpayer group are the Illinois Agricultural Association (Farm Bureau) and the AFL-CIO. The main concern of the IAA in the tax field is to secure some relief from property taxation for its members. In recent years this organization has actively promoted a state income tax as a means of securing property tax relief. The Illinois Federation of Labor and Congress of Industrial Organizations (AFL-CIO), with over one million members, has a great deal of potential political "clout" which has been little utilized in the tax field, perhaps because of the difficulty of mobilizing the full support of local unions. Although the AFL-CIO has not pressed the legislature on matters of tax policy, the organization's policy is to support a graduated income tax and the exemption of food and medicine from the sales tax.

The Taxpayers' Federation of Illinois and the Chicago Civic Federation are taxpayers' organizations in the narrower sense of the term. They are organized primarily to promote government economy and to keep taxes low. The Taxpayers' Federation of Illinois has gone beyond the narrow approach to this objective, however, to act as a major source of information for legislators and local government officials, especially in the highly technical aspects of property taxation.

Pro-expenditure organizations press for increased expenditures and expanded programs in the areas which they represent. Organizations representing highway contractors, cement producers, and truckers are interested in highway expenditure and often press for greater expenditure or for a different allocation of expenditure. The Illinois Education Association and the Parent-Teachers Association often support expanded educational expenditure. Other, more specialized, groups are active in promoting programs such as those for the mentally retarded or the improvement of public camping facilities.

The civic group includes organizations such as the League of Women Voters and the Union League Club of Chicago, which are composed of persons actively interested in "good government." They do not claim to represent a specific economic interest, although the members may be rather homogeneous in social and economic char-

[2] Illinois State Chamber of Commerce, *Meeting the Challenge of Economic Growth in Illinois; Part III: Illinois Taxes and Economic Growth* (October, 1964), p. 9.

acteristics. These groups are, in a sense, self-appointed representatives of "the public."

Local government organizations include organizations of elected officials such as the Illinois Municipal League, the Township Officials of Illinois, and the Illinois Association of County Supervisors and Commissioners. All of these are powerful organizations with large memberships which include important local politicians. The Illinois Municipal League has made active efforts to secure greater property and nonproperty taxing powers for municipalities and to protect and increase the cities' share of intergovernmental grants. The county and township organizations have been interested in increased property tax levies and intergovernmental revenues and have resisted efforts to consolidate or professionalize property tax administration. Other local government organizations are organized around a particular profession or skill and include organizations of city managers, finance officers, assessors, and engineers. These organizations are usually much smaller and confine their lobbying efforts to matters of direct professional interest.

There is, of course, considerable overlapping of membership among these groups, and it would be unfair to assume that any organization always places its own, narrow policy objective above all other objectives. Furthermore, there are often differences of opinion within organizations, and intra-organization political struggles sometimes parallel external political conflict.[3]

Organized groups may influence tax policy in several different ways. The power which an organization has depends both upon the political "clout" of the organization and the skill of the lobbyist. One form of "clout" exists if the organization has the power to influence the votes or political contributions received by a legislator. Stated or implied threats to use this power are a part of the legislative process, but the skillful lobbyist will avoid their actual use, if possible.

Threats which involve the state's welfare or prestige are often effective in influencing policy. These threats may be given wide publicity and sometimes serve as "cover" for legislators who may have other motives for their actions. For example, many legislators feel that business is the source of Illinois prosperity and respond quickly to statements by lobbyists that a piece of legislation will be harmful to the economic development of the state. Such threats are

[3] During the campaign for ratification of the proposed revenue article amendment in 1966, for example, a rather bitter struggle within the Chicago Bar Association resulted in the neutralizing of the organization on this issue.

exemplified by a news report on the strategy of business organizations in opposing a 1959 attempt to increase the corporate franchise tax: "They [business] are threatening to move out, stay out or build somewhere else, a flurry of telegrams from top executives indicates." [4] Similar threats have appeared each time a tax on business appears imminent and have been quite successful.

The lobbyist who possesses important information, either technical or political, will find several ready points of access to political decision-makers. Less tangible but also important is the personal rapport which a lobbyist has established with legislators. If he is trusted and respected, his demands are more sympathetically received than demands by less popular lobbyists.

THE POLITICAL PROCESS

The story of the politician who explained his success by saying that he never voted for a tax bill or against an appropriation often brings wry smiles, but it contains a truth that is essential for understanding tax politics. Taking the responsibility for imposing taxes is never popular and often brings about unhappy political consequences for those who do it, but policy-makers are subject to strong pressures in favor of spending and, unlike the politician in the story, they know that there are real dangers for a man or a party that is labeled as fiscally irresponsible. For these reasons, fiscal decisions made during the biennial sessions of the Illinois General Assembly are the outcome of an elaborate contest in which the goal is to raise adequate revenue and to avoid responsibility for higher taxes. It is a contest, moreover, in which "sides" are not constant. At times the entire legislature seems to unite in an effort to confuse the public, but at other times lines harden and the contest is between political parties or between the legislature and the Governor.

Tactics vary according to the role in which an individual participant or group of participants finds itself cast. A major distinction in the role which must be played is the difference between that of the gubernatorial party and the other party. The Governor is under the legal and practical necessity of proposing the state budget and the taxes needed to balance it. Whether his party is in the majority or minority in the two houses of the state legislature, its members must sponsor his tax measures and make any necessary bargains and compromises to get them, or substitute measures, enacted.

The other party's responsibility for the tax program varies. It is

[4] *Chicago Sun-Times,* June 8, 1959.

greatest when it has the majority in both houses, but even in this role, the nongubernatorial party can be more critical of proposed taxes than can the gubernatorial party. It has no allegiance to the Governor and is under less pressure to come up with an adequate financial program. The nongubernatorial party will seldom propose a tax measure, except as a substitute to one made by the Governor.

The tactics of each party are chosen with an eye to maximizing the party's position while minimizing public irritation. To do this legislators must keep in mind two conflicting public positions. First, the public wants some "adequate" level of services and the public conception of what is adequate seems to be rising steadily. Second, the public does not want to pay higher taxes. There is, however, less effective political resistance to certain kinds of taxes than to others. Usually there will be less public resistance to a small increase in the rate of an existing tax than to a comparable increase in tax collections via a new tax.

Even though the gubernatorial party is responsible for shepherding the Governor's proposals through the legislature, its members will desert those proposals which arouse too much public outcry or which adversely affect those interests to which the member is especially responsive. The other party will criticize and disown support of the Governor's tax program, usually without proposing one of its own, until it becomes evident that inaction will result in charges of negligence and irresponsibility.

Organized interest groups' positions are determined by their perceptions of the burdens which will be imposed by various tax alternatives and their appraisal of the relative political strength of various possible positions. This, in turn, is influenced by the beliefs of group leaders about the likely position of other groups and the possible alliances that can be put together to support a given position.

The Appropriation Process

The processes which determine appropriation and revenue for the state cannot be fully discussed as separate systems. Each set of decisions is profoundly influenced by the other. Nevertheless, the processes are at many points quite separate and distinct.

Since basic appropriations go to agencies rather than to programs, the process begins with the agency head. This official proceeds by assuming the agency appropriation of the present biennium as a minimum which forms his "basic" appropriation for the next year. New programs and increases in existing programs are included in the "supplemental" budget. This approach reflects the assumption that the present appropriation is basic and virtually assures every agency of an increase.[5] There is rarely an intensive review of basic agency budgets, even by the Budgetary Commission, which is set up specifically to review budgets.

The budgeting system is largely bound by personalities and governed by rules of the political system rather than by economic and fiscal analysis. Pressures of time and the lack of information give the legislature little opportunity to review the budget. This means that the word of the Governor and the Budgetary Commission carry great weight. Some appropriation bills are temporarily detained on their way through the legislature while large volleys of verbiage are shot at them, but the results are seldom crippling. In fact, the legislature customarily passes a large number of commission bills and bills appropriating money for projects in the sponsor's own district which were not included in the Governor's budget.

The Revenue Process

If the appropriation process sounds like an amicable affair, the process of raising revenue to cover the proposed expenditures is not. As Anton says, "For legislators, as for governors, the question of 'who shall pay?' is more sensitive than 'for what?'." [6]

Invariably, appropriations exceed estimated revenues from existing tax sources. It is always assumed that the Governor will veto some appropriation bills, especially the courtesy bills which were passed because they were dear to the heart—or political future—of a popular legislator. In addition, the legislature often makes last minute cuts in appropriations for unpopular agencies, but in the last few days of the legislative session, it is always necessary to face up to the fact that additional revenue must be raised.

There are four possible alternatives—new taxes, increased rates on existing taxes, a broadened base for existing taxes, or improved administration of existing taxes. From a political viewpoint any one of the three latter alternatives is often more desirable than imposing a new tax. The public is habituated to existing taxes and is likely to raise less of an outcry about increased rates or broadened bases

---

[5] For an extensive analysis of the appropriation process see two works by Thomas J. Anton: *Politics of State Expenditure in Illinois* (Urbana: University of Illinois Press, 1966) and "Roles and Symbols in the Determination of State Expenditure," *Midwest Journal of Political Science* (February, 1967), pp. 27–43.
[6] Anton, "Roles and Symbols in the Determination of State Expenditure," p. 35.

than about a new tax. In some cases, interest groups are anxious that existing taxes should be more vigorously enforced.[7]

Revenue from this source is limited by the base of the tax and the quality of previous administration, and large revenue increases cannot usually be expected. Thus, the process of choosing one of the remaining sources of revenue becomes a highly sensitive matter in which each participant tries to maximize his own position.

Interest groups generally subscribe to the maxim that the best tax is "one which falls on the other guy." In most cases, interest groups will attempt to protect their constituents from any increase in taxation. Sometimes, however, an organized interest group may support a tax increase that will benefit the group. Highway lobbies, for example, often support a motor fuel tax increase if they are assured that the proceeds will be spent for highway purposes.

The Governor and, generally, legislative members of his party want a revenue source which will yield sufficient funds without causing the party to be labeled as a "high tax" party. The party in opposition to the Governor wants to maximize its bargaining power with the Governor and tax measures are a prime element in that power. If it can block new tax proposals of the Governor, it appears as an advocate of economy in government and leaves the Governor with reduced funds to operate the executive branch. Another possibility is to offer an alternative revenue program which, in terms of public opinion, is better: for example, the same tax with a lower rate or a tax which affects an unpopular group such as the liquor industry. The nongubernatorial party must be careful, however, to avoid being labeled as obstructionist and vindictive. This possibility is greater if, as often happens in Illinois, the party controls one or both houses of the legislature.

These diverse interests all meet in the legislative arena as probing and bargaining maneuvers flourish. One common tactic is to send up "trial balloons" in the form of rumors or statements of possibilities to test public reaction. Another common practice is for the nongubernatorial party to hold tax proposals "hostage" as a bargaining point for gubernatorial approval on other issues. During the 1965 session the Republicans used this tactic quite successfully to gain leverage in the legislative battle over reapportionment of the General Assembly.

[7] In 1961 during the fiscal crisis early in Governor Kerner's first term, the Director of Revenue, Theodore Isaacs, tightened administration of the sales and use taxes. Several members of his staff were former employees of Sears Roebuck and were well aware of the impact which untaxed mail-order houses have upon large Illinois firms.

The combination of public antipathy toward major changes in the tax structure, and the powerful interest groups which prefer the status quo, has prevented any major change in the tax structure since the depression years; but there are forces favoring change. As the rates of existing taxes rise, public consciousness of their burden rises. "Border problems" increase in severity as the general sales tax and taxes on commodities such as cigarettes and liquor rise above those of surrounding states. Furthermore, the relatively low income elasticity of the major Illinois taxes and the much higher elasticity of public expenditure which has existed in the prosperous postwar years mean that tax rate increases must be frequent unless there is a substantial broadening of the base.

As noted above, several important organized interest groups favor major changes in the tax structure. For example, the Illinois Agricultural Association has actively promoted an income tax as a means of relieving the burden which property taxes place on agriculture, and the Illinois Education Association has supported the more elastic income tax as a means of obtaining additional funds for school purposes.

Another source of opposition to the existing tax structure includes those groups and individuals such as the League of Women Voters and a small group of liberal legislators who call for a reappraisal of the tax structure in terms of the equity of the tax burden and adequate support of state programs. Those who make such a reappraisal usually conclude that the Illinois tax system is defective on both counts. Usually they call for an income tax to reduce the regressivity and increase the elasticity of the tax system. Sometimes, exemption of food from the sales tax is proposed for the same reason. Measures to simplify and improve the equity of the property tax include greatly improved assessment procedures, exemption or classification of intangible property, and the elimination or revamping of the capital stock tax.

By themselves, the reform groups stand little chance of success, precisely because their criteria for criticism of the tax structure are alien to the political process which creates it. Participants' goals center on the maximization of interest group position rather than on equity of tax burden. Thus, it is inevitable that the groups bearing the greatest tax burden are those with the least political power.

FISCAL CRISIS OF 1961

On April 19, 1961, Governor Otto Kerner, in office less than four months, addressed the legislature to tell them that the state was perilously low on money in the general revenue fund—so low, in fact, that the daily balance had fallen to $8 million during February.[8] Further, the state could expect a $12 million deficit by the end of the fiscal year in July.[9]

This dramatic situation was the culmination of Illinois financial practices dating back to World War II. During the war construction and replacement of machinery was delayed because of lack of materials. A surplus in the general revenue fund of $154 million was enjoyed by Governor Dwight Green during his last biennium in office. This surplus dwindled steadily—$147 million in 1949, $81.6 million in 1953—until it totaled only $15 million as Governor Otto Kerner took office.[10]

In 1959 the legislature had approved Governor Stratton's budget without giving him the broadened base of the sales tax he had requested. Thus, appropriations exceeded expected revenue by some $130 million. Governor Stratton did not veto these excess appropriations, but froze spending on many new projects for which appropriations had been made. Before his campaign for reelection in 1960, he unfroze $65 million of these projects, leaving his successor an accelerating deficit.

The fiscal situation was further complicated by the new governor's own lack of experience and limited knowledge of the complexities of the state's fiscal machinery.[11] The Governor had come to office with little political expertise; his previous experiences had taught him little of the political skills of bargaining and compromise.

A sense of crisis soon pervaded official statements as well as editorial comments on them by newspapers in the state. In January newspaper columnists speculated that for all intents and purposes the state was broke, that there was only $15 million in unobligated cash in the general revenue fund.[12] In the same month the Governor withheld approval of $2 million in contracts while putting a freeze on all capital improvements paid through the general revenue fund.[13] On February 1, 1961, Justice George W. Bristow of the Illinois Supreme Court "hinted that the court might take a lenient view in interpreting the constitutionality of any state emergency tax measures."[14] Headlines such as "State Deficit Nearing $40 Million: Loh-

[8] *Chicago Daily News,* February 27, 1961.
[9] State of Illinois, *Budget Message, 72nd Biennium* (April 19, 1961).
[10] *Chicago Daily News,* January 17, 1961.
[11] Anton, *Politics of State Expenditure in Illinois,* p. 120.
[12] *Chicago Tribune,* January 18, 1961.
[13] *Chicago Tribune,* January 31, 1961.
[14] *Chicago Sun-Times,* February 2, 1961.

man Tells Steps to Avoid Payless Paydays," [15] were common. One newspaper pointed with alarm to the fact that the daily balance had hit a new low of $8 million in February; this same month, the paper stated, outgo had exceeded income by $10,416,000.[16]

Regardless of either the validity of the figures or the reality of "brinkmanship" in state finance, there was a great deal of concern in regard to the state's solvency. The experience of Michigan under Governor G. Mennen Williams was still fresh in the minds of the public and state officials alike, and many remarks were addressed to the possibility of payless paydays for Illinois employees. A further worry was that bonds totaling $365 million, approved in a 1960 referendum, would soon be going on sale. State officials were fearful of the effect of a fiscal crisis on the marketability of the bonds.

In this atmosphere it became apparent that the legislature would have to act during the 1961 session. Remedies which the Governor had proposed and which were within his power—collecting back alcoholic gallonage taxes and tightening administration of the sales tax—would take some time to become effective. The Governor faced a Republican-dominated legislature that seemed an enigma. Numerically, the Republicans controlled the House by a one-vote margin, 89 to 88, but a coalition of Democrats and maverick Republicans had elected a Democrat, Representative Paul Powell of Vienna, as Speaker, and Powell had assigned all committee chairmanships to Democrats. This made control of the House indefinite.

Because of the pressure of a crisis situation, both parties were aware of the necessity of remedying the state's financial ills. It seemed apparent that something had to be done about the drain on the general revenue fund during the biennium ending July 1, 1961, and, in the longer run, the problem of more adequate revenue sources still remained to be solved.

Republicans in the House grabbed the initiative on the first question. Representative William Pollack introduced a bill to transfer $5.1 million from the driver education fund to the general revenue fund. Transfers, which require a two-thirds vote by each house, were quickly seized as the solution to the fiscal crisis of the 1960–61 biennium after the early approval of Representative Pollack's bill (March 2nd).[17] Bills were introduced by Representatives Dunne and Harris to allow transfers up to $34 million from the motor fuel tax fund,[18]

[15] *Chicago Daily News*, March 27, 1961.
[16] *Chicago Daily News*, February 27, 1961.
[17] H.B. 107 (1961).
[18] H.B. 1653 (1961).

and by Representative Dunne[19] and Senator O'Brien[20] to transfer $16 million from the service recognition retirement fund. All but Representative Dunne's duplicate bill passed with emergency provisions which allowed immediate transfers from three funds to the general revenue fund of a total of $55.1 million.

The "solution" of transferring funds was far from permanent, however, since all transfers were essentially loans which would have to be repaid.

In April the legislature settled down to long-term patching of the revenue structure. In his budget message of April 19, 1961, Governor Kerner proposed closing loopholes in the sales tax, raising and broadening the corporate franchise tax, raising the tax on cigarettes, imposing a tax on cigars, and assessing a 5 per cent tax on the gross receipts of hotels and motels. Further, the Governor suggested a one-half cent raise in the sales tax to be effective for two years.[21] He estimated that these taxes would raise $265 million during the biennium.

Corporations had many sympathetic ears in the Senate, and the proposal to raise the rate of the corporate franchise tax as well as to broaden the base to include undistributed earnings stood little chance. Also, Senate Republicans had developed their own program in caucus and had taken a stand against an increase in the rate of the sales tax. Their program included four major points:

1. Postponement of repayment of funds to the service recognition and drivers education funds.

2. Trimming all appropriations by 5 per cent.

3. Passing legislation to turn unclaimed, idle trust funds over to the state.

4. Acceptance of the Governor's estimates of returns on the proposed broadening and hotel measures.[22]

The Republican caucus did back the bills to close loopholes in the sales taxes (sometimes called the "broadening bills"), which passed the Senate with little opposition and were sent to the House on June 5. When it became clear that the revisions in the corporate franchise tax would not be passed, the issue of a balanced budget turned more and more on the extra half cent of the sales tax. House Republicans had chafed during the session under Powell's leadership and were

[19] H.B. 1285 (1961).
[20] S.B. 369 (1961).
[21] State of Illinois, *Budget Message, 72nd Biennium* (April 19, 1961).
[22] *Chicago Sun-Times,* March 26, 1961.

not anxious to cooperate in passing a Democratic program of taxation. Also, the House had passed a one-half cent boost in the rate to be levied by municipalities; to pass another one-half cent increase would risk creating a public outcry, since the total sales tax rate would then be 4.5 per cent rather than 3.5 per cent. The Senate, on the other hand, had passed the broadening bills and a 3 per cent tax on gross receipts of hotels and motels. The Senate did not want to bear the full burden of tax imposition and therefore resisted a sales tax rate increase. However, the Governor still maintained he needed $129 million from the sales tax rate increase.[23]

To break what appeared to be a stalemate, Democrats resorted to rather risky strategy. Before the House were two bills. One, passed by the Senate, would continue the tax rate at 3 per cent. The other, a House bill, would raise the rate to 3.5 per cent. It was originally intended that the Democrats in the House, with some Republican help, would defeat the Senate bill, thus forcing the Senate to choose between letting both bills die, in which case the rate would drop back to 2.5 per cent, or accepting the Democratic-sponsored House bill, which would raise the rate to 3.5 per cent. Limitation of time forced House Democrats to push for an amendment to the Senate bill to raise the rate to 3.5 per cent.[24] Although the Senate rules state that one day is to elapse between House action on a bill and action on the same bill in the Senate, Lt. Governor Samuel Shapiro, presiding over the Senate, recognized the House amendment when it was sent over on the last day of the legislative session. This recognition touched off a melee that was to prompt the headline "Sales Tax Is Increased as GOP Senators Riot."[25] Objections were vociferously raised by Republicans who objected to Shapiro, a Democrat, recognizing the motion, but the die was cast in favor of the tax hike and the Senate voted 30 to 27 to sustain Shapiro's ruling.[26] Had the ruling not been sustained, the bill would have been effectively killed. Despite intimations of nazism on the part of Shapiro for refusing recognition of would-be filibusterers, four Senate Republicans voted with their Democratic colleagues to approve the sales tax hike.

As the 1961 session ended, Governor Kerner had asked for and received a 3.5 per cent rate on the Retailers' Occupation and Use

[23] *Champaign-Urbana Courier*, June 4, 1961.
[24] Constitutionally, each bill must be read on three separate days in each chamber, but concurrence on an amendment added to one chamber's bill by the other can constitutionally be enacted the day it is received.
[25] *Chicago Sun-Times*, July 1, 1961.
[26] *Ibid.*

taxes, a broadening of the tax base,[27] a 3 per cent tax on the gross receipts of hotels and motels, and an additional one cent tax per package on cigarettes. The only items deleted from the Governor's original tax proposal were the raising and broadening of the corporate franchise tax and the one cent cigar tax. The tax on cigars had been dropped from consideration, in part because of administrative difficulties and because of the inequity of a flat rate tax on a commodity which differs so greatly in price. The proposed increase in the corporate franchise tax had fallen before a strong business lobby which had barraged legislators with personal and written communications which stressed that business in Illinois would be adversely affected vis-à-vis competitive states.

The events of the 1961 session clearly demonstrate the jockeying between parties to avoid taking the "blame" for higher taxes; yet, in the face of a clearly spelled out fiscal crisis, methods were found to raise substantial additional revenue. Not surprisingly, these methods centered around broadening the base and raising the rates of existing taxes—there was no change in the general structure of the tax system.

THE REVENUE STUDY COMMISSION

The idea of a commission to study revenue had been current in Illinois for some time before a commission was finally appointed in 1961. An historical precedent had been set in 1949 when a Commission on Revenue Laws subjected Illinois' tax laws to careful scrutiny. In 1957 a Commission on Personal Property Tax was established. It reported to the legislature in 1959 and recommended several changes in personal property tax laws.

The 1959 General Assembly's debate on tax matters was stormy. Pressure was put on the legislature to end the personal property tax. The *Chicago Daily News*[28] described the flood of protests to Lee Daniels, chairman of the study commission on the property tax, as a "taxpayers' rebellion." A flat rate income tax was seriously proposed by interest groups such as the Illinois Agricultural Association, the Illinois Education Association, the Committee on Illinois Government, and by some legislators. Governor Stratton ruled out an income tax but admitted the state needed more money. In May the

[27] The broadening bills had been passed at a rate of only 3 per cent, however, and the rate differential was confusing. The rate was raised to 3.5 per cent at a later special session.
[28] *Chicago Daily News,* January 17, 1958.

Governor made a speech in which he called for a "crash study" of the United States' tax structure at all levels to be undertaken by a private foundation.[29]

In early summer, after the adjournment of the legislature, State Representative John K. Morris (D.–Chadwick), outspoken critic of property taxation, and State Treasurer Joseph Lohman, later a candidate for the Democratic nomination for governor, went to New York in search of a foundation which would be willing to finance a study of the Illinois tax structure.[30] Whereas many studies of the tax structure of a state have been welcomed as a delaying tactic, if nothing else, it soon became apparent that there was significant opposition to such a study in Illinois and that if such a study were to be conducted, there would be a struggle over the composition of the commission.

Opposition to making any study came mostly from groups anxious to avoid a change in the status quo. The *Chicago Tribune*, traditional opponent of income and business taxation, stated editorially: ". . . the subject is not one that can be farmed out. Deciding who is to pay for state government and how much, is a responsibility that the legislature and the governor cannot dodge. . . . Taxes are best imposed by men with whose purposes and policies the public has some familiarity, and over whose tenure in office it has some control." [31]

In contrast, enthusiastic responses were received from such groups as the IAA and the Taxpayers' Federation of Illinois.[32] At this time, it was announced that Governor Stratton was considering the appointment of a committee of from nine to 12 citizens in preparation for a formal application for funds from the Twentieth Century Fund. Lohman remarked that although no formal action had been taken by the foundation, "officials we talked to are receptive to the idea." [33]

By September of 1959 the Twentieth Century Fund had organized a staff to aid the commission. It was not until November 17, however, that Governor Stratton appointed a committee, headed by Meyer Kestnbaum, a Chicago clothing company executive and former chairman of President Eisenhower's Commission on Intergovernmental Relations. About this time, the Fund withdrew its offer of monetary support, explaining that there was insufficient time to complete a study before the 1961 session. Also, the foundation board of direc-

---

[29] *Champaign-Urbana Courier,* May 23, 1959.
[30] *Chicago Tribune,* July 20, 1959.
[31] July 23, 1959.
[32] *Chicago Daily News,* October 30, 1959.
[33] *Ibid.*

tors were reportedly unhappy with the high ratio (six of nine) of politicians to private citizens on the commission.[34] In the meantime, Governor Stratton had vetoed a bill appropriating $50,000 for a tax study. The legislation had been introduced by Representative Terrel E. Clarke (R.–Western Springs) and was co-sponsored by several prominent legislators of both parties.[35] It provided for a 15-man commission composed of five public members appointed by the Governor, five state senators, and five representatives. In his veto message Governor Stratton objected to the bill on the grounds that the studies contemplated were being carried out by the Department of Finance and that there was no provision in the budget for the appropriation of $50,000.

Meyer Kestnbaum remained interested in seeing a study made until his untimely death. During September, 1960, he had contacted the University of Illinois and other universities concerning the feasibility of obtaining a university research staff for the study.

In his budget message to the 1961 General Assembly the newly elected Democratic Governor, Otto Kerner, announced the appointment of a gubernatorial revenue study commission and asked the legislature for $120,000 to finance it. The commission was composed of representatives of "industry, labor, agriculture, municipalities and finance" under the chairmanship of Dean Simeon Leland of Northwestern University.[36] This idea was assailed as "presumptuous" by Senator W. Russell Arrington, prominent Republican legislator, who added that it was the responsibility of the legislature and not of the executive to revise and study the revenue structure of the state.[37] Accordingly, the Governor was given only $20,000 of his original request to finance the gubernatorial study committee. This severely crippled the commission, Dean Leland resigned, and the commission withered away.[38]

The 1961 legislature again passed Representative Clarke's bill for a legislative study commission. Governor Kerner vetoed it on August 25, stating that he had appointed a Revenue Study Commission and that it was his hope that its recommendations for changing the revenue structure would be adopted by the legislature before the deadline for reporting set up in the Clarke bill. He also indicated that he

[34] Chicago Sun-Times, September 13, 1960.
[35] H.B. 850 (1959).
[36] State of Illinois, Budget Message, 72nd Biennium (April 19, 1961), p. 2.
[37] Chicago Daily News, June 13, 1961.
[38] Louis H. Masotti, Illinois' 1961 Special Legislative Session: Some Tentative Conclusions Concerning the Effect of Process on Policy, National Center for Education in Politics, January, 1962.

intended to propose a new revenue article to a special session of the legislature.[39]

A special session was made almost mandatory by the failure of the 1961 legislature to agree on a reapportionment of congressional districts. In issuing the call for the special session in the fall of the year, Governor Kerner included in the list of topics to be considered the creation of a new revenue commission of 25 citizens and 12 legislators with an additional $130,000 appropriation.[40] This proposal was rejected amid allegations of "braintrusting," but the General Assembly, in the closing days of the special session, passed a bill providing for $50,000 [41] for a commission of 18. Only six were to be public members.

The Commission organized itself soon after the special session ended in November, 1961. Robert Cushman, a prominent tax attorney, was made chairman. Representative John K. Morris and Senator W. Russell Arrington served as vice-chairman and secretary, respectively. Professor H. K. Allen of the University of Illinois, who had served as director of the 1949 and 1957 studies, served as staff director and coordinated the work of a 24-man research staff whose services were contributed by four state universities.

The Commission organized itself into subcommittees and one of these, the Committee on Economy Measures, submitted questionnaires to all state officers and agencies asking for suggestions for economizing state funds. Public hearings on the same subject were held. This subcommittee and two others prepared written reports for the Commission.

Staff reports which, in printed form, totaled 813 pages were presented to the Commission by their authors. Separate reports dealt with each of the major categories of expenditures and discussed present programs and probable future needs. Another report combined the expenditure projections from these reports with original projections of state revenue to provide estimates of the probable "revenue gap" which would have to be filled with new taxes. Other reports dealt with local government finance and with the constitutional aspects of the Illinois tax system. There were eight separate reports dealing with a major state tax or with the taxation of a particular industry or commodity, and reports dealing with tax ear-

[39] State of Illinois, *Veto Messages, 72nd Biennium* (Springfield, 1961), p. 19.
[40] The Governor, in calling a special session, specifies the topics which may be considered at the session.
[41] This was in addition to the $20,000 appropriated for the gubernatorial commission.

marking and nontax revenue sources. A brief report by Professor Allen on potential sources of additional tax revenue included estimates of the probable yield of individual and corporate income taxes and other taxes not now levied in Illinois.

It was apparent from the beginning of the Commission's deliberations that it was unlikely to recommend major changes in the existing tax structure. A number of the members were known to be conservative in their fiscal views and several were considered as representative of the viewpoint of business groups. Some of the more energetic legislative members busied themselves with the work of the economy and earmarking subcommittees. These activities received a great deal of press coverage and, in principle, were approved by persons of many political persuasions. Approval was less certain when specific suggestions were made and, in any case, were unlikely to go far toward solving the state's financial problems.

On February 8 and 9, 1963, after many meetings to receive reports from staff members and subcommittees, the Commission met for the purpose of making tentative decisions on the recommendations. A series of proposed recommendations, drawn from the research studies, were voted upon with the understanding that a final vote would be taken later. On February 19, the final vote was taken and the Commission proceeded to print its report and the reports of the staff members for distribution to the legislature.

A number of recommendations were adopted. In the field of education, the Commission supported the idea of the state bearing a higher share of the cost of local schools but, in view of the fiscal situation, recommended that nothing be done in the current biennium. It recommended that state support of driver's education be discontinued and that the portion of the driver's license fee earmarked for that purpose be put in the general fund. It recommended that consideration be given to using statewide achievement tests to measure the quality of schooling and that minimum achievement be a condition of receiving state aid. It was also recommended that tuition at institutions of higher education be raised to the average level of neighboring states, that the State Board of Higher Education be given power to allocate funds to the state universities, and that a state system of junior colleges be created.

There were general recommendations that departments raise fees to cover the full cost of services rendered and a specific recommendation that there be no sales tax exemption for food. Minor changes in the inheritance tax were recommended and increases in motor vehicle user taxes were proposed.

The Commission recommended, with Senator Arrington and Chairman Cushman dissenting, limited increases in general corporation taxes. Specifically, earned surplus was to be included in the base of the corporate franchise tax or, alternatively, the rate was to be increased from one-twentieth to three-twentieths of 1 per cent. As an alternative to either of these, a corporate franchise tax measured by net income was suggested. Senator Laughlin joined in the dissent from this recommendation.

In the property tax field, it was recommended that county assessors be required in every county and that township assessors be abolished or brought under control of the county assessor. The principal recommendations for raising additional revenue proposed higher taxes on tobacco, alcoholic beverages, pari-mutuel betting, and public utilities. The Commission recommended that the Public Aid Commission be abolished and replaced by a code department under the control of the Governor.[42] The list concluded with the recommendation that all possible earmarked funds be abolished and with a list of 20 proposals for reducing state expenditure.

State Representative John K. Morris, Vice-Chairman of the Commission, wrote a strongly worded minority report in which he charged:

The Commission has made a detailed and extensive analysis of the revenue requirements in the State of Illinois over the next ten years. The need for additional revenue is not disputed and the amounts are realistic. However, the Commission was not only charged with stating the problem but was also obligated to come up with solutions. Instead, the Commission has made some piecemeal, patchwork recommendations, the effect of which can only be to compound the regressiveness of the Illinois tax structure.

The Commission duly noted the plight of property owners in this state and the disproportionate share of the tax burden which falls on home owners, farmers and persons on retirement. Similarly, the Commission acknowledged that some 80% of the revenue of the state is derived from sales tax of one form or another. Notwithstanding this acknowledged imbalance, the effect of the Commission's recommendations is to make more disproportionate these very disproportions.

. . . . .

I believe that the very composition of the Revenue Study Commission made it impossible for long range solutions to be found. The effort to get agreement from elements of the economy who do not want the present disproportion alleviated was doomed to failure. It defies human nature to expect the very elements who are not now paying their share of taxes

[42] Increases in public aid (welfare) payments were a major cause of the financial crisis of 1961, and the Public Aid Commission had been involved in a series of controversies. See Gilbert Y. Steiner, *Social Insecurity: The Politics of Welfare* (Chicago: Rand McNally & Co., 1966), pp. 205–37.

to voluntarily agree to such reform. The same elements have resisted a revenue article which would give a broader scope to legislative power in this field. I believe it is fruitless to expect such commissions to resolve their differences in the kind of forthright manner that the revenue problems of this state require. It is like asking a committee made up of hot-rodders and members of the Safety Council to work out a safety program.[43]

Neither the recommendations of the Commission nor the staff reports had much impact during the 1963 legislative session. The suggestions for a system of junior colleges and the reorganization of the Public Aid Commission into a code department were adopted, but both had strong support from other quarters and probably would have been adopted regardless of Revenue Commission action. Taxes on pari-mutuel betting and public utilities were increased but, even here, it is doubtful that the Commission recommendations were a major factor.

The Commission had been charged to recommend a new revenue article but had been unable to reach agreement before making its report to the legislature. The Governor then asked that the Commission reconvene and make such a recommendation. After many differences of opinion, a compromise article was approved by an eight to six vote. The proposal would have given the legislature the authority to classify real and personal property and to exempt any class of personal property from taxation. It prohibited the levy of a graduated income tax but specifically permitted a flat rate tax and liberalized the debt limit upon school districts maintaining both elementary and high schools.

No one seemed particularly anxious to support the article, and, except for the last minute efforts of a member of the Governor's staff to find a sponsor for the joint resolution, it might not have been introduced in the General Assembly.

The longer range results of the Commission were undoubtedly greater than is suggested by its failure to have a significant impact upon the 1963 session of the General Assembly. Several hundred copies of a volume containing the commission and staff reports were circulated, and the demand for additional copies was so great that the 1965 legislature appropriated funds for a second, paperbound, printing.

Several of the reports provided carefully documented examples of the inequity and irrationality of the Illinois tax system, but three reports appear to have been especially significant.

One of these reports contained the revenue and expenditure pre-

[43] *Report of the Commission on Revenue* (Springfield, 1963), pp. 56–57.

dictions prepared by Professor Case M. Sprenkle. The predicted revenue gap clearly demonstrated the need for an elastic tax base. The figures printed in the report of the Commission itself, as well as in Professor Sprenkle's report, indicated that there would be a massive gap between expenditures and the revenue produced by the tax system as it existed in 1961. These figures were to become the ghost which would biennially haunt the legislature, visiting newspaper editorial columns in the off season. By pointing out the inelasticity of the existing tax system, these figures bolstered the indictment which other staff reports had brought against the system on grounds of inequity. More important, however, they indicated to legislators and interest groups alike that maintaining the status quo with respect to the tax structure would mean frequent increases in the tax rates.

Another staff report which was to have a major impact was one prepared by Professor J. Nelson Young of the University of Illinois Law School. Professor Young's analysis of the constitutional problems which might be involved in implementing some of the most frequently proposed changes in the Illinois tax system revealed the extent to which constitutional matters have shaped tax policy and tax politics in Illinois; more important was his critical analysis of the Bachrach case. Among his conclusions were these: "On the basis of the foregoing analysis and appraisal of the decisions in *Bachrach v. Nelson* it appears likely that, if a question were presented the Illinois Supreme Court would reconsider its position and sustain an income tax as a privilege tax.

"It is reasonably clear that a corporate franchise tax based on net income would be sustained as a valid privilege tax." [44]

Professor Young, of course, was not the first to express these opinions. Many attorneys have conceded the probability that the Illinois Supreme Court would uphold a properly drawn corporate or individual income tax, but the publicity given to Professor Young's analysis greatly reduced the value to tax lobbyists of the "threat" of unconstitutionality.

Professor Sprenkle's projections raised the specter of biennial tax increases and Professor Young's analysis raised the possibility, unpalatable to many, that the income tax could, without constitutional amendment, provide a more elastic source of revenue. A third staff report offered another alternative. Professor A. James Heins presented an analysis showing that a sales tax broadened to include services

[44] J. Nelson Young, "Constitutional Problems," *Report of the Commission on Revenue* (Springfield, 1963), pp. 373, 382.

would produce a very large amount of revenue and, at the same time, would reduce the regressivity and capriciousness of the sales tax. In addition Professor Heins expressed the opinion that a broadened sales tax would probably be easier to administer than the existing tax. The appeal of this proposal to many members of the Commission was immediate and obvious to those in the room when it was presented. This seemed to be the politician's dream come true —a highly productive source of revenue which was not a "new tax," did not involve a rate increase, was easy to administer, would not have the adverse effect on business claimed for the income tax, was clearly constitutional, and, incidentally, would improve the equity and elasticity of the tax system. Events four years later were to prove this appraisal overly enthusiastic, but the Heins report was to play a significant role in Illinois tax politics.

THE REVENUE AMENDMENT OF 1965

Even though the "gateway" amendment of 1950 somewhat eased the requirements for amending the state constitution, the process is still a difficult one. The revenue article (Article IX) has not been amended since the adoption of the present constitution in 1870, although proposed amendments were submitted to the voters on seven occasions before 1965.

The process of adopting a constitutional amendment is a two-step one. The proposed amendment must first be introduced as a joint resolution in the legislature where it must receive an extraordinary majority (two-thirds). Then it must be submitted to the electorate and must receive 50 per cent of all votes cast in the election or two-thirds of the votes cast on the amendment.

Legislative Approval

At the legislative level, a proposed amendment faces even more hazards than does a tax bill. Like a tax bill, an amendment vitally affects the interests of powerful organized groups, and like a tax bill, it deals with a highly technical subject about which few legislators are fully informed. In addition, a proposed revenue amendment must be drafted so as to maximize its chances of adoption in a public referendum in a state which has shown a marked reluctance to vote such changes. Experience has shown that major changes will be made only if there is wide agreement among interest groups, political parties, and reform or "good government" groups. Under these conditions it is possible to mount a campaign for adoption which takes on the nature of a crusade against apathy and antipathy to change.

During the 1961 and 1963 sessions of the General Assembly, several proposed amendments were introduced, but none came close to adoption. It was clear that several major interest groups had the power to block any proposal which did not meet their approval, but that none of them had the power to push through a proposal of their own. The failure of the Commission on Revenue to agree on any proposal for a revenue amendment on the first try and the very close vote by which a proposal finally was adopted were symptomatic of the degree of division which existed.

Among the important interest groups there was general agreement that the article needed "cleaning up." Generally, this phrase seemed to mean that the article should be rewritten to avoid the necessity of the legal fiction that the sales tax is an occupation tax, to permit classification or exemption of personal property, and to eliminate the discrimination against unit school districts in the debt limit clause. Beyond this point, however, there was little agreement. The powerful business coalition opposed any change that might result in the imposition of income or general business taxes and was thus basically content with the status quo. The agriculture-education-labor coalition favored changes in the tax structure which would shift the burden from sales and property taxes to income or business taxes, but the motives of various members differed considerably.

The Governor naturally wanted a revenue article which would provide maximum flexibility in financing state government, but Governor Kerner, like his predecessor, had pledged to oppose an income tax and at no time did he provide forceful leadership in fiscal matters. The Cook County Democratic organization, under the leadership of Mayor Richard Daley, was actively concerned about obtaining additional nonproperty tax powers for the city of Chicago and with staving off Republican attempts to impose a limit on the city corporate levy. It could also be expected to react unfavorably to any development which might threaten the existing de facto system of property tax classification.

Still another interested group was made up of the legislators themselves. Every elected official desires to avoid irritating his constituents and few actions irritate constituents as much as do tax increases. Thus, legislators are ever on the lookout for means of reducing that irritation or, better, of shifting the blame for it. Every "tax expert" who has testified before a legislative committee or revenue study commission knows that the joking request to "invent a tax that everybody likes to pay" is no joke.

In these circumstances, it is not surprising that none of the proposed revenue articles received serious attention in the 1961 and 1963 sessions; but forces were at work which were to change the situation before 1965. One important force was the growing conviction that the sales tax was inadequate as a source of future revenue. The large gap between revenue and expenditure projected by the Commission on Revenue and its staff and the history of repeated increases in the rate raised the possibility that Illinois would soon have the highest sales tax in the nation. Memories of the 1961 brush with financial crisis were still fresh and there was little evidence that the financial situation was improving. In 1963 welfare checks were briefly held up due to a lack of funds. The establishment by the 1961 legislature of the Illinois Building Authority as a way of bypassing the constitutional limitation on the creation of bonded indebtedness alarmed many who held orthodox fiscal views. This alarm was heightened when the 1963 legislature used the Authority not only for major capital projects but also for relatively small items which were almost in the nature of current maintenance.[45] Another development which alarmed many defenders of the status quo was the growing expression of the belief that a state income tax would be upheld by the state Supreme Court.

To those sensitive to these changing circumstances, the position of the status quo coalition seemed to be eroding. One of these persons was Norman J. Beatty, tax manager and lobbyist for the Illinois State Chamber of Commerce. Following adjournment of the 1963 session of the General Assembly, Mr. Beatty had contacted John Cox of the Illinois Agricultural Association and suggested that the time for joint action had come. The Illinois State Chamber of Commerce and the Illinois Agricultural Association thus formed the initial liaison between the two major coalitions, and in March, 1964, nine organizations were invited to discuss a possible revision of the revenue article. The organizations were the Illinois Agricultural Association, Illinois Education Association, Illinois Association of School Boards, Chicago Association of Commerce and Industry, Civic Federation, Illinois Manufacturers' Association, Taxpayers' Federation of Illinois, Illinois State Chamber of Commerce, and

---

[45] The Building Authority issues bonds and uses the funds to construct capital facilities which are then "leased" to a state agency or department until the full cost has been recovered.

the state AFL-CIO. From this meeting and several subsequent ones was to come the proposal which, with modifications, would be submitted to the voters in 1966.

Since the representatives of the "selected organizations" were lobbyists who were well known to each other, they were also aware of the general position of each organization. Each was understood to have at least one "must" position to be satisfied. The business groups wanted protection against business taxes and against high and graduated income taxes. Labor insisted upon a "true" sales tax which would permit exemption of food and medicine. The Illinois Agricultural Association wanted an income tax in the belief that the adoption of this form of taxation would relieve pressure on the property tax, and the Illinois Education Association wanted an income tax as a means of raising more money for educational purposes. On other issues there was a considerable measure of agreement or, at least, a greater willingness to bargain away a favored position if necessary.

As the meetings continued, it became apparent that several of the business representatives were willing to accept an article which permitted an income tax, provided rates were strictly limited. Originally, they proposed the requirement that a public referendum must be held before an income tax could be imposed,[46] but eventually abandoned this position with regard to the first 3 per cent of tax rate. Agricultural interests were willing to accept the provision that an income tax be flat rate with a ceiling and a provision that the individual and corporate tax be the same.

It was quickly agreed that personal property should be divided into tangible and intangible property with the legislature being given power to classify intangible property as needed.[47]

All representatives agreed that it would be desirable to exempt household goods and personal items from taxation, but both business and agricultural groups were concerned about the possibility that their property might be singled out for heavier taxation. To avoid this possibility the groups worked out a fourfold classification which they felt would protect both interests. The draft read: "The General Assembly may classify tangible personal property into the following classes: (a) household goods and personal effects not used in the

[46] Referred to as a "double referendum," since the public would have to approve the constitutional amendment itself before voting specifically on an income tax proposal.
[47] Minutes of the meeting of the selected organizations concerned with amendment of the Revenue Article, March 11, 1964, Bismarck Hotel, Chicago, Illinois.

production of income, (b) business and farm inventories, including grain, livestock and poultry, (c) motor vehicles, ships, boats, and aircraft, and (d) all other tangible personal property, and may abolish property taxes on any or all classes thereof." [48]

It will be noted that class (b) contains both business and farm inventories and class (d) includes both business and farm machinery, thus eliminating the possibility that either farm or business property could be given special treatment vis-à-vis the other.

The principle of raising the limit on bonded indebtedness of school districts which operate both elementary and secondary schools was adopted with little controversy, although there was some bargaining over rates.

As the selected organizations proposal began to take shape, attention shifted to legislative strategy. It was agreed that efforts should be made to forestall the introduction of other revenue amendments and that attempts should be made to reach an agreement with the Governor before introduction of a proposal. Both efforts failed. A copy of the selected organizations proposal was sent to the Governor's office as early as November, 1964. Several months later representatives of the selected organizations met with the Governor. The Governor's attitude was described by one of those present as "amiable but noncommittal." Apparently the Governor was unwilling either to negotiate with the selected organizations or to reveal his own plans. At his request, however, the selected organizations did delay introduction of their own proposal, but when he had made no statement on his revenue plans by April 8, the proposal was introduced simultaneously in both houses of the General Assembly as H.J.R. 40 and S.J.R. 26. The main features of the proposed resolution were:

1. A flat rate income tax would be permitted. The rate could not exceed 5 per cent and individual and corporate rates would be the same.

2. A referendum would be required for imposition of any income tax at a rate in excess of 3 per cent.

3. Classification of real estate would not be allowed.

4. Classification of tangible and intangible personal property would be permitted. The permissible classes of tangible personal property were specified.

5. Debt limits for unit school districts would be raised.

6. A "true" sales tax would be permitted and exemptions could be made by legislative action.

[48] H.J.R. 71 (1965).

Several other proposed revenue amendments were already in the hopper. S.J.R. 1, written and sponsored by Senator W. Russell Arrington, called for multiple submission of the more controversial parts of the article. This approach stemmed from the feeling of Senator Arrington and Robert Cushman, who had been chairman of the Commission on Revenue, that the voters of Illinois would never accept an income tax but that this should not stand in the way of other needed reforms.

H.J.R. 3, sponsored by Representative Bernard Peskin (D.–Northbrook), was backed by liberal legislators. Essentially, it provided for classification and gave the legislature the authority to levy whatever taxes were necessary. This article had been presented to several general assemblies with little success, since the opposition had branded it a "blank check" which the legislature might well abuse. Representative Harold Katz (D.–Glencoe) was the sponsor of H.J.R. 30, which had been drafted by the Chicago Bar Association. Although resembling the selected organizations draft in many respects, the Bar Association draft was more flexible. It allowed legislative classification of all types of property and placed no limit on an income tax. It did clearly prohibit a graduated tax and required that individuals and corporations were to be taxed at the same rates.

Representative John K. Morris (D.–Chadwick) also introduced an amendment which would have allowed abolition of or rate reductions on personal property taxes, classification of real estate, and the levy of a flat rate income tax. Although the amendment was generally in line with the previous Illinois Agricultural Association policy, it was, of course, unacceptable to several members of the selected organizations group. Other amendments introduced (H.J.R. 23, H.J.R. 53, and H.J.R. 57) either made minor changes or did not receive widespread support.

Early in May the Governor presented his long-awaited message on revenue reform. He proposed a revenue article which would:

1. Permit classification of personal property.

2. Permit a state wheel tax in lieu of property taxation of motor vehicles.

3. Increase debt limits for unit school districts.

4. Permit the General Assembly to classify real property.[49]

The first three points coincided, in general, with the selected organizations draft, but the fourth raised the troublesome point of real estate classification which had been largely ignored by the selected organizations.

[49] Text of Governor's address on revenue reform, *Illinois State Register*, May 6, 1965.

Late in May the House and Senate created a joint legislative committee of 10 members to study proposed amendments and make recommendations to the General Assembly. This committee included among its members several men who were knowledgeable and highly respected in the field of revenue.[50] The committee had no staff other than those lobbyists who had information which would be of use to it.

Senator Arrington appeared before the committee at an early meeting in which he asked the committee to consider the device of multiple submissions to avoid the sabotage of all improvements by a few controversial provisions. The Senator was convinced that the public would never pass an article which provided for an income tax. The multiple submission device was especially opposed by the Illinois Agricultural Association, which felt that it would give Cook County a means of getting classification of real property legalized without giving anything in return.

In spite of the Arrington statement, the committee's attention centered on the draft prepared by the selected organizations. From the legislative point of view, this draft had already cleared a number of obstacles by gaining approval of several of the most important interest groups concerned with taxation.

Several additional issues were raised in the joint committee. One of these was the possibility of requiring that the personal property tax be abolished when an income tax was adopted. This idea does not seem to have been strongly pushed by any interest group, but after it was suggested by Representative John Morris, it quickly caught on among the legislators who felt that the chances of adoption would be enhanced if the voters knew the imposition of an income tax would be accompanied by the abolition of the highly unpopular personal property tax. Eventually, it was agreed in the joint committee that taxation of classes (a), (b), and (c) should be abolished if an income tax were imposed. That would leave only class (d), consisting largely of farm and business machinery, in the taxable category. After this agreement had been worked out, the committee had a very short time to deal with the problem of replacing the property tax revenue which local governments would lose with the abolition of the personal property tax. An amendment was drafted guarantee-

---

[50] Members of the committee were Senators Arthur Sprague, Thomas Lyons, Everett Laughlin, William Harris, and Robert McCarthy; Representatives Terrel Clarke (Chairman), James Loukas, Clinton Youle, John Morris, and Paul Elward. Senators Harris and Laughlin and Representatives Clarke, Elward, Loukas, and Morris had served on the 1963 Commission on Revenue. Senator Lyons had worked as an attorney for the Cook County Assessor's office.

ing that the proceeds of not less than 1 per cent of any such income tax should be distributed to local taxing districts. Unfortunately for the future of the proposal, drafting was done so hurriedly that no one noticed that the wording guaranteed local governments only one one-hundredth of the proceeds of the tax, although it was intended that the proceeds of a 1 per cent rate (one-third of a 3 per cent tax) should be so earmarked.

Another major issue which had not been settled by the selected organizations was the matter of classification of real estate. De facto classification of real estate was well established in Cook County but decisions of the Supreme Court in the "railroad cases" raised the possibility that a taxpayer challenge of the system might be upheld. In the joint legislative committee, the presence of Democratic legislators from Cook County insured that the issue would be an important one. Senator Thomas Lyons, a former employee of the Cook County Assessor's office, took the lead in demanding that real estate classification be permitted, and he appears to have been regarded as representing "Cook County" on this issue. Even more important, however, were the actions of the Governor. His message early in May revealed that the major difference between the selected organizations and the Governor was real estate classification. This difference was to play a major role in negotiations from that point onward. Representative Loukas and Senator Lyons were in touch with the Governor's office on the issue, and on occasion representatives of the selected organizations and the joint legislative committee met with the Governor.

Originally, the Governor made it clear that he wanted classification in every county and cited examples of existing classification systems in such downstate cities as Peoria and East St. Louis. Mr. Beatty, representing the state Chamber of Commerce, countered with a flatly negative response, saying that business could not support an article containing such a provision. After further discussion, the Governor suggested classification in all counties over 100,000 population. This, too, was flatly rejected by the business interests with the backing of agriculture. Finally, with both parties nearing exhaustion and the deadline fast approaching, classification in Cook County only was accepted by both parties. The exact wording provided that "Any classification of real property for purposes of taxation in effect in the County of Cook on January 1, 1965 shall continue in effect unless modified as hereinafter provided."

With the issue of classification and the abolition of personal property taxation settled, the legislative committee was ready to report a proposed amendment to the legislature. This proposal was introduced in the House as H.J.R. 71 on June 29, only the day before the traditional adjournment date. The final wording had been drawn up and approved in an all-night meeting.

The final results were a compromise which was acceptable to the major interest groups represented in the selected organizations, legislative members of the joint committee, and the Governor, but concessions had been made to other groups on a number of "minor" points. For example, banking interests were particularly interested in clarifying the tax treatment to be accorded intangibles held in trust. Accordingly, a clause was included which defined the taxpayer as the recipient of the benefit of the trust and relieved banks of liability for the payment of taxes on intangibles for which the bank acted as trustee. At one point in the negotiations, railroad interests asked that language be inserted which would write into the constitution the favorable court rulings on the recent railroad cases. This request was granted although the wording which ultimately emerged was ambiguous and, unaccountably, appeared in the Cook County section of the amendment, although it presumably was meant to apply to the entire state.

H.J.R. 71 was introduced at about 2 P.M. on June 29. The committee's motion for adoption was objected to by several representatives. Representative Bernard Peskin asked the Speaker for a delay until after dinner to give the members a chance to study the legislation. The request was granted, and the House did not consider the proposed amendment until 7 P.M. when it reconvened.

During the recess a group of liberal Democratic legislators met with Representative Peskin in his office.[51] They were alarmed, after the brief study which they were able to give the amendment, at the ambiguities and the detail written into the amendment. Representative Peskin went to talk with the Governor and told him that he felt that because of drafting errors and ambiguities, the amendment could not guarantee a true sales tax or a satisfactory allocation of the income tax to local governments. Although the Governor seemed concerned, his support for the joint committee draft was not swayed.

The debate on the issue was brief and consisted largely of arguments against. The opponents, in their brief recess meeting, had mapped out most of the arguments later raised against the article— ambiguous wording in many sections, restrictiveness, and difficulties in implementing some sections such as the return of revenue to

[51] Representatives Marvin Lieberman, James Moran, Adlai E. Stevenson III, and Abner Mikva.

local governments in lieu of the personal property tax. The proponents countered with a single argument—"it is agreed." On the strength of this agreement, the House passed the resolution by a vote of 143 to 18. The 18 votes against the amendment came from opposite ends of the political spectrum. The liberal Democrats in voting against H.J.R. 71 were voting against a nongraduated income tax and other restrictions on legislative freedom in dealing with revenue needs. Conservative Republicans objected to the inclusion of any kind of income tax in the article.

The resolution then went to the Senate where the majority leader, Senator Arrington, refused to sponsor the act but did promise not to oppose it. One significant amendment was added in the Senate. The House-passed version had called for the abolition of all taxes on personal property classes (a), (b), and (c) within four years of the adoption of an income tax. The remaining class, (d), was by far the largest class, since it contained both industrial and agricultural machinery. When this became known, senators were deluged with protests, and as a result, language was changed to exclude all classes of personal property.[52] The amended version passed the Senate by a vote of 46 to 7 with two abstentions.[53] The House concurred in the amendment and the first step toward amending the revenue article had been taken.

Campaign for Ratification

An attempt to pass a constitutional amendment to the revenue article is another dimension of state tax politics. The skills and techniques needed to persuade millions of voters to vote for an amendment are different from those needed to pass a measure in the state legislature. In the legislature, bargaining and compromise leading to agreement among the major interest groups is the key. Technical mastery of every detail of tax law is an important asset. Once the measure is submitted to the people, however, compromise is impossible and simplicity is essential to avoid confusion.

As Thomas Kitsos has noted in his analysis of the fate of proposed constitutional amendments in Illinois, there are certain tendencies which must be taken into consideration.[54] One of these, of course, is that most amendments are defeated. The extraordinary majority re-

---

[52] Reports as to the source of complaints differ. One version is that they came primarily from manufacturing interests. Another version is that utility corporations were the major protestors.
[53] One of whom was Senator Arrington.
[54] Thomas Kitsos, "Constitutional Amendments and the Voter, 1952–66," *Illinois Government*, No. 27 (July, 1967).

quired to pass a constitutional amendment is one factor, and another is the tendency to vote against all constitutional amendments which is especially strong in downstate counties.

This suggests that opponents of an amendment have the easier task and that an extraordinary effort, almost in the nature of a crusade, must be mounted if an amendment of major importance is to be adopted. Unfortunately for the proponents of the proposed revenue amendment, their political success at the legislative level produced the seeds of almost certain defeat at the referendum level. Why this is so will become clear in the following narrative of the events which preceded the vote on the issue in November, 1966.

The issue of revenue reform appeared nearly dormant for many months after the campaign for legislative action ended on June 30, 1965. The proposed amendment had received relatively little publicity during the session and its sudden introduction and adoption occurred during the final hours of the session when public attention was on the more immediately pressing issues which are always decided at that hectic time. Despite the seeming quiet, however, events were taking place which were to be influential in determining the fate of the amendment. In mid-July, liberal and conservative legislative opponents of the amendment met to write the statement of opposition to the amendment which would be included with the copy of the proposed amendment sent to each registered voter by the Secretary of State. At the same time, proponents were meeting to draft the arguments for the amendment. Unlike previous official explanations, however, there was no unbiased explanation to the voter of the provisions of the amendment. Instead, the "explanation" and "argument for" were one and the same. The result was rather confusing and some of the statements were rather clearly in conflict with the actual wording of the amendment. For example, the explanation stated that a sum equal to the yield of a 1 per cent income tax rate must be returned to local governments if an income tax was imposed and the personal property tax abolished. The amendment itself clearly stated that 1 per cent of the proceeds of the income tax was to be distributed to local units.

Some weeks later, Representative Abner Mikva, one of the early opponents of the amendment, wrote Professor J. Nelson Young of the University of Illinois Law School to ask his evaluation of the amendment. Professor Young's answer largely confirmed the criticisms which the liberal representatives had made on the floor of the House.[55] Mikva sent copies of Young's letter to several people, in-

[55] J. Nelson Young to Abner J. Mikva, September 22, 1965.

cluding influential labor leaders, and they began an evaluation of their position on the revenue amendment. In February the Committee on Political Education of the United Steelworkers came out against the new article, prompting the steelworkers to take a stand against it.[56] The opposition of this influential union attracted considerable attention in labor and liberal circles and affected the attitude of other labor leaders as the 1965 state convention of the AFL-CIO approached.

The *Report of the Executive Board* of the Illinois State Federation of Labor and Congress of Industrial Organizations to the state convention contained these words: "Much publicity was given to the story that the state organization fully supported the proposal. The fact is that the principle only was given approval by our President in April in order to get something started in the legislature. At that time, it appeared hopeless that the General Assembly would act in this field. Any news item which implies that the State AFL-CIO is pleased with the proposed New Revenue Article is not true." [57] The convention adjourned without taking any official action on the amendment, but it was clear that little support was apt to be forthcoming from organized labor.[58]

Despite the desires of leaders of the selected organizations group, supporters of the amendment were not organized until March of 1966. To some of the proponents it appeared that the Governor moved very slowly in the selection of a head for the proposed Governor's Citizen Committee. There was some embarrassment over the premature announcement of the appointment of a chairman, who did not accept and, in fact, was opposed to the article. However, in March, 1966, William J. Crowley, an executive of Northern Illinois Gas Company, was appointed head of the Governor's Citizen Committee. He also acted as chairman of an incorporated Citizen's Committee for a New Revenue Article. The former group consisted of one hundred prominent citizens, and the latter consisted of representatives of the major interest groups (except labor) which had drafted and worked for the article at the legislative level. The latter group raised the funds and organized the campaign for adoption. The state Chamber of Commerce and the Illinois Agricultural Association carried the major burden of organizing the campaign and

[56] *Illinois State Register,* February 3, 1966.
[57] Illinois State Federation of Labor and Congress of Industrial Organizations, *Report of the Executive Board* (October 4, 1965), p. 52.
[58] In March the executive board of the state AFL-CIO voted to oppose the amendment and in October, 1966, just a month before the election, the state convention voted to oppose it.

both donated a good deal of staff time. The IAA agreed to organize the 81 rural counties and, at the height of the campaign, had 19 full time staff members assigned to these counties. The Chamber of Commerce accepted responsibility for the urban counties except for Cook County, which was organized by the incorporated Citizen's Committee.

The opposition did not coalesce until late in August of 1966. The opposition consisted mainly of civic groups such as the City Club of Chicago, the League of Women Voters, the State Congress of Parents and Teachers, with additional backing from the Chicago Teachers Union, the Municipal League, organized labor, and several individuals interested in defeating the proposed article. This group of organizations and individuals formed a rather loose-knit group called Defeat the Revenue Amendment (DRA). A principal aim of this coalition was to legitimize "liberal" opposition to the amendment—opposition based on a desire for greater flexibility, legislative discretion, and a graduated income tax.

Two major problems plagued the proponents. The first of these arose from the necessity of selling rank and file members upon the proposed article. The article had been drafted by lobbyists for the various organizations. Understandably, lobbyists are more sophisticated about the political process and the necessary role of compromise than are rank and file members and they had, in every case, accepted a compromise which at some point violated the goals which their organization had been advocating. Thus, each organization was faced with the problem of explaining the compromise to its own members at the same time that it was attempting to convince the general public of the advantages of the proposal. Although the Citizen's Committee tried to coordinate the literature distributed by all proponents, a large amount of confusion as to the intent and possible effects of the article still leaked into the campaign. Business groups were anxious to convince their members that the article would hinder rather than encourage an income tax, whereas farm groups were eager to demonstrate the opposite. This confusion was inevitably of more help to opponents than to the proponents.

The second major problem faced by the proponents involved the enthusiasm and loyalty of the leadership of some of the groups supporting the article. Although some of the most important business organizations were supporting the article, the compromise on an income tax did not please more conservative business leaders who were the potential sources of a good deal of campaign money. Groups such as the Illinois Manufacturers' Association and the Oil Council were not only unfavorably disposed to contributing to the campaign, but within the ranks there was a good deal of opposition to the article. Proponent groups such as the state Chamber of Commerce were quite anxious lest business be split and worked hard to ensure at least a neutral position for such dissident groups.

There was also worry about the enthusiasm of the Cook County Democratic organization. Traditionally, Cook County returns a higher percentage of favorable votes on constitutional amendments than do downstate counties.[59] This, plus the heavy concentration of voters in the county made strong support from the Democratic leadership essential if the amendment was to be adopted. Yet, there were reasons to believe that they might consider passage of the article a mixed blessing. True, the article purported to legalize the de facto classification system, but some attorneys had raised questions as to how the courts might rule. Constitutionally, there could be no "system of classification in effect on January 1, 1965." Neither were there any administrative orders setting forth the levels at which various types of property were, in fact, assessed. The classification system existed only as embodied in the detailed instructions and tables in the assessors' manuals, and the only evidence that this produced systematic differences in the levels of assessment were the statistical studies of the relationship between sales prices and assessed values of various classes of property. Thus, there was considerable uncertainty as to what ruling the courts might make. The Illinois Municipal League had decided to oppose the article, primarily because of uncertainty as to whether the revenue lost from personal property tax exemption would be adequately made up by state grants. This, logically, should have concerned Chicago; in addition, Chicago officials had reason to be even more concerned over the fact that the amendment would have foreclosed the possibility of a city income tax at any time in the future.

Even now, it is not possible for the outside observer to determine the true feelings of the Cook County Democratic leaders. Some observers are of the opinion that only a stroke of luck prevented outright opposition. Democratic Senator Paul Douglas was running for his political life against a strong Republican opponent, Charles Percy, and the time which would be given to substantive questions was minimal. The most important substantive question to Chicago Democrats was a school bond issue which was also on the ballot. According to some, these factors led Democratic Party chiefs to tell people to vote "yes" on all questions, thus avoiding confusion. Evi-

[59] Kitsos, *op. cit.*

dence that they did not consider approval of the revenue amendment of prime importance is provided by the fact that outspoken opponents of the amendment received invitations to speak at local party meetings, a courtesy which is unheard of in matters of great importance to the Democratic Party in Cook County. Further, the number of sample ballots indicating the "right" vote picked up from the Citizen's Committee fell far below expectations.

Although the proponents succeeded in raising less than one-third of the projected $500,000 budget, they utilized much full-time staff help donated by the state Chamber of Commerce and the Illinois Agricultural Association. A public relations firm was hired to map out an advertising campaign. Several pamphlets, flyers, and a film were prepared, and stickers bearing the slogan "Prevent Unfair Taxation" were printed.[60] These materials were made available to local organizations which varied in strength and effectiveness in various parts of the state. Lack of funds, however, prevented the massive advertising campaign in the last few days before the election that had been recommended by the public relations firm.

The opponents had much less in the way of material resources than did the proponents, but they did not need as much. The budget of the DRA totaled about $10,000 and office space was provided by the League of Women Voters. In some areas they were able to utilize volunteer labor, and through the League of Women Voters, the Parent Teachers Association, and labor unions, they had access to rather large audiences. Perhaps the greatest advantage enjoyed by the opponents was that the mere existence of organized opposition destroyed the crusade spirit which is necessary to pass a revenue article. As Morton Kondracke, writing in the *Chicago Sun-Times,* put it: "For most voters, the subject of taxation is so complicated that if one major organization mounts a campaign against it, revenue article reform is doomed." [61]

The Vote

On November 8, 1966, a total of 3,076,879 Illinois voters cast a ballot on the amendment. Of these, 1,642,549, or 53.4 per cent, were favorable. This was, of course, far short of the two-thirds favorable vote which is required for adoption of a constitutional amendment and also far short of the 65.6 per cent favorable vote which had been cast on 13 proposed amendments which had been on the ballot since 1952.

---

[60] The originally suggested theme, "Stop Runaway Taxes," was vetoed by the state administration because of its implicit criticism of state policy.
[61] *Chicago Sun-Times,* March 21, 1965.

On a county basis, the proposal received a constitutional majority in only one county—little Jo Daviess. In crucially important Cook County, 62.9 per cent of Chicago ballots were in favor, but only 52.5 per cent of those in suburban Cook County were affirmative. Downstate, the favorable vote was 46.9 per cent of the total.

In view of the known tendency for certain areas of the state to vote against proposed revenue amendments, it is appropriate to analyze the vote on the amendment by considering the change from the average favorable vote in recent referenda. Chart XXI shows this information on a county-by-county basis. It reveals that several of the small rural counties were more favorable to the revenue amendment than they have been to other amendments voted on since 1952. On the other hand, every urban county, including Cook, voted less favorably to the amendment than usual. These results can be attributed to several factors, although it is not possible to prove cause-effect relationships. For one thing, the Illinois Agricultural Association has a great deal of experience with grass roots organization. The state Chamber of Commerce, alternatively, has had very little experience with grass roots campaigns, and most of their legislative effectiveness is based upon lobbying at the state level. Also, the more vocal opposing organizations such as the League of Women Voters and the PTA are more strongly organized in urban areas. Labor's opposition was probably a significant factor in such downstate urban areas as Madison and St. Clair counties. It is also possible that communications are better in the urban areas and that the somewhat conflicting arguments of the proponents came through more clearly.

Summary

The attempt to amend the revenue article can be rated as a spectacular success at the legislative level and a spectacular failure at the referendum level, and there may well be a close relationship between the two. The techniques of negotiation, compromise, hasty drafting, and last minute introduction worked well at the legislative level. The result, however, was a proposed amendment that was poorly drafted, restrictive, and at points, contrary to long established policy of the organizations involved. The poor draftsmanship and restrictiveness resulted in the opposition of important civic groups. The attempt on the part of the interest groups to sell their members upon the article for opposite reasons created confusion and mistrust.

This indictment of the proposed article is not to say, of course, that another article, drafted in another way, would have fared bet-

CHART XXI

FAVORABLE VOTE, PROPOSED REVENUE AMENDMENT, AS PERCENTAGE
CHANGE FROM COUNTY AVERAGE, 1952–65

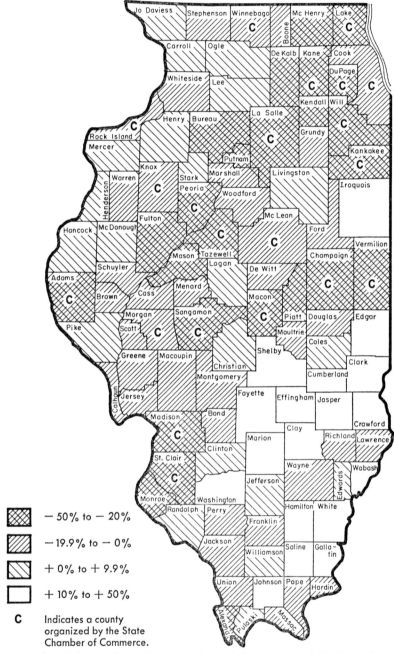

- -50% to -20%
- -19.9% to -0%
- +0% to +9.9%
- +10% to +50%

C   Indicates a county
     organized by the State
     Chamber of Commerce.

Source: Compiled from Thomas Kitsos, *Constitutional Amendments and the Voter, 1952–
1966* (Urbana: University of Illinois, Institute of Government and Public Affairs, 1968).

ter. Had Senator Arrington's multiple submission idea been adopted, it is possible that some of the less controversial proposals would have passed, but it seems equally likely that confusion would have been multiplied and that the number of negative votes and abstentions would have been even higher. A single proposal containing a few relatively uncontroversial proposals such as classification of personal property, a true sales tax, and increased debt limits for unit schools would have aroused less opposition but, probably, would have attracted far less organized support and might well have been lost to apathy.

SALES TAX BROADENING FAILS, 1967

As the 75th General Assembly opened on January 4, 1967, a Republican-dominated legislature and a Democratic governor were faced with the sure knowledge that substantial additions to existing revenue sources would be necessary. As is customary, the Budgetary Commission went over budget requests, agency by agency, with the avowed purpose of "cutting fat" from the agency requests. In spite of the fact that some agencies such as the Youth Commission were treated none too gently, the projected budget, when the Commission finished its work, was well over $5 billion. The major increases were for education—an area that legislators on both sides of the aisle were loath to cut. Highways were being studied by a commission that was almost certain to recommend vastly increased expenditures.

Although there was much speculation over the size of the Governor's budget and his probable recommendations for increasing state revenues, all major appropriations and state tax legislation were in a state of suspended animation until the legislature could be sure of the magnitude of the Governor's request. A city tax package giving cities permission for a one-half cent increase in the city sales tax and authority to levy taxes on cigarettes, cigars, liquor, and hotel receipts was introduced early in the session. Attempts by Democratic leaders to move these bills rapidly through the legislative process were blocked by the Senate Republican leadership, avowedly to "wait and see" what the Governor would ask in state taxes. Although this package was supported by the Illinois Municipal League and many downstate mayors testified for it, it was labeled the "Daley double," and the package was clearly a good hostage to hold for Democratic votes on Republican proposals.

On April 19 the Governor delivered his budget message, indicating that his biennial budget would be almost $5.6 billion. This did not include any increase in highway expenditure that might result from proposals of the Highway Study Commission nor did it include capital improvements to be financed by the Illinois Building Authority. To cover the $685 million gap between projected expenditures and projected revenues, the Governor proposed broadening the sales tax base to include almost all services.

This proposal had its beginnings in a 1963 suggestion to the Commission on Revenue by Professor A. James Heins. The economic reasoning behind the tax is straightforward. If taxation is to fall upon consumption, there is little logic to singling out consumption of tangible goods. Services are an ever-growing component of consumption and often are luxury items as contrasted with tangible necessities such as food and clothing. Professor Heins' suggestion met with a relatively enthusiastic reception when he presented it to the Commission, and bills based on his proposal were introduced in the 1965 legislature. In 1967 bills were introduced the day the Governor's budget message was delivered and were assigned to the Revenue Division of the Committee on Public Finance, chaired by Senator Hudson Sours, a conservative Republican from Peoria.

It soon became evident that the Governor's proposal was not such a "painless" method of raising taxes as had been assumed. In the first place, the bills were surprisingly broad. They not only covered all consumer services including physicians' and lawyers' services (sums paid to nonprofit hospitals were exempt), but also the service component (commissions) of such items as insurance premiums and security sales. The full cost of services rendered to business such as printing and engineering were to be taxable also.

The bills had been drafted so as to repeal all existing general sales tax legislation and replace it with the new tax. This "repeal" feature was significant in two respects. In the first place, it would wipe out much of the existing case law. From the standpoint of revenue, this approach had the advantage of simplifying the law and possibly eliminating some of the "loopholes" which are firmly embedded in existing case law, but it created the risk that litigation would tie up a great deal of revenue until new case law was established. The second significant factor is that it would have repealed the tax legislation to which the city sales tax increase bills were geared. The proposal did include permission for cities to levy the existing one-half cent tax upon the new, broadened base, but it would have made passage of the bills permitting a one-half cent increase in the cities' rate meaningless.

At the first hearing on the bills, scheduled to hear proponents only,

Senator James Loukas, principal sponsor of the administration bills, moved acceptance of Amendment 1 which changed the nature of the bills. Instead of repealing the Retailers' Occupation Tax and other existing sales taxes, the bills retained them and a new Business and Occupation tax was to apply to the newly taxable items. Cities were not to share in the added "service" base, but passage of the city sales tax bills would permit them to double the rate on the old base.[62]

The witnesses appearing for the broadening bills on June 1 represented the Retail Merchants Association, Caterpillar Tractor, Illinois Education Association, Illinois Agricultural Association, and the League of Women Voters. The retail merchants were anxious to avoid any higher sales tax rate, and the Illinois Agricultural Association felt that if the state didn't support increased expenditures for education, local governments would have to increase the property tax. The Illinois Education Association was also interested in adequate financing of education. In fact, the IEA witness said his organization would support almost any revenue source that would provide adequate revenue for schools. Both the League of Women Voters and the representative of the Caterpillar Tractor Company made pleas for the basic soundness and equity of the bills.

During this hearing Senator Sours was openly hostile, charging that the whole package was only an income tax on selected segments of the economy. Senate Majority Leader Arrington, who had been quoted in the press as telling the Governor that his proposal was "magnificent," was noncommittal, asking only that he be permitted to examine the figures used to arrive at the $685 million estimated yield.

At the request of Senator Arrington, Professor Heins testified before the Committee on the following week. He testified that the Governor's yield estimates were far too low. This obviously laid the groundwork for a possible Republican attempt to cut the rate or eliminate some of the services to be taxed. If this were the plan, however, opposition from major interest groups and a split in Republican ranks caused a change. At the June 19 meeting, strong protests against the tax were lodged by many groups affected. Representatives of newspaper and television interests testified that collecting the tax on advertising would drive advertisers elsewhere. Advertising agencies and engineering firms made much the same argument, and some witnesses made the point that if they attempted to absorb a 4 per cent tax, it would be equivalent to an 8 per cent

[62] The new draft would have resulted in a more complicated law and a different total (city and state) rate on sales of services and sales of tangible goods.

net income tax. Representatives of the insurance industry argued that to collect the tax on their commissions would amount to discrimination against this form of saving as compared to banks.[63]

The president of the State Bar Association testified that many lawyers would not be able to pass the tax on, and the representative of the Chicago Association of Commerce and Industry testified simply, "Business climate in this state cannot live with these bills." A representative of newspaper interests claimed that *any* tax upon newspapers is a violation of freedom of the press.

The effectiveness of the presentations varied considerably. Several witnesses made an effective case against the tax. For example, a representative of trucking interests pointed out that if they were forced to charge a tax on their services, large firms would buy their own trucks and thus escape the tax. Other groups such as the Chicago Association of Commerce and Industry were obviously appearing in their customary role of opposition to any tax and, even when pressed by members of the committee, were unwilling to suggest an alternative. Still other groups were represented by witnesses who obviously knew little of politics or taxation. The dry cleaning industry had been responsible for the return of thousands of postpaid postcards which had been attached to customers' dry cleaning, but the testimony of the witness was almost incomprehensible and closed with a clumsy threat based upon the industry's ability to "reach the people." One witness made repeated reference to "my Senator Harris" until informed by a member of the committee that the Harris present was not the one from his district. The amusement and laughter that greeted each *faux pas* of the more ineffective witnesses released the tension, but it was obvious that the Governor's proposals were in deep trouble. Newspapers had begun reporting that legislators were under unbelievable pressure and made almost no mention of the very respectable list of supporters who had appeared at the fiscal hearing.

On June 15 inter-party political maneuvering became obvious during a debate in the Revenue Division of the Public Finance Committee. The Democrats charged the Republicans with brinkmanship, and Republicans, in turn, blasted Democrats for the late budget and for completely changing the draft of the bill at a late date. About the same time, budget slashing began in the House where $117 million was reportedly cut from appropriation bills before they were moved to the Senate.[64] Characteristically, the significance of these claimed

[63] The federal constitution and federal statutes prohibit this form of taxation of national banks. For competitive reasons no effort was made to apply it to state banks.
[64] *Illinois State Register,* June 15, 1967.

cuts was more symbolic than real, and it was very difficult for the outsider to determine what was actually happening. For example, the $117 million "budget cut" for which the Republican-dominated legislature claimed credit included many millions for common school funds which were not in the Governor's budget. Thus, it took credit for reducing the School Problems Commission bills down to the figure recommended by the Governor. Also, over half of the $42 million cut in the mental health budget involved an appropriation which greatly exceeded the resources of the fund and thus could not have been spent in the absence of highly controversial legislation regarding the use of federal funds received for inmate care. In an eleventh hour attempt to save his revenue proposal, Governor Kerner spoke to a joint session of the General Assembly. In a short but forceful speech, Kerner told both houses that an increase in the sales tax rate would be "unconscionable" and that the legislature should take immediate action to approve the broadening bills. Although Democrats stood in the aisles and cheered, the Republicans went on with the search for other sources of revenue.

In spite of efforts by Senator W. Russell Arrington to gather support for Kerner's proposals behind closed doors of a Republican conference, the Governor's broadening bills were turned down by the Revenue Division of the Public Finance Committee by a margin of eight (Republicans) to five (Democrats). Senator Arrington abstained. The last few days of the session were chaotic as far as revenue measures were concerned. Democrats insisted that it was the Republicans' responsibility to develop a plan. Senate Republican revolt against the leadership of Senator Arrington over the open housing question and the desire of the House leadership to get involved in the revenue picture increased the confusion as proposals and "trial balloons" multiplied.

As the last week of the session approached, there was still no agreement. Since it takes a minimum of five days for a bill to clear both houses, a bipartisan agreement was reached to advance all tax legislation so that some of it could be amended and passed when agreement was reached. Still technically alive at the time were the Governor's broadening bills, the city tax bills, a bill to give direct grants to cities and counties, and a series of bills introduced in the House by Speaker Ralph Smith calling for a one-half cent increase in the sales tax and for increases in several selective excises.

In weekend conferences between the Governor and legislative leaders, the package introduced in the House by the Republican leadership emerged as the basic plan, although there was still much bargaining over rates. The package passed the House on June 28. In the Senate a coalition consisting of Republicans willing to vote for a one cent total increase in sales tax rates and of Democrats who were willing to support an increased state sales tax in return for an increase in the city sales tax was put together.

But the cliff-hanging finish did not arrive until the last day of the session. After a late afternoon Republican caucus, Senator Arrington said, "The raw fact is that we are not able to adopt the Governor's program. Every ingenuity has been used. I can now provide you with 14 votes for a penny sales tax increase. I need 16 Democratic votes." On the first roll call, the 16 Democratic votes were not forthcoming. The pressure was intense as Arrington gave warning that there would be no third call for votes, although many on both sides of the aisle had not voted. After more than an hour, the roll call stood at 31 for (18 Democrats and 13 Republicans)—one more than the necessary 30. The bills went back to the House at 11 P.M. for concurrence on amendments and passed, according to the stopped clock in the House Chamber, just before midnight.

Thus, in the last week of the session the legislature had passed a tax package which had not even been in committee. No hearings were held and no bills had been printed for House members to read on June 30. After wrestling with the Governor's bills since April, the legislature had reverted to the familiar pattern of increasing the rates of existing taxes plus some minor broadening of the base of existing taxes. No one could be sure how much revenue would be raised by the changes that had been made nor was it certain that some of the changes would not be declared unconstitutional. Clearly there had been no time, in the last frenzy of political maneuver, to worry about the niceties of bill drafting or revenue estimation. However, according to the tally published by the newspapers shortly after adjournment, the following changes had been made:[65]

Tax	Estimated Yield (millions)
Sales tax rate increase (three-quarters of one cent)	$300.0
Service occupation tax extension	140.2
Two cent cigarette tax increase	56.8
Enlargement of inheritance tax base	37.5
One cent increase in utility tax	43.0
Increase in corporate franchise tax	18.0
Total	595.5

[65] These estimates were made shortly after the June 30th adjournment in 1967. Since then, in a reconvened session the legislature repealed the changes it had made in the inheritance tax base. Also, the Illinois Supreme Court has declared the 1967 service occupation tax amendments (which particularly expanded the base) unconstitutional because of lack of uniformity.

In addition, a one cent increase in the motor fuel tax had been voted for highway purposes, and municipalities had been given the authority to increase the city sales tax by .25 per cent.

7

AN APPRAISAL

The preceding chapters have been concerned with facts about taxation and government expenditure in Illinois and have described some aspects of the process by which decisions concerning taxes and expenditures are made. There is no theory which satisfactorily relates the economic and political aspects of public finance, but the literature of these and related disciplines provides useful perspectives for viewing the complicated mass of facts and relationships that are involved. Some pertinent parts of this literature are reviewed in the first part of this chapter in order to provide a background for an appraisal of the Illinois tax and expenditure system.

ECONOMIC PERSPECTIVES

Basically, economic analysis deals with the question of how scarce resources are used to produce goods and services and with the consumption of those goods and services. It is sometimes said that the three basic economic questions are: "What shall be produced?", "How shall it be produced?", and "Who shall consume it?" The simplicity of this definition can easily obscure the complex reality which the subject matter of economics involves. For example, answers to the "how" question include a multitude of detailed decisions about the organization of production that range from matters of corporation finance to technical problems involving the flow of work on the assembly line. Answers to the "what" and "who" questions involve determining the income and consumption patterns of every member of society and thus involve important aspects of society itself. The economist does not pretend to be able to make all these decisions or even to know what detailed decisions must be made. He is concerned with the methods whereby the decisions are coordinated and related to one another rather than with each detail of the decision.

With the aid of mathematical models economists have been able to show that under certain conditions the pricing mechanism will secure an "optimum allocation of resources." This demonstration is based upon a definition of optimum which rests upon the concept of consumer sovereignty. Consumers make their wants known by their purchases in the market place. Producers, in an effort to maximize their incomes, respond to market demand by producing goods of the kind and quality required and by using the best possible production methods, given existing resources and technology. An optimum will be achieved only if consumers are rational in their choices and have complete knowledge of all of the possibilities open to them. Furthermore, an optimum will be assured only if certain precisely defined conditions concerning the nature of competition and the knowledge and motivations of producers are met.

Although the conditions for achieving an optimum are unlikely to be met, analysis based upon these assumptions yields results which are tolerably accurate for a wide range of purposes. Much policy advice from economists is thus based upon the belief that the powers of government should be used to create conditions which come as close as possible to the conditions prescribed in competitive market models.

Unfortunately, however, not all economic decisions can be determined by the price system. There are cases in which the concept "economic optimum" becomes meaningless or, at least, ceases to be helpful to those who would give policy advice or analyze economic phenomena. Some tax and expenditure programs are undertaken because the market system fails completely in certain cases, others because the market system produces results which are considered unacceptable by those who make political decisions.

The Theory of Public Finance

Professor Richard Musgrave's authoritative book, entitled *The Theory of Public Finance*, sets forth a theory of the public household which attempts to state the rules and principles that make for efficient conduct of the public economy and discusses problems involved in implementing these rules.[1] The entire exercise is frankly conceded to

[1] Richard A. Musgrave, *The Theory of Public Finance* (New York: McGraw-Hill Book Co., 1959), 628 pp.

be normative rather than descriptive of "what goes on in the capitals of the world." Furthermore, it turns out that many of the rules are not operational in the sense that they provide practical answers for those who must make decisions. In spite of these limitations, Musgrave's development and synthesis of the theory of public finance does provide a useful perspective for understanding the economic issues which are present, although sometimes in latent form, in the decisions which must be made.

Musgrave points out that there are three objectives of budget (tax and expenditure) policy. They are:[2]

1. To secure adjustments in the allocation of resources.
2. To secure adjustments in the distribution of income.
3. To promote economic stabilization.

For convenience of exposition, it is assumed that each of these policies is the responsibility of a different "branch" of government, but there must be a final reconciliation of the action of the three branches to produce a consolidated budget.

As the responsibilities of the *allocation branch* deal with the use of resources to produce goods and services, the principles of market pricing are sometimes applicable, at least in part. For example, a workshop in a state institution may be operated on market principles except for those modifications which are made necessary by the medical or rehabilitative purposes of the operation. There are other cases, however, in which the market mechanism fails altogether, as when social wants are involved. *Social wants* are those satisfied by goods which are not consumed privately, but which benefit everyone in the community. Thus, national defense must be provided to the whole nation or not at all. There is no possible mechanism by which individual consumers could buy varying quantities of national defense and no means by which those who choose not to buy could be excluded from the benefits. The economic problem arises from the fact that market demand cannot be counted on to determine the true demand for a social good. In the case of privately produced goods, consumers reveal their demands by purchases. In the case of social goods, the connection between payment and enjoyment ceases to exist and individuals have no incentive to reveal their preferences. In fact, any hint that payments (taxes) were to be related to preference would provide an incentive for concealing demands, since no individual's consumption of social goods would be reduced substantially if he made a lower payment.

There are not many pure social goods, but a great many goods and

[2] *Ibid.*, Chapter 1.

services provided by government have a social component. For example, education has monetary value to the individual and could be sold as a private good, but there are also benefits to the community which are in the nature of social goods and which justify provision of education in larger quantities than would result from pure market forces.

Governments also provide goods and services which satisfy *merit wants*. These are wants which society has decided should be satisfied more fully than would occur in a market economy because it is considered desirable to encourage consumption. Thus, milk may be supplied to children at a reduced cost and library services may be provided at no cost. The satisfaction of merit wants, by its very nature, involves interference with consumer preference and thus cannot be left to the determination of the market mechanism.

The *distribution branch* has the task of determining and securing the proper distribution of income. It can be shown that under conditions of market perfection which include perfect knowledge and perfect mobility of all factors of production, every person would receive an income equal to the marginal productivity of his labor and other resources owned. It is by no means clear, however, that this result would be desirable. Strict adherence to such a policy would mean the elimination, by starvation, of all unproductive persons who were not lucky enough to own property or to be cared for by relatives or private charity. Furthermore, even this extreme degree of *laissez faire* could not be defended as "natural," since the distribution of income would still be determined, in part, by laws of property ownership and inheritance and by the operations of the allocation branch.

There is widespread support for welfare and other programs which would be the primary responsibility of the distribution branch, but decisions in this field lead to a very different set of ethical, social, and economic problems than do those with which the allocation branch would be concerned. Economic theory can provide some guidance as to the likely effects of some programs, but it is clearly impossible to leave the problem to market decision or to provide a solution based on simulated market conditions.

The *stabilization branch* has the function of maintaining a high level of resource use and a stable value of money. In a federal system the prime responsibility for stabilization rests with the federal government and is not a major concern of state and local governments. Nevertheless, stabilization operations of the federal government will have an impact upon state and local finance through changes in federal grants, changes in interest rates, and changes in the federal tax system. State operations have an effect, however small, upon stabilization of the national economy.

Musgrave used both numerical examples and a system of equations to show the interrelations among the three branches.[3] The subbudgets prepared by each branch are consolidated into a single budget, and it is shown that the operations of each branch will affect the results achieved by the other branches. Then there must be a further adjustment in the operations of each until the correct balance is reached.

Further complications result from the fact that the public and private sectors of the economy are closely interdependent parts of the same whole. Tax and expenditure policy should be concerned not only with the initial impact but with the ultimate results of policy. Several chapters are devoted to an attempt to trace the effects of various possible tax and expenditure policies upon the private sector.[4]

It is clear from Musgrave's analysis that there are many public finance decisions which cannot be made through the price mechanism. In Chapter 6 he considers whether or not there is a technique whereby individuals can be induced to reveal their preferences for social wants. It is assumed that there is a set of "true" demand schedules for the satisfaction of social wants based upon the preference systems and incomes of the various individuals and that these are unaffected by considerations of strategy. Since these preferences will not be revealed voluntarily, the problem is to find a voting process that gives an approximation based on the true evaluation. Utilizing Arrow's analysis of the minimum conditions of collective rationality in majority voting,[5] Musgrave analyzes various possible voting methods for determining policy. The results of this analysis show that, depending upon the nature and number of issues voted upon (i.e., size of budget, method of sharing cost, and composition of budget), the results could be unambiguous or arbitrary (depending on order of voting on the issues). Even when the results are non-arbitrary in the Arrow sense, however, it is optimal only in the sense that it is the solution agreed to by more people than any other. It is an exceedingly crude kind of optimum as compared with the optimum achieved in the market where consumers can, in effect, cumulate their votes by spending a high proportion of income on favored products.

The analysis goes on to consider other systems of voting. One sys-

[3] *Ibid.*, Chapter 2.
[4] *Ibid.*, Chapters 10–16.
[5] Kenneth Arrow, *Social Choice and Individual Values* (New York: John Wiley & Sons, 1951).

tem analyzed is based upon the possibility that each voter be given a number of votes which can be spread among issues in proportion to his intensity of feeling about a particular issue (point voting). It is concluded that point voting would give determined results over a wider range of issues than majority voting and that the results would be a better reflection of underlying preferences. But when a strategy such as trading votes is allowed, new complications arise which could render the process unworkable.

If these results are not discouraging enough, Musgrave reminds us, at this point in the analysis, that the voting analysis applies primarily to the problem of satisfying social wants by the allocation branch. The problem of merit wants and distribution branch problems fall outside the framework of consumer sovereignty, and it can be expected that economic analysis will be of even less value as a guide.

Disappointment that the theory of public finance provides little help in analyzing how decisions should be made is somewhat reduced by the realization that it does help to understand issues and inter-relations. It is clear, for example, that the state must take action in economic affairs and that every action has an effect upon the distribution of income, allocation of resources, and upon the stability of the economy. Every action in the field of public finance has repercussions throughout both the public and private sectors which may not be noted or understood by those responsible for policy decisions.

THE REFORMIST VIEWPOINT

Another perspective from which to view Illinois public finance can, for want of a better name, be called "reformist." This viewpoint is that of persons who are concerned that "good" methods of decision-making be utilized. The position described here is not that of the muddle-headed amateur, but that of professionals in the appropriate fields. It is not possible to single out a concise body of knowledge or a single author as a representative of this viewpoint, but it can be identified as being that of a great many persons who have had formal training in public administration, of governmental accountants, of some businessmen-turned-public-servant, and of those economists whose major interest is policy advice rather than theory or analysis.

The thing that unites this diverse group is the belief that decisions in the field of public finance should be made on the basis of a maximum amount of information concerning the costs and benefits of the proposed action. The exact form that the information would take depends upon the situation and the skill and background of the professional reformer concerned. Accountants are apt to think largely in terms of costs and benefits as they are measured in conventional accounting categories. The practicing economist may think in somewhat broader terms and attempt to include items of social costs and benefits which are not included in the government's own books or to measure the impact which a policy has upon various groups within the economy.

Most proponents of this view make a relatively sharp distinction between the provision of data and policymaking. That is, they recognize that the data which they can provide will not, in itself, be an automatic answer and that policymakers must take other factors and values into consideration. At the same time, they see the ideal policymaker as one who utilizes a maximum amount of administrative information.

In view of the rather diverse character of approaches being considered, it may be useful to focus somewhat more sharply upon two examples—one dealing with expenditure decisions and one with tax decisions.

Budgeting

A governmental budget is both a plan for spending and a device for insuring that expenditures are in accord with authorizations. Since the number of items purchased in a biennial period by the Illinois state government is in the millions, it is clearly necessary to group and classify proposed expenditures in some systematic way. The classification system used in Illinois emphasizes the nature of the item purchased, the agency authorized to make the purchase, and the fund to be utilized.

Recent developments in public administration have included the development of highly sophisticated budgeting techniques which can provide the decision-maker with a very different kind of information. One of these techniques, known as program budgeting, classifies expenditure in terms of the output which will be produced by a given program. That is, an attempt is made to focus upon the services which will be provided rather than upon items which will be purchased. A highway budget, for example, would reveal how many miles of road are to be constructed, what maintenance is to be provided and, ideally, what this would mean in reduced accidents and vehicle operating costs.[6]

---

[6] See Thomas J. Anton, *The Politics of State Expenditure in Illinois* (Urbana: University of Illinois Press, 1966), pp. 225–35, for a description of an abortive attempt to introduce this system in Illinois.

More recently, this idea has been expanded into a method known as the program-performance-budgeting system (PPBS). Development of this system is associated with the name of Robert McNamara, since it was first applied on a large scale by the U.S. Department of Defense.[7] It combines program budgeting with a very detailed measurement of the cost and efficiency of performance. This not only permits expenditure decisions to be based upon evaluation of the relative merits of outputs, but permits policy-makers and administrators to compare costs of performing similar tasks in various agencies and to study trends in the costs of various activities and programs through time.

Tax Studies

In the postwar years a great many states and localities have commissioned tax studies. Typically, the authors of these studies lay down the criteria to be used in judging the system and then appraise the system by comparing it with the criteria.

In an earlier work, this writer suggested that four criteria might appropriately be utilized to appraise the Illinois tax system.[8] The suggested criteria are: equity, adequacy, administrative feasibility, and impact upon the state's economy.

Equity has two dimensions. Horizontal equity refers to the equal treatment of individuals in substantially equal circumstances. Although there are problems in writing an exact definition of equal circumstances,[9] it is easy to identify instances in which the criterion is violated. Few readers of Chapters 3, 4, and 5 of this volume will have difficulty in finding examples in the Illinois state and local tax systems.

Opinion as to what constitutes vertical equity differ more widely. Probably a majority favor some degree of progression. Some would argue that taxation should be proportional to income. Probably, very few would defend the extreme degree of regressiveness of the Illinois tax system.

Several writers have noted that a tax system must provide adequate revenue, but there has seldom been a clear definition of the adequacy principle. Brazer has suggested that an adequate tax system is one which provides sufficient revenue to meet the cost of providing public

[7] Charles J. Hitch, *Decision-Making for Defense* (Berkeley: University of California Press, 1965); David Novick, ed., *Program Budgeting, Program Analysis and the Federal Budget* (Washington: U.S. Government Printing Office, 1965).
[8] Glenn W. Fisher, "An Economist's Appraisal of the Illinois Tax System," *University of Illinois Law Forum* (Winter, 1961), pp. 543–85.
[9] Musgrave, *op. cit.*, Chapter 8.

services for a growing population and an expanding economy without frequent changes in tax rates or bases.[10] This definition is based upon the premise that affirmative political action should be required for every expansion of the level of services, but that maintaining existing services should require no such action. Those who desire to keep government as small as possible might well favor a tax system which, like that of Illinois, requires a periodic reratification of existing levels of services. Others might prefer a system which permits a constant or growing percentage of personal income to be spent for governmental purposes without the necessity of positive political action.

The administrative feasibility criterion requires that it be possible to secure a high degree of compliance with a minimum of cost to the state and the taxpayers and without unreasonable violations of the taxpayer's privacy. Again, it is not possible to draw up rigid statements as to what is reasonable, but it is often relatively easy to rate various taxes and to recommend changes which would simplify the administrative problem.

The impact upon the state's economy criterion is often defined to mean that the tax system should interfere as little as possible with decisions about such matters as the location of manufacturing and mercantile establishments, the ratio of labor to capital employed, and the pattern of consumption. Such an approach clearly reflects the belief that market forces should be allowed to operate whenever possible and that the inevitable impact of tax (and expenditure) policies should be kept to a minimum. In certain cases, however, this criterion may be reversed and a tax system may be designed to encourage economic development of a certain type or to change the pattern of consumption in favor of "merit" goods.

Clearly, the criteria for judging a tax system are not entirely unambiguous and there is often conflict among the criteria. A tax that rates highly on one criterion may be a very bad tax when measured by another. The question of the relative weights to be given to the various criteria seems to be largely a matter of personal preference. The importance of such disagreements should not be overstated, however. The history of many state tax studies shows that there is usually a high degree of agreement among the professional staff members of the committee, some agreement among the members of the committee, and, usually, no agreement at all among the legislators who are asked to enact the recommendations. This emphasizes the

[10] Harvey Brazer, *Taxation in Michigan: An Appraisal* (Ann Arbor: Institute of Public Administration, University of Michigan, 1961).

importance of viewing financial decisions from the political perspective.

POLITICAL PERSPECTIVES

In the simplest "theory" of representative democracy it is assumed that the electors choose officials on the basis of their policy positions and that, as a result, policies carried out by the government will be in the public interest or, at least, in accord with the desires of the majority. In spite of the obvious naïveté of this simple statement one hears many discussions of politics and government which appear to be based upon uncritical acceptance of this statement or to assume that it would be true except for the selfishness of politicians, the activities of evil lobbyists, and the apathy of citizens.

Actually, of course, this simple statement begs many questions of definition and skips many steps in the chain of logic. Political philosophers as widely separated in time and approach as Plato, Aristotle, Rousseau, and Mill have attempted to define the public interest and to specify the structure of government and other conditions which would best promote it. More recently, political scientists have turned more of their attention to attempts to explain the operations of the political mechanism and to derive laws or generalizations which are useful for explanatory or predictive purposes. Although these attempts have led to a greatly increased understanding of political phenomena, there is no model of the political system which commands the acceptance among political scientists that the pricing model commands among economists. The two political theories discussed below were chosen because they provide insights which are helpful in understanding the politics of public finance in Illinois, not necessarily because they are the most widely accepted or the most representative political theories.

The Downsian Model of Democracy

One source of insight into the nature of political decision-making is provided by the work of an economist, Anthony Downs.[11] The model which he constructs is based upon the assumption that men are rational in the pursuit of their chosen ends, but the political structure which he posits is far more realistic than are the voting

[11] Anthony Downs, *An Economic Theory of Democracy* (New York: Harper & Brothers, 1957).

models utilized by economists such as Musgrave and Buchanan.[12] Downs assumes that governmental decisions are made by the political party that has control of the government by virtue of having won a majority vote in an election, and that the objective of the party is to conduct government in such a way that it will be reelected at the next election. Analysis of the logic of voting (by citizens) and the logic of decision-making (by parties) in a situation in which there is no uncertainty and information is costless reveals that a government's best strategy is to adopt choices which are favored by a majority of the voters. However, conformity to the will of the majority does not guarantee reelection for the incumbents. Sometimes the opposition can form a coalition of dissenters and win by upholding the majority view on key issues. At other times, no clear majority position exists. In general, Downs believes that majority rule on specific issues will prevail most of the time whenever the majority strongly favors a certain policy, that is, when most citizens agree on what issues are most important as well as on what policy to follow.

Another long step toward political reality is achieved when the assumption of perfect certainty and costless information is dropped in the analysis. Under these conditions the voter no longer knows which party will best serve his interest, and political leadership arises among those who are able to provide correct (but biased) information and to persuade others to follow them. Governments are now uncertain about the true preferences of the voters and must rely upon intermediaries between them and the citizen. The intermediaries exact a price by demanding an influence over policy that is far greater than their numbers warrant.

Uncertainty and cost of information also lead to the rise of ideology. Voters find ideology a useful means of cutting information costs and parties find that the promotion of ideology is a useful means of gaining support from various social groups. In the model it is assumed that ideologies are never internally contradictory, but that they may be loosely integrated so as to appeal to many groups. Furthermore, the development of an ideology tends to prevent rapid and smooth change in the party policy.

Of great interest to one who wants to understand the nature of tax and expenditure decision-making is Downs' more detailed analysis

[12] Musgrave, *op. cit.*, Chapter 6; James M. Buchanan and Gordon Tullock, *The Calculus of Consent* (Ann Arbor: University of Michigan Press, 1962).

of the specific effects of information costs.[13] Although traditional economic theory assumes unlimited amounts of free information, Downs maintains that information of the kind needed to vote "rationally" is very costly and that the voter must face the question of how to decide what data to select and what to reject. Analysis of the influence which his vote is likely to have reveals that the return from obtaining and assimilating information is very low. Thus, it is irrational for the average voter to spend much time or money to inform himself about political matters except to the extent that he gets pleasure from participating in the process.

Those who do wish to influence policy find that they must become experts in the area in which they wish to have an influence. Since those who can afford to specialize in this way are those who have a great deal to gain, it follows that political influence accrues to those who earn their livelihood in the area. Clearly, this points to the rise of professional, highly specialized lobbyists, and it becomes understandable that legislatures will write tariff laws that benefit a few producers at the expense of thousands of consumers.

Downs' model emphasizes that decisions are made by politicians who have goals of their own and that there is no reason to expect that pursuit of these goals will lead either to an economic optimum or to majority rule. It emphasizes the cost of information and lays the groundwork for explaining the role of interest groups in political decision-making. The rationality assumption which is utilized is consistent with practice and is probably the most useful single assumption about human behavior that can be utilized, but it does oversimplify to such an extent that much political behavior is not satisfactorily explained. In terms of his own analysis, for example, it is difficult to see why most people vote at all. Also, the assumption that one party is in complete control of the government, that it speaks with one voice, and that it has complete control over the administrative machinery, obscures much of the decision-making process.

Easton's System Analysis

There have been many studies of the political process which describe particular legal and administrative structures within which decisions are made, or have concentrated upon the analysis of the roles played by various participants in the process or upon the dis-

[13] Downs, *op. cit.*, Chapters 11–14. See also James M. Buchanan, *Public Finance in Democratic Process: Fiscal Institutions and Individual Choice* (Chapel Hill: University of North Carolina Press, 1967), Chapter 10.

tribution of power within a system. Professor David Easton has gone beyond this in an attempt to formulate a general theory of political systems.[14] Basically, he attempts to answer the question of how a political system can persist whether the world be one of stability or change. He sees the political system as being surrounded by physical, biological, social, and psychological environments. The effects of these environments upon the political system are seen as inputs which cross the boundary between the two.

Inputs are of two kinds. Demands are expressions of opinion that an authoritative allocation (with regard to a particular subject) should or should not be made by those who have the responsibility for doing so. Demands may take the form of a request for a specific action such as the construction of a new school building in a specific location, or the form of vague requests for "better education" or even for "better government." Ideologies are ill-defined demands which can be met only by specific actions.

The second kind of input, support, can be roughly characterized as willingness to accept the rules of the game even though particular demands are not met. Easton analyzes different kinds of support and points out that support may be generalized or directed toward specific political objects and emphasizes that a minimum level of support is necessary for the persistence of the political object or the system in general.

Outputs of a political system can be considered as the way in which the system acts back upon its environment and includes binding decisions and their implementation. Of much importance in understanding the persistence of the system, however, is the fact that outputs feed back to affect the inputs into the system and thus cause modifications in the system itself. The system survives by adapting itself to the changing environment in order to maintain support at the necessary level.

The Easton analysis is detailed and abstract. It is intended to be a very general theory rather than an operational research model. Nevertheless, it focuses attention sharply upon the fact that political systems are dynamic organisms which have their own life processes. Every decision about taxes or expenditure affects not only the economic environment but also the nature and existence of the political system within which the decision is made.

[14] David Easton, *A Framework for Political Analysis* (Englewood Cliffs, N.J.: Prentice-Hall, 1965); *Political Systems* (New York: Knopf, 1953); *A Systems Analysis of Political Life* (New York: John Wiley & Sons, 1965).

A NORMATIVE APPRAISAL

Despite the fact that the summaries from the literature of political science, economics, and related fields which have been presented represent vast oversimplifications, it should be clear that public finance has many facets and that the literature provides many perspectives from which Illinois finance might be viewed. It can be considered as an economic problem in the allocation of resources and the distribution of income. It can be judged on the basis of the kind and quality of information which is utilized in making decisions and the administrative techniques used to insure that the decisions are implemented efficiently. It can be considered as a process of decision-making within a well defined political structure or as a process of decision-making which affects the evolution and survival of the political system itself.

The remainder of this chapter is an attempt to provide a summary appraisal from various perspectives. Initially, the appraisal will be normative—that is, an attempt will be made to identify "good" and "bad." This normative appraisal will be based upon criteria which have been elaborated in the literature, but will also involve the author's own opinions and sense of values. The normative approach will be followed by a positive or nonnormative appraisal which attempts to explain why results are as they are.

Expenditure Decisions

In the judgment of the author, the output of public services in Illinois is far too low. One can walk down the streets of many Illinois cities and observe broken pavements, dangerous sidewalks, poor street lighting, and boulevard plantings that are unsightly and dangerously obstruct vision. Any tourist who has driven on Illinois roads and spent a night in Illinois parks can testify that both are well below the standards in many other states. The showplace suburban schools north of Chicago are far outnumbered by overcrowded, understaffed central city schools and undersized, poorly staffed rural schools. To those who read the daily paper, there is little need to emphasize the complicated problems of race relations, poverty, inadequate recreation, unemployment, and disrespect for law that characterizes the slums of Chicago and many smaller cities.

The low level of many public services in Illinois is clearly not the result of inability to afford better services. Table 35 revealed that in only three states were state and local taxes a smaller proportion of personal income. If Illinois were to increase taxes by 25 per cent, there would still be 19 states paying a higher proportion of personal income in taxes, and taxes would still be lighter than they are in such high wealth, high growth states as New York and California.

Unfortunately, the author's judgment that services are inadequate is not a very substantial guide to policy. Even if it is correct, it leaves unanswered such questions as: "Is it possible to substantially increase services by more efficient use of existing revenue?", "How much should expenditure be increased?", and "In which functional area will increased expenditure yield the greatest return?"

To ask these questions is to reveal a weakness in the Illinois financial system. Illinois has made very limited use of available administrative and budgeting techniques which could help to answer these questions. Professor Anton's analysis of budgeting in Illinois suggests that the actual system of arriving at budgeting decisions is very different from that which would be suggested by budgeting experts. It is impossible to say what influence the adoption of a program budget or the PPBS system would have, but it is likely that it would be substantial. It might be, for example, that a careful cost-benefit analysis would show that there are many potential highway improvement projects which would yield benefits in terms of lower vehicle operating costs, reduced accidents, and saving of time which would exceed the cost of the project. There are other potential expenditures which might yield even greater benefits, even though they are more difficult to measure than are highway benefits. For example, well conceived projects of property conservation and human development in the slums of Illinois cities might yield economic and social benefits far in excess of those yielded by equal expenditures on highways.

Even increased expenditure for functions such as recreation and leisure might easily be justified in both economic and social terms. Illinois lacks many of the scenic and climatic amenities of some competing states, and man-made cultural and recreational attractions may well be below the level justified by the wealth, population, and desires of the residents. Improvements in these amenities would be judged by many to be worth the sacrifice of some private sector consumption, and in an economy in which the most desirable industries are highly mobile ones employing a high proportion of well educated, high income persons who put much emphasis upon such matters, it is by no means certain that such improvements might not lead to increased private wealth as well.[15]

---

[15] It is entirely possible that the lack of correlation between tax burdens and economic growth results from the fact that the negative effects of higher taxes are offset by the positive effects of improved governmental services.

It is also very likely that budgeting techniques which stress the output of services would result in substantially greater economy in expenditure of existing funds. The present orientation toward inputs means that there are few pressures for greater efficiency unless they are applied by agency heads themselves.

Tax Structure

Criteria for judging tax systems are more definite and widely accepted than are criteria for judging the proper level and pattern of government expenditure, and several detailed studies of various aspects of the Illinois tax system are available. The following brief appraisal utilizes the four criteria named above. The reader who wants further documentation will find it in the studies mentioned.[16]

Judged with regard to the criterion of equity, both state and local taxes in Illinois come off very badly. It is not difficult to name any number of horizontal inequities. For example, the sales tax law is an accumulation of statutes, regulations, and court decisions which make distinctions between taxable and nontaxable sales on a basis which is difficult to defend from either an equitable or an economic viewpoint. Attempts to expand the base into a more equitable one have been repeatedly frustrated by special interests in the legislature and the state Supreme Court.

The universal, uniform, general property tax *might* have been equitable in a primitive agricultural community, but it is clearly not equitable in Illinois today. The modifications which have been introduced by statute and by enforcement practice have eliminated some of the inequities which would exist if the tax were completely uniform and universal but have created others of great magnitude. The varying level of assessments of single-family houses shown in Table 32 is certain to result in unequal treatment of persons in similar circumstances, and, it must be remembered, the table deals with the class of property which is probably the most accurately assessed.

Even if it is argued that a regressive state and local tax system is permissible if offset by a progressive federal system, the Illinois tax system cannot be defended when the question of vertical equity is under consideration. Arlyn Larson's estimates, reported in Chapter 5, suggest that the burden of Illinois state and local taxation on low income groups is so great that it becomes extremely unlikely,

[16] Fisher, "An Economist's Appraisal of the Illinois Tax System," pp. 543–85; Glenn W. Fisher and Robert P. Fairbanks, *Illinois Municipal Finance* (Urbana: University of Illinois Press, 1968), especially Chapters III-VI; and *Report of the Commission on Revenue* (Springfield, 1963), Appendix A, Chapters XI–XXIII.

if not mathematically impossible, that the combined burden upon upper income groups would be greater than that upon the lowest income group—unless the aggregate level of taxation is greatly increased and the federal burden falls almost completely upon upper income groups.

The Illinois tax system falls far short of providing sufficient revenue to meet the cost of providing the existing level of public services without frequent changes in the tax rate. In fact, the elasticity of expenditures and the inelasticity of the tax system virtually guarantee that major rate changes or new taxes will be needed each biennium. Whether or not this is desirable depends upon one's philosophy and attitude toward the expansion of government services. In the opinion of the author, biennial reratification of the existing level of expenditure might have much to commend it, if that reratification took the form of a careful appraisal of the entire tax and expenditure picture. At present, however, the biennial arguments over taxes produce neither careful review of expenditure nor review of the tax and equity aspects of the tax system.

From the viewpoint of administrative feasibility (not the same thing as quality of administration), the Illinois tax system rates reasonably well. The sales tax is considered relatively easy to administer. The legal fictions and unusual definitions which constitutional interpretations have imposed upon the Department of Revenue make the task more difficult, but this is probably offset by the absence of the specific exemptions found in many states. The local property tax, on the other hand, is surely among the most difficult taxes in the country to administer. Because of the subjective nature of assessments, a property tax is difficult to administer even when confined to real estate and when provision is made for technically trained, properly equipped assessors. However, the Illinois statutes provide for listing and assessment, by locally elected assessors, of all items of tangible and intangible value. As a result, the statutes become almost impossible to administer and de facto modification of the law is almost inevitable.

Although many studies have failed to prove that the tax system has a major effect upon the economic growth of a state, there are clearly instances in which tax considerations have had an effect upon the location or expansion of particular industries. In view of the very low level of business taxation in Illinois, however, the Illinois tax system would clearly rate high on the "impact on business location" criterion. Nevertheless, the increasing level of sales taxation is a matter for concern by merchants located near state lines. In addition, individual firms may be hit hard by property tax assessments.

POSITIVE ANALYSIS

In the preceding section it was argued that the level of government expenditure in Illinois is probably too low, that little effort is devoted to appraising the results of actual and proposed expenditures, and that administrative techniques which would promote efficient use of resources are often not utilized. On the revenue side, it is apparent that the Illinois tax system is inequitable and regressive. Some taxes, especially the property tax, are difficult to administer as written, and the existing system can produce enough revenue to support government in a growing economy only by frequent changes in rates. Only on the "impact upon industrial location" criterion does the system generally rate well, but even here there are exceptions.

This section is addressed to answering the question "Why?" In it are sketches of some of the factors which must be considered if one is to understand the nature of tax and expenditure decision-making in Illinois and the nature of the decisions which result.

Complexity of Issues

One of the most important facts about public finance decisions is that the issues are very complex. In a sizable volume, Musgrave shows that a decision to tax or spend in an effort to improve the allocation of resources may result in a changed distribution of income and may affect the stability of the economy. He shows that the question of defining equitable taxation begins with difficult technical questions such as the proper definition of income. He considers questions such as the effect of tax and expenditure policy upon investment, upon work-leisure choice, and thus upon the growth of the economy. Yet, such an analysis only hints at the full complexity of the issue. Decisions to tax and spend in particular ways affect not only economic matters, but noneconomic matters that affect the political and social future of Illinois for many years to come. Decisions about common school equalization grants or about appropriations to the Youth Commission may have an effect upon the possibility of race riots five years later. Changes in the system of property taxation might have a major effect upon the kind of city Chicago will be 20 years from now. More generally, failure of tax and expenditure decisions to respond to the changing environment could lead to major changes in the political system, as well as the political future of those who make decisions.

In another sense, also, economic analysis greatly understates the true complexity of the problem. Most discussions of tax and expenditure policy are in rather aggregative terms. In fact, such policies can be implemented only by translating them into the amount of taxes that must be paid by every single taxpayer. Expenditure policy must be translated into the purchase and use by state agencies of single items like cakes of soap and paving machines or into checks and rent payments for the recipients of welfare payments. This means that laws must be written not in terms of textbook definitions of the tax or the U.S. Bureau of the Census definition of a functional expenditure category, but in legal language which is constitutional in Illinois and which is appropriate in view of the existing administrative system. The history of both the Illinois sales tax and the general property tax clearly indicates the difficulties which this may involve.

Finally, the issues are complex because they involve people—and people react in ways that may seem illogical and perverse to other people. Thus, a slum clearance and rehousing program may be seen by the supposed beneficiaries as an evil scheme to destroy communities and ruin the happiness of gentle old people who only wish to pass their remaining years in peace. An attempt to improve property tax assessment by professionalizing assessors means unemployment and loss of status for several hundred local assessors. Many others, who would suffer no personal loss of status or income by the change, will see such a change as a move to weaken local government and thus strike at the foundations of American democracy. Theoretically, these values might be put into a "social preference function" and analyzed economically—though the problem of measurement is immense—but when one considers the social conflict as individuals interact and the symbolic meanings which are created and changed in the process, it becomes bewildering to consider how one might take account of such matters in a systematic analysis.

Costs of Information

Closely related to the complexity of issues is the very high cost of information. Downs' analysis suggests that the average voter is likely to find that it is irrational to spend very much time trying to obtain information about issues before voting. In areas in which he earns his living it may become rational to make a greater expenditure in gathering information which might be utilized in influencing political outcomes. This often results in the employment of professional lobbyists whose jobs are to provide information to those who employ them and to utilize this information to influence decisions in a way that is favorable to the interests which they represent. Some lobbying groups employ, at considerable cost, sizable teams of experts to collect and analyze information about the issues in which they are interested. However, given the complexity of the issues and the cost of gathering information, it is obvious that even the most elaborate research organization will not be able to assemble all the information which might be of relevance to the decision. Further, as will be shown later, much of the information which might be collected about ultimate effect would be of little use to the lobbyist.

The decision-maker also finds that information is costly. A legislator, for example, must make decisions involving every subject with which modern government deals. In the 1967 session of the Illinois legislature, for example, over 5,000 bills were introduced and disposed of in a six-month period. The printed text of these bills alone represents more information than most legislators can utilize in the time allowed and few, if any, legislators ever read all the bills upon which they vote. They reduce the time-cost of information by depending heavily upon "secondary" information from fellow legislators, trusted lobbyists, party platforms, party leaders, and upon symbolic and ideological clues.

Specialized decision-makers in administrative or judicial branches are in positions to utilize more specific and detailed information, but even here cost considerations severely limit the amount of information which can be obtained and used. Thus, judges depend almost entirely upon legal information in deciding tax cases, and highway engineers make decisions affecting the lives of thousands of people largely on the basis of engineering data.

Real Conflict

Another important fact about public decisions is that they involve real conflict of interest. Economic theory is based upon the fact that the process of exchange results in gains to both parties. Politics, on the other hand, is the *authoritative* allocation of values, and the decisions with which this study has been concerned are made politically because the exchange process does not work or produces results which are not politically acceptable. Most, if not all, of the decisions which are made impose real losses upon some of the parties involved and represent real gains to others. In this case, no amount of information alone would resolve the issue.[17] In fact, information which spells out exactly who gains and who loses from particular tax and expenditure policies sometimes intensifies conflict.

The Motives of Decision-Makers

Because most persons who think and write about policy issues do so from a normative viewpoint, it is easy to fall into the habit of assuming that decision-makers make decisions on the basis of their appraisal of what they consider to be in the public interest. Even economists, who have utilized the concepts of rational self-interest so successfully in analysis, often seem to assume that politicians are, or should be, concerned only with the public interest. In fact, politicians come in many sizes and shapes. Some act altruistically most of the time; most act altruistically some of the time. But the assumption that politicians generally act in accordance with what they perceive to be their self-interest is a very useful one for political analysis.[18] In any event, it must be assumed that most politicians want to win elections and that elections are won only by making responses to political forces rather than by basing actions upon ultimate effects of policy decisions.

Survival of the System

It should now be clear that it is impossible for political decision-makers to base decisions upon a complete understanding of the effects which the decision will have. The issues are far too complicated and information is far too costly. There are many demands, often highly controversial, which must be dealt with. Furthermore, those who must make the decisions are ordinary men with the usual desire to keep their jobs and perhaps to advance to better ones.

It follows that any political system which has survived for any considerable period of time must have within it mechanisms which permit politicians to deal with the inherent complexity and conflict and to produce decisions which will maintain support at acceptable levels. The exact nature of these mechanisms will differ depending

[17] Conceivably, there is some amount of information about ultimate consequences, on earth and in heaven, which would produce absolute harmony of action, but at present, speculation about such matters must be considered as philosophy rather than social science.

[18] One problem with such an assumption is that political self-interest is more difficult to measure or define than is the self-interest of the pure competitor. The politician's situation is more akin to that of an oligopolist making long range investment decisions in an industry characterized by much innovation and market uncertainty.

upon the environment in which the system has developed and the particular history of its evolution. The following appear to play an important role in simplifying decisions and ameliorating conflict over tax and expenditure decisions in Illinois.

1. Constitutionalism   The existence of federal and state constitutions simplifies issues and reduces conflict in two ways. The first of these is that these documents and relevant judicial opinions set up rules for making and carrying out decisions.

In addition, the constitution reduces available alternatives by ruling out many possible decisions. Certain forms of taxation and certain expenditures are excluded from consideration in the biennial legislative sessions.

The state Supreme Court has played an unusually important role in Illinois. In *Bachrach* v. *Nelson* the court interpreted the revenue article in a way that outlawed both the general sales tax and the income tax at a time when the environment was changing in such a way as to create strong pressures for the use of one or both taxes as a main source of state tax revenue. Almost immediately, however, the court permitted the levy of a sales tax under the fiction that it was an occupation tax on the retailer. Since that time, there has been a confusing series of rulings which seem to have resulted in the basic tax being a use tax upon the privilege of using tangible personal property in the state. Throughout the entire period, however, the court interpretations have been unusually restrictive of the revenue power of the state.

The result has been to restrict the legislature's available alternatives and to make it difficult to fix responsibility. A legislator can plead that certain alternatives are not available to him because they are unconstitutional. The court stands, in the public mind, as a symbol of rational decision-making that is sacred to the American way of government, and a decision (or lack of decision) which results from court action has upon it the stamp of legitimacy. Further, the restrictive interpretations of the court tend to shift conflict into technical and verbal channels. Many debates about Illinois taxes turn into debates about wording the proposal to make it constitutional rather than remaining debates about issues of equity, administrative feasibility, or even yield.

2. Incremental Decision-Making   The number of decisions which must be made and the conflicts which result are greatly reduced by the fact that tax and budgeting decisions are incremental. This term is used here to imply that decisions are made as changes from the existing situation. It differs considerably from the term "marginal decision-making" as the term is used by economists. As applied to the appropriation process, for example, incremental decision-making implies that all past appropriations are continued (at least in a period of economic expansion), and the only question is how much the appropriation for each department or program is to be increased. Marginal decision-making would imply that the "least justifiable" item of expenditure in each department or program would be compared with the least justifiable items in all other departments or programs and with all proposed alternatives. This would continue until no possible change could improve the situation. Marginal decision-making might result in many changes in existing programs—and create much political disturbance. Incremental decision-making insures that there will be few changes in existing programs and minimizes political disturbance.

Incremental decision-making is general throughout all branches of government. In some cases it is highly formalized and in other cases it is by common, but unspoken, consent. In the judicial branch the rule is highly formalized as the legal doctrine of *stare decisis*. In the administrative branch it may be formalized in rules and regulations which are occasionally amended but rarely rewritten.

3. Compartmentalization Incremental decision-making reduces the burden of decision-making by spreading it over time. There are also a number of formal and informal devices for spreading responsibility among many individuals and groups. For example, the requirement that new legislation must be approved by two houses of the legislature and by the executive branch places additional hurdles in the way of legislation and increases the possibility that any legislation which is passed has widespread support among politically important groups. It also increases the difficulties of the irate citizen who wants to focus his anger or to retaliate for unpopular actions. Similarly, the constitutional provision dividing power among the legislative, judicial, and executive branches also divides responsibility. It means that the legislature enacts tax and expenditure programs in broad general terms rather than having to decide upon the tax to be paid by each individual or the exact details of service to be performed by the state. The administrator, in turn, is protected by the fact that he must follow the law, as set forth in the statutes and judicial decisions.

Compartmentalization goes outside the formal legal structures of government. There are compartments of influence and responsibility in which private groups play a major role. Often the approval of a relatively small number of group representatives would insure passage of particular financial measures, and the opposition of an even smaller number would block it. This process was well illustrated by the negotiations which led to the adoption of the revenue amendment proposal in the 1965 legislature and its rejection by the electorate.

4. Symbolism and Ideology Decision-making can be simplified by the use of ideology and symbolism. Terms such as "income tax" or "sales tax" have acquired symbolic meanings which carry much emotional content. The legislator lucky enough to come from a district in which there is substantial agreement about these meanings need know little about the technical aspects of either tax in order to choose his position.

Symbolic meanings are often manipulated by proponents or opponents of a particular measure. The success of opponents of the city sales tax bills in the 1967 legislature in tagging the measures as the "Daley double" meant that the bills became associated in the public mind as "Cook County bills." This made it easy for downstate legislators of either party to vote against them even though the bills had substantial support from downstate Republican mayors.

Demands and Outputs

Although the political system which has evolved in Illinois seems to be veto-ridden, every chapter of this volume testifies to the fact that change occurs. Expenditure rises apace and tax rates are raised, even though there is little change in the general structure of the tax system.

A key factor in understanding this process of stability through change is the built-in biennial gap between estimated revenue and appropriations. The gap arises because there are strong demands that insure substantial increases in expenditure and an inelastic tax system which insures that even existing levels of services cannot be maintained on the income from existing tax rates.

There are two sources of demand for increased expenditure. One of these sources is in the environment, outside the political system itself. Demands from this source might be called grass roots demands for better public services. As a nation or community grows more affluent, a smaller proportion of total economic resources need be devoted to the necessities of life, and there are more economic resources which can be devoted to optional uses. Among the options chosen are items such as better schools, parks, roads, civic cleanliness, security for the poor, and hospital care for the ill, which are provided largely by government. Another facet of this demand for increased government expenditure is that increased urbanization and specialization make certain governmental services more essential. For example, police costs are higher in urbanized areas, highways are essential elements in production, and much of the "capital" used in modern industry takes the form of knowledge developed and transmitted by state educational institutions.

The second source of demands for increased expenditure is from organized interest groups which have an interest in promoting expenditure. These groups include organizations of governmental employees, suppliers of government, local or state "development" groups, and "user" groups. These groups have a very specific occupational or avocational interest in a particular kind of spending which leads them to devote considerable time and effort to promoting spending for a specific purpose. Some methods of doing this involve promoting and mobilizing grass roots demands which would otherwise probably not have become politically effective.

Invariably, the strength of the demands for increased expenditure results in substantial increases in appropriations with the largest increases going to the strongest groups. The expenditure elasticities shown in Table 16 indicate that the most rapid increases have come in the fields of education and highways. This will come as no surprise to those who have observed the political scene in Illinois. Approval of large scale "investment" in education is easily reconciled with the ideology of those on both ends of the political spectrum in Illinois; education has an obvious and visible impact upon a large number of articulate persons (both as producers and consumers), and the proponents of higher spending are well organized at all levels of government and all levels of education. Highway expenditure has been promoted by liberal federal grants and by well organized lobbies. The strength of the "non-diversion of highway revenues" slogan and the "investment" character of highway construction are all political assets.

In contrast with these functions, public safety, welfare, and natural resources are notably poorer in political assets and have had much lower elasticities.

The compartmentalization of the legislative decision-making process means that increases are voted with little reference to revenue requirements, but in the final weeks (or hours) of each legislative session it is necessary to achieve some kind of balance. In this setting the strength of lobbies can be very effectively utilized.

All this means that criteria of a "good" tax system have relevance only to the extent that they are effectively translated into political demands, and that a tax system will conform to the criteria only to the extent that the combination of political forces, working within the existing political system, bring it about. Thus, if one is to understand why the Illinois tax system deviates from the criteria, it is necessary to understand something of the relative strengths of those making demands upon the system.

Demands, and the strengths of those making them, cannot be measured in an exact and precise way, but it is possible to make generalizations which should be reasonably accurate. For example, the relatively high rating which must be given the Illinois tax system in regard to its effect upon industry and economic growth is clearly related to the great strength of business lobbies in Illinois. There are several factors which help explain the power of the business groups in the tax field. In the first place, the normal organizational pattern of business groups is apt to coincide with the impact of the proposed tax. In the second place, these organizations are apt to include, and employ, men who are sophisticated about both taxation and the political process. In the third place, business organizations are apt to be relatively well supplied with funds for lobbying purposes. These three factors together mean that when a tax on business or a tax that would fall primarily upon upper income groups is proposed, there automatically exist organizations with a united view. Furthermore, these organizations are apt to know the significance of the proposal and have the technical skill and political knowledge to make an effective fight against it. An additional factor in the success of the business lobby is that one of the criteria of a good tax system—the location of industry argument—can be effectively utilized. The newspaper headlines about the effect of the tax upon employment and the inevitable announcement by one or more companies that they are holding up plans for a new factory in Illinois not only affect public opinion, but provide cover for legislators who may wish to vote against the proposal for entirely different reasons. It should be noted in this connection that studies which show that taxation is not a major factor affecting industrial location are of little relevance unless there is a politically effective group which, for reasons of its own, finds it advantageous to utilize these studies.

The importance of the "location of industry" argument as a political force is borne out by an examination of differences in the tax burden upon various kinds of businesses. For example, utilities which, by law, must be incorporated in the state and whose product must be delivered within the state are taxed more heavily than most other kinds of business. Not only has the capital stock tax been enforced far more rigorously upon utility corporations than on other corporations, but utility services were the first kind of service to be taxed by the state. In addition, municipalities are permitted to tax utility services at rates up to 5 per cent.[19]

The structure of the property tax, as administered, also reflects the influence of concern about economic effects. The Cook County classification system results in the heaviest tax falling upon those businesses which, by their nature, cannot easily move out of the central city. There is also evidence that the assessments upon tangible personal property, in Cook County and elsewhere, reflect the probability of the property being moved. The exemption or virtual exemption of intangibles results, in part, from concern about the effects upon the legal and economic location of securities.

The relatively low rating which the Illinois tax system would receive on the grounds of equity and particularly the heavy burden placed upon low income groups is also related to the balance of political forces. Equity is an abstract concept and many of the persons who are penalized by inequitable taxation are unaware of it. Furthermore, there is no ready-made organization of those who are so penalized. Some groups which are penalized by inequitable taxation are potentially politically effective, however. For example, there is a great mass of low income voters who would gain by a shift from sales taxation to income taxation. In some states this group has found effective political representation in the labor organizations, farm organizations, or a political party. In Illinois the political parties compete with each other in promising that there will be no income tax or other major change in the tax system. Illinois labor unions have not made taxation a major concern and no governor or other major political leader has made tax reform a major rallying cry. The Illinois Agricultural Association has made a major effort in support of income taxation as a means of relieving property taxation, but in a heavily urban state its influence has not been sufficient. Other groups

---

[19] There are, of course, other factors which help explain the popularity of taxes upon utilities and utility services. The relatively large size of utility corporations and the accounting and billing techniques used makes administration relatively easy. It might also be hypothesized that the virtual certainty that utility taxes can be passed to the consumer might make utility enterprises less zealous in their lobbying efforts than are enterprises whose ability to pass the tax to consumers is less certain. The author knows of little evidence to support this hypothesis, however. Utilities are well represented in Springfield and there seems to be no reason to believe that their lobbyists are less zealous or less skillful than other business lobbyists. It may be, however, that the testimony of utility lobbyists is discounted because the legislators know that the tax can be passed on to customers.

have supported income taxation mainly as a way of obtaining additional funds for a favorite expenditure.

On the basis of available evidence, it is impossible to say whether the failure of major political organizations and leaders to utilize tax "reform" as a means of gaining political support results from their overlooking an opportunity, or whether the climate of opinion indicates that such an effort would not be successful. It is clear, however, that the attempts of political figures to use the tax reform issue have not been notably successful.

State Treasurer Joseph Lohman made taxation a major issue in his attempt to secure the Democratic nomination for governor in 1960 but lost in the primary to organization-backed Otto Kerner. Governor Kerner's call for a tax study early in his first term bore some of the earmarks of a campaign for tax reform, but after several rebuffs and failures in connection with the study, he had little to say about tax reform in later years. Democratic Representative John Morris was an outspoken foe of property taxation and an advocate of corporation and income taxation. He received the second highest vote in the at-large election for state representative in 1964 but, after reapportionment, was defeated in his own district by a popular representative who had formerly been in another district. Republican leader W. Russell Arrington, although a foe of income taxation, has been active in an effort to orient the party toward public issues. His role in the Tax Rate Limit Commission which led to improvements in property tax law and his support of the sales tax broadening bills in 1967 have been described.

A WORD TO REFORMERS

Clearly, reform of the tax system or of the budgeting mechanism does not come easily in Illinois. However, as tax rates get higher, demands for more equitable taxation and more efficient use of revenue will surely arise. These demands will have an effect; but whether they will lead to minor, piecemeal modifications or to a political crisis which will result in major changes is difficult to predict.

One thing is certain. The "reformer" of whatever persuasion who wants to affect these developments will do well to study carefully the world in which decisions are made. That world is populated by politicians who are faced with complex, controversial problems which have ramifications far beyond the analytical power of any social scientist. It is a world made bearable by a system of decision-making which has passed only one test—the test of its ability to survive. Unfortunately, not all proposed reforms would pass even that test.

A

APPENDIX A: Statistical Tables

TABLE A1

MIDYEAR POPULATION ESTIMATES[a]

Year	Illinois	United States	United States Excluding District of Columbia
		(thousands)	
1929	7,606	121,770	121,287
1930	7,644	123,077	122,589
1931	7,687	124,040	123,536
1932	7,736	124,840	124,327
1933	7,768	125,579	125,050
1934	7,772	126,374	125,806
1935	7,797	127,250	126,642
1936	7,840	128,053	127,424
1937	7,857	128,825	128,209
1938	7,866	129,825	129,187
1939	7,890	130,880	130,222
1940	7,905	131,954	131,264
1941	7,995	133,417	132,653
1942	8,054	134,670	133,824
1943	7,765	134,697	133,809
1944	7,718	134,075	133,213
1945	7,612	133,387	132,522
1946	8,164	140,638	139,745
1947	8,344	143,665	142,792
1948	8,552	146,093	145,253
1949	8,670	148,665	147,858
1950	8,751	151,234	150,427
1951	8,755	153,384	152,565
1952	8,910	155,761	154,933
1953	9,002	158,313	157,467
1954	9,159	161,884	161,093
1955	9,316	165,069	164,284
1956	9,482	168,088	167,329
1957	9,647	171,187	170,424
1958	9,948	174,149	173,392
1959	9,986	177,135	176,374
1960	10,081	179,992	179,225
1961	10,115	183,057	182,276
1962	10,260	185,890	185,100
1963	10,369	188,658	187,866
1964	10,538	191,372	190,577
1965	10,641	193,795	192,993
1966[b]	10,722	195,857	195,049

[a] Excludes armed forces overseas.
[b] Provisional estimates, U.S. Bureau of the Census.

Source: For 1929–53, U.S. Department of Commerce, *Personal Income by States Since 1929* (Washington: U.S. Government Printing Office, 1956); for 1954–58, 1960–66, U.S. Bureau of the Census, *Population Reports*, Series P-25, Nos. 41, 130, 151, 172, 354; for 1959, U.S. Bureau of the Census, *Statistical Abstract of the United States*, 1964 (Washington, 1965).

TABLE A2

ILLINOIS ESTIMATED POPULATION, BY AGE GROUP, JULY 1

Year	Under 5	5–17	18 and Over[a]
		(thousands)	
1940		1,554	
1941		1,531	
1942		1,518	
1943		1,486	
1944		1,467	
1945		1,450	
1946		1,452	
1947	745	1,498	6,101
1948	760	1,520	6,272
1949	— b	— b	— b
1950	843	1,564	6,344
1951	906	1,612	6,237
1952	905	1,710	6,295
1953	926	1,797	6,279
1954	947	1,867	6,345
1955	970	1,935	6,411
1956	1,001	2,031	6,450
1957	1,039	2,134	6,474
1958	1,070	2,246	6,632
1959	— b	— b	— b
1960	1,130	2,309	6,642
1961	1,132	2,358	6,625
1962	1,143	2,446	6,671
1963	1,139	2,530	6,700
1964	1,140	2,629	6,769
1965	1,120	2,664	6,857
1966	— b	— b	6,920

a Population 18 and over was computed by subtracting the civilian population 17 and under from the total population excluding armed forces overseas. This results in omitting members of armed forces under 18 from the total, but the net effect is insignificant.
b Not available.

Source: U.S. Bureau of the Census, *Population Reports*, Series P-25, Nos. 41, 130, 151, 172, 354; Table A1. "Under 5" population for 1947 and 1948 was estimated by assuming that Illinois has same proportion of United States under 5 population as it does of 5–17 population.

TABLE A3

TOTAL AND PER CAPITA INCOME, ILLINOIS AND
UNITED STATES, CALENDAR YEARS 1929–65

	Illinois		United States			
Year	Total	Per Capita[a]	Total	Per Capita[a]	Total Excluding D.C.	Per Capita[a] Excluding D.C.
	(millions)		(millions)		(millions)	
1929	$ 7,280	$ 957	$ 85,661	$ 703	$ 85,046	$ 701
1930	6,235	816	76,780	624	76,164	621
1931	5,187	675	65,597	529	64,993	526
1932	3,780	489	50,022	401	49,483	398
1933	3,434	442	47,122	375	46,646	373
1934	3,945	508	53,482	423	52,959	421
1935	4,484	575	60,104	472	59,512	470
1936	5,112	652	68,363	534	67,674	531
1937	5,743	731	73,803	573	73,087	570
1938	5,116	650	68,433	527	67,734	524
1939	5,566	705	72,753	556	72,018	553
1940	5,964	754	78,522	595	77,715	592
1941	7,153	895	95,953	719	95,032	716
1942	8,367	1,039	122,417	909	121,263	906
1943	9,772	1,258	148,409	1,102	147,070	1,099
1944	10,743	1,392	160,118	1,194	158,772	1,192
1945	11,188	1,470	164,549	1,234	163,135	1,231
1946	12,487	1,530	175,701	1,249	174,193	1,247
1947	13,647	1,636	189,077	1,316	187,551	1,313
1948	15,521	1,815	208,878	1,430	207,234	1,427
1949	14,607	1,685	205,791	1,384	204,091	1,380
1950	15,948	1,822	226,214	1,496	224,424	1,492
1951	17,711	2,023	253,233	1,651	251,312	1,647
1952	18,608	2,088	269,767	1,732	267,789	1,728
1953	19,812	2,201	285,458	1,803	283,544	1,801
1954	19,933	2,176	287,613	1,777	285,696	1,773
1955	21,167	2,272	308,265	1,867	306,316	1,865
1956	23,024	2,428	330,481	1,966	328,462	1,963
1957	24,056	2,494	348,462	2,036	346,401	2,033
1958	24,378	2,451	358,474	2,058	356,341	2,055
1959	25,776	2,581	380,963	2,151	378,735	2,147
1960	26,718	2,650	398,725	2,215	396,414	2,212
1961	27,517	2,720	414,411	2,264	412,036	2,261
1962	28,992	2,826	440,192	2,368	437,658	2,364
1963	30,228	2,915	463,053	2,454	460,384	2,451
1964	32,136	3,050	493,408	2,578	490,604	2,574
1965	34,903	3,280	532,147	2,746	529,173	2,742

[a] Per capita figures computed using population data from Table A1.

Source: For 1929–47, U.S. Department of Commerce, *Personal Income by States Since 1929* (Washington: U.S. Government Printing Office, 1956); for 1948–65, *Survey of Current Business*, August, 1966.

TABLE A4

ESTIMATED TOTAL PERSONAL INCOME, ILLINOIS AND
UNITED STATES, FISCAL YEARS 1942–65

Year	Illinois	United States Including D.C.	Excluding D.C.
		(millions)	
1942	$ 7,760.0	$109,185.0	$108,147.5
1944	10,257.5	154,263.5	152,921.0
1946	11,837.5	170,125.0	168,664.0
1947	13,067.0	182,389.0	180,872.0
1948	14,584.0	198,977.5	197,392.5
1949	15,064.0	207,334.5	205,662.5
1950	15,277.5	216,002.5	214,257.5
1951	16,829.5	239,723.5	237,868.0
1952	18,159.5	261,500.0	259,550.5
1953	19,210.0	277,612.5	275,666.5
1954	19,872.5	286,535.5	284,620.0
1955	20,550.0	297,939.0	296,006.0
1956	22,095.5	319,373.0	317,389.0
1957	23,540.0	339,471.5	337,431.5
1958	24,217.0	353,468.0	351,371.0
1959	25,077.0	369,718.5	367,538.0
1960	26,247.0	389,844.0	387,574.5
1961	27,117.5	406,568.0	404,225.0
1962	28,254.5	427,301.5	424,847.0
1963	29,610.0	451,622.5	449,021.0
1964	31,182.0	478,230.5	475,494.0
1965	33,519.5	512,777.5	509,888.5

Source: Computed by averaging calendar year income of the two years involved (Table A3).
There are more accurate methods of estimating state fiscal year income, but this method somewhat
reduces irregularities and is thus more suitable for some of the applications for which it is employed in this study.

TABLE A5

COMPREHENSIVE TABLE OF STATE FUNDS, AS OF JUNE 30, 1965

Funds Supporting Appropriations

General Revenue Fund:
  General Revenue
  General Revenue—Armories
  General Revenue—Old Age Assistance
  General Revenue—Aid to Dependent Children
  General Revenue—Blind Assistance
  General Revenue—Disability Assistance

Common School Fund

Highway Funds:
  Road
  Road Bond Interest and Retirement
  Motor Fuel Tax—State
  Motor Fuel Tax—Counties
  Motor Fuel Tax—Municipalities
  Motor Fuel Tax—Townships
  Emergency Relief Bond Interest and Retirement
  Grade Crossing Protection

Building Funds:
  Public Building (not subject to appropriation)
  Public Welfare Building
  Universities Building

Debt Service Funds:
  Public Welfare Building Bond Interest and Retirement
  Universities Building Bond Interest and Retirement
  Service Recognition Bond Interest and Retirement
  Soldiers Compensation Bond Interest and Retirement

Educational Income Funds:
  Southern Illinois University Income
  Teachers College Income
  University Income

Other Special State Funds:
  Aeronautics
  Agricultural Premium
  Drivers Education
  Fair and Exposition
  Feeds and Fertilizers (no appropriation)
  Fire Prevention
  Game and Fish
  Illinois Bred Thoroughbreds
  Illinois Fund for Illinois Colts
  Illinois Korean Compensation
  Illinois-Michigan Canal
  Illinois Veterans Rehabilitation
  Mental Health
  Motor Vehicle
  Narcotic Control (no appropriation)
  Public Utility
  Soldiers Compensation (no appropriation)

State Boating Act
State Forest and Nurseries
State Parks
State Pensions

Special Federal Funds:
Agricultural Marketing Services
Airport
Armed Forces Rejectee (no appropriation)
Child Welfare Services
Civil Defense (no appropriation)
Civil Defense Administrative
Civil Defense Adult Education (no appropriation)
Drivers Education Internship (no appropriation)
Economic Opportunity (no appropriation)
Education Fellowship (no appropriation)
Emergency Planning (no appropriation)
Forest Reserve (no appropriation)
G.I. Educational (no appropriation)
Higher Education (no appropriation)
Hospital Construction
Library Services (no appropriation)
Manpower Development and Training Revolving
Maternal and Child Health Services
Mental Health Services
National Defense Education Act
Old Age Survivors Insurance
Public Health Services and Dental Health Services
Recoveries Trust (no appropriation)
School Lunch
School Milk (no appropriation)
Special Assistance (no appropriation)
Surplus Property Utilization (no appropriation)
Title III, Social Security and Employment Service
Unemployment Compensation, Special Administration
U.S. Veterans Bureau
Vocational Education
Vocational Rehabilitation
Youth Development (no appropriation)

Funds Held Outside the State Treasury (not subject to appropriation):
W. K. Kellogg Foundation
Psychiatric Training and Research
Urban Planning Assistance
Area Redevelopment Administration—Subsistence Payment Account
Manpower Development and Training Administration Account

Revolving Funds:
Air Transportation
Legislative Services
Paper, Printing, and Office Supplies
State Garage
Welfare
Working Capital

Trust Funds in State Treasury

State Trust Funds:
Agricultural Master

Armory Rental
Conservation School Income
Corporation Trust
County Retailers' Occupation Tax
Flood Control Land Lease
Forfeiture Narcotic
General Assembly Retirement
Group Insurance
Illinois State Toll Highway—Construction Account
Illinois State Toll Highway—Revenue Account
Judges Retirement System
Kaskaskia Commons Permanent School
Local Airport
Local Bond
Medical Payment
Morrill Fund
Municipal Retailers' Occupation Tax
Municipal Retirement System
Prevention of Blindness
Protest
Public Assistance Recoveries
Relief Compensation
Safety Responsibility
Social Security Contributions
State Employees Retirement
State Fair Trust
Teachers College Board—Revenue
Teachers Retirement System
Unclaimed Property Trust
Union Dues
United Fund Deductions
U.S. Savings Bonds
Warrants Escheated Fund
Workmen's Compensation

Other Trust Funds:
  Public Assistance
  Withholding Tax
  Unemployment Trust Deposit with U.S. Treasury

Source: Illinois Department of Finance, *Forty-Eighth Annual Report*, Table I.

TABLE A6

BIENNIAL EXPENDITURE,[a] BY AGENCY, 1948–65

(in thousands)

Agency	Sixty-fifth Biennium (1948–49)	Sixty-sixth Biennium (1950–51)	Sixty-seventh Biennium (1952–53)	Sixty-eighth Biennium (1954–55)	Sixty-ninth Biennium (1956–57)	Seventieth Biennium (1958–59)	Seventy-first Biennium (1960–61)	Seventy-second Biennium (1962–63)	Seventy-third Biennium (1964–65)
Legislative Agencies	$ 2,543	$ 2,732	$ 3,104	$ 3,363	$ 5,592	$ 5,132	$ 5,629	$ 6,141	$ 6,907
Judicial Agencies	4,056	4,433	5,124	5,499	5,718	7,650	9,046	10,926	22,189
Elected Officials:									
Governor, Lieutenant Governor, Attorney General	2,178	1,936	2,249	2,439	2,361	2,696	3,053	3,774	4,350
Secretary of State	12,266	14,310	15,645	19,143	24,759	32,096	33,983	35,664	41,097
State Treasurer	52,267	78,856	73,178	71,958	68,017	66,410	43,144	47,450	79,987
Auditor of Public Accounts	124,113	181,381	155,894	186,335	245,799	223,132	335,623	397,334	459,259
Superintendent of Public Instruction	1,332	1,562	1,746	1,998	2,078	43,340	68,364	83,468	111,608
Universities:									
University of Illinois	74,666	78,311	90,057	88,447	98,281	120,672	128,518	173,962	231,455
Southern Illinois University	—b	9,919	13,154	12,132	19,800	30,452	36,226	52,813	87,004
Teachers College Board	—b	—b	19,683	19,338	25,914	37,938	38,229	70,091	88,077
Code Departments:									
Aeronautics	4,357	6,827	2,770	3,028	4,243	7,596	5,789	7,196	8,086
Agriculture	10,340	9,748	10,504	16,525	17,633	18,439	19,796	23,705	24,980
Children and Family Services	—	—	—	—	—	—	—	—	44,173
Conservation	5,157	5,974	9,236	10,406	12,067	16,234	18,386	14,627	18,271
Finance	88,591	91,431	90,175	135,947	156,965	180,423	180,210	196,338	212,914
Financial Institutions	—	—	—	—	—	3,581	4,007	4,083	4,643
Insurance	1,597	1,512	1,699	1,583	1,617	1,735	2,182	2,298	2,642
Labor	19,966	20,533	21,387	21,678	23,701	29,256	31,697	39,855	50,569
Mental Health	—	—	—	—	—	—	—	224,466	295,496
Mines and Minerals	1,109	917	1,031	1,174	1,091	1,166	1,284	1,396	1,450
Personnel	—	—	—	—	319	1,614	1,685	1,615	1,726
Public Aid	199,585	214,813	275,636	284,274	319,331	393,388	483,128	604,931	620,222
Public Health	11,541	19,236	29,409	23,890	26,238	30,534	30,620	34,755	41,106
Public Safety	28,388	28,463	33,863	32,616	38,617	51,327	57,278	63,199	71,786

Public Welfare	93,161	118,446	134,829	120,472	132,935	172,285	188,129	—ᵈ
Public Works	165,796	128,171	201,707	259,175	288,601	461,147	620,860	743,914
Registration and Education	23,486ᵉ	26,719ᶠ	5,413	5,126	6,158	6,904	7,484	9,272
Revenue	25,097	26,198	33,815	40,245	41,876	42,811	43,632	46,314
Business and Economic Development	—	—	—	—	—	—	499ᵍ	2,403ᵍ
Boards, Commissions, and Noncode Departments:								
Department of Audits	—	—	—	—	—	562	627	672
Military and Naval Department	4,290	5,411	5,244	6,137	4,543	5,386	5,583	5,548
Youth Commission	—	—	—	7,161	10,032	14,770	16,045	20,874
Civil Service Commission	319	498	567	610	582	136	140	159
Commerce Commission	2,121	1,609	1,873	2,783	3,113	3,535	3,626	3,902
Board of Higher Education	—	—	—	—	—	88	119	175
Illinois Building Authority	—	—	—	—	—	—	13,809	19,125
Scholarship Commission	—	—	—	—	—	716	2,725	5,163
School Building Commission	—	—	—	—	—	886	7,041	5,027
Illinois Veterans Commission	2,755	1,726	1,843	2,178	2,162	2,977	—	2,763
Board of Vocational Education	15,313	15,130	12,504	11,695	13,285	15,224	18,418	37,793
Retirement Systems:								
State Employees	2,691	3,194	3,762	3,846	4,908	6,234	7,547	14,605
Teachers	—	—	—	11	16	15	16	6,905
University	276	797	564	—	—	16	—	633
Other Boards and Commissions	318,533ʰ	15,984	4,318	4,516	5,197	6,856	6,949	11,063
Total	1,297,891	1,116,777	1,261,984	1,405,727	1,613,553	2,045,460	2,480,627	3,466,315

a Years shown indicate the fiscal years in the biennium. Thus, the sixty-fifth biennium ran from July 1, 1947, to June 30, 1949, and includes fiscal years 1948 and 1949. Appropriations for this biennium were made by the sixty-fifth General Assembly which met from January through June of 1947.

b Appropriations made to the Department of Registration and Education before creation of separate board of trustees.

c Public Aid "Commission" prior to 1963.

d The Department of Public Welfare at various times, performed functions now carried out by four other agencies. From 1946 to 1962 this department performed functions now carried out by the departments of Mental Health and Child and Family Services. From 1946 to 1953, the services now provided by the Youth Commission and some of those provided by the Department of Public Safety were the responsibility of Public Welfare.

e Includes appropriations for five institutions of higher education later under control of the Teachers College Board and the Board of Governors of Southern Illinois University.

f Includes appropriations for four institutions later under the control of the Teachers College Board, now known as the Board of Governors of State Colleges and Universities.

g Changed from a board to a department in 1965.

h Includes expenditure of $311 million for the payment of veterans' bonuses.

Source: Illinois Department of Finance, Annual Report, various years.

TABLE A7

ILLINOIS STATE GOVERNMENT EXPENDITURE, BY TYPE AND
FUNCTION, FISCAL YEAR 1965

Function	Total	Per Capita
	(thousands)	
Education	$619,841	$58.82
State Institutions of Higher Education:		
Current Operations		
Auxiliary Enterprises	29,747	2.82
Other	164,661	15.63
Capital Outlay	98,206	9.32
Total State Institutions of Higher Education	292,614	27.77
Other Education:		
Assistance and Subsidies	7,872	.75
Other	24,043	2.28
Local Schools	3,571	.34
Total Other Education	35,486	3.37
Intergovernmental Expenditure	291,741	27.68
Highways	481,595	45.70
Direct Expenditure:		
Regular Highway Facilities		
Current Operation	59,432	5.64
Capital Outlay	287,416	27.27
Total Regular Highway Facilities	346,848	32.91
Toll Highway Facilities		
Current Operation	6,589	.63
Capital Outlay	407	.04
Total Toll Highway Facilities	6,996	.67
Intergovernmental Expenditure	127,751	12.12
Public Welfare	347,358	32.96
Direct Expenditure:		
Cash Assistance Payments	176,375	16.74
Vendor Payments[a]	67,830	6.43
State Welfare Institutions	7,281	.69
Other Public Welfare	27,517	2.61
Intergovernmental Expenditure	68,355	6.49
Hospitals	174,932	16.60
Current Operation of State Hospitals:		
Regular Mental Hospitals	77,500	7.35
Other Mental Institutions	35,613	3.38
General Hospitals	7,919	.75
Other	4,401	.42
Total Current Operation of State Hospitals	125,433	11.90
Capital Outlay, State Hospitals	45,939	4.37
Nongovernmental Hospitals	1,302	.12
Intergovernmental Expenditure	2,258	.21

Function	Total	Per Capita
	(thousands)	
Health	26,124	2.48
Natural Resources	42,325	4.02
Agriculture	25,283	2.40
Fish and Game	6,062	.58
Forestry and Parks	4,420	.42
Other	6,560	.62
Correction Expenditure	36,841	3.50
Current Operation:		
Correctional Institutions	24,286	2.30
Other	6,065	.58
Capital Outlay	6,490	.62
Police Protection	15,955	1.51
General Control	44,031	4.18
Judicial	11,923	1.13
Legislative	4,146	.39
Finance	23,322	2.22
Other	4,640	.44
Employment Security Administration	23,327	2.21
Insurance Trust Expenditure	165,029	15.66
Employee Retirement	68,132	6.46
Unemployment Compensation	96,815	9.19
Workmen's Compensation	82	.01
Miscellaneous General Expenditure	88,652	8.41
Housing and Urban Renewal	961	.09
Airports	5,016	.48
Water Transport and Terminals	2,395	.23
Protective Inspection and Regulation	20,723	1.97
General Public Buildings:		
Current Operation	3,600	.34
Capital Outlay	5,033	.48
Total General Public Buildings	8,633	.82
Veterans' Services	1,408	.13
Libraries	1,894	.18
Current Operation, n.e.c.	8,450	.80
Capital Outlay, n.e.c.	1,471	.14
Intergovernmental Expenditure, n.e.c.	2,293	.22
Interest on Debt[b]	35,408	3.36

[a] Of this total $67,315,000 was expended for medical care.
[b] Includes interest on toll highway revenue bonds and other nonguaranteed debts of state agencies.

Source: U.S. Bureau of the Census, *Compendium of State Government Finances in 1965* (Washington: U.S. Government Printing Office, 1965).

TABLE A8

ILLINOIS STATE GOVERNMENT EXPENDITURE, BY FUNCTION, FISCAL YEARS 1942–65

Function	1942	1944	1946	1948	1950	1951	1952
	(thousands)						
Public Safety	$ 10,235	$ 11,054	$ 11,105	$ 19,563	$ 19,245	$ 24,442	$ 24,200
Public Welfare	83,227	75,675	81,569	109,813	141,146	132,284	136,205
Education	36,016	38,199	39,979	93,334	121,012	134,856	141,786
Regular Highways	45,079	38,909	41,051	77,407	108,711	87,473	115,368
Toll Highways	—	—	—	—	—	—	—
Health and Hospitals	18,730	21,013	29,024	46,902	59,460	68,518	60,999
Natural Resources	5,891	5,763	7,743	15,790	15,180	16,476	14,291
Employment Security Administration	4,093	2,803	4,222	8,258	9,535	9,530	9,665
General Control	8,438	8,518	10,926	14,002	14,582	15,555	15,640
Nonhighway Transportation	—[a]	—[a]	—[a]	—[a]	—[a]	5,102	1,859
Housing and Community Redevelopment	—[a]	—[a]	—[a]	—[a]	—[a]	171	162
Miscellaneous and Unallocable	13,003	14,065	22,224	250,536 (38,422)[b]	38,474 (31,049)[b]	28,425 (27,672)[b]	23,884
Total General Expenditure	224,712	215,999	247,843	635,605 (423,491)[b]	527,345 (519,920)[b]	522,832 (522,079)[b]	544,059
Insurance Trust Expenditure	35,530	9,927	83,275	53,974	128,084	73,678	69,787
Total Expenditure	260,242	225,926	331,118	689,579 (477,465)[b]	655,429 (648,004)[b]	596,510 (595,757)[b]	613,846

(thousands)

Function	1953	1954	1955	1956	1957	1958	1959
Public Safety	$ 23,650	$ 23,184	$ 21,587	$ 22,352	$ 26,452	$ 32,440	$ 37,429
Public Welfare	147,205	140,533	152,553	158,001e	159,219e	173,245e	211,168e
Education	145,783	150,838	165,725	194,160	220,663	240,695	286,185
Regular Highways	168,318	191,820	209,411	204,784	224,915	276,835	355,199
Toll Highways	—	—	—	3,222	52,034	199,062	127,100
Health and Hospitals	72,445	67,330	67,155	70,648e	85,185e	106,300e	115,792e
Natural Resources	16,061	20,671	19,959	19,974	26,136	26,337	31,657
Employment Security Administration	9,178	8,862	9,571	10,081	10,936	12,690	15,933
General Control	17,568	17,575	18,367	20,763	22,715	22,857	28,316
Nonhighway Transportation	2,057	2,342	2,462	2,075	3,553	3,989	7,433
Housing and Community Redevelopment	163	153	152	136	152	176	236
Miscellaneous and Unallocable	24,218	26,087	31,113	34,696	40,491	44,864	49,242
Total General Expenditure	626,646	649,395	698,055	740,892 (737,670)d	872,451 (820,417)d	1,139,490 (940,428)d	1,265,690 (1,138,590)d
Insurance Trust Expenditure	65,599	114,759	131,334	81,258	97,695	178,572	225,140
Total Expenditure	692,245	764,154	829,389	822,150 (818,928)d	970,146 (918,112)d	1,318,062 (1,119,000)d	1,490,830 (1,363,730)d

TABLE A8 (Concluded)

Function	1960	1961	1962	1963	1964	1965
	(thousands)					
Public Safety	$ 30,138	$ 37,348	$ 33,116	$ 40,709	$ 37,418	$ 52,796
Public Welfare	232,731	264,277	299,285	317,907	294,060	347,358
Education	302,873	390,142	389,992	486,159	509,327	619,841
Regular Highways	381,529	399,935	367,820	430,368	455,375	474,599
Toll Highways	44,494	15,388	7,519	7,091	7,493	6,996
Health and Hospitals	91,376	110,404	101,851	136,091	142,906	201,056
Natural Resources	27,938	35,531	29,143	37,367	35,796	42,325
Employment Security Administration	13,795	17,146	17,997	21,531	19,437	23,327
General Control	24,897	29,947	27,656	34,814	34,524	44,031
Nonhighway Transportation	3,144	5,716	3,720	5,470	3,918	7,411
Housing and Community Redevelopment	273	343	240	575	694	961
Miscellaneous and Unallocable	57,798[e]	60,237[e]	54,102[e]	64,972[e]	69,470[e]	80,280[e]
Total General Expenditure	1,210,986 (1,166,492)[d]	1,366,414 (1,351,026)[d]	1,332,441 (1,324,922)[d]	1,583,054 (1,575,963)[d]	1,610,418 (1,602,925)[d]	1,900,981 (1,893,985)[d]
Insurance Trust Expenditure	151,612	228,127	204,620	197,317	187,621	165,029
Total Expenditure	1,362,598 (1,318,104)[d]	1,594,541 (1,579,153)[d]	1,537,061 (1,529,542)[d]	1,780,371 (1,773,280)[d]	1,798,039 (1,790,546)[d]	2,066,010 (2,059,014)[d]

[a] Included in "Miscellaneous and Unallocable."
[b] Excluding World War II veterans' bonus.
[c] From 1956 through 1959, vendor payments provided as part of public welfare programs were classified by the Bureau of the Census as "Health and Hospitals." These figures have been adjusted to conform with the other years in the series.
[d] Excluding toll highways.
[e] Includes Korean War veterans' bonus.

Source: U.S. Bureau of the Census, *Revised Summary of State Government Finances, 1942–1950* (Washington: U.S. Government Printing Office, 1953); U.S. Bureau of the Census, *Compendium of State Government Finances, 1951–65* (Washington: U.S. Government Printing Office, 1952–66).

TABLE A9

PER CAPITA STATE GENERAL EXPENDITURE, BY FUNCTION, ILLINOIS AND UNITED STATES, FISCAL YEARS 1942–65

Function	1942	1944	1946	1948	1950	1951	1952	1953	1954	1955
Illinois										
Public Safety	$ 1.28	$ 1.42	$ 1.46	$ 2.34	$ 2.22	$ 2.79	$ 2.76	$ 2.65	$ 2.58	$ 2.36
Public Welfare	10.41	9.75	10.72	13.16	16.28	15.12	15.56	16.52	15.61	16.66
Education	4.50	4.92	5.25	11.19	13.96	15.41	16.19	16.36	16.76	18.09
Highways	5.64	5.01	5.39	9.28	12.54	10.00	13.18	18.89	21.31	22.86
Health and Hospitals	2.34	2.71	3.81	5.62	6.86	7.83	6.97	8.13	7.48	7.33
Natural Resources	.74	.74	1.02	1.89	1.75	1.88	1.63	1.81	2.30	2.18
Employment Security Administration	.51	.36	.55	.99	1.10	1.09	1.10	1.03	.98	1.04
General Control	1.06	1.10	1.44	1.68	1.63	1.78	1.79	1.97	1.95	2.01
Miscellaneous and Unallocable	1.63	1.81	2.92	30.03ᵃ	4.44ᵃ	3.85ᵃ	2.96	2.97	3.18	3.69
Total General Expenditure	28.10	27.82	32.57	76.18	60.82	59.75	62.14	70.33	72.14	76.21
United States										
Public Safety	1.10	1.11	1.22	1.74	2.22	2.35	2.48	2.67	2.86	2.97
Public Welfare	6.88	7.06	7.97	11.28	15.95	15.89	15.64	16.23	16.21	16.51
Education	8.91	10.09	11.10	18.46	23.00	24.74	26.39	28.28	29.57	31.59
Highways	8.55	6.26	7.18	14.12	18.04	19.87	21.57	23.13	26.20	30.00
Health and Hospitals	2.34	2.59	3.37	4.90	7.05	7.57	8.25	8.47	8.90	9.13
Natural Resources	1.21	1.23	1.58	2.42	3.23	3.44	3.59	3.50	3.63	3.80
Employment Security Administration	.44	.26	.45	1.05	1.16	1.10	1.16	1.21	1.21	1.29
General Control	1.25	1.23	1.47	1.89	2.18	2.30	2.41	2.62	2.71	2.84
Miscellaneous and Unallocable	3.61	3.85	5.22	10.46	9.94	9.30	8.31	8.61	8.99	8.99
Total General Expenditure	34.29	33.69	39.58	66.32	82.85	86.56	89.80	94.72	100.28	107.12

TABLE A9 (Concluded)

Function	1956	1957	1958	1959	1960	1961	1962	1963	1964	1965
Illinois										
Public Safety	$ 2.40	$ 2.79	$ 3.36	$ 3.76	$ 3.02	$ 3.70	$ 3.27	$ 3.97	$ 3.61	$ 5.01
Public Welfare	16.96	16.79	17.96	21.23	23.31	26.22	29.59	30.99	28.36	32.96
Education	20.84	23.27	24.95	28.77	30.33	38.70	38.56	47.38	49.12	58.82
Highways	22.33	29.20[b]	49.33[b]	48.48[b]	42.66[b]	41.20	37.10	42.64	44.64	45.70
Health and Hospitals	7.58	8.98	11.02	11.64	9.15	10.95	10.07	13.26	13.78	19.08
Natural Resources	2.14	2.76	2.73	3.18	2.80	3.52	2.88	3.64	3.45	4.02
Employment Security Administration	1.08	1.15	1.32	1.60	1.38	1.70	1.78	2.10	1.88	2.21
General Control	2.23	2.40	2.37	2.85	2.49	2.97	2.74	3.39	3.33	4.18
Miscellaneous and Unallocable	3.95	4.66	5.08	5.72	6.13	6.58	5.74	6.92	7.14	8.41
Total General Expenditure	79.53	92.01	118.12	127.23	121.27	135.54	131.73	154.29	155.31	180.39
United States										
Public Safety	3.22	3.56	3.97	4.19	3.86	4.19	4.40	4.59	4.90	5.25
Public Welfare	16.35	16.64	17.40	18.47	20.91	21.74	23.41	24.92	26.00	28.40
Education	34.74	39.37	43.21	46.23	50.00	54.20	58.62	64.27	70.90	75.94
Highways	32.74	35.79	39.37	43.76	41.30	41.65	43.49	47.56	49.69	51.44
Health and Hospitals	9.80	11.47	12.69	13.36	11.70	12.46	12.85	13.65	14.30	15.37
Natural Resources	4.17	4.79	5.25	5.71	4.87	5.13	5.42	6.05	6.40	6.53
Employment Security Administration	1.32	1.41	1.59	1.74	1.77	1.95	2.18	2.21	2.26	2.39
General Control	2.97	3.23	3.41	3.60	3.75	4.08	4.21	4.53	4.68	5.01
Miscellaneous and Unallocable	10.06	10.43	11.95	12.27	15.56	16.37	16.21	17.15	18.28	20.33
Total General Expenditure	115.36	126.69	138.85	149.33	153.72	161.78	170.79	184.93	197.41	210.66

[a] Includes veterans' bonus.
[b] See Table A8 which shows disproportionate expenditures for toll highways from 1957 to 1960.

Source: U.S. Bureau of the Census, *Revised Summary of State Government Finances, 1942–1950* (Washington: U.S. Government Printing Office, 1953); U.S. Bureau of the Census, *Compendium of State Government Finances, 1951–65* (Washington: U.S. Government Printing Office, 1952–66). Population data used in computations are from Table A1.

TABLE A10

ILLINOIS STATE GENERAL EXPENDITURE PER $1,000 OF PERSONAL INCOME, BY FUNCTION, 1942–65

	1942	1944	1946	1948	1950	1951	1952	1953	1954	1955
Public Safety	$ 1.32	$ 1.08	$ .94	$ 1.34	$ 1.26	$ 1.45	$ 1.33	$ 1.23	$ 1.17	$ 1.05
Public Welfare	10.73	7.38	6.89	7.53	9.24	7.86	7.50	7.66	7.07	7.42
Education	4.64	3.72	3.38	6.40	7.92	8.01	7.81	7.59	7.59	8.06
Regular Highways	5.81	3.79	3.47	5.31	7.12	5.20	6.35	8.76	9.65	10.19
Toll Highways	—	—	—	—	—	—	—	—	—	—
Health and Hospitals	2.41	2.05	2.45	3.22	3.89	4.07	3.36	3.77	3.39	3.27
Natural Resources	.76	.56	.65	1.08	.99	.98	.79	.84	1.04	.97
Employment Security Administration	.53	.27	.36	.57	.62	.57	.53	.48	.45	.47
General Control	1.09	.83	.92	.96	.95	.92	.86	.91	.88	.89
Nonhighway Transportation	—a	—a	—a	—a	—a	.30	.10	.11	.12	.12
Housing and Community Redevelopment	—a	—a	—a	—a	—a	.01	.01	.01	.01	.01
Miscellaneous and Unallocable	1.68	1.37	1.88	17.18 (2.63)b	2.52 (2.03)b	1.69 (1.64)b	1.32	1.26	1.31	1.51
Total General Expenditure	28.96	21.06	20.94	43.58 (29.04)b	34.52 (34.03)b	31.07 (31.02)b	29.96	32.62	32.68	33.97

TABLE A10 (Concluded)

	1956	1957	1958	1959	1960	1961	1962	1963	1964	1965
Public Safety	$ 1.01	$ 1.12	$ 1.34	$ 1.49	$ 1.15	$ 1.38	$ 1.17	$ 1.37	$ 1.20	$ 1.58
Public Welfare	7.15[c]	6.76[c]	7.15[c]	8.42[c]	8.87	9.75	10.59	10.74	9.43	10.36
Education	8.79	9.38	9.94	11.41	11.54	14.39	13.80	16.42	16.33	18.49
Regular Highways	9.27	9.55	11.43	14.16	14.54	14.75	13.02	14.53	14.60	14.16
Toll Highways	.15	2.21	8.22	5.07	1.70	.57	.27	.24	.24	.21
Health and Hospitals	3.20[c]	3.62[c]	4.39[c]	4.62[c]	3.48	4.07	3.60	4.60	4.58	6.00
Natural Resources	.90	1.11	1.09	1.26	1.06	1.31	1.03	1.26	1.15	1.26
Employment Security Administration	.46	.46	.52	.64	.53	.63	.64	.73	.62	.70
General Control	.94	.96	.94	1.13	.95	1.10	.98	1.18	1.11	1.31
Nonhighway Transportation	.09	.15	.16	.30	.12	.21	.13	.18	.13	.22
Housing and Community Redevelopment	.01	.01	.01	.01	.01	.01	.01	.02	.02	.03
Miscellaneous and Unallocable	1.57	1.72	1.85	1.96	2.20	2.22	1.91	2.19	2.23	2.40
Total General Expenditure	33.53 (33.38)[d]	37.06 (34.85)[d]	47.05 (38.83)[d]	50.47 (45.40)[d]	46.14 (44.44)[d]	50.39 (49.82)[d]	47.16 (46.89)[d]	53.46 (53.22)[d]	51.65 (51.41)[d]	56.71 (56.50)[d]

[a] Included in "Miscellaneous and Unallocable."
[b] Excluding veterans' bonus.
[c] Adjusted for change in classification. See Table A8.
[d] Excluding toll highways.

Source: Tables A4 and A8.

ILLINOIS STATE GOVERNMENT GENERAL EXPENDITURE, BY CHARACTER AND OBJECT, FISCAL YEARS 1942–65

(thousands)

Character and Object	1942	1944	1946	1948	1950	1951	1952
Current Operation	$ 85,671	$ 89,437	$107,374	$166,157	$182,697	$ 199,252	$ 206,874
Capital Outlay	24,091	25,617	20,972	70,674	82,781	77,446	92,992
Assistance and Subsidies	47,763	59,847	67,245	298,454	110,752	101,302	103,332
Interest on Debt	6,259	5,236	4,360	8,492	9,477	8,807	8,538
Intergovernmental Expenditures	60,928	35,862	47,892	91,828	141,638	136,025	132,323
Total General Expenditure	224,712	215,999	247,843	635,605	527,345	522,832	544,059

(thousands)

Character and Object	1953	1954	1955	1956	1957	1958	1959
Current Operation	$221,463	$243,150	$263,816	$282,433	$305,251	$ 341,782	$ 395,858
Capital Outlay	119,602	131,040	133,457	138,239	201,528	400,948	403,852
Assistance and Subsidies	114,916	91,888	85,255	84,994	97,732	101,932	119,309
Interest on Debt	8,024	7,467	6,759	13,085	21,338	20,209	22,207
Intergovernmental Expenditures	162,641	175,850	208,768	222,141	246,602	274,619	324,464
Total General Expenditure	626,646	649,395	698,055	740,892	872,451	1,139,490	1,265,690

(thousands)

Character and Object	1960	1961	1962	1963	1964	1965
Current Operation	$ 390,466	$ 465,307	$ 463,533	$ 562,120	$ 562,867	$ 716,204
Capital Outlay	320,654	331,286	284,576	370,187	428,505	469,024
Assistance and Subsidies	126,720	135,424	176,192	187,091	173,019	184,303
Interest on Debt	22,412	22,690	23,107	29,389	34,256	35,408
Intergovernmental Expenditures	350,734	411,707	385,033	434,267	411,771	496,042
Total General Expenditure	1,210,986	1,366,414	1,332,441	1,583,054	1,610,418	1,900,981

Source: U.S. Bureau of the Census, *Revised Summary of State Government Finances, 1942–1950* (Washington: U.S. Government Printing Office, 1953); U.S. Bureau of the Census, *Compendium of State Government Finances, 1951–65* (Washington: U.S. Government Printing Office, 1952–66).

TABLE A12

PER CAPITA STATE EXPENDITURE, BY CHARACTER AND OBJECT, ILLINOIS AND UNITED STATES, FISCAL YEARS 1942–65

Character and Object	1942	1944	1946	1948	1950	1951	1952	1953	1954	1955
Illinois										
Current Operation	$ 10.72	$ 11.52	$ 14.11	$ 19.91	$ 21.07	$ 22.77	$ 23.63	$ 24.85	$ 27.01	$ 28.80
Capital Outlay	3.01	3.30	2.76	8.47	9.55	8.85	10.62	13.42	14.56	14.57
Assistance and Subsidies	5.97	7.71	8.83	35.77	12.77	11.58	11.80	12.90	10.21	9.31
Interest on Debt	.78	.67	.57	1.02	1.09	1.01	.98	.90	.83	.74
Intergovernmental Expenditure	7.62	4.62	6.29	11.01	16.34	15.54	15.11	18.25	19.54	22.79
Total General Expenditure	28.10	27.82	32.56	76.18	60.82	59.74	62.14	70.33	72.14	76.21
United States										
Current Operation[a]	11.60	12.76	15.38	22.03	25.67	27.13	29.17	30.87	32.28	34.08
Capital Outlay	4.84	2.47	2.78	10.20	15.13	16.66	17.42	18.38	21.26	24.90
Assistance and Subsidies	3.51	3.94	5.00	10.50	12.79	10.66	9.19	9.69	9.44	9.24
Interest on Debt	.92	.75	.63	.60	.74	.86	.94	1.05	1.23	1.57
Intergovernmental Expenditure	13.42	13.77	15.79	22.99	28.52	31.26	33.06	34.75	36.06	37.33
Total General Expenditure	34.29	33.69	39.57	66.32	82.85	86.57	89.78	94.74	100.27	107.12

Character and Object	1956	1957	1958	1959	1960	1961	1962	1963	1964	1965
Illinois										
Current Operation	$ 30.32	$ 32.19	$ 35.47	$ 40.06	$ 39.09	$ 46.15	$ 45.81	$ 54.78	$ 54.22	$ 68.28
Capital Outlay	14.84	21.25	41.61	40.87	32.10	32.85	28.12	36.08	41.27	44.72
Assistance and Subsidies	9.12	10.31	10.58	12.07	12.68	13.43	17.41	18.23	16.67	17.57
Interest on Debt	1.40	2.25	2.10	2.25	2.24	2.25	2.28	2.86	3.30	3.38
Intergovernmental Expenditure	23.84	26.01	28.49	32.84	35.11	40.83	38.05	42.32	39.66	47.29
Total General Expenditure	79.53	92.01	118.24	128.09	121.22	135.51	131.67	154.27	155.12	181.24
United States										
Current Operation[a]	36.18	39.82	43.88	46.31	49.61	52.84	56.85	62.13	66.33	72.67
Capital Outlay	27.92	30.99	35.08	40.53	37.30	38.15	39.41	43.63	46.75	47.94
Assistance and Subsidies	9.37	9.85	10.70	10.86	11.38	11.36	11.57	11.36	11.53	11.69
Interest on Debt	1.90	2.11	2.34	2.60	3.03	3.24	3.47	3.88	4.06	4.29
Intergovernmental Expenditure	40.00	43.92	46.86	49.03	52.40	56.19	59.49	63.93	68.74	74.06
Total General Expenditure	115.37	126.69	138.85	149.33	153.72	161.78	170.79	184.93	197.41	210.66

[a] Census "Character and Object" data include liquor store expenditure. In the above compilation "Current Operation" figures are reduced by the amount of liquor store expenditure, even though part of these expenditures may have been for capital outlay or interest. Enough detail on liquor store expenditure is available to indicate that the error involved in the procedure is small.

Source: U.S. Bureau of the Census, *Revised Summary of State Government Finances, 1942–1950* (Washington: U.S. Government Printing Office, 1953); U.S. Bureau of the Census, *Compendium of State Government Finances, 1951–65* (Washington: U.S. Government Printing Office, 1952–66); Table A1.

TABLE A13

PUBLIC EMPLOYMENT (FULL-TIME EQUIVALENT), BY TYPE OF GOVERNMENT AND BY FUNCTION, ILLINOIS, OCTOBER, 1962

Function	State	Counties	Municipalities	Townships	School Districts	Special Districts	Total Local Units	Total State and Local
Higher Education	14,739	—	—	—	1,647	—	1,647	16,386
Local Schools	—	—	—	—	120,350	—	120,350	120,350
Total Education[a]	16,035	—	—	—	121,996	—	121,996	138,031
Highways	8,342	3,660	8,741	1,690	—	—	14,091	22,433
Public Welfare	2,701	5,164	16	408	—	—	5,588	8,288
Hospitals	14,706	7,290	3,020	—	—	2,672	12,981	27,687
Health	1,061	523	1,528	—	—	145	2,195	3,256
Police Protection	1,608	1,680	18,237	24	—	—	19,941	21,549
Local Fire Protection	—	2	7,746	14	—	265	8,026	8,026
Sewerage and Sanitation	—	8	3,929	4	—	2,499	6,440	6,440
Local Parks and Recreation	—	702	1,290	6	—	5,421	7,419	7,419
Natural Resources	2,875	43	17	—	—	348	408	3,283
Housing and Urban Renewal	—	—	436	—	—	1,899	2,335	2,335
Local Airports	—	—	443	—	—	144	590	590
Water Transport and Terminals	262	2	317	—	—	19	336	598
Correction	3,134	822	463	—	—	—	1,285	4,420
Local Libraries	—	12	2,286	—	—	32	2,329	2,329
Employment Security Administration	2,755	—	—	—	—	—	—	2,755
Financial Administration	2,725	2,329	1,685	852	—	—	4,866	7,590
General Control	709	4,379	3,695	9	—	1	8,084	8,793
Local Utilities	—	19	6,116	18	—	12,741	18,893	18,893
Other and Unallocable	3,764	815	3,511	306	—	7	4,639	8,403
Total	60,676	27,449	63,473	3,330	121,996	26,193	242,442	303,118

[a] Includes "Other Education," such as state departments of education and state-operated schools for the handicapped.

Source: U.S. Bureau of the Census, Census of Governments: 1962. Vol. III, Compendium of Public Employment (Washington: U.S. Government Printing Office, 1963).

TABLE A14

PUBLIC EMPLOYMENT (FULL-TIME EQUIVALENT) PER 10,000 POPULATION, BY TYPE OF GOVERNMENT AND BY FUNCTION, ILLINOIS, OCTOBER, 1962

Function	State	Counties	Munici-palities	Town-ships	School Districts	Special Districts	Total Local Units	Total State and Local
Higher Education	14.4	—	—	—	—	—	1.6	16.0
Local Schools	—	—	—	—	117.3	—	117.3	117.3
Total Education[a]	15.6	—	—	—	118.9	—	118.9	134.5
Highways	8.1	3.6	8.5	1.6	—	—	13.7	21.9
Public Welfare	2.6	5.0	—[b]	.4	—	—	5.4	8.1
Hospitals	14.3	7.1	2.9	—	—	2.6	12.7	27.0
Health	1.0	.5	1.5	—[b]	—	.1	2.1	3.2
Police Protection	1.6	1.6	17.8	—	—	—	19.4	21.0
Local Fire Protection	—	—[b]	7.5	—[b]	—	.3	7.8	7.8
Sewerage and Sanitation	—	—[b]	3.8	—[b]	—	2.4	6.3	6.3
Local Parks and Recreation	—	.7	1.3	—[b]	—	5.3	7.2	7.2
Natural Resources	2.8	—[b]	—[b]	—	—	.3	.4	3.2
Housing and Urban Renewal	—	—[b]	.4	—	—	1.9	2.3	2.3
Local Airports	—	—	.4	—	—	.1	.6	.6
Water Transport and Terminals	.3	—[b]	.3	—	—	—[b]	.3	.6
Correction	3.1	.8	.5	—	—	—	1.3	4.3
Local Libraries	—	—	2.2	—	—	—	2.3	2.3
Employment Security Administration	2.7	—	—	—	—	—	—	2.7
Financial Administration	2.7	2.3	1.6	.8	—	—[b]	4.7	7.4
General Control	.7	4.3	3.6	—[b]	—	—[b]	7.9	8.6
Local Utilities	—	—[b]	6.0	—[b]	—	12.4	18.4	18.4
Other and Unallocable	3.7	.8	3.4	.3	—	—[b]	4.5	8.2
Total	59.1	26.7	61.9	3.2	118.9	25.5	236.3	295.4

[a] Includes "Other Education," such as state departments of education and state-operated schools for the handicapped.
[b] Less than 0.05 employees per 10,000 population.

Source: U.S. Bureau of the Census, *Census of Governments: 1962.* Vol. III, *Compendium of Public Employment* (Washington: U.S. Government Printing Office, 1963).

TABLE A15

PUBLIC EMPLOYMENT (FULL-TIME EQUIVALENT) PER 10,000 POPULATION, BY TYPE OF GOVERNMENT AND BY FUNCTION, UNITED STATES, OCTOBER, 1962

Function	States	Counties	Municipalities	Townships	Special Districts	School Districts	Total Local Units	Total State and Local
Higher Education	18.9	.1	.7	—	—	1.2	1.9	20.8
Local Schools	.4	8.0	11.5	3.4	—	101.1	124.0	124.5
Total Education[a]	20.9	8.1	12.2	3.4	—	102.3	125.9	146.9
Highways	14.0	6.5	5.8	1.6	.3	—	14.2	28.2
Public Welfare	2.6	3.2	1.2	.1	—	—	4.5	7.2
Hospitals	17.2	7.5	6.0	—[b]	2.3	—	15.9	33.0
Health	1.6	1.3	1.4	—[b]	.1	—	2.7	4.3
Police Protection	1.9	2.5	12.1	.6	—[b]	—	15.2	17.1
Local Fire Protection	—	.2	7.5	.3	.2	—	8.3	8.3
Sewerage and Sanitation	—	.3	7.2	.2	.5	—	8.2	8.2
Local Parks and Recreation	—	.6	3.7	.1	.4	—	4.8	4.8
Natural Resources	5.3	.6	—	—	.6	—	1.3	6.6
Housing and Urban Renewal	—	—[b]	.8	—[b]	1.1	—	1.8	1.8
Local Airports	—	.1	.3	—	.2	—	.5	.5
Water Transport and Terminals	.2	—[b]	.1	—	.2	—	.4	.6
Correction	3.2	1.3	.5	.1	.3	—	1.9	5.1
Local Libraries	—	.4	1.5	—	—	—	2.3	2.3
Employment Security Administration	3.2	—	—	—	—	—	—	3.2
Financial Administration	4.0	2.6	2.5	.5	—	—	5.6	9.7
General Control	1.1	4.6	2.9	.3	—	—	7.8	8.9
Local Utilities	—	.2	9.7	.2	2.5	—	12.6	12.6
Liquor Stores	.7	—	—	—	—	—	—	.7
Other and Unallocable	3.5	2.1	4.4	.4	.3	—	7.1	10.6
Total	79.5	42.2	79.9	7.8	8.9	102.3	241.1	320.6

[a] Includes "Other Education," such as state departments of education and state-operated schools for the handicapped.
[b] Less than 0.05 employees per 10,000 population.

Source: U.S. Bureau of the Census. *Census of Governments: 1962*. Vol. III, *Compendium of Public Employment* (Washington: U.S. Government Printing Office, 1963).

TABLE A16

ESTIMATED "REAL" GENERAL EXPENDITURE, STATE OF ILLINOIS,
FISCAL YEARS 1942–65 (1958 dollars)

Year	Total General Expenditure		Excluding Veterans' Bonuses and Toll Highways	
	Total	Per Capita	Total	Per Capita
	(thousands)		(thousands)	
1942	$ 518,399	$ 64.84	$ 518,399	$ 64.84
1944	439,458	56.59	439,458	56.59
1946	455,732	59.87	455,732	59.87
1948	898,274	107.66	635,756	76.19
1950	727,420	83.90	718,517	82.87
1951	685,517	78.34	684,653	78.24
1952	670,725	76.61	670,725	76.61
1953	749,009	84.06	749,009	84.06
1954	761,186	84.56	761,186	84.56
1955	799,952	87.34	799,952	87.34
1956	817,783	87.78	814,207	87.40
1957	916,550	96.66	864,935	91.22
1958	1,154,672	119.69	952,784	98.76
1959	1,249,723	125.63	1,124,254	113.01
1960	1,164,833	116.65	1,122,132	112.37
1961	1,275,575	126.53	1,261,274	125.11
1962	1,208,268	119.45	1,201,512	118.79
1963	1,394,621	135.93	1,388,445	135.33
1964	1,383,106	133.39	1,376,750	132.78
1965	1,587,613	150.66	1,581,845	150.11

Source: Tables A1, A4, A6, A9; U.S. Department of Commerce, *Statistical Abstract of the United States, 1966* (Washington, 1954), p. 356, and *Survey of Current Business*, August, 1965, and December, 1966. Estimates were made using the implicit price deflator to deflate current operation expenditure, capital outlays, and intergovernmental expenditures. The consumer price index was used to deflate expenditures for assistance and subsidies and interest payments. Indexes for the fiscal year were computed by averaging the figures for the two calendar years in which the fiscal year falls.

TABLE A17

ILLINOIS STATE REVENUE COLLECTIONS IN DETAIL, FISCAL YEAR 1965

Sources	Total	Per Capita
	(thousands)	
Sales and Gross Receipts Taxes	$1,030,604	$97.80
General Sales and Use	622,857	59.11
Selective Sales	407,747	38.69
Motor Fuel (net of refunds)	170,002	16.13
Alcoholic Beverages	47,952	4.55
Cigarettes	59,128	5.61
Insurance—Gross Premiums:		
General	33,795	3.21
Fire Marshal	762	.07
Surplus	374	.04
Total Insurance	34,931	3.32

Sources	Total	Per Capita
	(thousands)	
Public Utilities:		
Utility Service	60,016	5.70
Illinois Central R.R.	3,849	.36
Total Public Utilities	63,865	6.06
Pari-Mutuels:		
Running Races	18,436	1.75
Harness Racing	8,883	.84
Total Pari-Mutuels	27,319	2.59
Amusements:		
Racing	660	.06
Athletic Exhibitions	21	—*
Total Amusements	681	.06
Other—Hotel	3,869	.37
License Taxes	153,529	14.57
Motor Vehicles	123,157	11.69
Registrations	120,064	11.39
Common or Contract Carriers	681	.06
Certificate of Title and Other	2,412	.23
Motor Vehicle Operators	6,446	.61
Drivers	5,436	.52
Chauffeurs	1,010	.10
Corporations in General	8,084	.77
Alcoholic Beverages	1,144	.11
Amusements	823	.08
Race Track	815	.08
Athletic Exhibitions	8	—*
Occupations and Businesses, n.e.c.	10,386	.99
Insurance Agents and Brokers	1,001	.09
Real Estate Licenses	416	.04
Beauty Culture	586	.06
Oil Inspection Fees	1,258	.12
Grain Inspection Fees	1,051	.10
Bank, Building and Loan Examinations	1,025	.10
Securities Department	272	.03
Insurance Companies	1,559	.15
Other	3,218	.30
Hunting and Fishing	3,364	.32
Hunting	1,755	.17
Fishing	1,365	.13
Other	244	.02
Other—Watercraft	125	.01
Property Taxes	1,525	.14
General—Prior Years	10	—*
Special—Private Car Lines	1,515	.14
Inheritance Tax	33,031	3.13
Intergovernmental Revenue	482,066	45.74

Sources	Total	Per Capita
	(thousands)	
From Federal Government	473,872	44.97
Education	64,807	6.15
Highways	225,461	21.40
Public Welfare	145,254	13.78
Health and Hospitals	6,790	.64
Natural Resources	4,384	.42
Airports	2,627	.25
Employment Security Administration	22,152	2.10
Other	2,397	.23
From Local Governments	8,194	.78
Education	1,209	.11
Highways	6,368	.60
Public Welfare	32	—ᵃ
Health and Hospitals	326	.03
Other	259	.02
Charges and Miscellaneous General Revenue	146,578	13.91
Current Charges	114,082	10.83
Education:		
State Institutions of Higher Education		
Auxiliary Enterprises	37,751	3.58
Other	20,595	1.95
Total Higher Education	58,346	5.54
Other Education	138	.01
Total Education	58,484	5.55
Highways:		
Toll Facilities	32,135	3.05
Other	4,141	.39
Total Highways	36,276	3.44
Hospitals	15,597	1.48
Natural Resources:		
Agriculture	1,794	.17
Forestry and Parks	344	.03
Other	317	.03
Total Natural Resources	2,455	.23
Water Transport and Terminals	208	.02
Other Current Charges	1,062	.10
Sale of Property	12	—ᵃ
Interest Earnings	25,686	2.44
Other Charges and Miscellaneous Revenue	6,798	.65
Fines and Forfeits	123	.01
Donations	5,238	.50
Other	1,437	.14

ᵃ Less than $0.005.

Source: Table A1; U.S. Bureau of the Census, *Compendium of State Government Finances in 1965* (Washington: U.S. Government Printing Office, 1966); U.S. Bureau of the Census, *State Tax Collections: 1966* (Washington: U.S. Government Printing Office, 1966).

TABLE A18

ILLINOIS STATE GENERAL REVENUE, BY SOURCE, FISCAL YEARS 1942–65

Source	1942	1944	1946	1948	1950	1951	1952
				(thousands)			
Sales and Gross Receipts Taxes:							
General Sales and Use	$ 85,589	$ 89,932	$107,378	$159,528	$166,951	$187,556	$ 191,934
Motor Fuel	43,418	29,835	37,305	48,821	56,339	61,602	82,435
Alcoholic Beverages	23,574	19,505	26,197	23,122	22,966	25,915	22,098
Cigarette	12,448	13,712	15,367	27,343	28,328	27,828	28,919
Insurance	7,768	10,123	9,920	13,315	15,062	16,121	17,666
Public Utilities	12,801	14,596	15,391	20,157	22,848	25,704	27,425
Other	2,069	2,741	4,756	9,885	8,396	8,781	12,279
License Taxes:							
Motor Vehicle and Operators	27,443	23,091	24,079	34,141	41,278	45,770	48,984
Other	6,616	7,421	8,719	9,850	10,691	11,057	11,551
Property Taxes	325	123	248	216	321	297	442
Inheritance Taxes	7,816	5,481	7,459	8,954	7,090	8,618	11,439
Other Taxes	406	67	—	—	—	—	—
Total Taxes	230,273	216,627	256,819	355,332	380,270	419,249	455,172
Intergovernmental Revenue	43,658	56,502	46,512	80,188	106,246	92,593	107,426
Charges and Miscellaneous	5,832	5,593	9,463	18,934	17,175	18,546	19,554
Total General Revenue	279,813	278,722	312,794	454,454	503,691	530,388	582,152

(thousands)

Source	1953	1954	1955	1956	1957	1958	1959
Sales and Gross Receipts Taxes:							
General Sales and Use	$205,475	$208,557	$205,532	$258,652	$299,035	$319,308	$ 308,273
Motor Fuel	97,217	116,288	117,306	128,152	129,441	138,424	138,158
Alcoholic Beverages	24,340	24,461	23,362	26,262	25,653	25,137	26,558
Cigarette	30,867	31,777	30,261	32,904	33,437	36,727	37,477
Insurance	18,544	20,546	20,925	24,632	24,014	21,388	30,819
Public Utilities	29,407	31,513	33,952	37,023	38,824	41,175	43,726
Other	15,586	14,685	15,799	16,590	17,014	17,233	16,777
License Taxes:							
Motor Vehicle and Operators	67,989	72,420	75,776	82,659	91,773	98,266	99,781
Other	12,146	13,071	13,282	15,309	14,605	16,320	18,659
Property Taxes	427	335	563	615	697	740	1,111
Inheritance Taxes	12,437	12,191	15,065	19,976	19,245	20,372	21,123
Other Taxes	—	—	—	—	—	—	—
Total Taxes	514,435	545,844	551,823	642,774	693,738	735,090	742,462
Intergovernmental Revenue	118,596	120,781	118,068	134,993	154,060	187,710	260,057
Charges and Miscellaneous	22,740	27,543	30,861	36,771	49,634	52,213	58,584
Total General Revenue	655,771	694,168	700,752	814,538	897,432	975,013	1,061,103

TABLE A18 (Concluded)

Source	1960	1961	1962	1963	1964	1965
	(thousands)					
Sales and Gross Receipts Taxes:						
General Sales and Use	$ 374,949	$ 383,957	$ 466,430	$ 545,076	$ 558,584	$ 622,857
Motor Fuel	141,865	146,302	149,942	155,786	161,087	170,002
Alcoholic Beverages	31,623	40,612	41,419	42,376	41,691	47,952
Cigarette	49,320	43,064	54,869	56,002	55,449	59,128
Insurance	26,604	29,040	29,946	30,471	34,610	34,931
Public Utilities	48,570	50,159	52,284	55,764	59,983	63,865
Other	17,375	17,991	22,364	26,038	29,221	31,869
License Taxes:						
Motor Vehicle and Operators	104,854	108,656	110,413	115,886	122,902	129,603
Other	18,267	20,048	19,824	18,912	21,775	23,926
Property Taxes	918	1,026	1,213	1,612	1,250	1,525
Inheritance Taxes	22,027	33,455	31,682	31,981	35,783	33,031
Other Taxes	—	—	—	—	—	—
Total Taxes	836,372	874,310	980,386	1,079,904	1,122,335	1,218,689
Intergovernmental Revenue	344,401	336,672	337,173	385,001	415,049	482,066
Charges and Miscellaneous	73,507	84,740	94,910	108,963	122,306	146,578
Total General Revenue	1,254,280	1,295,722	1,412,469	1,573,868	1,659,690	1,847,333

Source: U.S. Bureau of the Census, *Revised Summary of State Government Finances, 1942–1950* (Washington: U.S. Government Printing Office, 1953); U.S. Bureau of the Census, *Compendium of State Government Finances, 1951–65* (Washington: U.S. Government Printing Office, 1952–66); U.S. Bureau of the Census, *Details of State Tax Collections in 1958* (Washington: U.S. Government Printing Office, 1958); Illinois Department of Finance, *Thirty-Ninth, Fortieth, and Forty-First Annual Reports*; letter from Allen C. Manvel, Chief of Governments Division, Bureau of the Census, February 11, 1959; U.S. Bureau of the Census, *Summary of State Government Finances in 1958* (Washington: U.S. Government Printing Office, 1959).

TABLE A19

PER CAPITA ILLINOIS STATE GENERAL REVENUE, BY SOURCE, FISCAL YEARS 1942-65

Source	1942	1944	1946	1948	1950	1951	1952	1953	1954	1955
Sales and Gross Receipts Taxes:										
General Sales and Use	$10.71	$11.58	$14.11	$19.12	$19.26	$21.43	$21.92	$23.06	$23.17	$22.44
Motor Fuel	5.43	3.84	4.90	5.85	6.50	7.04	9.42	10.91	12.92	12.81
Alcoholic Beverages	2.95	2.51	3.44	2.77	2.65	2.96	2.52	2.73	2.72	2.55
Cigarette	1.56	1.77	2.02	3.28	3.27	3.18	3.30	3.46	3.53	3.30
Insurance	.97	1.30	1.30	1.60	1.74	1.84	2.02	2.08	2.28	2.28
Public Utilities	1.60	1.88	2.02	2.42	2.64	2.94	3.13	3.30	3.50	3.71
Other	.26	.35	.62	1.18	.97	1.00	1.40	1.75	1.63	1.72
License Taxes:										
Motor Vehicle and Operators	3.43	2.97	3.16	4.09	4.76	5.23	5.59	7.63	8.05	8.27
Other	.83	.96	1.15	1.18	1.23	1.26	1.32	1.36	1.45	1.45
Property Taxes	.04	.02	.03	.03	.04	.03	.05	.05	.04	.06
Inheritance Taxes	.98	.71	.98	1.07	.82	.98	1.31	1.40	1.35	1.64
Other Taxes	.05	.01	—	—	—	—	—	—	—	—
Total Taxes	28.80	27.90	33.74	42.59	43.86	47.90	51.99	57.74	60.64	60.24
Intergovernmental Revenue	5.46	7.28	6.11	9.61	12.25	10.58	12.27	13.31	13.42	12.89
Charges and Miscellaneous	.74	.72	1.24	2.27	1.98	2.12	2.23	2.55	3.06	3.37
Total General Revenue	35.00	35.90	41.09	54.47	58.10	60.61	66.49	73.60	77.12	76.51

TABLE A19 (Concluded)

Source	1956	1957	1958	1959	1960	1961	1962	1963	1964	1965
Sales and Gross Receipts Taxes:										
General Sales and Use	$27.76	$31.54	$33.10	$30.99	$37.55	$38.09	$46.11	$53.13	$53.87	$59.11
Motor Fuel	13.76	13.65	14.35	13.89	14.21	14.51	14.82	15.18	15.54	16.13
Alcoholic Beverages	2.82	2.71	2.60	2.67	3.17	4.03	4.09	4.13	4.02	4.55
Cigarette	3.53	3.53	3.81	3.77	4.94	4.27	5.43	5.46	5.35	5.61
Insurance	2.64	2.53	2.22	3.10	2.66	2.88	2.96	2.97	3.34	3.32
Public Utilities	3.97	4.09	4.27	4.39	4.86	4.98	5.17	5.43	5.78	6.06
Other	1.78	1.79	1.78	1.69	1.74	1.78	2.21	2.54	2.82	3.02
License Taxes:										
Motor Vehicle and Operators	8.87	9.68	10.19	10.03	10.50	10.78	10.92	11.29	11.85	11.69
Other	1.64	1.54	1.69	1.87	1.83	1.99	1.96	1.84	2.10	2.88
Property Taxes	.07	.07	.08	.11	.09	.10	.12	.16	.12	.15
Inheritance Taxes	2.14	2.03	2.11	2.12	2.20	3.32	3.13	3.12	3.45	3.13
Other Taxes	—	—	—	—	—	—	—	—	—	—
Total Taxes	69.00	73.16	76.20	74.63	83.75	86.73	96.92	105.25	108.24	115.65
Intergovernmental Revenue	14.49	16.25	19.46	26.14	34.49	33.40	33.34	37.53	40.03	45.74
Charges and Miscellaneous	3.95	5.23	5.41	5.89	7.36	8.40	9.38	10.62	11.79	13.91
Total General Revenue	87.43	94.64	101.07	106.66	125.60	128.53	139.64	153.40	160.06	175.30

Source: Tables A1, A18.

TABLE A20

ILLINOIS STATE GENERAL REVENUE, BY SOURCE AS PERCENTAGE OF TOTAL GENERAL REVENUE, FISCAL YEARS 1942–65

Source	1942	1944	1946	1948	1950	1951	1952	1953	1954	1955
Sales and Gross Receipts Taxes:										
General Sales and Use	30.6%	32.3%	34.3%	35.1%	33.1%	35.4%	33.0%	31.3%	30.0%	29.3%
Motor Fuel	15.5	10.7	11.9	10.7	11.2	11.6	14.2	14.8	16.8	16.7
Alcoholic Beverages	8.4	7.0	8.4	5.1	4.6	4.9	3.8	3.7	3.5	3.3
Cigarette	4.4	4.9	4.9	6.0	5.6	5.2	5.0	4.7	4.6	4.3
Insurance	2.8	3.6	3.2	2.9	3.0	3.0	3.0	2.8	3.0	3.0
Public Utilities	4.6	5.2	4.9	4.4	4.5	4.8	4.7	4.5	4.5	4.8
Other	0.7	1.0	1.5	2.2	1.7	1.7	2.1	2.4	2.1	2.3
License Taxes:										
Motor Vehicle and Operators	9.8	8.3	7.7	7.5	8.2	8.6	8.4	10.4	10.4	10.8
Other	2.4	2.7	2.8	2.2	2.1	2.1	2.0	1.9	1.9	1.9
Property Taxes	0.1	—ᵃ	0.1	—ᵃ	0.1	0.1	0.1	0.1	—ᵃ	0.1
Inheritance Taxes	2.8	2.0	2.4	2.0	1.4	1.6	2.0	1.9	1.8	2.2
Other Taxes	0.1	—ᵃ	—	—	—	—	—	—	—	—
Total Taxes	82.3	77.7	82.1	78.2	75.5	79.0	78.2	78.4	78.6	78.7
Intergovernmental Revenue	15.6	20.3	14.9	17.6	21.1	17.5	18.5	18.1	17.4	16.8
Charges and Miscellaneous	2.1	2.0	3.0	4.2	3.4	3.5	3.4	3.5	4.0	4.4
Total General Revenue	100.0	100.0	100.0	100.0	100.0	100.0	100.0	100.0	100.0	100.0

TABLE A20 (Concluded)

Source	1956	1957	1958	1959	1960	1961	1962	1963	1964	1965
Sales and Gross Receipts Taxes:										
General Sales and Use	31.8%	33.3%	32.7%	29.1%	29.9%	29.6%	33.0%	34.6%	33.6%	33.7%
Motor Fuel	15.7	14.4	14.2	13.0	11.3	11.3	10.6	9.9	9.7	9.2
Alcoholic Beverages	3.2	2.9	2.6	2.5	2.5	3.1	2.9	2.7	2.5	2.6
Cigarette	4.0	3.7	3.8	3.5	3.9	3.3	3.9	3.6	3.3	3.2
Insurance	3.0	2.7	2.2	2.9	2.1	2.2	2.1	1.9	2.1	1.9
Public Utilities	4.5	4.3	4.2	4.1	3.9	3.9	3.7	3.5	3.6	3.5
Other	2.0	1.9	1.8	1.6	1.4	1.4	1.6	1.7	1.8	1.7
License Taxes:										
Motor Vehicle and Operators	10.1	10.2	10.1	9.4	8.4	8.4	7.8	7.4	7.4	6.7
Other	1.9	1.6	1.7	1.8	1.4	1.6	1.4	1.2	1.3	1.6
Property Taxes	0.1	0.1	0.1	0.1	0.1	0.1	0.1	0.1	0.1	0.1
Inheritance Taxes	2.5	2.1	2.1	2.0	1.8	2.6	2.3	2.0	2.2	1.8
Other Taxes	—	—	—	—	—	—	—	—	—	—
Total Taxes	78.9	77.3	75.4	70.0	66.7	67.5	69.4	68.6	67.6	66.0
Intergovernmental Revenue	16.6	17.2	19.3	24.5	27.4	26.0	23.9	24.5	25.0	26.1
Charges and Miscellaneous	4.5	5.5	5.4	5.5	5.9	6.5	6.7	6.9	7.4	7.9
Total General Revenue	100.0	100.0	100.0	100.0	100.0	100.0	100.0	100.0	100.0	100.0

* Less than 0.05 per cent.

Source: Table A18.

TABLE A21

PER CAPITA STATE GENERAL REVENUE, BY SOURCE, UNITED STATES, FISCAL YEARS 1942–65

Source	1942	1944	1946	1948	1950	1951	1952	1953	1954	1955
Sales and Gross Receipts Taxes:										
General Sales and Use	$ 4.76	$ 5.38	$ 6.78	$ 10.35	$ 11.29	$ 13.30	$ 14.61	$ 15.70	$ 16.13	$ 16.45
Motor Fuel	7.09	5.11	6.69	8.82	10.44	11.37	12.26	13.03	14.09	14.67
Alcoholic Beverages	1.94	2.00	3.03	2.98	2.84	3.12	2.90	3.00	2.94	2.94
Cigarette	.98	1.19	1.49	2.36	2.80	2.86	2.94	3.03	2.95	2.86
Insurance	.85	.93	1.09	1.35	1.63	1.69	1.86	2.07	2.24	2.31
Public Utilities	.75	.93	1.00	1.09	1.25	1.32	1.49	1.61	1.67	1.76
Other	.34	.55	1.07	1.36	1.32	1.38	1.49	1.65	1.74	1.82
License Taxes:										
Motor Vehicle and Operators	3.25	2.94	3.31	4.15	5.11	5.59	6.06	6.53	6.97	7.38
Other	2.09	2.31	2.60	2.85	3.20	3.44	3.61	3.99	3.87	3.98
Individual Income Taxes[a]	1.88	2.36	2.94	3.49	4.90	5.35	5.98	6.25	6.38	6.82
Corporation Net Income Taxes[a]	2.03	3.33	3.34	4.10	3.96	4.57	5.49	5.23	4.90	4.60
Property Taxes	1.99	1.82	1.88	1.93	2.08	2.30	2.43	2.36	2.48	2.57
Inheritance Taxes	.83	.82	1.06	1.25	1.14	1.30	1.38	1.43	1.57	1.55
Other Taxes	.64	.75	.99	1.13	1.67	1.81	2.09	2.24	2.51	2.61
Total Taxes	29.42	30.42	37.26	47.22	53.63	59.38	64.61	68.11	70.42	72.33
Intergovernmental Revenue	6.47	7.33	6.52	12.19	16.39	16.67	16.29	17.82	18.30	18.64
Charges and Miscellaneous	2.79	3.09	3.64	5.42	6.15	6.41	7.12	7.73	8.43	10.03
Total General Revenue	38.68	40.84	47.41	64.82	76.17	82.45	88.02	93.66	97.16	101.00

TABLE A21 (Concluded)

Source	1956	1957	1958	1959	1960	1961	1962	1963	1964	1965
Sales and Gross Receipts Taxes:										
General Sales and Use	$ 18.57	$ 20.27	$ 20.69	$ 21.23	$ 24.28	$ 25.05	$ 27.92	$ 29.80	$ 32.25	$ 35.07
Motor Fuel	16.44	16.99	17.22	17.56	18.83	19.06	20.02	20.72	21.51	22.47
Alcoholic Beverages	3.34	3.42	3.34	3.44	3.67	3.83	4.04	4.27	4.58	4.79
Cigarette	3.15	3.34	3.63	3.88	5.21	5.56	5.87	6.05	6.34	6.71
Insurance	2.45	2.57	2.68	3.14	3.00	3.25	3.23	3.44	3.75	3.89
Public Utilities	1.84	2.06	2.04	2.02	2.06	2.23	2.29	2.35	2.64	2.60
Other	1.93	2.04	2.02	2.05	2.27	2.31	2.39	2.63	2.91	3.16
License Taxes:										
Motor Vehicle and Operators	7.93	8.22	8.35	8.56	8.88	9.12	9.11	9.57	10.16	9.77
Other	4.45	4.93	4.64	4.76	5.21	5.46	5.47	5.61	6.07	7.05
Individual Income Taxes[a]	8.41	9.39	9.11	10.13	12.48	13.08	14.90	15.90	18.10	19.11
Corporation Net Income Taxes[a]	5.44	5.91	6.01	5.74	6.66	7.04	7.14	8.10	8.98	10.08
Property Taxes	2.86	2.88	3.14	3.25	3.43	3.51	3.50	3.70	3.83	4.00
Inheritance Taxes	1.90	2.03	2.07	2.00	2.37	2.78	2.82	3.20	3.49	3.82
Other Taxes	3.12	3.26	3.07	3.24	3.46	3.60	3.62	3.64	3.89	4.00
Total Taxes	81.83	87.31	88.02	91.00	101.81	105.88	112.32	118.98	128.50	136.52
Intergovernmental Revenue	20.16	23.60	28.11	35.90	38.03	37.68	40.87	44.34	50.17	53.93
Charges and Miscellaneous	10.51	11.55	12.32	13.48	14.59	15.86	17.02	18.95	20.89	23.43
Total General Revenue	112.50	122.47	128.45	140.38	154.48	159.42	170.21	182.27	199.56	213.88

[a] Individual income tax data include corporation net income tax collections for from one to five states in various fiscal years.

Source: U.S. Bureau of the Census, *Revised Summary of State Government Finances, 1942–1950* (Washington: U.S. Government Printing Office, 1953).; U.S. Bureau of the Census, *Compendium of State Government Finances, 1951–65* (Washington: U.S. Government Printing Office, 1952–66).

TABLE A22

STATE GENERAL REVENUE, BY SOURCE AS PERCENTAGE OF TOTAL GENERAL REVENUE, UNITED STATES, FISCAL YEARS 1942–65

Source	1942	1944	1946	1948	1950	1951	1952	1953	1954	1955
Sales and Gross Receipts Taxes:										
General Sales and Use	12.3%	13.2%	14.3%	16.0%	14.8%	16.1%	16.6%	16.8%	16.6%	16.3%
Motor Fuel	18.3	12.5	14.1	13.6	13.7	13.8	13.9	13.9	14.5	14.5
Alcoholic Beverages	5.0	4.9	6.4	4.6	3.7	3.8	3.3	3.2	3.0	2.9
Cigarette	2.5	2.9	3.2	3.6	3.7	3.5	3.3	3.2	3.0	2.8
Insurance	2.2	2.3	2.3	2.1	2.1	2.0	2.1	2.2	2.3	2.3
Public Utilities	1.9	2.3	2.1	1.7	1.6	1.6	1.7	1.7	1.7	1.8
Other	0.9	1.3	2.3	2.1	1.7	1.7	1.7	1.8	1.8	1.8
License Taxes:										
Motor Vehicle and Operators	8.4	7.2	7.0	6.4	6.7	6.8	6.9	7.0	7.2	7.3
Other	5.4	5.7	5.5	4.4	4.2	4.2	4.1	4.3	4.0	3.9
Individual Income Taxes[a]	4.9	5.8	6.2	5.4	6.4	6.5	6.8	6.7	6.6	6.8
Corporation Net Income Taxes[a]	5.2	8.2	7.0	6.3	5.2	5.5	6.2	5.6	5.0	4.6
Property Taxes	5.1	4.4	4.0	3.0	2.7	2.8	2.8	2.5	2.6	2.5
Inheritance Taxes	2.1	2.0	2.2	1.9	1.5	1.6	1.6	1.5	1.6	1.5
Other Taxes	1.7	1.8	2.1	1.7	2.2	2.2	2.4	2.4	2.6	2.6
Total Taxes	76.1	74.5	78.6	72.8	70.4	72.0	73.4	72.7	72.5	71.6
Intergovernmental Revenue	16.7	18.0	13.8	18.8	21.5	20.2	18.5	19.0	18.8	18.5
Charges and Miscellaneous	7.2	7.6	7.7	8.4	8.1	7.8	8.1	8.3	8.7	9.9
Total General Revenue	100.0	100.0	100.0	100.0	100.0	100.0	100.0	100.0	100.0	100.0

TABLE A22 (Concluded)

Source	1956	1957	1958	1959	1960	1961	1962	1963	1964	1965
Sales and Gross Receipts Taxes:										
General Sales and Use	16.5%	16.5%	16.1%	15.1%	15.7%	15.7%	16.4%	16.4%	16.2%	16.4%
Motor Fuel	14.6	13.9	13.4	12.5	12.2	12.0	11.8	11.4	10.8	10.5
Alcoholic Beverages	3.0	2.8	2.6	2.5	2.4	2.4	2.4	2.3	2.3	2.2
Cigarette	2.8	2.7	2.8	2.8	3.4	3.5	3.4	3.3	3.2	3.1
Insurance	2.2	2.1	2.1	2.2	1.9	2.0	1.9	1.9	1.9	1.8
Public Utilities	1.6	1.7	1.6	1.4	1.3	1.4	1.3	1.3	1.3	1.2
Other	1.7	1.7	1.6	1.5	1.5	1.4	1.4	1.4	1.5	1.5
License Taxes:										
Motor Vehicle and Operators	7.0	6.7	6.5	6.1	5.8	5.7	5.4	5.3	5.1	4.6
Other	4.0	4.0	3.6	3.4	3.4	3.4	3.2	3.1	3.0	3.3
Individual Income Taxes[a]	7.5	7.7	7.1	7.2	8.1	8.2	8.7	8.7	9.1	8.9
Corporation Net Income Taxes[a]	4.8	4.8	4.7	4.1	4.3	4.4	4.2	4.4	4.5	4.7
Property Taxes	2.5	2.4	2.4	2.3	2.2	2.2	2.1	2.0	1.9	1.9
Inheritance Taxes	1.7	1.7	1.6	1.4	1.5	1.8	1.7	1.8	1.7	1.8
Other Taxes	2.8	2.7	2.4	2.3	2.2	2.3	2.1	2.0	1.9	1.9
Total Taxes	72.7	71.3	68.5	64.8	65.9	66.4	66.0	65.3	64.4	63.8
Intergovernmental Revenue	17.9	19.3	21.9	25.6	24.7	23.6	24.0	24.3	25.1	25.2
Charges and Miscellaneous	9.3	9.4	9.6	9.6	9.4	10.0	10.0	10.4	10.5	11.0
Total General Revenue	100.0	100.0	100.0	100.0	100.0	100.0	100.0	100.0	100.0	100.0

[a] Individual income tax data include corporation net income tax collections for from one to five states in various fiscal years.

Source: U.S. Bureau of the Census, *Revised Summary of State Government Finances, 1942–1950* (Washington: U.S. Government Printing Office, 1953); U.S. Bureau of the Census, *Compendium of State Government Finances*, 1951–65 (Washington: U.S. Government Printing Office, 1952–66).

B

APPENDIX B: Multiple Correlation Analysis of Agency Expenditure Trends

It has often been hypothesized that legislatures are more generous with appropriations to agencies when federal or earmarked funds are involved. It has also been suggested that larger state agencies tend to obtain an ever growing share of appropriations.[1] Data for 26 agencies of the state of Illinois were utilized to test several specific variations of this hypothesis.[2]

Two different "models" were constructed. Each is based upon a somewhat different set of assumptions about the relationships which are to be expected. ·

Model 1

This model might be designated the "growth model," since it is hypothesized that the *relative* expenditure growth of the agency is associated with the *relative* growth of earmarked state and federal funds as well as with the size of the agency in the base year. The dependent variable (Y) is the percentage increase in agency expenditure from the 1958–59 biennium to the 1963–65 biennium.[3]

Two independent variables were utilized:

$X_1 =$ Expenditure of the agency in the first biennium of the period (agency size).

$X_2 =$ Percentage increase in expenditure from federal and state earmarked funds during the four-biennia period.

Multiple correlation analysis of these variables produces a coefficient of multiple correlation (R) of .38 and a coefficient of multiple determination (R^2) of .14. Since R^2 can be considered as the proportion of variation explained, it is clear that there is little support for the hypothesis that the rate of growth of total agency expenditure is closely related to the independent variables.

Examination of standardized regression coefficients and coefficients of partial correlation reveal that almost all of the association which exists is between Y and X_2. In other words, including size of agency, X_1, in the analysis adds almost nothing to the level of correlation obtained.

Two variations of this model were utilized. In the first variation, expenditure from federal funds was excluded in computing the dependent variable, and the independent variable X_2 was replaced by two variables: percentage increase in expenditure from federal funds and percentage increase in expenditure from state earmarked funds. These changes raised R to .43. Percentage increase in earmarked funds became the most important independent variable.

[1] Thomas J. Anton, *The Politics of State Expenditure in Illinois* (Urbana: University of Illinois Press, 1966), pp. 255–62.
[2] The agencies utilized were those listed in Table A6 with the exception of Southern Illinois University and the Superintendent of Public Instruction. These were deleted because the very large growth (starting from a small base) produced percentage expenditure increases which were far beyond the range of all other agencies and thus made it unlikely that a straight line regression equation would produce a good fit.
[3] Test runs utilizing one- and two-biennia increases were also made, but correlations were usually substantially lower for the shorter periods. Apparently, whatever association exists between the independent and dependent variables tends to be obscured by other sources of variation in the very short run.

In the second variation, all expenditures from earmarked state funds were excluded in computing the dependent variables. Independent variables remained the same as in the first variation. These changes reduced R to .36, and size became slightly more important than percentage increase in earmarked funds as an "explanation" of variation in the dependent variable.

Model 2

This model was based upon the hypothesis that the agencies which receive the largest proportion of their funds from federal sources or from earmarked state funds grow the most rapidly. The dependent variable (Y) is the percentage increase in expenditures from all sources. The independent variables are:

X_1 = Expenditure of the agency in the first biennium of the period (agency size).

X_2 = Percentage of agency expenditures from federal funds in the last biennium of the period.

X_3 = Percentage of expenditures from earmarked state funds in the last biennium of the period.

Straight line multiple correlation analyses were made for two-, four-, and eight-biennia periods ending with the 1963–65 biennium. The highest correlation was for the four-biennia period and only the results of this analysis are reported. The coefficient of multiple correlation (R) was .34. Most of the correlation which exists is attributable to state earmarked funds, but the relationship was inverse, that is, the agencies with a high proportion of earmarked funds tend to grow less rapidly than those with little or no revenue from these sources. The coefficient of simple correlation between Y and X_3 was −.31. The standardized coefficients of regression were:

$$
\begin{array}{cc}
X_3 & -.35 \\
X_1 & .15 \\
X_2 & .04 \\
\end{array}
$$

Conclusion

None of the correlation analyses done, including several variations not reported, provide much support for the hypothesis that larger agencies and agencies which receive large amounts of federal or state earmarked funds fare better than do other agencies. The percentage of variation explained is low and the relative importance of the independent variables changes from model to model and from time period to time period.

C

APPENDIX C: Glossary of U.S. Census Terminology

Agriculture

Development and conservation of natural resources for agricultural purposes. Includes provision and support of agricultural extension services, experiment stations, fairs, associations, and other agricultural activities; promotion, improvement, regulation, and protection of agricultural production, processing, and marketing; and the like. Excludes activities relating to *Fish and Game, Forestry and Parks*, irrigation, flood control, and other conservation activities. See also *Natural Resources*.

Airports

Provision, operation, and support of airport facilities.

Alcoholic Beverages

See under *License Taxes* and *Sales and Gross Receipts Taxes*.

Amusements

See under *License Taxes* and *Sales and Gross Receipts Taxes*.

Assistance and Subsidies

For state governments this category comprises direct cash assistance payments to public welfare recipients; veterans' bonuses; direct cash grants for tuition and scholarships; and aid to nonpublic educational institutions.

Auxiliary Enterprises, State Institutions of Higher Education

Dormitories, cafeterias, athletic contests, lunchrooms, student activities, and other auxiliary activities of state institutions of higher education financed mainly by revenue from charges.

Capital Outlay

Direct expenditure for contract or force account construction of buildings, roads, and other improvements, and for purchase of equipment, land, and existing structures. Includes amounts for additions, replacements, and major alterations to fixed works and structures. However, expenditure for repairs to such works and structures is classified as current operation expenditure.

Cash Assistance

Direct cash payments to beneficiaries of public welfare programs. See also *Public Welfare*.

Categorical Assistance Programs

Old Age Assistance, Aid to Families with Dependent Children, Aid to Blind, Aid to Disabled, and Medical Assistance to the Aged. See also *Public Welfare*.

Charges and Miscellaneous General Revenue

General revenue other than taxes and intergovernmental revenue.

Commercial Activities, n.e.c.

See under *Miscellaneous Commercial Activities*.

Compiled from U.S. Bureau of the Census, *Compendium of State Government Finances in 1965* (Washington: U.S. Government Printing Office, 1966). Note that terminology utilized in Illinois statutes and financial reports does not always correspond to Census terminology. See especially Chapter 2.

Contributions, Insurance Trust

Amounts derived from contributions, assessments, premiums, "taxes," etc., required of employers and employees for financing of compulsory or voluntary social insurance programs operated by the government. Any contributions by a government to a social insurance system it administers (either as employer contributions or for general financial support) are excluded from insurance trust revenue. However, such contributions are included in exhibit statistics on insurance trust system receipts.

Corporation Net Income Taxes

Taxes on net income of corporations and unincorporated businesses (when taxed separately from individual income). Includes distinctively imposed net income taxes on special kinds of corporations (e.g., financial institutions).

Correction

Confinement and correction of adults and minors convicted of offenses against the law, and pardon, probation, and parole activities.

Correctional Institutions

State prisons, reformatories, houses of correction, and other state institutions for the confinement and correction of convicted persons and juveniles. Includes only state-operated facilities; excludes cost of maintaining prisoners in institutions of other governments.

Current Charges

Amounts received from the public for performance of specific services benefiting the person charged, and from sales of commodities and services, except liquor store sales. Includes fees, assessments, and other reimbursements for current services, rents and sales derived from commodities or services furnished incident to the performance of particular functions, gross income of commercial activities, and the like. Excludes amounts received from other governments (see under *Intergovernmental Revenue*) and interdepartmental charges and transfers. Current charges are distinguished from license taxes, which relate to privileges granted by the government or regulatory measures for the protection of the public.

Current Operation

Direct expenditure for compensation of own officers and employees and for the purchase of supplies, materials, and contractual services, except amounts for capital outlay.

Death and Gift Taxes

Taxes imposed on transfer of property at death, in contemplation of death, or as a gift.

Direct Expenditure

Payments to employees, suppliers, contractors, beneficiaries, and other final recipients of government payments—i.e., all expenditure other than *Intergovernmental Expenditure*.

Document and Stock Transfer Taxes

Taxes on the recording, registering, and transfer of documents such as mortgages, deeds, and securities, except taxes on recording or transfer of motor vehicle titles, which are classified elsewhere.

Education

Schools, colleges, and other educational institutions (e.g., for blind, deaf, and other handicapped individuals), and educational programs for adults, veterans, and other special classes. *State Institutions of Higher Education* includes activities of institutions operated by the state, except that agricultural extension services and experiment stations are classified under *Natural Resources,* and hospitals serving the public are classified under *Hospitals.* Revenue and expenditure for dormitories, cafeterias, athletic events, bookstores, and other *Auxiliary Enterprises* financed mainly through charges for services are reported on a gross basis. *Local Schools* comprises direct state payments (rather than intergovernmental transactions) for operation of local public schools, construction of school buildings, purchase and operation of school buses, and other local school services. Direct state expenditure for *Other Education* includes state educational administration and services, tuition grants, fellowships, aid to private schools, and special programs.

Employee-Retirement Expenditure

Insurance Trust Expenditures (see below) for state-administered retirement systems for public employees.

Employee-Retirement Revenue

Insurance Trust Revenue (see below) for state-administered retirement systems for public employees, including employer contributions from local governments for such systems covering local government employees. Contributions from the state government for systems it administers are excluded but are included in exhibit statistics on employee-retirement system receipts.

Employee-Retirement System

A state-administered contributory plan for financing retirement and associated benefits for state or local government employees. Does not include noncontributory plans. See also *Insurance Trust System.*

Employment Security Administration

Administraion of unemployment compensation, public employment offices, and related services, and veterans' readjustment allowances. See under *Unemployment Compensation Expenditure* for benefit payments under this program.

Expenditure

All amounts of money paid out by a government—net of recoveries and other correcting transactions—other than for retirement of debt, investment in securities, extension of credit, or as agency transactions. Note that expenditure includes only external transactions of a government and excludes noncash transactions such as the provision of perquisites or other payment in kind.

Financial Administration

Activities involving finance and taxation. Includes central agencies for accounting, auditing, and budgeting; the supervision of local government finance; tax administration; collection, custody, and disbursement of funds; administration of employee-retirement systems; debt and investment administration; and the like.

Fines and Forfeits

Penalties imposed for violation of law and forfeits of amounts on deposit as performance guarantees. Does not include penalties on delinquent taxes.

Fiscal Year

The 12-month period at the end of which the state or any state agency determines its financial condition and the results of its operations and closes its books.

Fish and Game

Conservation and development of fish and game resources through regulation, protection, and propagation.

Forestry and Parks

Conservation, development, and promotion of forests and forest products and state park areas. Includes forest fire prevention and forest firefighting activities.

Functions

Public purposes served by governmental activities (education, highways, public welfare, etc.). Expenditure for each function includes amounts for all types of expenditure serving the purpose concerned.

Fund

An accounting device established to control receipt and disbursement of income from sources set aside to support specific activities or attain certain objectives. In the accounts of individual states, each fund is treated as a distinct fiscal entity. Herein, however, transactions of funds are consolidated in accordance with the principles described in the introduction to this report.

General Control

The legislative and judicial branches of the government, the office of the chief executive, and auxiliary agencies and staff services responsible for law, recording, general public reporting, personnel administration, and the like. Internal control activities of individual departments or agencies are classed under the particular function. See also *Financial Administration*.

General Expenditure

All state expenditure other than the specifically enumerated kinds of expenditure classified as *Liquor Stores Expenditure* and *Insurance Trust Expenditure*.

General Hospitals

See under *State Hospitals*.

General Public Buildings

Public buildings not allocated to particular functions.

General Revenue

All state revenue except *Liquor Stores Revenue* and *Insurance Trust Revenue*. The basis for distinction is not the fund or administrative unit receiving particular amounts, but rather the nature of the revenue sources concerned.

General Sales or Gross Receipts Taxes

See under *Sales and Gross Receipts Taxes*.

Health

Health services, other than hospital care, and financial support of health programs of other governments. Includes public health research, nursing, immunization, maternal and child health, and other categorical, environmental, and general health activities. Does not include vendor payments for health services administered under public welfare programs.

Highways

Streets, highways, and structures necessary for their use, snow and ice removal, toll highway and bridge facilities, and ferries. Includes support of or reimbursement for street and highway activities of local governments, including aid to local governments for debt service on local highway debt.

Hospitals

Establishment and operation of hospital facilities (and institutions primarily for care and treatment—rather than education—of the handicapped), provision of hospital care, and support of other public or private hospitals. Does not include vendor payments for hospital care administered as a part of public assistance programs. See also *State Hospitals and Institutions for the Handicapped* and *Public Welfare*.

Housing and Urban Renewal

State housing and renewal projects and regulation, promotion, and support of private and local government housing and renewal activities.

Individual Income Taxes

Taxes on individuals measured by net income and taxes distinctively imposed on special types of income (e.g., interest, dividends, income from intangibles, etc.).

Insurance Trust Expenditure

Cash payments to beneficiaries (including withdrawals of retirement contributions) of employee retirement, unemployment compensation, workmen's compensation, and disability benefit social insurance programs. (See also *Insurance Trust System*.) Excludes cost of administering insurance trust activities, state contributions to programs administered by the state or by the federal government, intergovernmental expenditure for support of locally administered employee-retirement systems, and noncontributory gratuities paid to former employees.

Insurance Trust Revenue

Revenue from contributions required of employers and employees for financing social insurance programs operated by the state (see also *In-*

surance Trust System) and earnings on assets held for such systems. Excludes any contributions by a state—either as employer contributions or for general financial support—to a social insurance system it administers. Note that tax proceeds, donations, and any forms of revenue other than those enumerated above are classified as general revenue, even though such amounts may be received specifically for insurance trust purposes.

Insurance Trust System

A state-administered plan for compulsory or voluntary social insurance (insurance protection of persons or their survivors against economic hazards arising from retirement, disability, death, accident, illness, unemployment, etc.) through accumulation of assets from contributions, assessments, premiums, and the like collected from employers and employees for use in making cash benefit payments to eligible persons covered by the system. Comprises Employee Retirement, Unemployment Compensation, Workmen's Compensation, and miscellaneous (accident, sickness, and other disability benefit) systems. In exhibit statistics, each insurance trust system is treated as an entity, with its transactions including intragovernmental amounts. However, intragovernmental transactions are excluded from the insurance trust components of state revenue and expenditure. See also *Insurance Trust Revenue* and *Insurance Trust Expenditure*.

Interest Earnings

Interest earned on deposits and securities including amounts for accrued interest on investment securities sold. However, receipts for accrued interest on bonds issued are treated as offsets to interest expenditure.

Interest Expenditure

Amounts paid for use of borrowed money.

Intergovernmental Expenditure

Amounts paid to other governments as fiscal aid in the form of shared revenues and grants-in-aid, as reimbursements for performance of general government activities, and for specific services for the paying government (e.g., care of prisoners and contractual research), or in lieu of taxes. Excludes amounts paid to other governments for purchase of commodities, property, or utility services, any tax imposed and paid as such, and employer contributions for social insurance (e.g., contributions to the federal government for old-age survivors' and disability insurance for state employees).

Intergovernmental Expenditure, n.e.c.

Intergovernmental expenditure for purposes not falling within any standard functional category and amounts for combined and unallocable purposes.

Intergovernmental Revenue

Amounts received from other governments as fiscal aid in the form of shared revenues and grants-in-aid, as reimbursements for performance of general government functions and specific services for the paying government (e.g., care of prisoners and contractual research), or in lieu of taxes. Excludes amounts received from other governments for sale of property, commodities, and utility services and employer contributions from local governments to state-administered retirement systems. All intergovernmental revenue is classified as general revenue.

Intergovernmental Revenue from Federal Government

Amounts from the federal government either for direct expenditure by the state or for distribution to local governments.

Intergovernmental Revenue from Local Governments

Amounts from local governments for shares in financial support of programs administered by the state; for reimbursements for services performed or expenditures made for them by the state; for application to debt service on state debts issued for their benefit; and for repayment of advances and contingent loans extended to them. Does not include local government contributions to state-administered employee retirement or other insurance trust systems, which are classified as insurance trust revenue or agency transactions. Excludes also proceeds from interest on local government securities held by the state and proceeds from state taxes on local government facilities.

Judicial

Courts and activities associated with courts, such as law libraries, medical and social service activities, juries, etc.

Libraries

Provision of state public library facilities and services, and support of local public library services.

License Taxes

Taxes exacted (either for revenue raising or for regulation) as a condition to the exercise of a business or nonbusiness privilege, at a flat rate or measured by such bases as capital stock, capital surplus, number of business units, or capacity. Excludes taxes measured directly by transactions, gross or net income, or value of property, except those to which only nominal rates apply. "Licenses" based on these latter measures, other than those at nominal rates, are classified according to the measure concerned. Includes "fees" related to licensing activities—automobile inspection, gasoline and oil inspection, professional examinations and licenses, etc.—as well as license taxes producing substantial revenues.

Alcoholic beverages—Licenses for manufacturing, importing, wholesaling, and retailing alcoholic beverages other than those based on volume or value of transactions or assessed value of property.

Amusements—License taxes imposed on amusement businesses generally or on specific amusement enterprises (e.g., race tracks, theaters, athletic events, etc.). Does not include "licenses" based on value or number of admissions, amount of wagers, or gross or net income, which are classified elsewhere.

Corporations in general—Franchise license taxes, organization, filing, and entrance fees, and other license taxes which are applicable, with only specified exceptions, to all corporations. Does not include corporation taxes based on value of property, net income, or gross receipts from sales, or taxes imposed distinctively on particular types of corporations (e.g., public utilities, insurance companies, etc.).

Hunting and fishing—Commercial and noncommercial hunting and fishing licenses and shipping permits.

Motor vehicles—License taxes imposed on owners or operators of motor vehicles, commercial and noncommercial, for the right to use public highways, including charges for title registration and inspection of vehicles. Does not include personal property taxes or sales and gross receipts taxes relating to motor vehicles, taxes on motor carriers based on assessed value of property, gross receipts, or net income, or other taxes on the business of motor transport.

Motor vehicle operators—Licenses for privilege of driving motor vehicles, including both private and commercial licenses.

Occupations and businesses, n.e.c.—License taxes (including examination and inspection fees) required of persons engaging in particular professions, trades, or occupations, and such taxes on businesses not elsewhere classified. Includes charges relating to inspection and marketing of seed, feed, fertilizer, gasoline, oil, citrus fruit, and other commodities, and chain store licenses, as well as licenses relating to operation of particular business enterprises.

Public utilities—License taxes distinctively imposed on public passenger and freight transportation companies, telephone, telegraph, and light and power companies, and other public utility companies including government-owned utilities. Does not include taxes measured by gross or net income, units of service sold, or value of property.

Other license taxes—License taxes not listed separately (e.g., animal licenses, marriage licenses, registration fees on pleasure boats and aircraft, individual permits to purchase liquor, and other nonbusiness privileges).

Liquor Stores

Alcoholic beverage distribution facilities operated by states maintaining state alcoholic beverage monopoly systems. Liquor stores revenue and expenditure are included in state revenue and expenditure.

Liquor Stores Expenditure

Expenditures for purchase of liquor for resale and provision and operation of liquor stores. Excludes expenditure for law enforcement and licensing activities carried out in conjunction with liquor store operations.

Liquor Stores Revenue

Amounts received from sale of liquor by state retail liquor stores and other revenues from state liquor store operations. Excludes any state taxes collected by state liquor monopoly systems.

Miscellaneous and Unallocable Expenditure

General expenditure for purpose and activities not falling within any standard functional category and unallocated amounts relating to two or more functions.

Miscellaneous Commercial Activities

Provision and operation of commercial facilities not classified under particular functions. Includes a bank (North Dakota), a cement plan, hail insurance systems, hydroelectric and other electric power agencies, and the like.

Motor Fuels Sales Taxes
See under *Sales and Gross Receipts Taxes.*

Motor Vehicle License Taxes
See under *License Taxes.*

Natural Resources
State activities to conserve, promote, and develop agriculture, fish and game, forestry and parks (see also these headings above), and other soil and water resources, including geological research, flood control, irrigation, drainage, and other conservation activities. Hydroelectric power activities are classed under *Miscellaneous Commercial Activities.*

n.e.c.
Not elsewhere classified.

Pari-mutuel Taxes
See under *Sales and Gross Receipts Taxes.*

Personal Services
Amounts paid for compensation of state officers and employees. Consists of gross compensation before deductions for withheld taxes, retirement contributions, or other purposes.

Police Protection
Preservation of law and order and traffic safety. Includes crime prevention activities, detention and custody of persons awaiting trial, highway patrols, and the like.

Poll Taxes
Capitation taxes levied as specific amounts, uniform or graded, against persons, or as ad valorem taxes on an arbitrary valuation of polls.

Property Taxes
Taxes conditioned on ownership of property and measured by its value. Includes general property taxes relating to property as a whole, real and personal, tangible or intangible, whether taxed at a single rate or at classified rates; and taxes on selected types of property, such as motor vehicles or certain or all intangibles.

Protective Inspection and Regulation, n.e.c.
Regulation of private enterprise for the protection of the public and inspection of hazardous activities except where done incident to major functions, such as health, natural resources, etc. Includes regulation of financial institutions, public service corporations, insurance companies, and other corporations, regulation of professional occupations (including professional examinations and licensing), regulation of working conditions, regulation of sales of alcoholic beverages, and other regulatory and inspection activities not included under other functional headings.

Public Utilities Taxes

See under *License Taxes* and *Sales and Gross Receipts Taxes*.

Public Welfare

Support of and assistance to needy persons contingent upon their need, including *Intergovernmental Expenditure* to help finance public welfare programs administered by local governments. Direct expenditure under this heading includes *Cash Assistance* paid by the state to needy persons under the categorical programs (Old Age Assistance, Aid to Families with Dependent Children, Aid to the Blind, and Aid to the Disabled) and under any other state-administered welfare program; segregable payments directly to private vendors for medical care, burials, and other commodities and services provided under welfare programs for the needy (including all direct vendor payments under Medical Assistance for the Aged); and expenditure for state administration of public welfare programs, including the provision and operation of welfare institutions. Health and hospital services provided directly by the state, and payments to local governments for such purposes, are reported under other functional headings rather than here. Benefits not contingent upon need, such as bonuses and other aids to veterans as a class, also fall outside the public welfare classification.

Regular Highway Facilities

State direct expenditure for highways, other than toll facilities, is classified under this heading. Does not include any intergovernmental expenditure.

Rents and Royalties

Rents from leased properties, mineral leases, royalties, and miscellaneous rentals not relating to facilities incident to the performance of particular functions. Rental revenue from such facilities is classified as revenue from current charges for the activity or function concerned.

Revenue

All amounts of money received by a government from external sources—net of refunds and other correcting transactions—other than from issue of debt, liquidation of investments, and as agency and private trust transactions. Note that revenue excludes noncash transactions such as receipt of services, commodities, or other "receipts in kind."

Sale of Property

Sale of real property and improvements. Excludes sale of securities and sale of commodities, equipment, and other personal property.

Sales and Gross Receipts Taxes

Taxes, including "licenses" at more than nominal rates, based on volume or value of transfers of goods or services, upon gross receipts therefrom, or upon gross income, and related taxes based upon use, storage, production (other than severance of natural resources), importation, or consumption of goods. Dealer discounts or "commissions" allowed to merchants for collection of taxes from consumers are excluded.

General sales or gross receipts taxes—Sales or gross receipts taxes which are applicable with only specified exceptions to all types of goods, all types of goods and services, or all gross income, whether at a single rate or at classified rates. Taxes imposed distinctively upon sales of or gross receipts from selected commodities, services, or businesses are reported separately under categories listed below.

Selective sales and gross receipts taxes—Sales and gross receipts taxes imposed on sales of particular commodities or services or gross receipts of particular businesses, separately and apart from the application of general sales and gross receipts taxes.

Alcoholic beverages—Selective sales and gross receipts taxes on alcoholic beverages.

Amusements—Selective sales and gross receipts taxes on admission tickets or admission charges and on gross receipts of all or specified types of amusement businesses.

Insurance—Taxes imposed distinctively on insurance companies and measured by gross premiums or adjusted gross premiums.

Motor fuels—Selective sales and gross receipts taxes on gasoline, diesel oil, and other fuels used in motor vehicles, including aircraft fuel. Note that any amounts refunded are deducted from gross collections.

Pari-mutuels—Taxes measured by amounts wagered at race tracks, including "breakage" collected by the government.

Public utilities—Taxes imposed distinctively on public passenger and freight transportation companies, telephone, telegraph, and light and power companies, and other public utility companies and measured by gross receipts, gross earnings, or units of service sold. Taxes levied on such companies on other bases are classified elsewhere in accordance with the nature of the tax.

Tobacco products—Selective sales and gross receipts taxes on tobacco products, including cigarette tubes and papers.

Other selective sales and gross receipts taxes—Selective sales and gross receipts taxes relating to specific commodities, businesses, or services not separately enumerated (e.g., lubricating oil, fuel other than motor fuel, meals, margarine, cement, etc.).

Severance Taxes

Taxes imposed distinctively on removal of natural products—e.g., oil, gas, other minerals, timber, fish, etc.—from land or water and measured by value or quantity of products removed or sold.

State Government

The state government in each case consists of the legislative, executive, and judicial branches of government and all departments, boards, commissions, and other organization units thereof. It also includes any semi-autonomous authorities, institutions of higher education, districts, and other agencies that are subject to administrative and fiscal control by the state through its appointment of officers, determination of budgets, approval of plans, and other devices. As to all such agencies, financial information included in Census reports represents their gross transactions with the public and other governments, rather than only the net effect of such transactions on central state funds. Each data item for a state government consists of the sum of amounts of the type described for all funds and accounts, including not only the general fund but also special revenue funds, sinking funds, public trust funds, bond funds, and all other special funds.

State Hospitals and Institutions for the Handicapped

Hospital facilities established and operated by the state government. Includes hospitals operated in conjunction with state institutions of higher education. Excludes support of other public or private hospitals and expenditure for hospitalization of persons in other public or private institutions. *Regular Mental Hospitals* include institutions for custody and treatment of the insane as well as hospitals for general care of mental patients. *Other Mental Institutions* provide care and treatment of mental defectives and other special classes of mental patients (e.g., feeble-minded, mentally retarded, and emotionally disturbed children).

General Hospitals provide general medical and surgical services to the public, including such hospitals administered by state universities. *Other State Hospitals* include tuberculosis sanatoriums, maternity and children's hospitals, orthopedic hospitals, hospitals for chronic diseases, and institutions for care and treatment of the blind, deaf, and other special classes. Note that infirmaries which serve only particular institutions (e.g., university infirmaries, prison hospitals, etc.) are classified under the function served rather than under hospitals.

State Institutions of Higher Education

See under *Education.*

State Welfare Institutions

State institutions for care of needy veterans, dependent children, aged, and others. Does not include hospitals and institutions for the handicapped, provision for care of the needy in local governmental or private institutions or homes, or general support of private welfare institutions.

Taxes

Compulsory contributions exacted by a government for public purposes, except employee and employer assessments for retirement and social insurance purposes, which are classified as insurance trust revenue. All tax revenue is classified as general revenue and comprises amounts received (including interest and penalties but excluding protested amounts and refunds) from all taxes imposed by a government. Note that state tax revenue includes any amounts to be shared with or redistributed to local governments as well as amounts to be expended directly by the state. However, state taxes exclude locally imposed taxes collected and returned to local governments by the state acting as collection agent.

Tobacco Products Sales Taxes

See under *Sales and Gross Receipts Taxes.*

Toll Highway Facilities

Toll turnpikes and toll roads, toll bridges, ferries, and tunnels operated by state agencies. Expenditure for this purpose includes only acquisition, construction, and maintenance of state facilities; it does not include any debt service on toll facility debt or any aid to local governments for toll facilities.

Unemployment Compensation Expenditure

Insurance trust expenditure for state-administered unemployment compensation programs. Includes only benefit payments; administration of unemployment compensation is classified as general expenditure for employment security administration (see above). State amounts exclude agency transactions relating to the federal unemployment compensation programs for veterans and for federal employees.

Unemployment Compensation Revenue

Employer and employee contributions ("payroll taxes") for state unemployment insurance programs and interest received or credited on state unemployment insurance deposits held in the United States Treasury.

Unemployment Compensation System

A state-administered plan for compulsory unemployment insurance through accumulation of assets from contributions collected from employers or employees for use in making cash benefit payments to eligible unemployed persons. Does not include distinctive sickness or disability insurance plans carried out in conjunction with unemployment insurance programs by certain states. Unemployment insurance contributions collected by the state are deposited in the United States Treasury in a trust account maintained for the state; interest is credited by the United States Treasury on balances in state accounts, and funds are withdrawn by the state as needed to make unemployment compensation benefit payments.

Vendor Payments

See under *Public Welfare.*

Veterans' Services

Cash bonuses to veterans and other financial grants not contingent on need, administration of bonus payments, veterans' information and guidance services, and other veterans' services not classified under public welfare, education, hospitals, or other functions.

Water Transport and Terminals

Provision, operation, and support of canals and other waterways, harbors, docks, wharves, piers, and related terminal facilities.

D

APPENDIX D: Selected Sections, Revenue Article, Illinois Constitution of 1870, and Amendments Proposed by Seventy-fourth General Assembly

ILLINOIS CONSTITUTION ARTICLE IX

Section 1. The General Assembly shall provide such revenue as may be needful, by levying a tax, by valuation, so that every person and corporation shall pay a tax in proportion to the value of his, her or its property—such value to be ascertained by some person or persons, to be elected or appointed in such manner as the General Assembly shall direct, and not otherwise; but the General Assembly shall have power to tax peddlers, auctioneers, brokers, hawkers, merchants, commission merchants, showmen, jugglers, inn-keepers, grocery-keepers, liquor dealers, toll bridges, ferries, insurance, telegraph and express interests or businesses, vendors of patents, and persons or corporations owning or using franchises and privileges, in such manner as it shall from time to time direct by general law, uniform as to the class upon which it operates.

H.J.R. NO. 71—PROPOSED AMENDMENT TO ARTICLE IX

Resolved, By the House of Representatives of the seventy-fourth General Assembly of the State of Illinois, the Senate concurring herein, that there shall be submitted to the electors of this State for adoption or rejection at the next election of members of the General Assembly of the State of Illinois, in the manner provided by law, a proposition to amend Sections 1, 2, 3, 9, 10, 12, and 13 of Article IX of the Constitution to read as follows:

Section 1. The General Assembly shall provide such revenue as may be needful by levying taxes, or by authorizing the levy of taxes, in accordance with the provisions of this Article.

Real estate shall constitute one class except as provided in this Article.

The General Assembly may classify tangible personal property into the following classes: (a) household goods and personal effects not used in the production of income, (b) business and farm inventories, including grain, livestock and poultry, (c) motor vehicles, ships, boats and aircraft, and (d) all other tangible personal property; and may abolish property taxes on any or all classes thereof.

Subject to the provisions of the succeeding paragraphs of this Section, any tax upon real estate and personal property shall be levied by valuation, such value to be ascertained by some person or persons to be elected or appointed in such manner as the General Assembly shall direct and not otherwise.

The General Assembly may levy a use, privilege or franchise tax, uniform throughout the State, upon ships, boats and aircraft, and upon motor vehicles, or upon any class or classes thereof, in lieu of all property taxes thereon, provided, however, that the proceeds of any tax so levied shall be distributed to local taxing districts and for such purposes as the General Assembly may direct by general law.

The General Assembly may classify intangible property for taxation and may abolish taxation of any or all classes thereof. Classifications of intangible personal property shall be reasonable and based solely upon the nature and characteristics of the property and not on the amount or number owned, and each class may be taxed in such manner as the General Assembly may direct by general law, uniform as to the class upon which it operates. Intangible personal property not employed in carrying on any business by the owner shall be deemed to be located at the domicile of the owner for purposes of taxation; and if such intangible personal property is held in trust, the owner for the purposes of taxation shall be deemed to be the person or persons, according to their respective interests, who have the present beneficial enjoyment of such property. However, intangible personal property employed in or resulting from carrying on a trade or business outside the state shall be deemed to be located outside the state for the purposes of taxation, notwithstanding that the domicile of the owner thereof is within the state.

No class of personal property in any county shall be assessed for taxation at a percentage of actual value greater than the percentage used in assessing real property, other than in Cook County.

Section 2. The specification of the objects and subjects of taxation shall not deprive the General Assembly of the power to require other subjects or objects to be taxed in such manner as may be consistent with the principles of taxation fixed in this Constitution.

Section 2. The General Assembly may levy or authorize the levy of occupation, sales, use, inheritance, privilege and franchise taxes, uniform as to the objects and subjects taxed within the jurisdiction of the authority levying the tax and uniform as to exemptions granted from any such tax. Any such tax on or measured by gross receipts shall be nongraduated and shall be imposed uniformly upon persons and corporations.

The General Assembly may levy a tax on or measured by income, the rate of which tax shall be nongraduated and shall be levied only by the State uniformly upon corporations and persons with deductions, exemptions and credits not to exceed those permitted from time to time under the Internal Revenue Code of the United States and with credits for taxes and fees as the General Assembly may direct by general law and shall not exceed the rate of 3% unless and until the question whether such a tax should be levied at a rate exceeding 3%, including the maximum rate of tax which might be so levied, has been submitted as a proposition at a general election to the people of the state and has received a majority of the votes cast at such election for or against such proposition. No such tax shall exceed in any event the rate of 6%. Except as provided in this paragraph, the General Assembly shall neither levy nor authorize the levy of any tax on or measured by income. If an income tax is levied, the General Assembly shall fix a date, not later than 4 years after the effective date of the Act levying such tax, after which no ad valorem tax shall be levied on any tangible or intangible personal property; and the proceeds of not less than 1% of any such income tax shall be distributed to local taxing districts and for such purposes as the General Assembly may direct by general law.

Section 3. The property of the State, counties, and other municipal corporations, both real and personal, and such other property as may be used exclusively for agricultural and horticultural societies, for school, religious, cemetery and charitable purposes, may be exempted from taxation; but such exemption shall be only by general law. In the assessment of real estate incumbered by public easement, any depreciation occasioned by such easement may be deducted in the valuation of such property.

Section 3. The property, both real and personal, and the income of the state, counties and other municipal corporations, intangible personal property and the income therefrom held for the purpose of providing pension or welfare benefits, and such other property or part thereof as may be used exclusively, as defined by general law, for agricultural or horticultural societies, school, religious, cemetery or charitable purposes, and the income of organizations organized for such purposes, may be exempted from taxation, but such exemption shall be only by general law. In the assessment of real estate encumbered by public easement, any depreciation occasioned by such easement may be deducted in the valuation of such property.

Section 9. The General Assembly may vest the corporate authorities of cities, towns and villages, with power to make local improvements by special assessment, or by special taxation of contiguous property, or otherwise. For all other corporate purposes, all municipal corporations may be vested with authority to assess and collect taxes; but such taxes shall be uniform in respect to persons and property, within the jurisdiction of the body imposing the same.

Section 9. The General Assembly may vest the corporate authorities of cities, towns and villages, with power to make local improvements by special assessment or by special taxation of contiguous property, or otherwise. For all other corporate purposes, all municipal corporations may be vested with authority to assess and collect taxes, but such taxes shall be uniform, in respect to persons and property, within the jurisdiction of the body imposing the same, except as otherwise authorized by Sections 1 and 2 of this Article.

Section 10. The General Assembly shall not impose taxes upon muni-

Section 10. The General Assembly shall not impose taxes upon mucipal corporations, or the inhabitants or property thereof, for corporate purposes, but shall require that all the taxable property within the limits of municipal corporations shall be taxed for the payment of debts contracted under authority of law, such taxes to be uniform in respect to persons and property, within the jurisdiction of the body imposing the same. Private property shall not be liable to be taken or sold for the payment of the corporate debts of a municipal corporation.

Section 12. No county, city, township, school district, or other municipal corporation, shall be allowed to become indebted in any manner or for any purpose, to an amount, including existing indebtedness, in the aggregate exceeding five per centum on the value of the taxable property therein, to be ascertained by the last assessment for state and county taxes, previous to the incurring of such indebtedness. Any county, city, school district, or other municipal corporation, incurring any indebtedness as aforesaid, shall before, or at the time of doing so, provide for the collection of a direct annual tax sufficient to pay the interest on such debt as it falls due, and also to pay and discharge the principal thereof within twenty years from the time of contracting the same.

This section shall not be construed to prevent any county, city, township, school district, or other municipal corporation, from issuing their bonds in compliance with any vote of the people which may have been had prior to the adoption of this Constitution in pursuance of any law providing therefor.

nicipal corporations, or the inhabitants or property thereof, for corporate purposes, but shall require the corporate authorities to levy taxes for the payment of debts contracted under authority of law. Private property shall not be liable to be taken or sold for the payment of the corporate debts of a municipal corporation. The General Assembly may distribute in whole or in part, the proceeds of any tax levied by the state to such local governments and for such purposes as it may direct by general law.

Section 12. No county, city, township, school district, or other municipal corporation, shall be allowed to become indebted in any manner or for any purpose, to an amount, including existing indebtedness, in the aggregate exceeding 5% or in the case of school districts maintaining grades 1 through 12 exceeding 10%, on the value of the taxable property therein, to be ascertained by the last assessment for state and county taxes, previous to the incurring of such indebtedness. Any county, city, school district, or other municipal corporation, incurring any indebtedness as aforesaid, shall before, or at the time of doing so, provide for the collection of a direct annual tax sufficient to pay the interest on such debt, as it falls due, and also to pay and discharge the principal thereof within 20 years from the time of contracting the same. In the event the tax on all personal property is abolished, the foregoing limitations of 5% and 10% shall be increased to 6% and 12% respectively.

Section 13. (1) The corporate authorities of the city of Chicago are hereby authorized to issue interest-bearing bonds of said city to an amount not exceeding five million dollars, at a rate of interest not to exceed five per centum per annum, the principal payable within thirty years from the date of their issue, and the proceeds thereof shall be paid to the treasurer of the World's Columbian Exposition, and used and disbursed by him under the direction and control of the directors in aid of the World's Columbian Exposition, to be held in the city of Chicago in pursuance of an act of Congress of the United States. Provided, That if at the election for the adoption of this amendment to the Constitution, a majority of the votes cast within the limits of the city of Chicago shall be against its adoption, then no bonds shall be issued under this amendment.

And said corporate authorities shall be repaid as large a proportionate amount of the aid given by them as is repaid to the stockholders on the sums subscribed and paid by them, and the money so received shall be used in the redemption of the bonds issued as aforesaid. Provided that said authorities may take in whole or in part of the sum coming to them any permanent improvements placed on land held or controlled by them.

And provided further, That no such indebtedness so created shall in any part thereof be paid by the State, or from any State revenue, tax or fund, but the same shall be paid by the said city of Chicago alone.

Section 13. Any classification of real property for purposes of taxation in effect in the County of Cook on January 1, 1965, shall continue in effect unless modified as hereinafter provided.

The County Assessor of Cook County may abolish existing classes, and may create new and additional classes as may be reasonable and equitable; but no property shall, by reason of the creation of a new or additional class or by the abolition of any existing class, be placed in a class assessed at a higher percentage of actual value than the class in which such property was previously assessed.

The County Assessor of Cook County may change the level of assessment of any class of real property provided that the difference between the percentage of actual value used in the County of Cook for taxation of the lowest taxed class of real property and the percentage of actual value used in the assessment for taxation of any other class of real property is not greater than the difference in effect on January 1, 1965.

The substance of procedures in effect on January 1, 1965, with respect to real property assessed for taxation by the State of Illinois shall continue in effect without modification.

Any person or corporation aggrieved by any violation of this Section shall be entitled to appropriate relief at law or in equity.

The classification of real property herein provided for may be abolished by a vote of registered voters of Cook County in the following manner. The county board of such county shall, upon petition signed by 33% of the registered voters in the county, cause a proposition for the abolition of such classification of real property, to be submitted to the registered voters of the county at a general election or at a special election called for such purpose. If two-thirds of all of the registered voters of such county vote affirmatively upon the proposition, then such classification shall thereupon be abandoned.

Schedule

Paragraph 1. This Amendment of Article IX, if adopted, shall become effective on July 1, 1967, hereinafter called the "Effective Date." After the adoption of this Amendment of Article IX, the General Assembly shall enact such laws and make such appropriations as may be necessary or proper to give effect to its provisions.

Paragraph 2. All laws in force on the Effective Date of this Amendment of Article IX and consistent therewith shall remain in full force and effect until amended or repealed by the General Assembly. All laws in force on the Effective Date of this Amendment of Article IX and inconsistent therewith, unless sooner repealed or amended to conform with this Amendment, shall remain in full force and effect until July 1, 1968.

Paragraph 3. All fines, taxes, penalties and forfeitures levied, due or owing prior to the Effective Date of this Amendment of Article IX shall continue to be as valid as if this Amendment had not been adopted.

INDEX

Charts and tables are not indexed. See pp. x and xi for list.

Adequacy: of tax system, 238
Administrative classification of taxes, 111
Administrative feasibility: of tax system, 230, 238
Advisory Commission on Intergovernmental Relations, 86n
AFL-CIO, 179, 201, 209
Agencies: role in budget process, 182–83
Agricultural counties: expenditure in, 122
Agricultural interests: favor change in tax structure, 199
Agricultural Premium Fund, 32
Agriculture, Department of: receives appropriations, 34
Ahern v. *Nudelman*, 76n
Alcoholic beverage taxation: trends in yield, 71, 73, 93; rates, 92; rationale for, 92; rates in other states, 94
Allen, H. K., 134, 193
Anton, Thomas J., 24, 35, 38n, 183, 186, 228n, 236
Appropriations: made by legislature, 11; as focus of decision process, 23–24; factors influencing, 24; to elected officials, 24–26; to code departments, 26–27; lapses, 27; as authority to spend, 27–29; itemization, 28–29; and federal grants, 32; as source of conflict,

35; not by function, 36; as limit on political power, 36–37; limits on use, 37; exceed estimated revenues, 183
"Appropriation book," 24
Arrington, W. Russell, 144, 192, 195, 203, 207, 215, 217, 219, 220, 249
Arrow, Kenneth, 226
Assistance and subsidies: defined, 45
Attorney General: role in inheritance tax administration, 106–7
Automobiles: not assessed in Chicago, 137

Bach, Jacob O., 59n
Bachrach v. *Nelson*, 74n, 124n, 197, 243
Bank accounts: taxation of, 134
Banking interests: and taxation of intangibles, 206
Bargaining: in legislative arena, 184
Basic appropriations: as minimum, 182–83
Beatty, Norman J., 200, 205
Birdzell, Ruth A., 104n, 131n, 132
Board of equalization: used lax methods, 131
Board of Vocational Education: administers grants, 151
Boards of review: correct assess-